OXFORD WORLD'S CLASSICS

THE OXFORD SHAKESPEARE

General Editor · Stanley Wells

The Oxford Shakespeare offers new and authoritative editions of Shakespeare's plays in which the early printings have been scrupulously re-examined and interpreted. An introductory essay provides all relevant background information together with an appraisal of critical views and of the play's effects in performance. The detailed commentaries pay particular attention to language and staging. Reprints of sources, music for songs, genealogical tables, maps, etc. are included where necessary; many of the volumes are illustrated, and all contain an index.

DAVID BEVINGTON, the editor of *Henry IV, Part 1* in the Oxford Shakespeare, is Professor of English in the University of Chicago and one of the most distinguished Shakespearian scholars of his generation. He has edited the Complete Works, and has a special interest in the history plays and their background. His books include *From Mankind to Marlowe* (1962), *Tudor Drama and Politics* (1968), and *Action is Eloquence: Shakespeare's Language of Gestures* (1984).

D0250033

THE OXFORD SHAKESPEARE

Currently available in paperback

The rest of the plays are forthcoming

OXFORD WORLD'S CLASSICS

WILLIAM SHAKESPEARE

Henry IV, Part 1

Edited by
DAVID BEVINGTON

OXFORD
UNIVERSITY PRESS

CONTENTS

LIST OF ILLUSTRATIONS

1. Map of England and Wales, showing places referred to in *1 Henry IV*

INTRODUCTION

Reception, Reputation, and Date

THE greatness of *Henry IV, Part 1* is witnessed by its undiminished popularity in both performance and reading, and by an equally undiminished critical debate about its structure, themes, language, and characterization. Are the two parts of *Henry IV* to be regarded as a unitary sequence, or as two separate plays, the second of which was either not conceived or only sketchily planned when the first was written? Does the sub-plot involving Falstaff and his companions keep pace with the political story in *Part 1*, or is the climax of the sub-plot deliberately reserved for the second play? In the scheme of dramatic balances, or 'foil' relationships, that contrasts Falstaff with Hotspur and Falstaff with King Henry, is Hal's position that of the virtuous mean between extremes of conduct, as in Aristotle's *Nicomachean Ethics*, or is Hal's conduct subject to a comic, or even satiric, point of view that encompasses all political machinations and warmongering? Behind such questions lies the ultimate test of the Prince's character: what are we to think of his rejection of Falstaff in *Part 2*, and how early (that is, how calculatedly, how heartlessly perhaps) is the rejection adumbrated in Hal's parrying relationship with his fat companion?

Other controversial issues follow, deriving their fascination from Shakespeare's arresting portrayal both of political struggle and of conflict within the family. Critics disagree as to whether Hal is educated by his sojourn in the tavern, or simply permits his true self to emerge over time; whether Falstaff is a true coward and liar, or one who seeks to please the Prince by acting the roles of coward and liar; whether King Henry is the guilt-ridden murderer of Richard II unable to command the loyalty of his peers, or a king with popular support who is betrayed by the ambitious barons who helped him to the throne; whether the play is a mirror for magistrates that providentially demonstrates the wages of regicide, or a matter-of-fact record of a historical transition from feudalism to centralized monarchy and from the absolutist myth of divine right to the brusque reality of a machiavellian struggle for power; whether, in Yeats's words, England is engaged in a triumphal

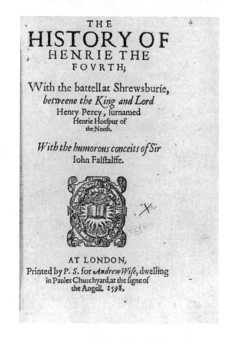

THE

HISTORY OF
HENRIE THE
FOVRTH;

With the battell at Shrewsburie,
betweene the King and Lord
Henry Percy, furnamed
Henrie Hotſpur of
the North.

With the humorous conceits of Sir
Iohn Falſtalffe.

AT LONDON,
Printed by *P. S.* for *Andrew Wiſe*, dwelling
in Paules Churchyard, at the ſigne of
the Angell. 1598.

2. Title-page of Q1

march of destiny, or a journey of 'blind ambitions, untoward accidents, and capricious passions' toward a world that is devoid of
meaning in the eyes of God.[1] These issues are illuminated by striking motifs and images, including those of vocation and recreation,
the redeeming of time, bodily illness and wounding, commercial
exchange and thievery, sun and moon, lion and hare, Scriptural
iteration and parody.

As to the enduring popularity of *1 Henry IV*, the historical record
seems clear. Entered in the Stationers' Register on 25 February
1598, the play went through seven quarto editions (two in 1598,
and one each in 1599, 1604, 1608, 1613, and 1622) before the
publication of the First Folio text in 1623, and appeared in two
subsequent quarto editions (1632 and 1639) even after the First
Folio became available. Of all Shakespeare's plays, only *Richard III*,
with six quartos before 1623, approaches *1 Henry IV*'s record of
publication. *2 Henry IV* received only one quarto printing, in
1600, though scholars have speculated that the number of copies

---

[1] William Butler Yeats, 'At Stratford-on-Avon' (1901), in *Essays and Introductions* (1961), 106–7.

2

A brefe Chronycle concernynge the
Examinacyon and death of the blessed
martyr of Christ syr Johan Oldeca·
stell the lorde Cobham/collected to·
gyther by Johan Bale.

Syr. Iohan. Oldecastel.the.worthy·
lorde.Cobham. and. moste.valyaunt.

suffred.death.at.London.Anno.1418.

warryoure.of.Iesu.Christ.

In the latter tyme shall manye be
chosen / proued / and puryfyed by fyre/
yet shall the vngodly lyue wyckedly styll
and haue no vnderstandynge. Dan.12.

3. Sir John Oldcastle, Protestant martyr, from the title-page of John Bale's
account of his life and death (1544)

then printed may have been large in anticipation of sales generated
by the popularity of *Part 1*.

This play is also singled out in contemporary allusions. By as
early as 1598, Falstaff's wit seems to have become a common
property of the English language. 'Honour pricks them on', wrote
Tobie Matthew on 20 September of Sir Francis Vere and other
military commanders then on the Continent, 'and the world thinks
that honour will quickly prick them off again' (see 5.1.129–30). [1]
In the same year, Francis Meres commended Michael Drayton's
'virtuous disposition' as a refreshing contrast to times 'when there
is nothing but roguery in villainous man' (see 2. 4. 120). [2] Seldom
has a fictional character gained such instantaneous immortality.

Not only Falstaff's wit, but the notoriety of his very name,
proved irresistibly attractive. Originally, it seems, Shakespeare
called his leading comic character 'Oldcastle', a name previously

[1] *Calendar of State Papers, Domestic Series, Elizabeth, 1598–1601*, 97; quoted in
Humphreys, note to 5.1.129–30. (For full references for works cited repeatedly in
the Introduction and Commentary, see Abbreviations and References, pp. 116–22).
[2] Francis Meres, *Palladis Tamia* (1598), 281b.

3

used for one of the humorous dramatis personae in his chief dramatic source, *The Famous Victories of Henry the Fifth* (anonymous, 1583–88). The choice may also reveal Shakespeare's interest in the historical Sir John Oldcastle, a Lollard leader martyred during the reign of Henry V. At any rate the sixteenth-century descendants of Oldcastle's widow—Sir William Brooke, seventh Lord Cobham, and his son Sir Henry Brooke, eighth Lord Cobham—apparently objected to the defamatory use of their ancestor's name. The felt grievance was all the more sensitive in view of the fact that the seventh Lord Cobham had been Lord Chamberlain from the death of Lord Hunsdon on 8 August 1596 to Cobham's own death on 5 March 1597. As Lord Chamberlain he oversaw the office of the Master of Revels and the licensing of plays. Cobham may have taken a more censorious attitude toward the stage than his predecessor or than Sir George Carey, second Lord Hunsdon. Although we have no direct evidence of puritanical leanings among the Cobhams, the family name of Oldcastle symbolized reforming zeal to many who were pressing for changes in the established Protestant church in the 1590s, whereas the second Lord Hunsdon served as an active patron of Shakespeare's company after the death of the first Lord Hunsdon and became Cobham's successor as Lord Chamberlain on 12 March 1597. Sir Henry Brooke was the brother-in-law of Sir Robert Cecil and an intimate of Sir Walter Ralegh, and hence an adversary of the Essex faction and the Earl of Southampton. Was the choice of 'Oldcastle' a deliberate slap at the family that had been responsible for the interruption in the patronage of the lords chamberlain? Falstaff's comically irreverent use of scriptural piety and his love of theatrics certainly lend themselves to such an interpretation.[1]

In any event, Shakespeare backed down. He changed the name to 'Falstaff', but the original name has left its traces in the text. The Prince's reference to Falstaff as 'my old lad of the castle' (*1 Henry IV* 1.2.40–1) seems pointless without historical explanation. A line of verse ('Away, good Ned. Falstaff sweats to death', 2.2.102) is metrically irregular perhaps because of the change. In *2 Henry IV* a speech prefix '*Old.*' stands for Falstaff at 1.2.114, in the quarto, and the Epilogue has been extended past the prayer for the Queen

---

[1] So too does the jesting at the expense of 'Master Brooke' in *Merry Wives* (altered to 'Master Broome' in the First Folio text), if Shakespeare was at work on that play in 1597. See S. Schoenbaum, *William Shakespeare: A Documentary Life* (New York and London, 1975), 142–6.

with which it originally ended to include a public disclaimer and apology: 'Oldcastle died martyr, and this is not the man.' Other name changes introduced at the same time have left their mark as well: Peto and Bardolph are substitutions for Harvey and Sir John Russell, whose names, still visible in Q1 of *1 Henry IV* at 1.2.153 and in the speech prefix 'Rɔss.' at 2.4.167, 169, and 173, as well as in the entry direction 'Sir John Russell' at 2.2.0 in the quarto of *2 Henry IV*, may similarly have caused offence to influential members of these families at court. Russell was a family name of the Earls of Bedford, and Harvey that of the Earl of Southampton's stepfather. Harvey, a parvenu who may have seemed an opportunist in the marriage, was no friend to Southampton, and Southampton had been Shakespeare's patron.[1]

References to Oldcastle and Falstaff appear with an abruptness and persistence that bespeak heated concern. The Earl of Essex wrote to Sir Robert Cecil between 25 and 28 February 1598 asking him to inform their friend Sir Alex Ratcliff that 'his sister is married to Sir John Falstaff'. Although Margaret Ratcliff did not in fact marry Sir Henry Brooke, gossip may have linked their names matrimonially at the time the letter was written.[2] Evidence on the point is circumstantial, but we can at least perceive the effect of Falstaff's name in making a topical hit. The equation of Falstaff with a descendant of Oldcastle would have a satirical point if, as seems likely, Henry Brooke was among the chief complainants against the abuse of Oldcastle's name.

A rival play, *1 Sir John Oldcastle* by Michael Drayton, Richard Hathway, Anthony Munday, and Robert Wilson, was produced by the Lord Admiral's Men in October of 1599 and defiantly proclaimed in its Prologue that 'It is no pampered glutton we present, | Nor agèd counsellor to youthful sin'. This rebuke of the Chamberlain's Men contains in it a blatant appeal to Puritan-leaning audiences in London who revered the Lollard Oldcastle as a prototype of Protestant martyrdom of the kind celebrated in John Foxe's influential *Acts and Monuments* (1563), better known as *The Book of Martyrs*. 'Let fair Truth be graced', insists the Prologue, 'Since forged invention former time defaced.' In March of 1600 the Lord Chamberlain entertained an ambassador from Burgundy

---

[1] Humphreys, xvi; John Jowett, 'The Thieves in *1 Henry IV*', forthcoming.

[2] Leslie Hotson, *Shakespeare's Sonnets Dated and Other Essays* (1949), 147–8, citing uncalendared papers in the Public Record Office, vol. 41, fol. 192.

with a play alluded to in a letter as 'Sir John Old Castell', presumably Shakespeare's play, since the players were the Chamberlain's own and not the Admiral's.[1]

A letter written by Richard James, librarian to Sir Robert Cotton, in about 1633, deftly sums up the commonly held opinion of the time as to why Shakespeare had abandoned the name 'Oldcastle' and fixed upon 'Falstaff' instead. How, a lady reader of Shakespeare had asked James, could Sir John Falstaff, or Fastolf as the name was recorded in historical registers, be dead in the time of Henry V and yet be alive in the time of Henry VI (in *1 Henry VI*) to be banished for cowardice? James's disparaging answer agrees with Plato's condemnation of poets for their 'humours' and mistakes; he reports 'that in Shakespeare's first show of Harry the fifth [i.e. *1 Henry IV*], the person with which he undertook to play a buffoon was not Falstaffe, but Sir Jhon Oldcastle, and that offence being worthily taken by personages descended from his title (as peradventure by many others also who ought to have him in honourable memory) the poet was put to make an ignorant shift of abusing Sir Jhon Falstaffe or [these two previous words crossed out] Fastolphe, a man not inferior of virtue, though not so famous in piety as the other, who gave witness unto the truth of our reformation with a constant and resolute martyrdom, unto which he was pursued by the priests, bishops, monks, and friars of those days'.[2]

The Puritan leanings of this writer and his consequent disapproval of Shakespeare's impiety notwithstanding, this record seems substantially correct in its facts. The forms 'Falstaff', 'Falstolf', and 'Fastolf' appear to have been used interchangeably as early as 1459, and, although the earliest quarto pages of *1 Henry IV* known as Q0 (1598) retain the form of '*Fast.*' for two speech prefixes (2.2.63 and 69), suggesting some inconsistency in Shakespeare's manuscript, we need not question James's assertion that Shakespeare, in *1 Henry VI* and then in the *Henry IV* plays, chose the name 'Falstaff' (possibly with symbolic overtones of 'Fall-staff' in mind) as his form of the historical name 'Fastolf'. The Stationers' Register entry in 1598 refers to Shakespeare's character as 'Sir John Falstoff'. Shakespeare had already accused

[1] Letter, 8 March, of Rowland Whyte to Sir Robert Sydney (*Sydney Papers*, ii. 175), quoted in Chambers, ii. 322. The play was probably put on at Hunsdon House, Blackfriars.

[2] Richard James, *Epistle* to Sir Harry Bourchier, quoted in Chambers, ii. 241–2. The young lady was of Bourchier's acquaintance.

the knight of cowardice in *1 Henry VI* without repercussions, and may have felt safe in resurrecting him, in place of Oldcastle, for further comic abuse in *1 Henry IV*.[1]

The interchangeability of Oldcastle and Falstaff persisted long into the seventeenth century. Nathan Field's play *Amends for Ladies* (*c*.1610–11) alludes to 'The play, where the fat knight hight Oldcastle | Did tell you truly what this honour was', in obvious reference to Falstaff's catechism on honour.[2] Performances of 'ould Castel' on 6 January 1631 at the Cockpit and again at court on 29 May 1639 in honour of the Prince's birth night[3] were more likely to have been Shakespeare's play, given the tastes of the court and Shakespeare's continued popularity, than the Puritan-leaning *1 Sir John Oldcastle* of 1599. George Daniel of Beswick, writing 'The Reign of Henry the Fifth' in his poetic work *Trinarchodia* (1647), reports as follows:

> Here to evince the scandal, has been thrown
> Upon a name of honour (charactered
> From a wrong person, coward, and buffoon);
> Call in your easy faiths, from what y' have read
>   To laugh at Falstaff, as an humour framed
>   To grace the stage, to please the age, misnamed.[4]

He relates further how Falstaff's name was used 'lest scandal might | Creep backward, and blott martyr', that is, libel Sir John Oldcastle.

Thomas Fuller, like Richard James, adopts an antitheatrical, disapproving attitude towards the maligning of a Protestant saint:

Stage poets have themselves been very bold with, and others very merry at, the memory of Sir John Oldcastle, whom they have fancied a boon companion, a jovial roister, and yet a coward to boot, contrary to the credit of all chronicles, owning him a martial man of merit. The best is, Sir John Falstaff hath relieved the memory of Sir John Oldcastle, and of late is

---

[1] Robert F. Willson, jun., 'Falstaff in *1 Henry IV*: What's in a Name?', *SQ*, 27 (1976), 199–200; Norman Davis, 'Falstaff's Name', *SQ*, 28 (1977), 513–5; George Walton Williams, 'Some Thoughts on Falstaff's Name', *SQ*, 39 (1979), 82–4; T. Walter Herbert, 'The Naming of Falstaff', *Emory University Quarterly*, 19 (1954), 1–11.

[2] 1639 edition, sig. G.

[3] From a bill evidently submitted by the King's Company as basis for payment, quoted in Chambers, ii. 353.

[4] Alexander B. Grosart, ed., *The Poems of George Daniel* (1616–1657), 4 vols. (Boston, 1878), iv. 113.

substituted buffoon in his place; but it matters as little what petulant poets as what malicious papists have written against him.[1]

Concerning 'John Fastolfe, Knight', Fuller, in his *Worthies of England* (1662), similarly complains that

the stage hath been overbold with his memory, making him a thrasonical puff and emblem of mock-valour.

True it is, Sir John Oldcastle did first bear the brunt of the one, being made the make-sport in all plays for a coward. It is easily known out of what purse this black penny came: the papists railing on him for a heretic, and therefore he must also be a coward, though indeed he was a man of arms, every inch of him, and as valiant as any in his age.

Now as I am glad that Sir John Oldcastle is put out, so I am sorry that Sir John Fastolfe is put in, to relieve his memory in this base service, to be the anvil for every dull wit to strike upon. Nor is our comedian excusable by some alteration of his name, writing him Sir John Falstafe (and making him the property of pleasure for King Henry the Fifth to abuse), seeing the vicinity of sounds intrench on the memory of that worthy knight, and few do heed the inconsiderable difference in spelling of their name.[2]

The story thus remains consistent, and, even if it is told by Puritan-leaning observers at the expense of Shakespeare and his company, it attests to the play's fame. Catholic observers naturally took the opposite view of Oldcastle, but were, nevertheless, in agreement on the facts: the Jesuit Robert Parsons, in 1604, speaks disparagingly of the 'Wycliffian' Oldcastle as 'a ruffian knight as all England knoweth', who has been 'commonly brought in by comedians on their stages', and who was 'put to death for robberies and rebellion under the foresaid King Henry the Fifth'.[3]

When and under what circumstances Shakespeare first turned to the writing of *1 Henry IV* has much to do with the controversy over 'Oldcastle', and with the play's relationship to the plays preceding and following it. It must have been written and performed before it was entered in the Stationers' Register on 25 February 1598, but performance may have been fairly recent; the storm about 'Oldcastle' and the need to assure the Cobham family of a suitably revised text may have led to unusually speedy publication. Francis Meres's *Palladis Tamia* (entered on 7 September 1598)

---

[1] Thomas Fuller, *The Church History of Britain* (1655), book IV, cent. xv, p. 168.

[2] Norfolk, under 'John Falstolfe'.

[3] *The third Part of A Treatise, Intitled . . . An Examen of the Calendar or Catalogue of Protestant Saints*, by N[icholas] D[olman] (pseudonym for Robert Parsons), 1603. Quoted in Chambers, ii. 213.

lists 'Henry the 4' among the plays demonstrating Shakespeare's excellence in tragedy. His neglecting to specify one or two parts leaves us uncertain as to whether *2 Henry IV* had come to his attention. Both the Stationers' Register entry of 25 February 1598 and the First Quarto title-page of 1598 refer to the first part simply as 'The History of Henry the Fourth', even though the subtitle makes plain that the play in question contains the Battle of Shrewsbury, Hotspur, and Falstaff. Meres lists 'Richard the 2. Richard the 3.' and 'King John', along with 'Henry the 4', but omits *Henry V*.

Meres and the Stationers' Register entry thus confirm what we would expect from the stir about Oldcastle–Falstaff, that *1 Henry IV* was written and performed during the time that Cobham was Lord Chamberlain (August 1596–March 1597), or at least before February of 1598, that *2 Henry IV* (which originally included allusions to Oldcastle also) was begun before February of 1598, and that *Henry V*, not mentioned by Meres, was written and acted in 1599. *Richard II*, entered in the Stationers' Register on 29 August 1597, may have been finished in late 1595, shortly after the appearance (entered 11 October 1594) of Samuel Daniel's *The First Four Books of the Civil Wars*, to which it is indebted. If Shakespeare indeed completed *Richard II* in late 1595—and there is nothing stylistically or topically to suggest a later date—then he would have been free to work on *1 Henry IV* in 1596. The London theatres were closed from late July to late October 1596, which means that *1 Henry IV* must have been performed before, or more probably after, this hiatus. If Shakespeare managed to complete *The Merry Wives of Windsor* in time to celebrate the installation of Lord Hunsdon, the company's new patron and Lord Chamberlain, as a member of the Order of the Garter at Windsor in May of 1597, then he must have written, or at least begun, *2 Henry IV* by then as well, for *Merry Wives* makes use of comic types introduced into *Part 2*. Such a comparatively early date for the composition of *2 Henry IV* would also explain the Oldcastle echoes, which must date from before the outcry. Some allowance must nevertheless be made for the possibility of a later date for *Merry Wives*; 1600–1 is still proposed by some.

Almost certainly, performances of *1 Henry IV* took place before the elder Lord Cobham died in office in March of 1597. From 28 July to October of 1597, the Privy Council banned all theatrical performances in reaction to a purportedly libellous and 'seditious' play called *The Isle of Dogs*, and Shakespeare's company, obliged to undertake a prolonged provincial tour, may have found this an apt time to disavow any stage plays of its own that might be construed as libellous. Little needed to be changed in *1 Henry IV* other than the names of Oldcastle, Harvey, and Russell. Perhaps at this time, 'Brooke' in *Merry Wives* was changed to 'Broome', in deference to Sir Henry Brooke and his family.

Sources: The Chronicles

Shakespeare's achievement so far transcends that of his sources that no comparison can do adequate justice to it. He did use a remarkable variety of sources, nonetheless, and his reshaping of them tells us something of the way in which he worked. His most substantial narrative indebtedness is to *The Third Volume of Chronicles* of Raphael Holinshed (1587 edition) and, to a less certain extent, to John Stow's *Chronicles of England* (1580) and *Annals of England* (1592). *A Mirror for Magistrates* (1559) may also have made a small contribution. Shakespeare need not have consulted Edward Hall's *Union of the Two Noble and Illustre Families of Lancaster and York* (1542) to write *1 Henry IV*, for the sense of nemesis demanding retaliation for King Henry's usurpation is found in Holinshed as well (ii. 869), but we know from his earlier historical plays that Shakespeare had read Hall's book and been stirred by its dramatic view of history. (Extracts from these works that are pertinent to particular scenes and passages of Shakespeare's play are quoted in the Appendix.)

Other than for a brief account of friction between Henry IV and the Prince of Wales which was resolved late in the King's reign, and a few suggestions in Stow's *Chronicles* and *Annals* of the Prince's riotous behaviour (see Appendix, 1.2.121, 123, and 3.2.0), Shakespeare did not turn to the chronicles for his comic plot. For his version of the conflict between King Henry and the rebel lords, on the other hand, he relied extensively on Holinshed. Here he found an account of the unquietness of King Henry's early reign and the King's resolve to undertake a crusade to the Holy Land (though in Holinshed it comes late in Henry's reign, and as a plan for uniting Europe against the infidel, with no hint of remorse for King Richard's murder, as in Shakespeare). Holinshed relates Owen Glendower's border depredations in 1401–2, the

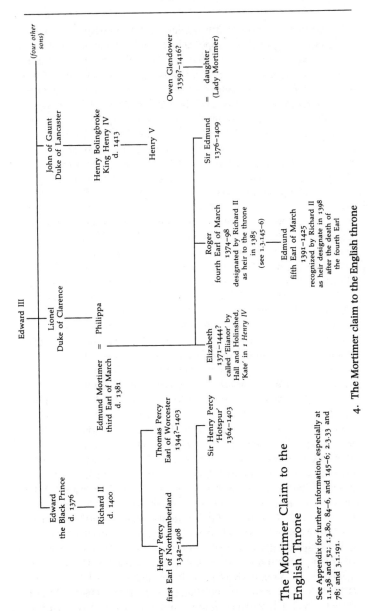

Edward III

(four other sons)

Edward
the Black Prince
d. 1376

Lionel
Duke of Clarence

John of Gaunt
Duke of Lancaster

Richard II
d. 1400

Philippa

Edmund Mortimer
third Earl of March
d. 1381

Henry Bolingbroke
King Henry IV
d. 1413

Henry V

Henry Percy
first Earl of Northumberland
1342–1408

Thomas Percy
Earl of Worcester
1344?–1403

Sir Henry Percy
'Hotspur'
1364–1403

Elizabeth
1371–1444?
called 'Elianor' by
Hall and Holinshed,
'Kate' in *1 Henry IV*

Roger
fourth Earl of March
1374–98
designated by Richard II
as heir to the throne
in 1385
(see 1.3.145–6)

Edmund
fifth Earl of March
1391–1425
recognized by Richard II
as heir designate in 1398
after the death of
the fourth Earl

Sir Edmund
1376–1409

Owen Glendower
1359?–1416?

=   daughter
(Lady Mortimer)

4. The Mortimer claim to the English throne

The Mortimer Claim to the
English Throne

**See Appendix for further information, especially at
1.1.38 and 52; 1.3.80, 84–6, and 145–6; 2.3.33 and
78; and 3.1.191.**

atrocities committed by Welsh women on the English corpses after battle (see 1.1.43–6), the capture by Glendower of Edmund Mortimer, and the suspicious fact that this same Mortimer, whom King Henry was not eager to ransom 'because his title to the crown was well enough known', soon married Glendower's daughter and joined forces with him against the English throne. Shakespeare even follows Holinshed (and Daniel) in confusing Sir Edmund de Mortimer, who married Glendower's daughter, with his nephew Edmund, the fifth Earl of March, who was proclaimed heir to the throne by Richard II (Appendix, 1.1.38; the confusion occurs in *1 Henry VI* 2.4 as well). Shakespeare takes from Holinshed his account of the battle of Holmedon (1.1.53–5) in which Hotspur and his allies turn back the Scottish incursion of Archibald, Earl of Douglas, and take a number of prisoners; here Shakespeare mistakenly surmises from Holinshed's ambiguously punctuated account that Mordake (or Murdoch) was Douglas's son (71–2).

In portraying the historical personages on both sides of the conflict, Shakespeare achieves a remarkable originality even while basing his insights on what he learned from his sources. Hotspur's unforgettable mannerisms and colourful speech are largely Shakespeare's invention, though Holinshed does report the quarrel over the prisoners and Hotspur's 'fury' at the King's 'fraudulent' reasons for not ransoming Mortimer (see 1.3.125 ff.). Hotspur's very name, as reported in the chronicles, would suggest the outlines of his character. Worcester is, for Shakespeare as for Holinshed, a major instigator of the break between the Percys and the King—compare Shakespeare at 1.3.15–21 with Holinshed's view of Worcester as one 'whose study was ever (as some write) to procure malice, and set things on a broil' (184)—and yet Shakespeare goes far beyond his chronicle source in understanding why it is that Worcester cannot agree to King Henry's terms once the rebellion has been declared openly. Telling shifts of emphasis are apparent everywhere in Shakespeare's account of Worcester, King Henry, and Northumberland, even though it is solidly grounded in Holinshed's chronicle. Holinshed is more open in his disapproval of rebellion; at the same time, Shakespeare gives Henry a better motive for refusing to ransom Mortimer, since Mortimer has already shown his failure of allegiance by marrying Glendower's daughter (in Holinshed the motive is chiefly that of fear of a rival claim to the throne). Moreover, Shakespeare's Henry enjoys more widespread popular support than he is credited with by Holinshed (see 4.3.66–73). In contrast, Northumberland is rendered less admirable in Shakespeare by the suggestion that his sickness was feigned.[1]

Invention of non-historical scenes adds to our understanding of the personal lives and idiosyncrasies of these leaders caught in political conflict. The scenes of repartee between Hotspur and his wife Kate (Holinshed merely refers to her as 'Elianor') and of Mortimer's touching inability to communicate with his Welsh wife offer meaningful comment on a world in which women play but a small part. Shakespeare's decision to show us the division of the kingdom (3.1) by the rebel leaders Hotspur, Glendower, and Mortimer, instead of by their deputies as reported in Holinshed, allows him to provide insight into the complex and difficult relationships among these men, who are united chiefly by their mistrust of Henry IV. Shakespeare also gives prominence to Glendower by placing the meeting apparently at his house rather than at the house of the Archdeacon of Bangor as in Holinshed.[2]

Glendower, like Hotspur, is based on the merest hints in Shakespeare's sources. Holinshed takes from Hall's *Union of the Two Noble and Illustre Families of Lancaster and York* some deprecatory reflections on the 'blind and fantastical dreams of the Welsh prophesiers',[3] and adds further rumours about Glendower's purported magical ability to cause foul weather at his enemies' expense. It is from such scattered impressions that Shakespeare creates the enigmatic, and not ignoble, character of his Welsh magician Glendower. Another ambiguity in Holinshed may have assisted him. Holinshed reports 'strange wonders' at 'the nativity of this man', such as that 'all his father's horses in the stable were found to stand in blood up to the bellies' on the night he was born; Holinshed appears to be referring to Mortimer, but his pronouns are sufficiently vague that Shakespeare could (and did) appropriate such qualities to Glendower.[4] Shakespeare accordingly emphasizes Glendower's fascination with magic and poetry, making of these qualities a temperament quite opposite to that of Hotspur.

---

[1] Charles Fish, 'Henry IV: Shakespeare and Holinshed', *SP*, 61 (1964), 205–18; Edna Zwick Boris, *Shakespeare's English Kings, the People, and the Law* (Rutherford, NJ, 1978), 156.

[2] Bullough, iv. 185.

[3] Bullough, iv. 185.

[4] Bullough, iv. 184.

The result is unlike anything found in Holinshed or *A Mirror for Magistrates*, in which Glendower is portrayed chiefly as a fierce outlaw. Shakespeare may well have gleaned from Thomas Phaer's Complaint about Glendower in the *Mirror* a few details about 'dreamer Merlin', the mouldwarp (mole), the dragon, the lion, and other such prophetic utterances (see 3.1.143–50), but the effect is strikingly different.

The Percys' mustering of arms, Northumberland's illness, the alliance with the Archbishop of York (who is mistakenly 'brother', instead of distant cousin, to the Scrope executed at Bristol in both Holinshed and Shakespeare, 1.3.269), the rebels' statement of grievances against Henry, Hotspur's battle oration to the rebel forces, and his cry of 'Esperance Percy', all owe much to the chronicle account. So do the parley before battle, the King's offer of pardon, and Worcester's duplicity in reporting to his nephew Hotspur 'clean contrary to that the King had said',[1] though Holinshed's evident bias against rebellion is corrected by a more evenhanded appraisal in Shakespeare's dramatized account. One significant difference is that Shakespeare's King summons the Percys into his own presence at Windsor, thereby demonstrating his grim determination to rule events, rather than following their initiative as in Holinshed.

Hal's offer to combat Hotspur single-handedly and the King's decline of this offer are not in the chronicles, and indeed Shakespeare has played up the rivalry between Hal and Hotspur, along with Hal's role in the Battle of Shrewsbury. Like Daniel (see next section), Shakespeare has considerably reduced Hotspur's age in order to intensify the rivalry of two young men. They are often in one another's thoughts. Shakespeare has Hal rescue his father from Douglas on the battlefield, whereas in Holinshed the credit for rescue belongs to unnamed persons or (earlier in the battle) to the Scottish Earl of March, George Dunbar. Holinshed credits the Prince with fighting 'like a lusty young gentleman' and with receiving a wound in the face, but the central figure of the loyalist forces remains the King himself, whose valour inspires his followers to fight vehemently and to slay Hotspur. In Shakespeare, by contrast, Hotspur is killed by the Prince of Wales.

For Shakespeare, indeed, the Prince's defeat of Hotspur is the decisive event of the battle, as well as a personal triumph in his

---

[1] Bullough, iv. 190.

reformation. Shakespeare has heightened the odds confronting Hotspur in order to accentuate his bravery and personal tragedy; the sickness of Northumberland, for instance, announced early enough in Holinshed to allow the rebels to plan for his absence, is a last-minute catastrophe in Shakespeare. Familiar ballad accounts of the military deeds of Hotspur and Douglas, such as 'The Hunting of the Cheviot' and 'The Battle of Otterburn', may have inspired Shakespeare with a sense of the heroic greatness of these northern warriors.[1] Shakespeare makes more of the stratagem of apparelling others in the King's likeness than does Holinshed, who simply reports it as fact. The Prince's heroism in Shakespeare eclipses the wariness of his ageing father, and prepares him for his role as Hotspur's nemesis.

Sir Walter Blunt's role as devoted follower of the King and self-effacing embodiment of honour is considerably amplified by Shakespeare, in earlier scenes as well as in the battle sequence,[2] and Sir Richard Vernon's role as interlocutor to Worcester is similarly enhanced. Prince John's valour at Shrewsbury is a detail not found in any source (he was in fact only thirteen in 1403), and may have been motivated in part by anticipation of John's increased role in *2 Henry IV*, though John's presence is also useful in *1 Henry IV* to provide Hal with a united family and with a younger brother whom he can introduce to armed conflict. Holinshed reports Douglas's capture and release for his valour, but attributes the action to the King, whereas in Shakespeare the release without ransom is one further testimonial to the Prince's magnanimity and political maturity.[3] Finally, Shakespeare telescopes events after Shrewsbury, omitting an expedition against York, so that the events of *2 Henry IV* can follow immediately.

Holinshed's account of a rebellion staged chiefly in the north and west of England may have seemed especially pertinent to Shakespeare and his audience because of England's own recent experience with the Northern Rebellion of 1569. This challenge to Elizabeth on behalf of Mary Queen of Scots and her Catholic claim to the throne, though unsuccessful, caused great alarm, and led her government to take strenuous measures against treason in the

[1] Humphreys, xxxviii.

[2] Margaret B. Bryan, ' "Sir Walter Blunt. There's Honor for You" ', *SQ*, 26 (1975), 292–8.

[3] Seymour V. Connor, 'The Role of Douglas in *Henry IV, Part One*', *UTSE*, 27 (1948), 215–21.

years that followed; decades later, a homily against wilful disobedience and rebellion was still required to be read in churches at periodic intervals. Prominent among the leaders of the rebellion were Thomas Percy, seventh Earl of Northumberland (who was loath to take extreme measures because of the danger in which Mary might be placed) and the more fiery Earl of Westmorland; among those commanding the forces of Elizabeth were Henry, Lord Scrope, and Henry Carey, first Lord Hunsdon, who was to become Lord Chamberlain in 1583 and patron of Shakespeare's acting company from 1594 until his death in 1596.[1]

Daniel's 'Civil Wars'

Samuel Daniel's *The First Four Books of the Civil Wars* gave Shakespeare an interpretation of these same events that accorded with his own view of the Prince's centrality. Like Holinshed, Daniel does not include the comic tradition of Hal's escapades, and he perpetuates the error of conflating the two Mortimers. The bias against rebellion is plainly marked, and Daniel leaves to Shakespeare the vivid fleshing out of Hotspur's mercurial character, though Daniel does bestow upon the warrior a 'fury' and 'undaunted' mettle enabling Hotspur to encourage his forces with 'cheerful voice' and 'great spirit' (iii. 100). Hotspur's oration before the battle is presented at some length, with a fine sense of the odds against him and his courageous response, compelling admiration even for one whose cause is irredeemably flawed.

Daniel's chief contribution is to highlight the meeting of the two young men as a turning-point in English history. He reduces the age of Hotspur (who was, in fact, older than King Henry, having been born in about 1364) to render him the Prince's equal: 'There shall young Hotspur with a fury led | Meet with thy forward son as fierce as he' (iii. 97). Daniel here implies that the two are to meet in single combat, though he does not describe the scene. Certainly 'young Henry' becomes 'Wonder of arms, the terror of the field', the one on whom the victory ultimately depends. Daniel's Prince lends speedy aid to his endangered father, 'Whom fierce encount'ring Douglas overlaid' (iii. 110–11). Perhaps Daniel misread (as Shakespeare may have done also) Holinshed's account of the death of Hotspur; 'The other on his part', who in Holinshed

[1] J. B. Black, *The Reign of Elizabeth, 1558–1603* (1959), 134–44.

'slew the Lord Percy, called Sir Henry Hotspur', presumably means 'others of the King's party',[1] but the reference is vague enough to permit an alternative interpretation, and the Prince is mentioned at the beginning of the same paragraph. (In Holinshed's *The History of Scotland* (ii. 254), which Shakespeare and Daniel seem not to have consulted here, the King is personally credited with the slaying of the Lord Percy.) Whatever the reason, for Daniel and Shakespeare the error served the purpose of accentuating the Prince's role in the battle.

Daniel also gave Shakespeare a hint for the enlarged role of 'Heroical courageous Blunt, arrayed | In habit like as was the king attired' (iii 111), and Shakespeare seems to follow Daniel rather than Holinshed (whose report is ambiguous) in saying that two Blunts died for the King (see *Civil Wars*, iii. 112, and *2 Henry IV* 1.1.16–17). Shakespeare's list of the casualties in Henry's army derives from Holinshed and from Daniel's praise of 'magnanimous Stafford' and 'valiant Shorly', i.e. Shirley;[2] Hall, by contrast, lists Stafford among those who died in the Percys' cause. Shakespeare is closer to Daniel (iii. 99) than to Holinshed in denying a Welsh presence at Shrewsbury (see Appendix, 4.4.16). Daniel's achievement was to present Holinshed's factual narrative in a coherent dramatic form, centred upon the conflict of two young and well-matched antagonists.[3]

'Famous Victories' and the Prince's Wild Youth

Thus far Shakespeare's chronicle and narrative sources have given him only fragmented suggestions for Hal's wild youth. This legend enjoyed a vigorous life of its own, however, especially on the stage. Richard Tarlton, the clown of the Queen's Company before his death in 1588, is reputed to have taken part in a play at the Bull Inn in Bishopsgate in which a scapegrace Prince of Wales struck his father's Lord Chief Justice on the ear with his fist.[4] Tarlton himself is supposed to have filled in for an absent player on one occasion as the Chief Justice, in addition to playing his own part of the clown—a kind of improvisation for which he and other

---

[1] Bullough, iv. 191.

[2] Daniel, iii. 113; see *1 Henry IV* 5.4.40.

[3] Mary Olive Thomas, 'The Elevation of Hal in *1 Henry IV* ', *Studies in the Literary Imagination*, 5.1 (1972), 73–89.

[4] *Tarlton's Jests*, in *Shakespeare Jest-Books*, ed. W. C. Hazlitt (1864), ii. 218–19.

Elizabethan clowns were noted. The text we have of *The Famous Victories of Henry the Fifth*, printed in 1598, perhaps in order to capitalize on the popularity of Shakespeare's play or plays about Prince Hal, announces on its title-page that it was 'played by the Queen's Majesty's Players', who were indeed a leading troupe in the 1580s, though on the decline in the 1590s.

Whether this text accurately records the version in which Tarlton acted is a matter of debate. Objections that Shakespeare could have garnered little from the text we have, with its overstated parricidal vehemence and its relatively minor role for Sir John Oldcastle, do not do justice to Shakespeare's imagination or to his access to other materials. On the other hand, the span between 1588 and 1597 is a long one, and one in which there are suggestions of new developments. A posthumously published collection of jests attributed to Tarlton, entitled *Tarlton's Jests*, includes a version of Scene 5 which is at variance with the scene we have, and seems to call for an impossible doubling on Tarlton's part of the Chief Justice and the clown Derick, both of whom are on stage at once, but the discrepancy may be the result of Tarlton's improvisations. Thomas Nashe may or may not refer to *Famous Victories* in his *Pierce Penniless* (1592) when he conjures up a finale not unlike that of the extant play: 'What a glorious thing it is to have Henry the Fifth represented on the stage leading the French King prisoner and forcing both him and the Dolphin to swear fealty.'[1] A Stationers' Register entry of 14 May 1594 to Thomas Creede for 'a book entitled *The Famous Victories of Henry the Fifth*' certainly sounds like a version of the play we have, but the entry in Henslowe's *Diary* for a 'ne[w]' *harey the v*, acted at the Rose by the Lord Admiral's Men on 28 November 1595 and twelve times more by 15 July 1596,[2] suggests at least some revision to justify the appellation of a new play. We cannot be sure that there were not two, or even three, quite separate plays.

We can be confident, however, that Shakespeare knew and consulted a play very like *Famous Victories*. Presumably he was free to use plays of a company that had disappeared from the scene. He seems to have borrowed from the Queen's Company's play called *The Troublesome Reign of John, King of England*, c.1587 (unless it is

---

[1] Nashe, i. 213.
[2] *Henslowe's Diary*, ed. R. A. Foakes and R. T. Rickert (Cambridge, 1961), 33 ff.

a bad quarto of his own play, as argued by E. A. J. Honigmann in his Arden edition of *King John*); and the old *King Leir* (*c.*1588–94) to which he turned may also have been in this company's repertory. Perhaps, as Sir Edmund Chambers speculates, an edition of *Famous Victories* appeared in 1594 subsequent to the Stationers' Register entry of that year, one that was used as a source by Shakespeare, and perhaps independently by a dramatist writing for the Admiral's Men.[1] Or Shakespeare may have had access to a playhouse document passed on by a Queen's player or players in a reshuffling of companies. He certainly had the opportunity to see some version of the Henry V story on the stage in 1595–6, and must have prepared his version in an atmosphere of competitive rivalry between the two leading companies; the Lord Chamberlain's Henriad had to be perceived as a theatrical answer to the successful run of *harey the v* at Henslowe's Rose.

Even if the *Famous Victories* text that we have has been cut and rearranged, it provides ample illustration of the legends Shakespeare vigorously adapted for his own use. The stories it inherited go back at least to Thomas Walsingham's *Historia Anglicana*, 1418, in which Prince Henry is said to have undergone a sudden reformation at the time of his accession to the throne.[2] Hints of licence and wild company appear in Tito Livio's *Vita Henrici Quinti* (*c.*1437) and in Lambeth MS 83 (*c.*1479). Fabyan's *Chronicle*, published in 1516, adds to the story of sudden reform the detail that Henry banished his riotous companions a distance of ten miles from his royal person on pain of death. Accounts of Hal taking the crown from the pillow of his dying father, and earlier of his having lain in wait with his wild companions to ambush his own receivers or revenue collectors (compare *Famous Victories*, in which his victims are the King's receivers), first appear in additions to a manuscript translation of Livio's *Vita* in 1513. This manuscript partly owes its inspiration to the *Chronicle* of Enguerrand de Monstrelet and to the recollection of the fourth Earl of Ormonde, who was knighted by Henry V at Agincourt and was presumably in possession of firsthand information.[3] In these accounts, the great distress of Hal's father leads to a scene of reckoning and

[1] Chambers, i. 148 and 384.

[2] *Historia Anglicana*, ed. H. T. Riley (1863), ii. 290.

[3] Humphreys, xxix; C. L. Kingsford, ed., *The First English Life of King Henry the Fifth* (Oxford, 1911), v–xx.

repentance, one in which the suddenness of the reform is accentuated by Hal's appearing before his father extravagantly garbed in blue satin with gold accoutrements. The episode of Hal boxing the ear of the Lord Chief Justice and being sent to prison as a result first appears in Sir Thomas Elyot's *The Book of the Governor* (1531), though it may have been current earlier in popular lore. Some of these legends surface again in Stow's *Chronicles* and *Annals*, including the interesting titbit (which Shakespeare made use of) that the Prince restored to his receivers the money that he had stolen from them and rewarded them for their trouble.[1] Holinshed, on the other hand, says nothing of highway robbery. Materials for the legend were thus available but scattered. To the anonymous author of *Famous Victories* belongs the credit of first gathering them together and then animating them through the medium of comic drama.

The similarities between *Famous Victories* and Shakespeare's three plays on Henry IV and Henry V are extensive. In its 1550-odd lines, the earlier play traverses the full narrative extent of Shakespeare's plays. In company with Sir John Oldcastle, Ned, and Tom, the Prince intimidates the two receivers he and his companions have robbed, thereby assuring the victims' silence, and repairs to 'the old tavern in Eastcheap' where good wine and a pretty wench are to be found (compare 1.2.39). The King has to deal with the Prince's arrest for rioting by the Mayor of London, and laments the rebelliousness of a son who will kill his father with grief (ll. 262–3, 544–5). The Prince interferes with justice to save Cutbert Cutter, one of his followers who has robbed 'a poor carrier' (one who hauls produce to market), even though he scorns such a base crime against a harmless citizen. When the Chief Justice persists in resolving to hang the culprit, the Prince boxes him on the ear. No sooner is the Prince out of prison for this offence than he proposes to make Ned Chief Justice, and 'turn all these prisons into fence schools' (ll. 459–66). His eagerness to see his father die ushers in a remarkable confrontation: the Prince demands an interview, comes to court in a fantastic cloak of eyelet holes and attended by 'a very disordered company', proclaims his intention that 'the breath shall be no sooner out of his mouth but I will clap the crown on my head', commands 'three noise of musicians' (i.e. three bands), and enters his father's chamber with a dagger in his hand (ll. 447–540). Reform is sudden. After a last scene between father

[1] Bullough, iv. 219.

and son in which Hal's removal of the crown from the dying King's bedside prompts suspicion once more of a parricidal wish, the King dies reconciled to his heir. The new King disappoints his expectant followers—Ned, Tom, and Sir John Oldcastle—and banishes them from his royal presence, though he promises to look after them if they will reform. The remaining 800 or so lines deal with the French Dauphin's insolent challenge and King Henry V's triumphant campaign in France, in which he is followed at a comic distance by John Cobbler, Derick, Robin Pewterer, and other such 'filching fellows' (but not by Sir John Oldcastle, Ned, or Tom).

The portion of *Famous Victories* corresponding to *1 Henry IV* does not include the Percys and Shrewsbury field. Instead, the play focuses on Hal's wild youth and in no way anticipates his conversion. Hal is proud of his exploits in robbing his father's receivers, and makes a sharp distinction between such a 'trick of youth' and Cutbert Cutter's victimizing of a poor honest carrier. Hal is in part a Robin Hood figure, whose escapades are justified by their being directed at aged authority. He has vigorously and courageously taken part in the robbery, so much so that he expects to feel the villains' blows on his shoulders for a month. He takes the lead in devising ways to spend the loot and in silencing the hapless officers whose careers have been so severely threatened by the loss. The latter recognized Prince Hal's horse and that of Sir John Oldcastle at the scene of the crime, but have dared say nothing against so mighty an adversary. The Prince seems to have done this sort of thing before, and is not unacquainted with the wenches of the tavern. It is he who broaches the theme of a rule of licence after King Henry IV's demise: 'I tell you, sirs, an the King | My father were dead, we would be all kings' (ll. 93–4; also 456–7). Ordinary citizens know the Prince to be 'one of these taking fellows', though they dare not say too much, and anticipate the day when the King his father 'will cut him off from the crown'. On stage, Hal's defiance of the Chief Justice takes the literal form of a blow, a blow for freedom and licence.

The details of Shakespeare's borrowings are often as significant as the outlines of the story. The thief Cutbert Cutter in the earlier play is known also as 'Gad's Hill' because of his reputation as a highwayman on Gad's Hill in Kent (see *1 Henry IV* 1.2.101 ff.). Like Shakespeare's Gadshill, he is employed by the highwaymen as 'the villain that was wont to spy | Out our booties' (ll. 23–4). The

King's receivers, like Falstaff, are expected to play along with the Prince's pranks, rather than speak out against him. The carrier attacked by Cutbert Cutter speaks of a great rase, or root, of ginger taken from his pack (l. 303), like the carrier in Shakespeare at 2.1.23–4. The 'hue and cry' that follows Falstaff and his fellow thieves to the tavern in *1 Henry IV* (2.4.488) recalls the 'hue and cry' raised in the town of Deptford, south of the Thames, in pursuit of Cutbert Cutter (ll. 19–20).

Most such interesting details are transformed, nevertheless, in accordance with Shakespeare's interpretation. *Famous Victories* presents us with a play-acting scene, for example, in which John Cobbler enacts the Lord Chief Justice, who is seated on a chair and is boxed on the ear by Derick as the young Prince. Levels of acting and reality are cleverly manipulated when John Cobbler, after having received the blow, is reminded that he is not in fact the Chief Justice, but a 'simple fellow' who has allowed himself to be taken in by Derick's wit: 'what a clown wert thou, to let me hit thee a box on the ear!' (ll. 417–18). The play-acting that goes on between Hal and Falstaff in 2.4 of Shakespeare's play is incomparably richer, and yet it, too, connects the comic tavern world with the political scene at court through mimicry and role-playing.

Many of Shakespeare's reshapings of material in *Famous Victories* take the form of transferring qualities from the Prince to his companions, and most of all to Falstaff. Because *1 Henry IV* ends without the death-bed reconciliation of father and son and the subsequent rejection of Falstaff, Shakespeare is under some obligation to assure his audience that reformation will come. He adds a soliloquy in which Hal announces his intention of amending his life (1.2.183–205), and gives Falstaff the initiative of asking whether there will still be gallows standing in England when Hal is king. Shakespeare's Prince has never robbed before, and must be persuaded to undertake the escapade as a jest. He assaults not those who own the wealth but Falstaff and his crew who perform the robbery. The deplorable reality of the crime is accentuated by its being directed not at the King's receivers but at ordinary carriers such as the Prince in *Famous Victories* would never accost, though traces of *Famous Victories*' 'receivers' are still visible in Shakespeare's play; the victims are 'pilgrims' and 'traders' in 1.2.119–20, but at 2.1.55 we hear of an 'auditor' or royal officer in their company, and at 2.2.51–2 Gadshill supposes that the 'money of the King's coming down the hill' is 'going to the King's Exchequer'. There is nothing romantic about the robbery, in any case, and Falstaff is its chief perpetrator. Hal takes the money from the thieves and restores it to its rightful owners, somewhat along the lines of Stow's report of the Prince's rewarding his own receivers for their trouble.

In Shakespeare, Hal's chief motives for his sojourn in the tavern and at Gad's Hill are to savour Falstaff's huge lies and to reprove them in jest. To be sure, he shields Falstaff from the law, just as the Prince in *Famous Victories* acts to save Cutbert Cutter, but Hal does so with assurances that the wrongdoing will be remedied. *Famous Victories*' utterances about wishing the father dead are dropped from Hal's conversation, and Falstaff, more often than Hal, uses the profanities ('Gogs wounds') that fall plentifully from Henry's lips in *Famous Victories*. Shakespeare's Prince jests with Falstaff about using women, but no evidence of any actual wenching is forthcoming; instead it is Falstaff who must deny that he is a whoremaster (2.4.451–3) and insist that he patronizes bawdy houses no oftener than once a quarter—of an hour (3.3.15–16). Bardolph, the Hostess, and the rest similarly go far beyond anything in *Famous Victories* (where drunkards and tavern women are mentioned but do not appear, unless Derick's quarrelling with John Cobbler's wife, ll. 583–604, is regarded as anticipating Falstaff's bantering with the Hostess), in part because they are called on to serve not as mere accessories to Hal's wildness but as inhabitants of a world from which Hal must learn to separate himself.

Falstaff and his crew, for all their engaging qualities, are scapegoat figures to whom Shakespeare has attributed the saturnalian anti-authoritarian features of *Famous Victories*' Prince. The various unsavoury companions in *Famous Victories* are of secondary importance; even Sir John Oldcastle is only a pale anticipation of Falstaff. Shakespeare's borrowings from *Famous Victories* for his character of Falstaff must be understood to encompass all those figures—not only Derick and Ned but the Prince himself—who express delight in licence, resourcefulness in thievery, and gleefulness in anticipation of the next king's reign.[1] This is not to say that

---

[1] See Rudolph Fiehler, 'How Oldcastle Became Falstaff', *Modern Language Quarterly*, 16 (1955), 16–28; D. B. Landt, 'The Ancestry of Sir John Falstaff', *SQ*, 17 (1966), 69–76; James Monaghan, 'Falstaff and His Forebears', *SP*, 18 (1921), 353–61.

Prince Hal is left guiltless by the transfer; his association with Falstaff and the rest still amounts to complicity in irresponsible amusement at a time of national crisis. Nonetheless, the transference of unredeemable qualities to Hal's tavern companions, especially Falstaff, does make possible a formal banishing of those qualities with the banishing of the scapegoat figures, thereby paving the way for a reformation that is vastly more plausible than that of the conversion-play strategies of *Famous Victories*. The anonymous play relies on a sudden last-minute reformation, in the vein of a Pauline conversion, in order to exploit fully beforehand the parricidal implications of youthful defiance of authority. Shakespeare's play explores instead the complex transition from seeming prodigal son to mature prince.

Falstaff and the Vice

That Shakespeare's Falstaff is incomparably more than an amalgamation of qualities borrowed from *Famous Victories* and various other sources does not lessen the importance of understanding the prototypes from which Shakespeare departed. Shakespeare's awareness of tradition is at times evident, even while he transcends it. Prince Hal invokes the morality play, for example, in his comic invective directed at Falstaff, 'that reverend Vice, that grey iniquity, that father ruffian, that vanity in years' (2.4.437–8). 'Iniquity' and 'vanity' are the sort of abstract terms applied to the Vice in the moral drama, as for example in *King Darius* (1565) and *Liberality and Prodigality* (1567?, revised *c*.1600), and the point of Hal's oxymoron is that the ruffians and swaggerers of such plays are usually young. Tavern scenes are a common feature of the dissipated life to which protagonists in morality plays are prone, as for example in the Digby *Mary Magdalene* (a late fifteenth-century conversion play with morality elements), *Mankind* (*c*.1470), and *The Nature of the Four Elements* (*c*.1517). Vintners ply their customers with wine and rich fare, while wenches named Idleness or Lechery draw young men into neglect of spiritual or humanistic pursuits. The London underworld in particular is the scene of riotous behaviour: *Mundus et Infans* (*c*.1500–22), for example, gives us vivid details of Holborn, Westminster (where Covetous corrupts the law), London Bridge and the 'stews' near it, Eastcheap (where the revellers dine and play at dice with Lombard or Italian bankers), and the Pope's Head Inn (ll. 566–670).[1] Falstaff's role as 'abominable misleader of youth' (2.4.445–6) owes some of its ambience to the morality play's vivid dramatization of a life of sin, even though the moral stridency has disappeared.

Because Hal is no simple morality play sinner, Falstaff is no mere tempter. His soliloquy on honour is not in the gloating, boastful vein of the Vice; his wonderful inventiveness does not run to schemes for hoodwinking the Prince with vicious deception, and he does not rub his hands with glee or share with the audience his stratagems for undoing virtue. Still, as Bernard Spivack argues, the shadow of a serious moral judgement does hover about him. The banishment and imprisonment to which he is later subjected are usual punishments for the Vice. Falstaff shares with the Vice a double image of witty *bonhomie* and incorrigibility, thereby giving rise to an inextricable mixture of farce and high moral seriousness, through which he becomes a source of both gaiety and gravity in the play.[2]

Falstaff may owe his gluttony and physical grossness in part to the allegorical figure of Gula or Gluttony, who appears in *The Castle of Perseverance* (c.1425), Henry Medwall's *Nature* (c.1495), and Spenser's *The Faerie Queene*, I.iv 21–3, and is closely identified with Sensual Appetite in *The Nature of the Four Elements*, Incontinence in *The Longer Thou Livest the More Fool Thou Art* (c.1559), and Greediness in *The Tide Tarrieth No Man* (1576). Falstaff's drunkenness (and that of Bardolph) is similarly anticipated in the toping of Hans in *Wealth and Health* (1554–5) and Tom Tosspot in *Like Will to Like* (1562–8).[3] Shakespeare's language recalls this tradition when the newly crowned Henry V refers to Falstaff as 'The tutor and the feeder of my riots' (*2 Henry IV* 5.5.63). *1 Sir John Oldcastle*, written, as we have seen, for the Admiral's Men in 1599 in homage to a Protestant saint, angrily rebukes the Chamberlain's profane incarnation of Sir John Oldcastle (who had been renamed Falstaff by this time) as a 'pampered glutton' and 'aged counsellor to youthful sin'. Behind the figure of the Vice lies the image of *psychomachia*, or soul-struggle, in which Mankind must choose between the

[1] See selection in Bullough, iv. 241–5.

[2] Bernard Spivack, *Shakespeare and the Allegory of Evil* (New York, 1958), 203–4.

[3] John W. Shirley, 'Falstaff, an Elizabethan Glutton', *PQ*, 17 (1938), 271–87.

seductive offerings of Gluttony or Good Fellowship and the path of Righteous Living, between vanity and government.[1]

Structurally, the morality play dramatizes these alternatives through the metaphor of choosing. It presents its action in alternating scenes of seriousness and riot that give dramatic point to a series of analogies or correspondences between radically opposed alternatives.[2] Perhaps *1 Henry IV*'s greatest debt to the morality play is to be found in its alternations between the serious plot of Henry IV and Hotspur (1.1, 1.3, 2.3, 3.1) and the comic plot of Hal and Falstaff (1.2, 2.1–2, 2.4), through which we are shown parallels between rebellion in the land and rebellion in the royal family. This rhythm is not broken until 3.2, when Prince Henry appears before his father at court to account for his behaviour and to promise to reform; thereafter Falstaff is more often on his own in broadly comic scenes that stress the inappropriateness of his behaviour in a time of civil conflict. Antithetical character types —Hotspur and Falstaff, the King and Falstaff—offer Hal a scheme of 'foils' expressed in the theatrical language of moral choice: they are both living characters and alternative possibilities, mimetically 'real' and at the same time morally symbolic.

The alternatives facing Hal are ultimately brought together on stage, as they are in the morality play, thus providing a fitting structural climax to a drama of choice. We see the protagonist standing over two seemingly dead bodies, those of Hotspur and Falstaff, in a tableau that is striking in its symbolism: excessive devotion to chivalric honour and irresponsible pursuit of pleasure both appear to have been defeated, with Hal as the intelligent survivor (5.4.86–109). What follows is no less indebted to homiletic tradition: Falstaff, not dead in fact, carries off the dead Hotspur on his back just as Satan carries off Worldly Man to hell in *Enough Is as Good as a Feast*, c.1560. (Similar actions occur in *The Longer Thou Livest* and *Like Will to Like*.) To see the scene as a homiletic contest between good and evil does not sufficiently account for its symbolic richness, but the legacy of moral choice expressed concretely through the pairing and contrasting of characters is central to *1 Henry IV*'s dramatic structure.

---

[1] Bernard Spivack, 'Falstaff and the Psychomachia', *SQ*, 8 (1957), 449–50; Wilson, *Fortunes*, 17.

[2] David Bevington, *From 'Mankind' to Marlowe* (Cambridge, Mass., 1952); Alan C. Dessen, 'The Intemperate Knight and the Politic Prince: Late Morality Structure in *1 Henry IV*', *ShakS*, 7 (1974), 147–71.

Falstaff as Soldier

Shakespeare also brought to his creation of Falstaff an awareness of the tradition of the *miles gloriosus*, or braggart cowardly knight. Falstaff's soliloquy on honour recalls the litany-like effect of Basilisco's ruminations on death in *Soliman and Perseda* (*c.*1590), 5.3.63–76, in which that braggart soldier ponders the fates of Hercules, Priam, Achilles, Ajax, Ulysses, Alexander, and Pompey, only to answer each query with the refrain: 'dead'.[1] The sham soldier, going back at least as far as Plautus, enjoyed a theatrical currency in such humanist or neo-classical plays as *Thersites* (1537), in which the ignominious and boastful figure from Homer is terrified by a snail, even though he is armed with helmet, habergeon, sword, and club; Nicholas Udall's *Ralph Roister Doister* (*c.* 1552), whose blustering title-figure is put to rout by women; and Lyly's *Endymion* (1588), in which Sir Tophas 'thinks himself the valiantest man in the world if he kill a woman' (2.2) and speaks in a vein of comic euphuism that inspired one of Falstaff's finest parodies (2.4.386–8). As Daniel Boughner points out, pedantry often goes with the character of the traditional braggart soldier; Italian humanism gives to the soldier the embellishments of classical allusion, florid speech, and the like, so that a braggart like Don Armado in *Love's Labour's Lost* can speak in the affected style for which he is noted.[2] Though neo-classical in origin, the braggart assimilates qualities of the bragging knight in medieval drama and even of the Vice when the latter behaves in cowardly fashion; for example Ambidexter in *Cambyses* (a play to which Falstaff alludes in his spoof of 'King Cambyses' vein', 2.4.373–4)[3] puts on a comic semblance of armour. The result is a rich amalgam in which many English features colour the Latin original.[4]

Even allowing for the complexity of the tradition, however, Dover Wilson is right in insisting that Falstaff is no Bobadill (in Jonson's *Every Man In His Humour*) or Ralph Roister Doister or Parolles. These are sham soldiers, whereas Falstaff is an *old* soldier, a resourceful, seasoned campaigner for whom war is a

[1] E. E. Stoll, *Shakespeare Studies* (New York, 1927), 459.

[2] Daniel C. Boughner, 'Traditional Elements in Falstaff', *JEGP*, 43 (1944), 417–28.

[3] M. P. Tilley, 'Shakespeare and His Ridicule of *Cambyses*', *MLN*, 24 (1909), 244–7.

[4] Daniel C. Boughner, 'Vice, Braggart, and Falstaff', *Anglia*, 72 (1954), 35–61.

heaven-sent opportunity to ply the tricks of his trade.[1] The tradition of comic cowardice in the *miles gloriosus* certainly adds to our merriment at Gad's Hill, where Falstaff roars in hasty retreat, and at Shrewsbury, where he falls flat in a self-preserving semblance of death on the battlefield, but Falstaff is more than a type figuratively bearing his name on his forehead. Among other things he is a corrupt Elizabethan military officer, whose abuses of his office— allowing recruits to buy out their service, enlisting convicts, padding muster rolls, deliberately leading men into danger in order to draw their 'dead pay' (see 4.2.11–45)—are chronicled in contemporary accounts.[2] Falstaff's corrupt ways as a highwayman may borrow some details from the topical portrait of Lord Trisilian in the anonymous *Woodstock* (1591–5, revised after 1603), a play Shakespeare had certainly consulted in writing *Richard II*; with his band of pillaging knaves, Trisilian fleeces rich farmers coming to market amid cries of 'rich chuffs', 'rich whoresons', 'bacon-fed pudding eaters', and 'caterpillars', while the victims respond with 'Jesus receive my soul' and 'we can be but undone' (Malone Society reprint (1929), ll. 1527–4 and 1615–37; compare *1 Henry IV* 2.2.79–86).[3] Shakespeare's elaboration of the ancient figure of the *miles gloriosus* owes much to contemporary and recent history, and to literary satire of current abuses.

Shakespeare's debt to his own time is reflected in piquant details that give added life to his comic action. When Falstaff speaks of 'three-and-fifty upon poor old Jack' in his inflated account of the odds he faced at Gad's Hill (2.4.180), his audience may well have picked up an allusion to the fight of the *Revenge* against the Spanish fleet in September of 1591, for Ralegh and Markham stress these same odds in their well-known accounts.[4] Thus we have Falstaff against the entire Spanish fleet! As Wilson has shown, the epithets applied by Prince Hal to Falstaff's girth come from the environment of Eastcheap with its butchers' stalls and cook shops: Falstaff

[1] Wilson, *Fortunes*, 82–8.

[2] John Draper, 'Sir John Falstaff', *RES*, 7 (1932), 414–24.

[3] J. J. Elson, 'The Non-Shakespearean *Richard II* and Shakespeare's *1 Henry IV*', *SP*, 32 (1935), 177–88; Humphreys, xxxvi–xxxvii; D. J. Lake, 'Three Seventeenth-Century Revisions', *Notes and Queries*, NS 30 (1983), 133–43. The evidence of revision after 1603 raises the possibility that the phrasing in *Woodstock* is indebted to *1 Henry IV* rather than the reverse.

[4] George R. Stewart, jun., ' "Three and Fifty upon Poor Old Jack" ', *PQ*, 14 (1935), 274–5.

5. The Elizabethan meat market in Eastcheap, pictured in Hugh Alley's manuscript 'A Caveat for the City of London' (1598)

is ribs, tallow, chops, guts, brawn, sow, Martlemas beef, Manningtree ox with the pudding in his belly, hogshead, tun, bombard (leather liquor jug), and the like, or, in risible contrast, he is differentiated from such meagre fare as shotten herring, soused gurnet (pickled fish), radish, rabbit-sucker (young rabbit), and more.[1] Or maybe Shakespeare is recalling his earlier days in Stratford. According to an unsubstantiated theatrical legend from the eighteenth century, Shakespeare drew Falstaff's character to vilify a fellow townsman 'who either faithlessly broke a contract, or spitefully refused to part with some land for a valuable consideration adjoining to Shakespeare's'.[2] To the social historian, Falstaff has a more generic contemporary resonance: he is the type of impoverished gentry sinking into decadence with the disintegration of feudal order,[3] or, alternatively, the resilient exponent of an opportunistic social philosophy that supplanted feudalism when Henry Bolingbroke and his son replaced Richard II.[4]

[1] Wilson, Fortunes, 25–31.

[2] 'Old Mr Bowman the player', as reported by Sir William Bishop, c.1750. From G. Steevens, ed., Works of Shakespeare (1778), i. 202, quoted by Chambers, ii. 279.

[3] T. A. Jackson, 'Marx and Shakespeare', Labour Monthly, 46 (1964), 165–73; Paul N. Siegel, 'Falstaff and His Social Milieu', Shakespeare Jahrbuch West, 110 (1974), 139–45.

[4] Axel Clark, 'The Battle of Shrewsbury', Critical Review, 15 (1972), 29–45; William B. Stone, 'Literature and Class Ideology: Henry IV, Part One', College English, 33 (1972), 891–900.

Another image of soldiership plays a part in the genesis of Falstaff: that of Sir John Oldcastle, the historical personage who actually fought for Henry IV in France and Wales, and whose presence at Shrewsbury field in Shakespeare's play therefore begins in historically plausible circumstances, however much we are invited to laugh at the incongruous outcome. Oldcastle was knighted, probably knew the Prince of Wales, was declared a heretic for his Wycliffite beliefs, was seemingly engaged in treasonous conspiracy, was condemned to be 'hung and burnt hanging', and was extravagantly execrated by contemporary chroniclers. As Gary Taylor has pointed out, Oldcastle's controversial career is well documented in Foxe's *Book of Martyrs* (in which Oldcastle appears as a Protestant hero) and in other sources consulted by Shakespeare, including Hall, Holinshed, and Stow. Shakespeare and his audience alike were thus familiar with accounts of Oldcastle, accounts that resonate in Shakespeare's play and that would have been even more apparent to audiences of those first uncensored performances in which the name 'Oldcastle' was retained. The historical Oldcastle's gruesome torture on the gallows before being burned to death may be alluded to in the play's frequent mention of gallows.

The terms in which Oldcastle's conservative detractors sought to blacken his name were not unlike those of Shakespeare's characterization. Oldcastle was called a traitor (compare 'By the Lord, I'll be a traitor then, when thou art king', 1.2.137–8), a thief, an immoral misleader of youth (he is said to have attempted to convert the Prince of Wales), a heretic, and a hypocrite.[1] Some resemblances between the historical figure and Shakespeare's character may be fortuitous, since any reprobate figure is likely to attract such epithets, but Shakespeare's stage creation is certainly adept at the roles for which Oldcastle was so often maligned. To Shakespeare's first audience, traditional traits of the Vice and the braggart soldier may have seemed perfectly blended with topical references to one of the most interesting controversial figures of the age.

---

[1] Gary Taylor, 'The Fortunes of Oldcastle', *ShS* 38 (1985), 85–100; Wilhelm Baeske, *Oldcastle–Falstaff in der englischen Literatur bis zu Shakespeare*, Palaestra, 50 (Berlin, 1905); Alice-Lyle Scoufos, *Shakespeare's Typological Satire: A Study of the Falstaff–Oldcastle Problem* (Athens, Ohio, 1979).

Other Falstaff Antecedents

Falstaff's literary and theatrical antecedents are as varied and particularized as the references to contemporary history. Besides the Vice and the braggart soldier, Shakespeare's Falstaff may well owe something to the picaresque tradition as represented by *Lazarillo de Tormes* (1533), which was translated into English in 1586 and served as a model for the adventures of Jack Wilton in Nashe's *The Unfortunate Traveller* (1594). The wanderings of the picaresque hero are less relevant here than the succession of roles portraying the outsider and opportunist—beggar, camp-follower, strolling player, card-sharp, poseur, and the like—all sardonically employed in the interests of survival. The picaresque hero is in part descended from the parasite and the witty slave of Plautus and Terence, but in a context of Elizabethan social satire giving it immediacy for Shakespeare's audience.[1]

Falstaff's tutelage of Hal may be distantly derived from the mythic education of the Greek hero in the centaur's cave. Even though Shakespeare's indebtedness was unconscious, being filtered through knight–squire relations of medieval romance, the mythic dimension is perhaps evident in the centaur's self-indulgence, untamed appetite, and antisocial vigour. With a double parentage common in myth, the hero is exposed to the teaching of one who appears not to teach at all, but who conveys his understanding of the boundless possibilities of human imagination and the frailty of human character.[2]

Emblem-book literature is replete with illustrations linking the moon with the changing tides of fortune, folly, lack of steadfastness, and even heresy, images that are pertinent to Falstaff and his 'minions of the moon' (1.2.25), in contrast to Hal who is identified with the sun. Similarly, the emblematic contrast between the regal lion and the hare (2.4.262, 421) playfully lends to Falstaff the aura of lechery, cowardliness, and melancholy traditionally associated with the hare.[3] Conventional emblems of wrath from this literature illuminate the contrast between Hotspur and Falstaff; the latter parodies Hotspur through emblematic gesture when he

[1] Herbert B. Rothschild, jun., 'Falstaff and the Picaresque Tradition', *MLR*, 68 (1973), 14–21.

[2] Douglas J. Stewart, 'Falstaff the Centaur', *SQ*, 28 (1977), 5–21.

[3] James Hoyle, 'Some Emblems in Shakespeare's Henry IV Plays', *ELH*, 38 (1971), 512–27.

overindulges in passion, manifests at Gad's Hill an irascible display of swordsmanship, wishes a plague on all cowards, exaggerates his achievements in arms, refuses to explain his behaviour upon compulsion, and generally serves to mock Hotspur's obsessive devotion to honour.[1] Falstaff embodies all the deadly sins, even wrath, however much in jest.

Some of Falstaff's inventiveness in parody must have been transmitted to Shakespeare through the stage business of Elizabethan players specializing in clown parts, notably Richard Tarlton and Will Kempe. Tarlton especially was famous, as we have seen, for his extemporaneous wit and his ability to joke his way out of difficult situations. Clown actors no doubt gave to Shakespeare an amalgamation based on theatrical experience of many of the character types—Vice, parasite, braggart and so on —that we have encountered. The routines of Tarlton may also have appealed to Shakespeare because of that actor's fondness for mock-serious reforming cant. Tarlton was noted for his satiric depiction of psalm-singing Puritans (and of Catholics as well), a role ironically enhanced by his own whoring, extravagance with money, and association with a particular tavern.[2] Perhaps Tarlton doubled the roles of Derick and Oldcastle in *Famous Victories*.[3]

Certainly the biblical allusions in *1 Henry IV* are chosen to enhance in Falstaff the sort of comic discrepancy between fleshly living and mock-pious talk that Tarlton had incorporated in his own acting style. Falstaff urges Hal not to trouble him any more with vanity (1.2.77) and praises wise speech (ll. 81–3); in response, Hal quotes Proverbs (1 : 20) to the effect that 'Wisdom cries out in the streets and no man regards it' (ll. 84–5). Falstaff speaks of amending his present life in which he is 'little better than one of the wicked' (l. 90), but is also ready to defend highway robbery as his 'vocation', saying that it is 'no sin for a man to labour in his vocation' (ll. 99–100; 1 Corinthians 7 : 20), thus answering Hal's quip, in reference to the Anglican liturgy and its sources in Matthew and Luke, 'I see a good amendment of life in thee' (l. 97). Falstaff abuses Scripture to justify his pursuit of the seven deadly sins, jests about the crucial Lutheran doctrine of justification by

---

[1] Lawrence L. Levin, 'Hotspur, Falstaff, and the Emblem of Wrath in *1 Henry IV*', *ShakS*, 10 (1977), 42–66.

[2] J. A. Bryant, jun., 'Shakespeare's Falstaff and the Mantle of Dick Tarlton', *SP*, 51 (1954), 149–62.

[3] James Monaghan, 'Falstaff and His Forebears', *SP*, 18 (1921), 353–61.

faith alone (ll. 102–3), bids farewell to Hal in the words of a collect about the 'spirit of persuasion' that can move the hearer into a state of belief (ll. 143–5), wishes he were a psalm-singing weaver, condemns liars as 'the sons of darkness', compares his own 'days of villainy' to the 'state of innocency' when Adam fell, flaunts his girth as palpable evidence that he is more vulnerable to the frailty of flesh than most men, and so on.[1]

Falstaff's favourite biblical stories include the parable of Dives and Lazarus, with its associations of hell-fire, and that of the prodigal son. As a 'younker' or prodigal himself, as a 'youth' who 'must live', Falstaff is also the companion of Hal, from whose riotous ways the Prince, like the prodigal son, must seek to redeem himself and the time lost thereby.[2] The biblical allusions suggest the richness of the roles Falstaff plays on Hal's behalf, for Falstaff is at once the 'father of lies' and 'Monsieur Remorse', riot and repentance, vanity and sanctimony, tempter and innocence beguiled.[3] Both incorrigible and meaning to repent, he play-acts for Hal the internal drama of 'casting off the old man',[4] and is finally left behind by the young man who succeeds in so doing.

Falstaff's biblical guise is perhaps only one aspect of his larger function as Lord of Misrule.[5] Parody of biblical texts and the liturgy was an essential feature of those festive days on which minor functionaries in the Church assumed authority for a time as Boy Bishop or made braying noises from the choir. In holiday revels the Lord of Misrule presided over similar occasions of permitted indecorum and Saturnalian inversion; licensed play of this sort was necessary in an institutionalized, hierarchical social order. Falstaff becomes Lord of Misrule when he presides over the tavern revelry of 2.4, and even plays the role of King with mock crown and mock chair of state. *1 Henry IV*'s interest in holidays

[1] Compare 1.2.102 with Romans 3: 28, 2.4.165 with 1 Thessalonians 5: 5, 3.3.35 with Matthew 8: 12 and 22: 13, and 3.3.158–61 with Matthew 26: 41 and Mark 14: 38. See Commentary on these lines and at 1.2.143–5 and 2.4.127; see also Milward, 90–1, 106–9, and *passim*, and Noble, 169–74.

[2] See 2.2.80–6, 3.3.29–31 and 77, 4.2.23–5 and 31–3, and *2 Henry IV* 2.1.139.

[3] Wilson, *Fortunes*, 32–3.

[4] D. J. Palmer, 'Casting Off the Old Man: History and St Paul in *Henry IV*', *CritQ*, 12 (1970), 267–83.

[5] C. L. Barber, *Shakespeare's Festive Comedy* (Princeton, 1959), 192–221; Roy Battenhouse, 'Falstaff as Parodist and Perhaps Holy Fool', *PMLA*, 90 (1975), 32–52.

(1.2.192) and their relation to labouring in one's vocation reveals a deep affinity for the Feast of Fools and other such times of respite from everyday life. Falstaff is accordingly given a role not unlike that of the professional fool in Renaissance courts or the wise fool in Erasmus's *Praise of Folly*, one whose function is to entertain the Prince with madcap inverted wisdom, and to ask the irreverent questions that more worldly counsellors are not permitted to ask. Folk elements are pronounced, not least of all in the bogus resurrection Falstaff engineers for himself in the manner of a St George play.[1]

Providential Views of History Versus Renaissance Scepticism

The rich ambivalence of Falstaff's character, which can be suggested only incompletely by a study of character types such as the Vice, braggart, parasite, court fool, Lord of Misrule, mock-Puritan, picaresque hero, and so on, needs to be understood in relation to ambivalences in the play as a whole, to what A. P. Rossiter has termed 'the dialectic of the histories'.[2] To ask whether Falstaff is a Vice figure to be exorcised or a wise fool to be cherished, or both, is to examine only one aspect of a large question centred on order and degree. Does Shakespeare's play show evidence of a retributive pattern of moral history, through which we perceive a divine endorsement of hierarchy in the state and a condemnation of rebellion, or is the lesson of history more matter of fact, iconoclastic even? Shakespeare's sources again reveal a wealth of contradictory material. We are concerned here not merely with the chronicles and fictional narratives from which he drew characters and events, but with works of political theory, homilies on obedience, defences of established religion, and all that contributes to that maddeningly imprecise entity called public opinion.

The conservative view of the subject presents itself under the banner of Elizabethan world-order. According to E. M. W. Tillyard, Shakespeare derived from many sources the notion of history as an epic, providential sequence centred on the state as protagonist.[3]

[1] Walter Kaiser, *Praisers of Folly* (Cambridge, Mass., 1963), 195–275; Leo Salingar, 'Falstaff and the Life of Shadows', in *Shakespearean Comedy*, ed. Maurice Charney (New York, 1980), 185–205.

[2] A. P. Rossiter, 'Ambivalence: The Dialectic of the Histories,' in *Angel with Horns* (1961), 40–64.

[3] E. M. W. Tillyard, *Shakespeare's History Plays* (1944).

Man, as the apex of the ladder of creation and as the synthesis of the four elements, was thought to contain in himself in microcosm the structure of the body politic. Any alternative to a cosmic view of a divinely ordained political order was branded as machiavellism, abhorrent because it was perceived as setting false limits to the human spirit. Tudor mythographers like Polydore Vergil, and especially Edward Hall, shaped their vision of Renaissance English history around the triumphant union of the two families of Lancaster and York after the disorders of civil war. *A Mirror for Magistrates* emphasized the horror of division, the significance of prophecy, and the importance of educating the Christian Prince through didactic examples from history. The morality drama and plays like *Gorboduc* (1562) and *Woodstock* likewise endorsed the instructive metaphor of a mirror. In this context, argues Tillyard, a reading of *1 Henry IV* must heed closely the cross-references to other plays in the sequence: to the prophetic warnings in *Richard II* of bloodshed whereby future generations of Englishmen will pay for the impiety of Richard's godless overthrow (4.1.137–50), to Henry V's prayer on the eve of Agincourt that God not hold against him 'the fault | My father made in compassing the crown' (*Henry V* 4.1.281–2). The natural consequence of such a reading is that *1* and *2 Henry IV* are viewed as parts of a single structure leading towards the rejection of Falstaff as the embodiment of dishonour and vanity while Hal completes his education to become the kingly type of magnificence and *sprezzatura*.[1]

Against this conservative interpretation of Tudor historiography and its narrowing implications for Falstaff, recent scholarship has propounded serious objections. Renaissance humanism never accepted the wholly providential view of Augustine's *City of God*, according to M. M. Reese; instead, it created a blend of classical didacticism and medieval providentiality that incorporated admonitions to rulers and the seeking of remedies for the state, thereby linking history with the science of politics in a way that was not deterministic. Such a humanism reconciled a belief in God as the ordainer of a rational and good design with an increased awareness of secondary causes in history attributable to behaviour of men.[2] As a consequence, political drama could do much more

---

[1] Ibid. See also Lily Bess Campbell, *Shakespeare's 'Histories': Mirrors of Elizabethan Policy* (San Marino, Calif., 1947).

[2] M. M. Reese, *The Cease of Majesty* (1961), 1–19.

than simply affirm providential truth: it could study the ironies of human striving for power.

Englishmen were far too independent, in Wilbur Sanders's view, to have accepted without question the truisms of the political homilies they heard in church. The treatises of John Ponet (*A Short Treatise of Politic Power*, 1556) and Thomas Starkey (*A Dialogue between Reginald Pole and Thomas Lupset*, 1533–6), among others, give evidence of deep concern about the controlling tendencies of monarchical power and about the need for a concept of power as something given by the people to the prince to be exercised humanely. Marlowe's *Edward II* (1591–3) shows us English history stripped bare of divine sanction, and, although Shakespeare does not follow Marlowe's extreme of iconoclasm, his admiration for that play is obvious in *Richard II*. Shakespeare, like Marlowe, has thought about the unproductive violence of political controversy and has seen through to the deeper issues it evades. He voices the dialogue of Tudor political controversy much more clearly than he takes sides; he gives us a whole range of possible answers to questions of rebellion and loyalty in a kind of empirical openness that is characteristic of the best political theorists of the age.[1]

Moral and providential judgements abound in Shakespeare's Henriad, but, as Henry Kelly observes, they are distributed according to the speakers' biases. Lancastrian supporters of Bolingbroke and his son reflect the Lancastrian myth that Providence overthrew Richard II and favoured his successor; Yorkist supporters, like the Bishop of Carlisle in *Richard II* (4.2), reflect the Yorkist myth branding the Henrys as usurpers and regicides who deserve providential punishment in the form of civil rebellion. The amalgams generated by sixteenth-century historiographers offered Shakespeare a heterogeneous mix of these ideas, in which he would have found not so much a consistent pattern of hereditary retribution as the simpler notion that God's favour was to be perceived in fortunate events and his disfavour in unfortunate ones. Holinshed in particular gave Shakespeare no unambiguous thesis of a continued providential curse on the Henrys or of punishment of a people in repayment for the crimes of its ruling family.[2]

[1] Wilbur Sanders, *The Dramatist and the Received Idea* (Cambridge, 1968), chap. 8.
[2] Henry Ansgar Kelly, *Divine Providence in the England of Shakespeare's Histories* (Cambridge, Mass., 1970).

1 Henry IV correspondingly demonstrates no clear sign of providential punishment. King Henry may ponder whether 'God will have it so | For some displeasing service I have done', and speculate that his son's rebellion is a 'revengement' and a 'scourge' (3.2.4−7), just as Henry V will later plead divine forgiveness for the 'fault' by which his father obtained the crown, but the events of their reigns, however stormy, prove ultimately benign for them. Hotspur (1.3.158−86, 4.3.52−105) gives eloquent voice to Yorkist mythology about the wrongs done to Richard, 'that sweet lovely rose' (1.3.175), but the more practical accusations made by Hotspur's conspiring kinsmen are those of treachery and double-dealing by Henry against his own former allies (5.1.30−71). In any event, the Percys' rebellion fails, and along with it any claim that God will avenge, during the course of this play at least, the wrong done his royal minister. Even Worcester frankly admits that their rebellious cause 'Must keep aloof from strict arbitrament' (i.e. impartial inquiry or adjudication), and must stop up every loophole whence 'The eye of reason may pry in upon us' (4.1.70−2). Glendower's occult magical powers tend to undercut any idea of the rebels as God's agents, and even a rebel Christian like the Archbishop of York seems motivated more by revenge for his brother than by moral outrage at regicide and usurpation. On the other hand, King Henry's final judgement on the Percys' cause —'Thus ever did rebellion find rebuke' (5.5.1)—is no certain providential conclusion; it is the public statement of a winner, glad to see his troubles behind him, at least temporarily.[1]

The Question of Structural Unity

The debate over Tillyard's insistence on Elizabethan world-order as the key to Shakespeare's history plays has interesting ramifications, not only for characterization—e.g. is Falstaff a Vice tempter or a free spirit?—but also for structure. Are *1* and *2 Henry IV* a unified whole, and integrally part of the larger structure of the Henriad, or is each play a separate theatrical event? Tillyard's argument, as we have seen, impels him towards the unitary view, towards seeing the rejection of Falstaff and the emergence of Henry V as the necessary conclusion to a story of political conflict whose

[1] Ibid. See also John Wilders, *The Lost Garden: A View of Shakespeare's English and Roman History Plays* (1978).

another play 'with Sir John in it', though Falstaff does not
materialize in *Henry V*.

1 and *2 Henry IV* are closely bound, however, by the rejection of
Falstaff, and by the use of a story that had already appeared in
Famous Victories as a single dramatic structure. Did Shakespeare
intend from the start to leave the rejection out of *1 Henry IV*,
despite anticipations of that event? Or did he plan originally to
include the rejection, as in *Famous Victories*, as has been argued by
Harold Jenkins? According to Jenkins's theory, Shakespeare
originally set up a series of parallels between comic and serious
plots designed to culminate, as promised in Hal's soliloquy, in the
besting of Hotspur and the rejection of Falstaff. Falstaff serves as a
foil for Hotspur at every turn in matters of robbery and cowardice,
and Hal's announcement of his intention towards Falstaff in the
play-acting scene (2.4) is paired with his announcement of his
intention towards Hotspur in the interview with King Henry (3.2).
Once the dooms of Falstaff and Hotspur are in sight, however,
Jenkins sees Shakespeare changing his mind; the comic material
for the rest of the play is less compressed, and *Part 2* improvises
its sub-plot on a theme of justice. This hypothesis explains, in
Jenkins's view, why the second play, for all the parallelisms with
the rebel scenes and tavern scenes of *Part 1*, does not contain the
same real double action. History does not repeat itself; Hal does not
go through a cycle of riot and reform again.[1]

Whether or not Shakespeare changed his mind this drastically
as he wrote, the structural integrity of the two separate plays we
now have in *1* and *2 Henry IV* is surely more substantial than
Jenkins's or Wilson's theories of improvisation would seem to
allow. The ending of *1 Henry IV* is suited to the play for which it is
provided. Falstaff is to be rejected ultimately, but not now. Mean-
time, the Battle of Shrewsbury brings to a resolution the issue of
honour with which *Part 1* has been concerned. Hotspur lies dead,
and Hal has vindicated himself as promised, having both proved
his worth in arms and reformed his wasteful ways. The symmetries
of the serious and comic plots have permitted the stories of Hotspur
and Falstaff to develop side by side, each with its beginning, middle,
and end. In one, a rebellion is conceived and developed,
whereupon the rebels prepare for battle and are defeated; in the

[1] Harold Jenkins, *The Structural Problem of Shakespeare's 'Henry the Fourth'*
(1956).

other, the Prince takes part in a conspiracy to rob in the name of companionship with Falstaff, yet declares his intent to reform, appears penitentially before his father, and puts some distance between himself and Falstaff thereafter. The coincidence of Hal's declarations against Hotspur and against Falstaff marks the simultaneous progression of the two plots, even though we must allow that the two follow divergent and irreconcilable time-schemes; an interval of some three or four weeks is needed to ripen the serious rebellion hatched in 1.3, for example, while the highway robbery is planned and executed in a matter of hours.[1]

Loose ends are apparent at the end of *1 Henry IV*, to be sure, for history is open-ended even in a play that achieves brilliant closure.[2] After all, even *Henry V* concludes, for all its triumphs in war and marriage, on a reminder of the failures of Henry VI that are to follow in the course of history. In *1 Henry IV* rebellion is never wholly quelled, and the introduction of the Archbishop of York in 4.4 is a reminder of unfinished business. Falstaff's deplorable behaviour at the expense of Hal's military reputation is both a fit testimonial to the distance that has come between them and a promise of further roguery. The uneasy relationship between Hal and his father attains a moment of trust appropriate to Hal's emergence as his father's son, but there is unfinished business here too. The actions in *Part 2* that involve repetition—the second rebellion of the Percys, the second long tavern scene, the second interview of father and son—all arise from the perception that what seemed so easy of solution is in fact deeply problematic. Falstaff just won't go away, and neither will Hal's reputation for wanton behaviour. In *Part 1* Hal's business was to reform his conduct; in *Part 2* he finds he must convince the world that he has reformed and is fit to be king.[3]

The Pattern of Oppositions: *Hotspur and Falstaff on Honour*

As a dramatic entity, *1 Henry IV* reveals a structure that is simultaneously manifested through character and theme. The

[1] F. M. Salter, 'The Play within the Play of *First Henry IV*', *Proceedings and Transactions of the Royal Society of Canada*, third ser. 40.2 (1946), 209–23.

[2] David Scott Kastan, *Shakespeare and the Shapes of Time* (Hanover, NH, 1982), 37–55.

[3] Sherman H. Hawkins, 'Virtue and Kingship in Shakespeare's *Henry IV*', *ELR*, 5 (1975), 313–43.

alternation of action from serious to comic and the parallel movement in two plots from rebellion to reformation take visible shape in the contrasts between Hotspur and Falstaff and the King and Falstaff, with the Prince occupying a central position. Such oppositions invite definition. One focus of definition is the concept of honour.

According to one often repeated formulation, Hotspur is the excess and Falstaff the defect of military spirit; the former represents exaggerated honour, the latter dishonour. The Prince, comparing the rival merits of chivalry and vanity, comes to embody magnificence, or tasteful bounty, and is thus representative of Aristotle's middle quality between extremes, as is Guyon in Book 2 of Spenser's *The Faerie Queene*.[1] This scheme need not oversimplify the extremes or present them as unattractive: Hotspur is idealistic, brave, and charismatic, Falstaff wisely sceptical and philosophic about war. Still, each suffers from an incompleteness or immaturity that leads to failure of one extreme or the other on the field at Shrewsbury.

The scheme of Aristotle's *Nicomachean Ethics* can be expanded to include the four cardinal virtues as integral to a prince's ethical training, if, as Sherman Hawkins argues, *Part 1* is seen as concerned with fortitude and temperance, *Part 2* with justice and wisdom. The Prince, who in *Part 1* tellingly speaks of himself as embodying all humours, and who proves a great mimic of those he would study, learns in the course of time to master the irascible and the appetitive; he does not repress, but instead masters, choler and fleshly indulgence, thereby assimilating the energies of both Hotspur and Falstaff. Each of these two figures represents the defect of one virtue and the excess of another, while the Prince becomes, in Macrobius' words, the 'good man' who is first made lord of himself and then ruler of the state.[2] *1 Henry IV* is Hal's *institutio principis*, and Hal is its epic hero.

These attractive schemes of opposition need careful qualification, however. Falstaff is happy enough, as Norman Council observes, to garner honour at Shrewsbury; he rejects merely the established code through which it is normally attained.[3] Hotspur,

---

[1] Cleanth Brooks and Robert B. Heilman, *Understanding Drama* (New York, 1948), 376–87; Tillyard, *Shakespeare's History Plays*, 265.

[2] Hawkins, 'Virtue and Kingship', *ELR*, 5 (1975), 313–43.

[3] Norman Council, 'Prince Hal: Mirror of Success', *ShakS*, 7 (1974), 125–46.

6. *Falstaff carrying dead Hotspur*, by H. W. Bunbury (1750-1811)

conversely, is the unstained embodiment of that code, respected even by King Henry as one 'who is the theme of honour's tongue' (1.1.80). To see Falstaff as the embodiment of dishonour is to ignore the value of his insight; Falstaff gives us a reasoned rejection of honour, by reversing the terms of the code according to which honour is more precious than life. The debate is one of conflicting values, to which Hal comes as one detached: he will employ honour as a useful commodity, and redeem his own lost reputation by using Hotspur's reputation for his own gain, but he shows what he has learned from Falstaff by his ironic appreciation of a shrunken 'ill-weaved ambition' that is now food for worms (5.4.86–7). As W. Gordon Zeeveld has put it, 'food for worms' nicely expresses the cost of Hotspur's misdirected idealism, while 'food for powder' (4.2.62–3) exposes the limits of Falstaff's sardonic view of war. Hotspur is brave, but never gives a thought to the lives of his soldiers; Falstaff, too, regards his soldiers as expendable, though in the interest of preserving his own life in all its jollity. Hal sees war as the inhuman business it is, and yet his own superior honour takes the form of proposing to save blood on both sides through

43

single combat. His honour, in contrast to Hotspur's cry of 'Die all, die merrily' (4.1.135), includes a regard for the value of human life.[1]

The opposition represented by Hotspur and Falstaff is thus one of paradox, rendering more complex the choice that Hal must make. Even the physical difference between Hotspur and Falstaff is instructive. In the opposition of prudence and economy to wasteful excess, Falstaff represents both the sickness of the state (like the caterpillars of the commonwealth in *Richard II*) and the remedy of some of its ills. His obesity is suggestive of luxurious surfeit, and yet he shows us the point of view from which thinness and economy can be inadequate and unpleasant. Hal stands to benefit from Falstaff's friendship, yet must know when to reject the reign of vanity that brought down Richard II.[2] He must cultivate princely liberality in response to Hotspur's churlishness (as in Hotspur's dealings with Glendower) and Falstaff's prodigality. Hal must exhibit good-tempered bravery in response to Hotspur's irascibility and Falstaff's lack of combativeness.[3] Paradox is evident here as well, for Falstaff is able to parody Hotspur's exaggerated manliness with his 'A plague of all cowards', his lament for old-fashioned 'manhood' that is now 'forgot upon the face of the earth', and his tale of 'two- or three-and-fifty upon poor old Jack' (2.4.110–81).

Hal studies manliness in Hotspur while learning, as Hotspur does not, to limit his sense of superiority; through Falstaff he discovers his weakness as a man and his capacity for witty laughter, without surrendering, as Falstaff does, to the fleshliness of appetite and the moral anarchy that wit can produce.[4] In his ability to enlarge and be flexible, in contrast to Hotspur and Falstaff, both of whom diminish other people as means to an egotistical end, Hal finds a happy mean between humourless zeal and frivolity.[5] Yet his choice is not simply between extremes, but between alternatives that cast light on each other's deficiencies and virtues alike, as when Falstaff's highway escapades illustrate, both by resemblance and contrast, the thievery that is part of the political story as well;

[1] W. Gordon Zeeveld, ' "Food for Powder"–"Food for Worms" ', *SQ*, 3 (1952), 249–53.

[2] R. J. Dorius, 'A Little More Than a Little', *SQ*, 11 (1960), 13–26.

[3] William B. Hunter, jun, 'Prince Hal, His Struggle Toward Moral Perfection', *South Atlantic Quarterly*, 50 (1950), 86–95.

[4] Charles Mitchell, 'The Education of the True Prince', *TSL*, 12 (1967), 13–21.

[5] John P. Sisk, 'Prince Hal and the Specialists', *SQ*, 28 (1977), 520–24.

at Gad's Hill and in Bolingbroke's dealings with the Percys, we see the ironic pattern of the robber robbed.

From Feudal Chivalry to Pragmatism: Language and Political Change

The symmetries of *1 Henry IV* are thus not those of a stable pyramidal structure of order and degree. Authority at the apex is uncertain, as Sigurd Burckhardt has shown, producing two kinds of order, each attempting to destroy the other. The instability bespeaks a shift in Shakespeare's world-picture from the divinely ordered state of *Richard II* to a state that is ordered in accordance with human needs, from the seemingly permanent structures of feudalism and primogeniture to a state of combat and questionable legitimacy, from the king as divinely sanctioned to the king as self-made.[1] The outmoded honour of chivalry gives way to machiavellian concern with power, and, in Hal, to the new virtue of courtesy; Hotspur remains a crusader in a romance, while Hal becomes a Renaissance gentleman, 'the king of courtesy' (2.4.10), showing this quality in his disposition of Douglas who has fled in the battle. As in Castiglione's *The Courtier* and Spenser's *The Faerie Queene*, courtesy is motivated in part by a desire for praise. It is exercised by 'knowing what is fitting for oneself and others', and by enacting this graciously.[2]

The old order of Hotspur confuses personal with public welfare, personal with public conflict.[3] Its ceremony must yield to history, divinity to mortality, the golden to the brazen. The ideal world of what ought to be gives way to the unselected, chaotic flow of history, to contingency and temporality. Our evaluation of this shift is ambivalent: on the one hand, we regret the destruction of a divinely sanctioned culture only to be replaced by cunning and political expediency; on the other, we applaud the acceptance of a vital historical movement. Hal's difficult task is to construct a symbolic order of monarchy out of diverse and unpromising materials, mingling the residues of a dying political theology of the king's two bodies with his own abilities in magisterial rhetoric and

[1] Sigurd Burckhardt, *Shakespearean Meanings* (Princeton, 1968), 144–205.

[2] G. M. Pinciss, 'The Old Honor and the New Courtesy: *1 Henry IV*', *ShS* 31 (1978), 85–91.

[3] Anthony La Branche, '"If Thou Wert Sensible of Courtesy": Private and Public Virtue in *Henry IV*, Part One', *SQ*, 17 (1966), 371–82.

the language of the tavern. Poetic self-indulgence is replaced by the art of persuasive speech.[1]

The shift in language from the medieval and ceremonial speech of *Richard II* to the Renaissance and practical speech of *1 Henry IV* is evident in the latter's extensive and brilliant use of prose (not used at all in *Richard II*, and scarcely at all in the earlier history plays except for the Jack Cade scenes of *2 Henry VI*), in its proliferation of tongues and accents (including Welsh), and, as Joseph Porter has pointed out, in the topic of naming.[2] The validity of names in the linguistically absolutist world of *Richard II* is a test case for the validity of language generally; only sick men play with their names, and Richard devoutly believes that 'the King's name' is 'twenty thousand names' (3.2.85). In *1 Henry IV*, by contrast, the magical authority of names comes increasingly into question, and the invention of abusive appellations is one of the chief vehicles in the combat of wits between Hal and Falstaff. Hotspur's speech is like Richard II's in his tuning of his ear to his own tongue and in his holding to an absolutist conception of language that does not take time into account; his verbal scepticism is also appropriate to one who is a political rebel.[3] Falstaff regards honour merely as a word, as air, and accordingly treats words as the proper object of linguistic playfulness, punning, and comparison. Hal enjoys the hilarity and irresponsibility of Falstaff's speech acts, revelling in a polyglot facility with languages, but ultimately he is asking very different questions about language from those of Hotspur or Falstaff. He is interested in learning how to cope practically with the potentially anarchic aftermath of the fall from Richard II's linguistic absolutism, and so Hal's characteristic speech acts involve promising, vowing, giving and keeping one's word (as the rebels and even King Henry do not).[4]

Hal's speech takes account of the passage of time, for changes in history demand changes in language. King Henry, having instigated the idea that a king's word lacks sacred ranking, must suffer the consequences: for him, the oath as a locutionary act can

[1] Eric La Guardia, 'Ceremony and History: The Problem of Symbol from *Richard II* to *Henry V*', in *Pacific Coast Studies in Shakespeare*, ed. W. McNeir and T. Greenfield (Eugene, Ore., 1966).

[2] Joseph A. Porter, *The Drama of Speech Acts* (Berkeley, 1979), 52–88.

[3] M. M. Mahood, *Shakespeare's Wordplay* (1957), 73–88.

[4] Porter, *Drama of Speech Acts*, 52–88. See also Joseph Candido, 'The Name of King: Hal's "Titles" in the "Henriad"', *TSLL*, 26 (1984), 61–73.

no longer be binding. Not coincidentally, Falstaff uses oaths in this play more freely and irresponsibly than anyone else. The boast is another characteristic locutionary act in this play, as Ronald Macdonald has observed, and it is one that is peculiarly vulnerable to deflation, whether in Glendower's assertion of a power to summon devils or in Falstaff's fiction of a triumph over two young men in Kendal green in the dark. Because Hal is wise and self-knowing in his mastery of new languages, he is able to avoid these pitfalls of empty oath-giving and boastfulness. Most of all he senses that people like Richard II and Hotspur who do not grow in language are defeated by history.[1]

Fathers and Sons: *Role-playing and Identity*

In such a changing world, King Henry provides both positive and negative examples in his roles of king and father to Hal. Here the King acts as a foil to Falstaff, providing a very different set of alternatives from those put to Hal by Hotspur and Falstaff. King Henry and Falstaff are alternative parental figures: the King is distant and awesome, serving as the guilt-based conscience of adult responsibility, whereas Falstaff is nurturing and permissive, offering the infantile world of the child. Hal must come to terms both with resentment towards the restrictions of social life and with the seemingly innocent wish to love and enjoy a life of self-gratification. By killing Hotspur, argues Franz Alexander, Hal kills or assimilates his own self-destructive tendencies and overcomes his own natural aggression and jealousy towards his father.[2] Shakespeare thus accounts for both the debauchery and the sudden conversion registered in the chronicles and in *Famous Victories*.

The legend of parricidal near-violence subsequently giving way to filial acceptance of the father whom the son must replace is a profoundly resonant one for any account of a young man's wavering struggle towards maturity. The centrality of the motif is apparent in the several configurations of father and son in *1 Henry IV*. King Henry has in effect two sons (Hal and Hotspur), just as Hal

---

[1] Ronald R. Macdonald, 'Uneasy Lies: Language and History in Shakespeare's Lancastrian Tetralogy', *SQ*, 35 (1984), 22–39.

[2] Franz Alexander, 'A Note on Falstaff', *Psychoanalytic Quarterly*, 3 (1933), 592–606.

has two fathers; and Hotspur also stands between a weak father and his uncle, Worcester. Glendower attempts to be a father to the fiery youth whose kinsman has married his daughter, only to be met with witty hostility and scepticism towards his claims of magical authority. With no mother present, Prince Hal's conflict (as Ernst Kris terms it) takes the form of filial attachment to a father substitute, one who satisfies his need for warmth and love, even while Hal acts out with this substitute his feelings towards the lineal father whom he must test against an ideal of royal dignity. Hal goes to the tavern, according to Kris's argument, rather than acquiesce in regicide; the tavern gives Hal some respite, some time to explore dimensions of himself that have no place in his father's world. By the time of the battle of Shrewsbury, he is ready to save his father's life and kill his *alter ego* instead.[1] W. H. Auden puts it well: we were all Falstaffs once upon a time, and then we became social beings with super-egos, dreaming the potentially hazardous dream of a narcissistic self-sufficiency.[2]

The form of this play is thus one of conflict successfully resolved, though, as Richard Wheeler points out, success is achieved only by the suppression of the young man's relationship to women.[3] Hal is provided with neither mother nor love attachment in this play about maturation. Women generally play a peripheral role in *1 Henry IV*; they are dependent on their husbands' whims, like Lady Percy, or separated from the male world by impassable barriers, like the Welsh wife of Mortimer. Brief scenes of tenderness between men and women merely accentuate by means of contrast the centrality of male conflict, between twinned rivals or fathers and sons.[4]

1 Henry IV aptly demonstrates how the adult world of political struggle can easily dismay one who is expected to assume a role of leadership. The predominant metaphors of the opening scene are of England as mother, daubing her lips with her own children's

[1] Ernst Kris, 'Prince Hal's Conflict', *Psychoanalytic Quarterly*, 17 (1948), 487–506.

[2] W. H. Auden, 'The Prince's Dog', in *The Dyer's Hand* (1948), 182–208. See also Robert N. Watson, *Shakespeare and the Hazards of Ambition* (Cambridge, Mass., 1984), 47–75.

[3] Richard Wheeler, *Shakespeare's Development and the Problem Comedies* (Berkeley, 1981), 158–67. See also Coppélia Kahn, *Man's Estate: Masculine Identity in Shakespeare* (Berkeley, 1981), 47–81.

[4] Robert J. Lordi, 'Brutus and Hotspur', *SQ*, 27 (1976), 177–85.

blood, and, conversely, of war trenching England's fields and bruising her flowers; the mother violates and is violated.[1] Civil butchery is cannibalistic and suicidal, as seen in the knife-edge of civil war that cuts its own master. Metaphors of disease occur throughout ('This sickness doth infect | The very life-blood of our enterprise', says Hotspur, 4.1.28–9), hearkening back to the motif of the physician and the sick land in *Richard II*.[2] The division of England is given literal form on stage in the map used by the rebels to chop up their country into three parts. Henry's wish for a pilgrimage to the Holy Land mocks him in *1 Henry IV* because it remains so unattainable;[3] again, a recurring motif from *Richard II* (1.3.49 and 264, 4.1.92–100) contributes to an ominous mood of unfinished business.

Troubled by a rebellious son, continually having to weigh the demands of humanity and those of authority, King Henry faces difficulties not unlike those of King David with Absalom.[4] Because he continually masks his personal and political self, King Henry is a hard character to read. Why does he speak so sternly to Hotspur over the business of the Scottish prisoners, when he has already confessed his father-like envy of Northumberland for siring so noble a son? We are inclined to view the reprimand and warning as expressive of the King's parental regard; he wants Hotspur as a kind of son, but on the terms of fatherly command and filial obedience. Hotspur is easily persuaded by Northumberland and Worcester to see the King's attitude as one of arrogance and hostility, and so a relationship that might have flourished is instead poisoned. The irony of a war that might have been averted never disappears, for the King's admiration of Hotspur prompts him even at the last minute to seek genuine peace.

The offer is undone by Worcester's perfidious refusal to transmit the offer fairly to Hotspur. Yet can we really blame Worcester? His logic in describing the King's implacable hostility towards him and Northumberland, however much the King may be ready to forgive

---

[1] L. C. Knights, '*Henry IV* as Satire', Part II of 'Notes on Comedy', *Scrutiny*, 1 (1933), 356–67.

[2] Ronald Berman, 'The Nature of Guilt in the *Henry IV* Plays', *ShakS*, 1 (1965), 18-28.

[3] James Black, 'Henry IV's Pilgrimage', *SQ*, 34 (1983), 18–26.

[4] David Evett, 'Types of King David in Shakespeare's Lancastrian Tetralogy', *ShakS*, 14 (1981), 139–61.

Hotspur, is unassailable.[1] The barons who helped Bolingbroke to usurp the throne must have expected great favours from him, and authority to do much as they pleased in their own territories; Henry's assertion of royal prerogative strikes at the heart of their political self-interest. Henry must suspect the Percys of feelings of ingratitude towards him as he moves to centralize power, and so he cannot rely on them. No less inevitably, they sense that Henry is no longer their friend. The response of the two sides to Mortimer's capture at the hands of Glendower is symptomatic: Henry sees it as evidence of an interest in Mortimer's claim to the throne, and finds his suspicions confirmed by the marriage to Glendower's daughter, whereas the Percys see the refusal to provide ransom as one more proof of Henry's cooling sympathy with their cause. War between the two sides is as unavoidable as it is unnecessary. Hal senses this fact, and makes an offer of single combat through which pointless bloodshed might be avoided. Once again a sane and generous solution proves impossible, and the battle goes forward. How is Hal to rule an England so divided against itself?

In his dealings with his son, King Henry is no less enigmatic, distant, and pursued by ironies that seem destined to kill his most fervent hopes. Why, in a time of grave national crisis, should such a careworn king be plagued by rebellion in the very person on whom his futurity depends? Shakespeare invites us to sympathize with the father as with the rebels, to see the point of view of all sides even in what is often self-destructive behaviour.

Henry's interviewing of his son in 3.2 is an astonishing performance. He offers his son a lesson in statecraft that depends on the staging of public appearances, on learning how to steal 'all courtesy from heaven' and dress oneself in humility, plucking allegiance from men's hearts, and avoiding at all costs the unwise behaviour of one who like Richard II cheapens his dignity through over-exposure and glibness. Royal governance, in this view, is the art of manipulating the awesome images of power, by whose means the astute monarch can 'steal' and 'pluck' what he desires from the populace (3.2.50–2). King Henry may be a 'well-graced actor' (*Richard II*, 5.2.24) compared with Richard II, but he can never shake off the theatrical associations of a dissembler who has cleverly created for himself a role as king.[2]

[1] Moody Prior, *The Drama of Power* (Evanston, Ill., 1973), 59–82 and 199–262.
[2] Anne Righter, *Shakespeare and the Idea of the Play* (1962), 127 ff.

Hal, despite the rehearsal of the night before, finds himself abashed and denied the 'glittering' reformation that his soliloquy of 1.2 had anticipated.[1] The son gives a poor account of himself at first, so much so that he subsequently laughs at his performance in the interview; 'I am good friends with my father', he tells Falstaff, 'and may do anything' (3.3.174–5). Yet father and son break through their reserve at the crucial moment, in part because of the unexpected candour of King Henry's account of his anxieties and the honesty of his weeping. Hal's vow to redeem the time is put in terms of a promise to his father: 'I will ... Be bold to tell you that I am your son' (3.2.132–4). Identity is attained by acknowledging the father, by assimilating the best that he has to teach, while at the same time preserving one's sense of self. Hal will save his father's life at Shrewsbury. At the same time his bravery on the field of battle will bear little resemblance to the 'counterfeits' of soldiership displayed by the older man protected by other warriors marching in his coat of arms.[2]

In order to differentiate himself from his father and be free of the demand for unquestioning obedience that parents often make when they view their children as extensions of themselves, Hal finds that he must explore his identity in the liberating company of Falstaff. The instructive games they play include masquerading and name-calling, both forms of altering and testing identity. In the long tavern scene, Hal proposes playing Hotspur to Falstaff's 'Dame Mortimer his wife' (after having shown how well he can mimic Hotspur's mannerisms of speech), agrees to a 'play extempore' if the 'argument' or plot is Falstaff's running-away at Gad's Hill, and undertakes with Falstaff to play-act an interview between himself and his father. Inveterate actors, Hal and Falstaff shift roles with a versatility that bespeaks their familiarity with this form of entertainment. Hal's role-playing takes him through the parts of Hotspur and King Henry, both essential models in his forging of his own identity, and brings him into continual juxtaposition with Falstaff. Hal's insight into Hotspur's fanatical self-absorption and King Henry's stern disapproval are as sympathetic as they are witty; Hal studies character even while he good-naturedly mocks it. The role-playing also allows Hal to depose his father in jest and to rehearse the rejection of Falstaff.

---

[1] Thomas Jameson, *The Hidden Shakespeare* (New York, 1967), 82–104.
[2] James Black, 'Counterfeits of Soldiership in *Henry IV*', *SQ*, 24 (1973), 372–82.

Closely allied is the game of name-calling. Hal and his companions have many names for Falstaff—Sir John Sack-and-Sugar Jack, Monsieur Remorse, grey iniquity, swollen parcel of dropsies, and the like—but Hal, too, must hear his legitimacy subjected to comic doubt, and must hear himself asked whether a son of England will prove a thief and take purses. To his assertion that Falstaff is a bed-presser and huge hill of flesh, Hal is answered with the labels of 'bull's pizzle', 'stockfish', and 'vile standing tuck' (2.4.238–40). Falstaff's fondness for 'if' clauses underlines flexible identity, as in 'If I be not ashamed of my soldiers, I am a soused gurnet' (4.2.11–12).[1]

Falstaff is incessantly the actor, creating roles to captivate the young Prince. William Hazlitt has suggested that Falstaff may have put the tavern reckoning in his pocket deliberately, for his comic gambit is always to offer himself and his gluttonous ways at the expense of glory.[2] He not only is called many names by others, but is always renaming himself, like Misrule assuming the disguise of Good Government. At one moment he is a highwayman identifying himself with youthful riot against age and respectability, at another he is a pious penitent; at one time he is a patriot wishing the tavern were his drum, at another he is a flagrant abuser of military conscription. He wittily defends his 'vocation', but what is it other than to amuse Hal? His grossness is essential to the comic effect, for a circus clown cannot seem to be an accomplished athlete; gaucherie and laughable failure are part of the routine. Being a humorous figure, for us and for Hal, he cannot be brave in a hero's way.[3] As Mark Van Doren says, Falstaff's wit is the wit of a man 'who knows that other men are waiting to hear what he will pretend, what he will become, how he will get out of it'. Falstaff doesn't live to drink or to steal; he is an artist who assumes most of his roles with comic detachment, understanding everything through parody and at a remove, hence never seriously.[4]

Falstaff's Cowardice and Lying: His Play World

What, then, are we to make of Falstaff's cowardice at Gad's Hill? Is it, too, an act for Hal's benefit, a guise calculated to offer Falstaff

---

[1] James P. Driscoll, *Identity in Shakespearean Drama* (1983), 35 ff.

[2] William Hazlitt, *Characters of Shakespeare's Plays* (1817), 190–1.

[3] Wyndham Lewis, *The Lion and the Fox* (1927), 221 ff.

[4] Mark Van Doren, *Shakespeare* (New York, 1939), 97–118. See also Theodore Weiss, *The Breath of Clowns and Kings* (New York, 1974), 260–97.

as the target of laughter and thus ingratiate him with the Prince upon whose favour he must depend? The wish to exculpate Falstaff of cowardice is strongly apparent in the 'character' criticism of Maurice Morgann, whose *Essay on the Dramatic Character of Sir John Falstaff* (1777) argues that our overall impression of Falstaff must take account of his natural vigour, alacrity of mind, freedom from malice, and reputation for bravery in his youth that led to his being knighted and pensioned. In this context we must note that Poins distinguishes between true-bred cowards, like Bardolph, and those who will fight no longer than they see reason, like Falstaff (1.2.170–3). Before the robbery, we see no alarm on Falstaff's part, no holding back. He seems to object when the Prince and Poins separate themselves from the company, thereby reducing the number of the attackers, but takes part in the robbery itself with glee. He sleeps unconcernedly while the sheriff and a 'most monstrous watch' seek to arrest him. The Prince commissions him with a company of foot-soldiers for the forthcoming battle. At Shrewsbury he behaves reprehensibly, but with no indication of terror or disorder of mind. Courage must have been required for him to have led his 'ragamuffins' where they are 'peppered' in the fighting (5.3.35–6). Corbyn Morris, also writing in the eighteenth century, gives us a similarly amiable Falstaff, one whom we like even in his cowardly predicaments for the occasions they provide to his wit.[1]

Opposing arguments, however, are no less strong. Robert Langbaum has shown how the 'character' criticism of Morgann and Morris arose out of a post-Enlightenment response to literature not in Aristotelian terms of action and moral meaning but in Romantic terms of self-expression and self-discovery. Literature should contain events that provide the central character with an occasion for experience. Falstaff, viewed in this light, attains a kind of heroism in going down to defeat. Romantic hatred of hypocrisy takes solace in Falstaff's attack on prudence; Falstaff becomes an autonomous force, guilty of a generous error but gifted with a vision of life, a virtuoso.[2] Such a theory is implicitly hostile towards drama, and finds its most eloquent expression at a time when the staging of Shakespeare failed to satisfy many acute readers of Shakespeare. In

[1] Stuart M. Tave, *The Amiable Humorist* (Chicago, 1960), 106 ff.

[2] Robert Langbaum, *The Poetry of Experience* (1957), 168–81.

the study one can provide Falstaff with a life that extends beyond the limits of Shakespeare's play.

In the theatre, on the other hand, as Arthur Colby Sprague has amply demonstrated, Falstaff's cowardice takes on an immediacy that few actors can resist. The cowardice was simply taken for granted by most critics in the play's first 150 years, especially those who were responding to theatrical performances. In the theatre, we are forced to watch Falstaff as he runs away from the disguised Hal and Poins, sweating to death and larding the lean earth as he walks along. 'How the fat rogue roared!' says Poins (2.2.105). Falstaff's response to Hal's twitting him about cowardice, in the tavern scene, is not that of one who has the last laugh: 'Ah, no more of that, Hal, an thou lovest me!' (2.4.273). During Falstaff's temporary absence in this scene, Bardolph relates how Falstaff hacked his sword to simulate the effects of combat and to browbeat his fellow robbers into tickling their noses with spear-grass to make them bleed (2.4.293–301). Falstaff's leading of his own soldiers into deadly fire at Shrewsbury is a self-serving tactic with minimal danger to himself. The motif of fear is recurrent in his speech: he asks Hal if he is not 'horrible afeard' of Douglas, Percy, and Glendower (2.4.355), wishes it were bedtime and all well (5.1.125), and fears the shot at Shrewsbury (5.3.30–1). However humorously played, such lines derive their energy from Falstaff's role as coward, and the role must be played for the audience as well as for Hal. We allow of course that Falstaff runs away at Gad's Hill '*after a blow or two*' and is thus unlike the natural coward Bardolph, who admits, 'Faith, I ran when I saw others run' (2.4.292). Whatever Falstaff means by his claim to be a coward on instinct, he is set apart from the rest. Nevertheless, the actor's instinct to invite laughter at cowardice deserves our most serious critical consideration. In the theatre we usually find, as Sprague says, 'a Falstaff of dexterous evasions and miraculous escapes, lawless in his exaggerations, redoubtable only in repute, and the funnier for being fat and old and a coward'.[1]

What about Falstaff as a liar? As Dover Wilson has observed, the issues of cowardice and lying are connected, for the craven behaviour at Gad's Hill and Shrewsbury could be part of an act in anticipation of evasive story-telling, all calculated to 'tickle' the young Prince (2.4.427–8). Certainly Hal and Poins invite us to

[1] Arthur Colby Sprague, 'Gadshill Revisited', *SQ*, 4 (1953), 125–37.

connect cowardice and lying: 'The virtue of this jest', says Poins of the robbery and the robbing of the robbers, 'will be the incomprehensible [i.e. boundless] lies that this same fat rogue will tell us when we meet at supper—how thirty at least he fought with, what wards, what blows, what extremities he endured; and in the reproof [i.e. disproof] of this lives the jest' (1.2.173–8). The speech is a virtual stage direction for what in fact occurs, suggesting that this sort of game has been played before.

If Poins and Hal can anticipate what Falstaff will do, why cannot Falstaff guess at their game as well? He observes that Hal and Poins agree to take part in the robbery, but then suddenly absent themselves on a slender pretext just when they are needed, whereupon two disguised athletic young men set upon Falstaff and his companions in the dark. Does the coincidence in numbers fail to impress Falstaff? Or does he hint at suspected perfidy when he boasts of peppering two of his adversaries, two rogues dressed in buckram suits (2.4.185–6)? 'Rogues' might seem an insult cunningly directed at the Prince and Poins, who cannot respond to the insult without revealing their identities. Does Falstaff hint again at an awareness of their identity when, having expanded his attackers from two to an imaginary eleven, he speaks of 'three misbegotten knaves in Kendal green' who treacherously came at his back (ll. 214–15)?

Perhaps, then, Falstaff fabricates an entertaining lie, with just such an exaggeration in numbers as Poins and Hal have predicted, and illustrates it with precisely those 'blows' and 'wards' they knew he would use. The palpable impossibility of the lie, the mounting inconsistencies in statistics, seem to beg for exposure. By the time he sees Falstaff in the tavern again in *2 Henry IV*, at any rate, hindsight has suggested to Hal that Falstaff indeed recognized him when he ran away at Gad's Hill (2.4.293–4). This evidence, even though it forms no part of an audience's response to *1 Henry IV*, does provide an interesting interpretation after the fact by the dramatist himself. To imagine Falstaff offering to be caught out in a lie, for the Prince's amusement and sense of superiority, is to conceive of a compassionate man who wishes to be loved at whatever cost to his own dignity.[1] Falstaff, according to this view, is wiser and more self-denying than the Prince who condescends to

---

[1] Wilson, *Fortunes*, 48–56.

him, and our knowledge of Falstaff's wisdom significantly redresses the balance of sympathy in his favour.

Again, however, the conditions of theatrical performance give support to an opposing interpretation. The lovable Falstaff of Morgann and A. C. Bradley is a product of the literary imagination, and in these terms Falstaff's lies and cowardice cannot be taken at face value. Falstaff is judged as a real person by the literary student of character, and no real person of Falstaff's endearing qualities would behave so outrageously other than in jest, or expect others to believe his outlandish lies. In the theatre, on the other hand, 'character' is created by what the actor does, and 'belief' is the result of an understanding between dramatist and spectators. We do not ask how Falstaff could believe his lie, A. J. A. Waldock argues; instead, we accept it as a burlesque or exaggeration. The point of Poins's and Hal's anticipation of Falstaff's lie is to heighten the spectators' eagerness to see the outcome.[1] Surely we are not meant to suppose that Falstaff persuaded Bardolph and the rest to lie about the wounds they received at Gad's Hill with an expectation of his being caught out; such an argument is too circumstantial for the theatre. Eighteenth-century adaptations of the text enabled an actor like James Quin to assert Falstaff's recognition of the Prince in disguise at Gad's Hill, but only by adding lines to Shakespeare's dialogue.[2] Otherwise, actors have generally not known what to do with the proposition that Shakespeare's meaning is multi-layered, offering the broad comedy of satirical exposure to the groundlings while sharing with more discriminating audiences a covert understanding of Falstaff's compassionate wisdom. Falstaff is a lovable and inventive liar, but still a liar.

In the long tavern scene Falstaff gives the performance of his career, a virtuoso performance of lying and recovering himself when caught. He outdoes himself in his comic role as a misunderstood defender of good old-fashioned manhood, and as an ageing sinner on the verge of repentance. Play-acting to him is more than a means of captivating Hal. It is the essence of the temptation he lays before Hal, one in which (as Paul Gottschalk observes) all things are reduced to play. Falstaff offers Hal a child's world in which he need never grow up, in which even King Henry's most

---

[1] A. J. A. Waldock, 'The Men in Buckram', *RES*, 23 (1947), 16–23. See also Michael Goldman, *Acting and Action in Shakespearean Tragedy* (Princeton, NJ, 1985), 3–16.   [2] Wilson, *NCS*, xxxvi.

7. The play-acting scene, Old Vic, 1955, directed by Douglas Seale. To the amusement of Mistress Quickly (Rachel Roberts, far left), Bardolph (Ronald Fraser) blows a mock fanfare as Falstaff (Paul Rogers) crowns himself with a cushion

serious worries can be parodied in the comic language of euphuistic bombast.[1] Falstaff's plea is for the companionship of eternal youth: sport with me, he says in effect to Hal, and let those who covet the world's rewards suffer the attendant risks.

This kind of all-consuming play world offers an invaluable critique and means of testing reality, but as an end in itself it becomes an escape. Because Falstaff puts his appeal in terms of choice, Hal must respond in the same theatrical language, by usurping Falstaff's role as King and Lord of Misrule in order to restate the proposition in his own terms. Stage properties—chair, dagger, cushion—that serve Falstaff merely as devices for creating illusion become for Hal the means of rehearsing his future. Falstaff, absorbed in the fantasy of a timeless world of game, wants to 'play out the play' even when the knock is heard at the door, for he still has 'much to say in the behalf of that Falstaff' (2.4.466–7). Hal uses the medium of play-acting to proclaim his regality and his

[1] Paul A. Gottschalk, 'Hal and the "Play Extempore" in 1 *Henry IV*', *TSLL*, 15 (1974), 605–14.

57

8. Falstaff attempts to convince the Princes that he killed Hotspur. Ralph Richardson bestrides Hotspur (Laurence Olivier), confronting Prince Henry (Michael Warre) in the 1945 production by the Old Vic Company at the New Theatre, directed by John Burrell

acceptance of the challenge represented by that knock at the door.[1]

At Shrewsbury field, Hal will have nothing to do with Falstaff's play-acting, and, indeed, we perceive that play-acting is now out of place. The refusal to take war seriously produces fine reflections on the incorporeality of honour, but to substitute a bottle of sack for a pistol or deliberately abuse one's authority to recruit is to endanger lives and a cause to which Hal is now fully committed.

[1] Ibid.; Richard L. McGuire, 'The Play-within-the-play in *1 Henry IV*', *SQ*, 18 (1967), 47–52; J. McLaverty, 'No Abuse: The Prince and Falstaff in the Tavern Scenes', *ShS* 34 (1981), 105–10.

Falstaff persists, nonetheless, and with his greatest lie of all challenges the very relationship between history and theatrical illusion. When he arises from apparent death, he surprises a theatrical audience as well as Hal, for the actor has lain as though dead (or should do so), and we all know that actors can rise—once they step out of their roles. Falstaff claims his literary heritage as Vice, clown, *miles gloriosus*, and the rest; Hotspur is 'really' dead, as recorded in the chronicles, while Falstaff rises. Hal's response, Sigurd Burckhardt and James Calderwood argue, must be to acquiesce in the lie, to accept it as a practical necessity in order that Falstaff's claim to a purely theatrical life may be contained once more within the necessary confines of mimesis.[1] Falstaff seems 'larger than life' in part because he is so adept at transcending the boundaries of illusion. Hal, too, shares a world in which theatre and mimesis interact. 'Lying' in *1 Henry IV* is thus far more than a yardstick by which to judge Falstaff's character, for it continually hints at the artist's way of using illusion to depict historical life.

The 'Education' of Prince Hal

For some interpreters of Shakespeare, Hal is a more culpable liar than Falstaff. From Maurice Morgann and William Hazlitt to A. C. Bradley, G. B. Shaw, L. C. Knights, and H. C. Goddard, those who are most willing to excuse Falstaff's excesses are critical of the Prince for heartlessness, ingratitude, manipulation of friendship for the sake of public image, and (as King) warmongering.[2] In this regard, the interpretation of Hal's soliloquy (1.2) is crucial. Are we to view it as evidence of bloodless calculation, or as reassurance for the audience of good intent, or perhaps as whistling in the dark?

The newness of this kind of soliloquy in Shakespeare, so unlike Richard III's chortling confidences or Richard II's meditation on the vanity of human existence, leaves us uncertain as to its intent. On the one hand, Hal's dismissal of Falstaff as 'foul and ugly mists' seems harsh towards one who makes claims to companionship, and the accent on the timing of Hal's intended reformation

[1] Burckhardt, *Shakespearean Meanings*, 144–205; James Calderwood, '*1 Henry IV*: Art's Gilded Lie', *ELR*, 3 (1973), 131–44.

[2] E.g. Knights, '*Henry IV* as Satire', *Scrutiny*, 1 (1933), 356–67; Harold C. Goddard, *The Meaning of Shakespeare* (Chicago, 1951), i. 161–214. For the other references, see notes 113 and 145.

suggests that his escapades are being used to generate a myth of rebirth.[1] Hal seems to be refining the methods of his father, husbanding the display of his virtues just as King Henry has withheld from the multitude the display of his royal person.[2] On the other hand, reassurance of the audience is a practical necessity in view of the wild traditions dramatized in *Famous Victories*. The first scene in which we see Hal with Falstaff has raised a worrisome issue: 'shall there be gallows standing in England when thou art king?' asks Falstaff, 'And resolution thus fubbed as it is with the rusty curb of old Father Antic the law?' (1.2.56–8). However much Hal may parry these suggestions, a chorus-like explanation directed at the spectators is plainly in order.[3] Perhaps Hal's plans are not as certain in his own mind as they appear to his critics; he may be postponing the necessary day of reckoning to some vague terminus in order to enjoy as long as possible the holiday of youth. Actors are seldom content to portray him as a machiavel in this soliloquy, if only because they perceive him as having such a good time with Falstaff. Who can better appreciate Falstaff's performance than the person to whom it is presented as a love-offering and a bribe?

Hal's encounter with Francis is another problematic test of his humanity. Does he simply use Francis in a crude practical joke, as he uses other tavern acquaintances? We hear a note of boredom and ironic impatience with himself as he devises an entertainment 'to drive away the time till Falstaff come' (2.4.26–7), for Hal has admittedly 'sounded the very bass string of humility' (ll. 5–6) in drinking below stairs with the tapsters, and he is probably drunk.[4] Even Poins cannot be sure what 'cunning match' Hal has made with this jest (ll. 87–8). Yet on closer inspection the episode resonates with much that Hal is thinking about. Like Francis, Hal is being pulled simultaneously in two directions, and has not devised as yet a better response than Francis's own 'Anon, anon, sir!'[5] The transition to Hotspur seems like a *non sequitur*, and yet

[1] Irving Ribner, *The English History Play in the Age of Shakespeare* (Princeton, 1957); Alan Gerald Gross, 'The Justification of Prince Hal', *TSLL*, 10 (1968), 27–35.

[2] Alfred Harbage, *William Shakespeare: A Reader's Guide* (New York, 1963), 200.

[3] Levin L. Schücking, *Character Problems in Shakespeare's Plays* (1927), 221.

[4] Fredson Bowers, 'Hal and Francis in *King Henry IV, Part 1*', *Renaissance Papers 1965* (1966), 15–20.

[5] Mark Rose, *Shakespearean Design* (Cambridge, Mass., 1972), 50 ff.

Hotspur is oddly like Francis in his uncommunicativeness, his obsession with the business at hand, and his being called away from conversation. Hal brings Francis into a situation that mimics Hal's own, creating a little drama that might be called 'Francis the Rebellious Drawer'. A prince who would and would not be king calls Francis to account, and questions his loyalty to hard duty in a way that also arraigns the conscience of the questioner.[1] By thus parodying himself as a fellow Corinthian and fellow apprentice to Francis, Hal reflects through the medium of play-acting on his own neglect of his vocation. He takes seriously the trope of the 'body politic' by trying to encompass the whole state and the 'humours' of all ages in his own person, as J. D. Shuchter has argued, and comes to realize that the sloughing-off of his companions will be no simple matter that will cost him nothing.[2] Hal is asking, Who am I?, without fully answering his question. The scene is, like Hal's other play-acting, a trial of possible selves.

Is Hal's experience in the tavern, then, together with his studying of Hotspur and King Henry, his education? Tillyard, as we have seen, has argued that the Prince is indeed completing his education in the knowledge of men, in order to become the fully developed man, the *cortegiano*, universal in a way that Hotspur the provincial can never be.[3] Yet in one sense, it has been suggested, Hal is 'perfect' from the start, knowing what he has to do, identified always with the sun of royalty.[4] In his most self-revealing speeches, notes Alan Gross, the Prince speaks like a man who has already made up his mind. We perceive a basic stability in him, and are never privileged to enter the process of decision-making. Yet, we gradually realize that he has not yet totally committed himself to the decision he has made, and so in the comic scenes he is at once witty and judgemental, oscillating between folly and

[1] Sheldon P. Zitner, 'Anon, Anon: or, a Mirror for a Magistrate', *SQ*, 19 (1968), 63–70; Waldo F. McNeir, 'Structure and Theme in the First Tavern Scene (II. iv) of *1 Henry IV*', in *Pacific Coast Studies in Shakespeare*, ed. W. McNeir and T. Greenfield (Eugene, Ore., 1966), 89–105.

[2] J. D. Shuchter, 'Prince Hal and Francis: The Imitation of an Action', *ShakS*, 3 (1968), 129–37; D. J. Palmer, 'Casting off the Old Man; History and St Paul in *Henry IV*', *CritQ*, 12 (1970), 267–83.

[3] Tillyard, *Shakespeare's History Plays*, 264–304.

[4] David Berkeley and Donald Eidson, 'The Theme of *Henry IV, Part 1*', *SQ*, 19 (1968), 25–31; Dean, 'From *Richard II* to *Henry V*: A Closer View', in *Studies in Honor of DeWitt T. Starnes*, ed. Thomas P. Harrison and others (Austin, Texas, 1967), 37–52.

seriousness in a way perhaps characteristic of one who is weighing a decision.[1]

His 'reformation' is thus not an amendment of life so much as a revelation of his true identity to men's eyes. Vernon's speech in praise of Hal's princely qualities (4.1.97–111) is as much a turning-point in the metamorphosis of Hal from irresponsible youth to mirror of Christian kings as is the vow to King Henry to redeem all the supposed faults of youth on Percy's head.[2] Even to his father, Hal does not so much apologize as insist that he has been falsely reported, and his promise is to 'Be more myself', that is, his father's son (3.2.92–134). Undoubtedly Hal needs to mature, to come of age, to learn the languages of his countrymen, to put away childish things. Still, as W. Gordon Zeeveld insists, he is never without a consciousness of the responsibilities of kingship or of restrictions on personal life inherent in the ceremonies that are an indispensable part of kingship. He puts aside ceremony until he has need of it, in a conscious policy of calculated reformation. He is redeeming time all the while, preparing to labour in his vocation.[3]

The climax and culmination of Hal's metamorphosis in *Part 1* is his defeat of Hotspur. Hal has tried on a variety of names, and has been referred to contemptuously by Hotspur as the 'sword-and-buckler Prince of Wales' (1.3.229) and 'the nimble-footed madcap Prince of Wales' (4.1.95); King Henry speaks of his son as though he were a changeling,[4] and Falstaff comically doubts his paternity. Hal's first words to Hotspur at Shrewsbury speak to this subject of naming. 'If I mistake not, thou art Harry Monmouth', Hotspur accosts him, to which the Prince replies, 'Thou speak'st as if I would deny my name' (5.4.58–9). Hal not only defends his name but proclaims his identity as 'Prince of Wales' (l. 62), one whose sober duty is now to vanquish his opposite number called Harry Percy, 'A very valiant rebel of the name' (l. 61). By claiming name and title, the Prince redeems his unprincely reputation, and

[1] Gross, 'The Justification of Prince Hal', *TSLL*, 10 (1968), 27–35.

[2] Peter J. Gillett, 'Vernon and the Metamorphosis of Hal', *SQ*, 28 (1977), 351–3.

[3] W. Gordon Zeeveld, *The Temper of Shakespeare's Thought* (New Haven, Conn., 1974); Paul A. Jorgensen, '"Redeeming Time" in Shakespeare's *1 Henry IV*', *TSL*, 5 (1960), 101–9.

[4] M. C. Bradbrook, '*King Henry IV*', in *Stratford Papers on Shakespeare*, 1965–67, ed. B. A. W. Jackson (Toronto, 1969), 168–85.

9. 'Harry, thou hast robbed me of my youth' (5.4.76), an engraving of Francis Rigaud's painting of the Battle of Shrewsbury for Boydell's Gallery of illustrations to Shakespeare (1796)

denies the defamatory names by which he has been known.[1] Confirming Vernon's speech about him, Hal assimilates the wild and wanton energies of youth into a living embodiment of natural vitality, becoming one who bears the coat of arms of the Prince of Wales and displays through able horsemanship a capacity for discipline and good government.[2]

Most of all, Hal settles accounts with Hotspur in a metaphor of financial liability. In his first soliloquy he resolves to 'pay the debt I never promisèd' (1.2.197). To his father he insists that 'Percy is but my factor' (i.e. agent) 'To engross up glorious deeds on my behalf', for which Hal will 'call him to so strict account | That he shall render every glory up' (3.2.147–50). He returns to this motif at Shrewsbury when he vows to 'crop' all the budding honours on Hotspur's crest 'to make a garland for my head' (5.4.71–2).

[1] Marjorie Garber, *Coming of Age in Shakespeare* (1981), 66 ff.; Warren J. MacIsaac, '"A Commodity of Good Names" in the *Henry IV* Plays', *SQ*, 29 (1978), 417–19.
[2] Palmer, 'Casting off the Old Man', *CritQ*, 12 (1970), 267–83.

Hotspur dies lamenting that the Prince has 'robbed' him of his youth and has 'won' his proud titles. The scene is climactic in part because it recalls so many occasions when the play expresses ethical obligation in terms of financial responsibility: reckonings at the tavern, repentance as a form of repaying a debt, knowing when to promise and when to pay (4.3.53 and 5.4.42), metaphors of counterfeiting, legal tendering, commercial cavilling, and engrossing.[1] The persistent themes of thievery in high life and of the robber robbed are similarly brought to their climax and resolution in Hal's triumph over Hotspur.[2] We admire the Prince for his victory and for his generosity to the vanquished corpse of his opponent: having vied with Hotspur for the 'budding honours' on his crest, the Prince now covers the mangled face with his own favours in a token of restoring honour where it is due, and even allows Falstaff to claim the prize that the Prince has so valiantly won.[3]

The Rejection of Falstaff

The rejection of Falstaff and Hal's accession to the throne, the second and decisive stage in Hal's emergence as king, are not encompassed in the action of *1 Henry IV*. They are adumbrated so forcefully, however, that they become central considerations in our evaluation of the Prince even when we view this play, as we must, as a single dramatic entity. On three occasions, arranged in climactic sequence, Hal indicates his intention of turning away from Falstaff's company: in his soliloquy (1.2), when he plays King Henry in the tavern revels (2.4), and when he promises his father that he will 'scour' his shame in glorious deeds (3.2.137). Each such statement of intention comes as though in answer to threatening suggestions of disorder, but each is followed by an apparent relapse: after the first, Hal takes part in a robbery, after the second, he protects Falstaff from the sheriff, and after the third, he procures for Falstaff a military commission. Shakespeare's strategy is to hide the process of Hal's inevitable transformation from those closest to him (and his enemies as well) while revealing

---

[1] E. Rubinstein, '*1 Henry IV*: The Metaphor of Liability', *Studies in English Literature*, 10 (1970), 287–95.

[2] Robert Hapgood, 'Falstaff's Vocation', *SQ*, 16 (1965), 91–8.

[3] Herbert Hartman, 'Prince Hal's "Shew of Zeale"', *PMLA*, 46 (1931), 720–3.

it to his audience.[1] The rhythm of this seemingly erratic advance pulls us both ways: we concede the ultimate necessity of his rejection of Falstaff, but like Hal himself we yearn to postpone it. *Part 1* satisfies us as a dramatic whole because the rejection is at once assured, though not yet completed. We still have Falstaff, and have not yet been shown the extent of his decline, as we will be in *Part 2*.

Those who, like A. C. Bradley, deplore the rejection of Falstaff find fault with Hal for his ruthless alacrity in using people, and suppose that Shakespeare overshot his mark by making Falstaff more lovable than the story would bear.[2] Even those who are more admiring of Hal's decision, like Jonas Barish, agree that Falstaff's vitality stands in the way of the deterioration that is necessary to the grim business of preparing the fat knight for his ultimate role as scapegoat. We are forced from the domain of comedy into that of history, where the killjoys win out — as they do not, for instance, in *Twelfth Night*. To banish plump Jack, as Falstaff says in his own defence, is in a true sense to 'banish all the world' (2.4.462). If history defeats those who attempt to defy time and change, those who would live an eternal youth, the survivors must also suffer an inevitable diminution of spirit by their acquiescing in change. The Prince rejects himself, turning away from his former self in a way that is self-mutilating.[3] From being a man of all humours in the tavern, Hal becomes a public figure whose every move must be governed by the dictates of ceremony. His marriage will be political, however much he strives to succeed in it personally as well.

Falstaff has asked of Hal the impossible thing. He has asked to be loved as he is and for what he is, so that their games may continue for ever. He has offered Hal various comic stratagems for evading responsibility—the enjoyment of appetite for its own sake, game-playing and parodies of success, carnival escape into holiday—but the Prince must learn to put these games behind him as he casts off the 'old man'.[4] Falstaff has embodied the mythology of the cycle of the year and its ever-returning fertility, but by so doing he has

---

[1] Gottschalk, 'Hal and the "Play Extempore"', *TSLL*, 15 (1974), 605–14.

[2] A. C. Bradley, 'The Rejection of Falstaff', in *Oxford Lectures on Poetry* (1909), 252–73.

[3] Jonas A. Barish, 'The Turning Away of Prince Hal', *ShakS*, 1 (1965), 9–17.

[4] Robert G. Hunter, 'Shakespeare's Comic Sense as It Strikes us Today: Falstaff and the Protestant Ethic', in *Shakespeare, Pattern of Excelling Nature*, ed. David Bevington and Jay Halio (Newark, Del., 1978), 125–32.

created for himself the role of one who must be sacrificed to ensure that renewal.[1] We accept the rejection as necessary because it represents a process of death by means of which a diseased land can be restored to health.[2] At the same time, as Michael Goldman has said, we feel protective and sentimental towards Falstaff's life, which has been so preciously placed in the Prince's hands, because it represents our own sensuality and anarchic impulses. Falstaff is the sleeping child we will have to punish, the silly dying father we are destined to replace.[3]

Although Hal's rejection of Falstaff is for these reasons self-mutilating, it can also be viewed as a compassionate act. The Prince is aware of the cost of success in terms of the human spirit. He neither scorns such success nor minimizes its difficulties. Politics has its own morality. Hal willingly embraces an understanding of the world that allows little room for the spirit of perpetual play.[4] There is even charity in his embrace of a public life thrust upon him and demanding that he play a leading role on behalf of the common weal.[5] Self is necessarily diminished as Hal takes up the awesome burdens of kingly office. This sacrifice has not yet been demanded or made when *1 Henry IV* comes to an end, and much remains to be done to clear Hal's name of the wild associations that have accrued to it. Nonetheless, Hal's readiness to become king has been fully proclaimed.

The Play in Performance

In the theatre, the story of Prince Hal's passage to manhood becomes a script for actors and directors who must choose among a host of practical options regarding set, costuming, and gesture. The play itself imposes certain constraints but also offers certain

[1] J. I. M. Stewart, 'The Birth and Death of Falstaff', in *Character and Motive in Shakespeare* (1949); Barber, *Shakespeare's Festive Comedy*, 192–221; Moody Prior, 'Comic Theory and the Rejection of Falstaff', *ShakS*, 9 (1976), 159–71.

[2] G. K. Hunter, 'Shakespeare's Politics and the Rejection of Falstaff', *CritQ*, 1 (1959), 229–36; Philip Williams, 'The Birth and Death of Falstaff Reconsidered', *SQ*, 8 (1957), 359–65.

[3] Michael Goldman, *Shakespeare and the Energies of Drama* (Princeton, 1972), 45–57.

[4] Norman Rabkin, *Shakespeare and the Common Understanding* (1967), 95 ff.

[5] Franklin B. Newman, 'The Rejection of Falstaff and the Rigorous Charity of the King', *ShakS*, 2 (1967), 153–61; Hugh Dickinson, 'The Reformation of Prince Hal', *SQ*, 12 (1961), 33–46; David Sundelson, *Shakespeare's Restoration of the Father* (Brunswick, NJ, 1983), 62–70.

opportunities for the acting company to provide a critical interpretation. Any director must take into account, for example, the rhythm of the alternation between serious and comic scenes, and the establishment of antithetical, or foil, relationships among the characters: Hotspur and Falstaff, the King and Falstaff, Hal in relation to all three.

Juxtapositions of this sort lend themselves to visual contrasts and to parody through stage business. Scenes at court are dominated by Henry's royal presence, his throne and regalia, his noble peers in order of rank. The rebels in their assemblies are also formally dressed and observant of protocol; only with their wives are they able, briefly, to be informal, to listen to music, to banter, or to confess emotion. By contrast, Falstaff sleeps on benches after noon and unbuttons himself after supper, and can be discovered snoring behind the arras. The comic world of *1 Henry IV* also finds room for ordinary commoners, like the men who haul provisions on the Rochester–London road and gripe about their hard life in foul-smelling hostelries (2.1). Language is vividly colloquial in such an environment. Disguise is a common motif in the comic scenes; Poins has vizards for the robbers and 'cases of buckram' for himself and the Prince (1.2.167–8). Disguise is appropriate in a holiday world of inversion, as in the comedies, but on the battlefield, adopted by King Henry and his peers, it seems out of place, incongruous in the 'real' world of history.

The action of the comic scenes is appropriately vivid, at times almost farcical, filled with burlesque and horseplay. Falstaff and his crew rob and bind the travellers with much ado, run away in panic when they are set upon, drink plenteously, gather round as Falstaff re-enacts his intrepidity at Gad's Hill, stage a play extempore, run to answer a knock at the door and return with news from court, hide from the sheriff, quarrel about money, play-act at soldiering, and so on. The tavern furnishings—tables, joint-stools, cushion, leaden dagger—become stage props in their revels, hinting at wider emblematic significance and helping to invoke a graphic sense of place on the otherwise unfurnished Elizabethan stage. The knock at the door also defines stage space: beyond the tiring-house wall lies the outside world with its demands for maturity, while for a time the stage is transformed into a magical world, an artist's world, a world of youthful merriment and camaraderie.

These contrasts, achieved without scenery (though with rich

costuming), lend themselves to parodic inversions. Falstaff's 'piti-ful bald crown' substitutes for a 'precious rich crown', his leaden dagger for a golden sceptre, and his joint-stool for a 'state', or chair of state—the throne or dais beneath a canopy appropriate to ceremonial scenes at the court of Henry IV (2.4.365–9). Falstaff playing king begs his queen (the Hostess) not to weep, 'for trickling tears are vain' (2.4.378); King Henry wishes that his tears of vexation over his son were not real (3.2.90–1). Images of sun and comets, motifs of accusation and renunciation and reaffirmation, all underscore the parallels between the two scenes of interview.[1] In each, the interview is cut off by the arrival of a messenger in haste. The parallels may also have been reinforced by positioning and by gestures such as kneeling.[2] Hal's mimicry of Hotspur and his wife provides a similar parallel. At the end of 3.3, Falstaff's comic exuberance in calling for his breakfast and wishing the tavern were his drum echoes through parody the noble resolution of Prince Hal as he departs for war. In the battle itself the serious and the comic are more jarringly juxtaposed, for the noblemen of England are now in armour, and Falstaff is among them, his craven and self-serving antics mocking at every turn the engage-ments of the fighters, just as his words mock the emptiness of honour. Percy dies, and Falstaff rises and dishonours his corpse. Yet from these juxtapositions Hal emerges at last as the visual embodiment of the Prince. His transformation is literally one of costume, of helmet and feathers and thigh-armour, all of which are brought to our attention in Vernon's ringing speech (4.1).

Rich in theatrical opportunities of this sort, *1 Henry IV* has almost always been one of Shakespeare's most popular stage plays. It successfully weathered the changes that affected many of Shakespeare's plays during the Caroline years, the Interregnum, and the Restoration. The so-called Dering manuscript, prepared in about 1622 for the library of the literary antiquarian Sir Edward Dering, in which parts of *1* and *2 Henry IV* are combined in a single play of 3,401 lines, seems to have been intended as a script for private performance. Evidently the project was not brought to

[1] Richard L. McGuire, 'The Play-within-the-play in *1 Henry IV*', *SQ*, 18 (1967), 47–52.

[2] John Shaw, 'The Staging of Parody and Parallels in *1 Henry IV*', *ShS 20* (1967), 61–73; Alan C. Dessen, 'The Intemperate Knight and the Politic Prince: Late Morality Structure in *1 Henry IV*', *ShakS*, 7 (1974), 147–71.

10. Frontispiece of *1 The Wits* (1662), including Falstaff and the Hostess, Mistress Quickly, among the famous characters featured in the volume's adapted playlets

completion, but it does reveal a lively interest in stage tradition and in technical aspects of production. Leonard Digges's commendatory verses to Shakespeare's *Poems* in 1640 note that, whereas Jonson's *Volpone* and *The Alchemist* can scarce defray the costs of production in revival, yet 'let but Falstaff come, | Hal, Poins, the rest, you scarce shall have a room, | All is so pestered'. A commendatory poem to the Folio edition of Beaumont and Fletcher (1647) similarly acknowledges the vogue of the fat knight: 'I could praise Heywood now,' Sir Thomas Palmer begins, 'or tell how long | Falstaff from cracking nuts hath kept the throng.' A frontispiece illustration to *1 The Wits, or Sport upon Sport*, published in 1662, prominently features Falstaff and the Hostess among the figures on an artificially lighted indoor stage, advertising the first, and evidently one of the most popular, of the 'drolls' within its covers. The droll, or farcical skit, entitled *The Bouncing Knight, or the Robbers Robbed* presented a surreptitious excerpt from *1 Henry IV* to spectators during the closing of the theatres between 1642 and

1660; its focus on the antics of Falstaff bears witness once again to his centrality in the play's continuing appeal.

1 Henry IV was among the plays acted at the Red Bull, Clerkenwell, at the time of (or even before) the Restoration, by a theatrical company of the Caroline era which formed the basis of Thomas Killigrew's King's Company in 1660. From 1660 to 1669, Samuel Pepys saw parts at least of *Henry IV* on four occasions among some forty-one performances of twelve of Shakespeare's works noted in his diary, a record surpassed only by *Hamlet* (five occasions) and *Macbeth* (nine). Pepys's high expectations led to disappointment at the first performance on 31 December 1660 (in the King's Company's new theatre in Gibbons's tennis court in Vere Street), evidently because he found the performed version untrue to the original, but on 4 June 1661 he accounted it 'a good play', and on 2 November 1667 (at the King's Company's playhouse off Drury Lane) he, 'contrary to expectation, was pleased in nothing more than in [William] Cartwright's speaking of Falstaff's speech about "What is honour?"'.[1] The King's Company, under Killigrew's direction, kept *1 Henry IV* as a stock play along with *Macbeth, Hamlet, Othello, Julius Caesar, Henry VIII,* and Nahum Tate's *King Lear*. It remained in the repertory in the time of Colley Cibber (i.e. until 1742).

Thomas Betterton made perhaps the most lasting contribution of the Restoration and early eighteenth century to the staging of *1 Henry IV*. In 1682, when the King's Company combined with the Duke of York's Company, Betterton took the part of Hotspur with 'wild impatient starts' and 'fierce and flashing fire'.[2] His interpretation provided an effective contrast to Edmund Kynaston's King Henry, whose grave dignity and sense of command reverberated with terrible menace in his whisper to Hotspur, 'Send us your prisoners, or you will hear of it!', while in the interview between King Henry and his son the audience was privileged to witness 'that sort of grief which only majesty could feel'.[3] Later, in the season of 1699–1700, Betterton revived the play 'with the humour of Sir John Falstaff' at the Little Theatre in Lincoln's Inn Fields. This time (at the age of sixty-five or so), he took the role of Falstaff, a role heretofore played by William Cartwright and John

---

[1] Odell, i. 22; Wilson, *NCS*, xxxii.
[2] Colley Cibber, *An Apology for the Life of Mr Colley Cibber* (1740), 87.
[3] Ibid., 104–5.

Lacy, and enjoyed a huge success. According to a contemporary account, Betterton's Falstaff took London by storm, 'more than any new play that has been produced of late ... and the critics allow that Mr Betterton has hit the humour of Falstaff better than any that have aimed at it before'.[1]

Moreover, Betterton's text of the play was remarkably close to the Shakespearian original. To be sure, he curtailed the long council speeches in 1.1 (including much of the King's opening address), the major portion of Lady Percy's speeches in 2.3, part of the 'play extempore' in 2.4, all of 3.1 after l. 135 (including Glendower's daughter and Lady Percy), much of King Henry's long address to Hal in 3.2, all of 4.4 with the Archbishop of York, and all of 5.4 prior to the entry of Hotspur at. l. 58.[2] The Folio text was consulted as a guide in the omission of vulgarity and profanity. Still, in an age accustomed to Tate's happily ending adaptation of *Lear* or William Davenant's and John Dryden's greatly altered version of *The Tempest*, Betterton's *1 Henry IV* was unusual in its lack of rearrangement of scenes or introduction of new characters and business. Some cutting was to be expected, and later revivals in the eighteenth century (including those in America, beginning with David Douglass as Falstaff in New York in 1761) made similar or expanded excisions, but in its avoidance of extensive rearrangement or recasting, the Betterton text set a healthy precedent for the rest of the eighteenth century and on into the nineteenth as well. Throughout this entire period, *1 Henry IV* generally fared better at the hands of theatre managers than did *Lear, Macbeth, The Tempest, Romeo and Juliet, The Merchant of Venice, Coriolanus, Richard III*, and other targets of the 'improvers' of Shakespeare's scripts. Most remarkable of all, perhaps, is Betterton's restraint in refusing to sacrifice the serious material to the comedy, or to exploit the play merely as a vehicle for the lead actor.

1 Henry IV enjoyed a vogue in the early eighteenth century exceeding that of Shakespeare's most popular comedies,[3] and it seems belatedly to have been responsible for the reintroduction of *2 Henry IV* to the repertory—though only seldom during the century were the two parts performed within a week of each other.

[1] Letter of 28 January 1700, in Edmond Malone, ed., *The Critical and Miscellaneous Prose Works of John Dryden* (1800), 329, n. 4.

[2] Odell, i. 84.

[3] Charles B. Hogan, *Shakespeare in the Theatre: A Record of Performances in London, 1701–1800*, 2 vols. (Oxford, 1952–7), i. 460.

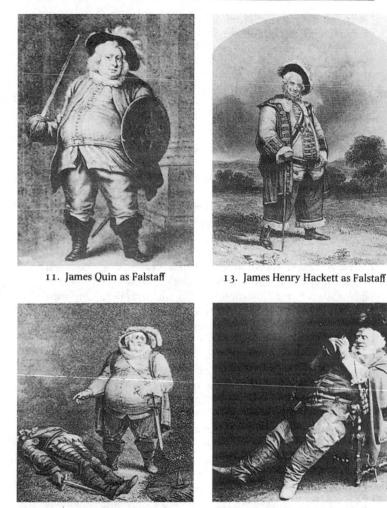

1 1. James Quin as Falstaff

1 3. James Henry Hackett as Falstaff

1 2. Stephen Kemble as Falstaff

14. Herbert Beerbohm Tree as Falstaff

James Quin was a notable successor to Betterton in the part of Falstaff from 1718 to 1751, whereas the celebrated David Garrick at Drury Lane evidently found the role and the play unsuited to his talent; for years Drury Lane had no *1 Henry IV*, and, when Garrick reluctantly agreed to play Hotspur to Quin's Falstaff in 1746, he proved relatively unsuccessful. Quin, tall and bulky and of manly countenance, excelled in satire and sarcasm; he betrayed a surliness beneath his assumed gaiety, and was accounted the most intelligent and judicious Falstaff since Betterton. Leaving to lesser actors like Edward Berry the vulgarities of a beerhouse Falstaff, he presided in 'impudent dignity' over the consumption of choice viands and liquors.[1] Quin played down Falstaff's participation in the Gad's Hill robbery, omitted the extempore play of 2.4 entirely, and began his response to Hal's exposure of lying with 'Ha, ha, ha! d'ye think I did not know ye?', thereby raising the dignity of Falstaff's role in the way in which it was similarly 'justified' by Maurice Morgann and Corbyn Morris.[2]

John Henderson, Quin's most able successor as Falstaff (1777–85), was a laughing Falstaff, frolicsome, gay, and humorous, carrying the audience with him in sympathetic bursts of laughter that dismayed at least one critic who felt that so much laughter was out of place for Falstaff.[3] Although Quin had had no trouble in getting Garrick, as the dead Hotspur, on his back in 5.4, occasioning much laughter in the process, and had managed with Spranger Barry as well (albeit with less ease), Henderson encountered so many difficulties in hoisting still another Hotspur on his shoulders that 'it was thought best, for the future, that some of Falstaff's ragamuffins should bear off the dead body'.[4] Even Quin, for all his stress on Falstaff's shrewd perception of Hal's stratagems, was noted above all for the detection of Falstaff's cowardice by the Prince and Poins. A satirical poem of 1761 asked in a similar vein why the actor James Love rolled his eye so 'when Falstaff stands detected in a lie?'.[5] Audiences seemed to have

---

[1] Thomas Davies, *Dramatic Miscellanies*, 3 vols. (1783–4), i. 232 and 249–50.

[2] Wilson, *NCS*, xxxvi.

[3] Henry Mackenzie, *The Lounger*, 68:272, 20 May 1786, quoted in Arthur Colby Sprague, *Shakespeare's Histories: Plays for the Stage* (1966), 54–5.

[4] Davies, *Dramatic Miscellanies*, i. 273–5; Sprague, *Shakespeare and the Actors* (Cambridge, Mass., 1963), 90–1.

[5] Charles Churchill, *The Rosciad* (1761), ll. 451–2.

little hesitance in applying the labels of coward and liar to Falstaff even while they applauded his arch-roguery.

Women in the eighteenth century were sometimes offended by the play, finding the person of Falstaff coarse and his language revolting; as Elizabeth Montagu wrote in the 1760s, 'Gluttony, corpulency, and cowardice are the peculiarities of Falstaff's composition . . . so it was very skilful to make him as ridiculous as witty, and as contemptible as entertaining.'[1] The occasional coarseness of the buffoonery is suggested in a piece of stage business in 1770: at Shrewsbury field, before the battle, Falstaff was made to sit on the same drum as King Henry, and to tumble down when Henry got up.[2] Costuming maintained the exaggerated tradition of a cowardly lying Falstaff: actors continued to wear something like the high boots loosely falling to the knee, the jerkin with points, the scarlet and buff, the round hat with a feather, the big gloves with wide wrists, the shield, and mountainous belly that we see in the frontispiece to *The Wits* (1662), even while Garrick played Hotspur at Covent Garden in 1746 in a 'laced frock and a Ramellies wig'. In America, where the Falstaff plays enjoyed a secure place in the repertory, the most notable contribution to stage history may have been the appearance of Mrs Osborne of the New American Company as Prince Hal, handsomely dressed in breeches, at Annapolis in 1769.[3]

The stage popularity of *1 Henry IV* declined briefly in the early nineteenth century; apparently the play did not suit the talents of the leading actors of the time. John Philip Kemble as Hotspur at Covent Garden in 1817 disappointed Ludwig Tieck by the leisurely, solemn, almost torturing slowness of his declamation and by his failure to comprehend Hotspur's fiery humour; an occasional bit of sharp utterance, something a fine actor would achieve as a matter of course, received too much approbation from an audience that in Tieck's view expected little from its actors.[4] To be sure, Tieck saw a late performance of Kemble's Hotspur, which earlier had won admiration from Sir Walter Scott.

[1] Elizabeth Montagu, *An Essay on the Writings and Genius of Shakespear* (1769), 107.

[2] Francis Gentleman in 1770, quoted in Sprague, *Shakespeare and the Actors*, 89.

[3] Davies, *Dramatic Miscellanies*, i. 225–7; A. C. Sprague and J. C. Trewin, *Shakespeare's Plays Today* (1970), 80–1; Charles Shattuck, *Shakespeare on the American Stage* (Washington, DC, 1976), 14.

[4] Ludwig Tieck, quoted in Theodore Martin, 'An Eye-Witness of John Kemble', *The Nineteenth Century*, 7 (Feb. 1880), 281–2.

Stephen Kemble, brother to John Philip Kemble and Mrs Sid-
dons, was sufficiently obese to undertake Falstaff at Drury Lane
without padding (see Figure 12), but critics generally found his
performance more painful than amusing. 'Every fat man cannot
represent a great man', wrote Hazlitt in *The Examiner* of 13 October
1816, dismissing Kemble as a mere paunch and lump of lethargy
'with water in the head' rather than 'guts in his brains'.[1] That
Kemble had no serious rival is a sad comment on the state of the
stage at that time. Robert Elliston was an acclaimed Falstaff after
Kemble, but according to W. C. Macready, who saw Elliston's final
performance in May 1826, the character of Falstaff 'was left, as it
has been since the days of Quin and Henderson, without an
adequate representative'.[2] Even though Stephen Kemble played
opposite Edmund Kean's Hotspur for three performances in 1819
and 1820, his Falstaff prompted the telling question from J. R.
Planché: 'Did anyone ever see Sir John Falstaff except in his mind's
eye?'[3] The American actor James Henry Hackett, famous for an
inflated Falstaff that on one occasion at least was deflated by an
envious fellow actor, argued vociferously in a pamphlet response
to his critics (1840) that Falstaff shows no signs of refinement,
intellect, or breeding. Hackett's Falstaff (shown in Figure 13),
portrayed as an example of wickedness attempting to corrupt
youth, never found favour with London critics during his visits
there, but at home in the United States it became a national
institution.[4] The literary Falstaff championed by Morgann, the
Falstaff of humane wit and courage, flourished in the vacuum
created by lack-lustre and unsubtle stage performances.

Period costuming and elaborate settings brought stage
verisimilitude to the productions of Shakespeare's historical plays
by Charles Kemble, Macready, and their nineteenth-century suc-
cessors. The problem of frequent change of location was usually
solved by reducing the number of scenes and enhancing the visual
splendour of those that were retained. Macready played King
Henry and Charles Kemble the Prince in an 1821 revival of
2 Henry IV featuring a splendid coronation procession and the
coronation itself, staged as a tribute to the actual coronation of

---

[1] *The Examiner*, 13 October 1816, 650.

[2] W. C. Macready, *Reminiscences and Diaries*, ed. Frederick Pollock (1875), 232.

[3] J. R. Planché, *Recollections and Reflections* (1901), 23.

[4] Sprague, *Shakespeare's Histories*, 54; Wilson, *NCS*, xlvi, quoting an 1840
pamphlet called *Falstaff*; Shattuck, *Shakespeare on the American Stage*, 59–62.

King George IV.[1] Kemble's *King John* in 1823–4 at Covent Garden was no less sumptuous in its attention to historical detail. These successes could not but encourage performances of *1 Henry IV* in period style as well. Kemble's production at Covent Garden in 1824 derived its sets and costumes from stained glass, the monumental effigy of Henry IV in Canterbury Cathedral, portraits of the Prince and other historical figures in various illustrated manuscripts, and the sumptuary laws of Henry IV's reign. The scenery, newly designed for the most part, called for the King's chambers in Westminster Palace, the inn-yard at Rochester with the castle at night (a favourite scene in eighteenth- and nineteenth-century productions, though cut by Herbert Beerbohm Tree in 1896), Hotspur's camp near Shrewsbury, a road and distant view of Coventry, Shrewsbury from the field of battle, the King's tent, and so on.[2] Kemble attempted Hotspur without great success, but the scenery was the main attraction in any case. Macready had better luck with Hotspur from 1815 to 1847.

A magnificent revival of the play in 1864 to celebrate the tercentenary of Shakespeare's birth, at the reborn Drury Lane under the management of Edmund Falconer and F. B. Chatterton, featured Samuel Phelps as Falstaff, Walter Montgomery as Hotspur, Walter Lacy as the Prince, John Ryder as King Henry, and Mrs Edmund Falconer as the Hostess. For the first time since before Betterton, the audience heard the Welsh songs of 'Lady Glendwyr' (Glendower's daughter) and all of 3.1. Only the Archbishop of York in 4.4 was missing from an essentially complete rendering. The elaborate staging included a new, and much-applauded, ambush during the Battle of Shrewsbury. The run continued for several months during the tercentenary jubilee.[3] Phelps had played Falstaff before, at Sadler's Wells (following the end of the monopoly for the two great patent theatres), from 1846 to 1862.

In general, however, during these years and into the 1870s and 1880s, *1 Henry IV* lost ground to the lavish pageantry of Charles Kean's *King John* (1852–3), *Henry VIII* (1855), and *Richard II* (1857), the last of which introduced an elaborate scene of Richard's humiliating entry into London in the train of the capering Bolingbroke. Henry Irving abandoned the idea of playing Fal-

---

[1] Odell, ii. 166–9.

[2] Ibid., ii. 173–4.

[3] Ibid., ii. 299.

staff in *1 Henry IV* in the face of Beerbohm Tree's success in *The Merry Wives of Windsor*, and was drawn instead to *Henry VIII* (1892), which he produced at the Lyceum with a splendour that outdid even the tableau-like richness of Kean's production in 1855. Beerbohm Tree's *1 Henry IV* of 1896, though not on the scale of his later extravaganzas (such as his three-act *King John* complete with the signing of Magna Carta), was a handsome production culminating in a tableau of the final battle. (Tree himself played Falstaff; see Figure 14.) *1 Henry IV* was not the play to compete in this era of opulent sets and ceremonial pageantry.

Stage business in the nineteenth century accommodated itself to the increasing emphasis on stage furniture, and to a traditional theatrical view (though not without exceptions) of Falstaff as a comic buffoon. Stephen Kemble's gross Falstaff, unaided by stuffing, was discovered on a couch in 1.2, as though awakening in order to ask the question, 'Now, Hal, what time of day is it, lad?' In the same scene, Falstaff (as performed by Elliston) regularly carried a stick, while Hal and Poins often sported canes, enabling the Prince to tap Falstaff in the belly at the line, 'And is not a buff jerkin a most sweet robe of durance?' (ll. 41–2).[1] The carriers in 2.1 signalled through gesture their discomfort at being 'stung like a tench'(l. 14), or caught fleas to examine them by the light of the lantern. At Gad's Hill Falstaff was known to run about with his sword drawn, shouting defiance at the travellers, after which he returned to sit (assisted to do so in Phelps's version) and divide the spoils. In that position, so vulnerable for a fat man, he could be attacked mercilessly by Hal and Poins, and even forced to crawl away to safety.[2] Clearly a sense of dignity was sacrificed at times to slapstick effect.

In the long tavern scene Falstaff dominated the stage and its opportunity for visual effects. He threw the dregs of his sack in Francis's face, sometimes prompting the tapster to protect himself with his apron from a second such assault. Falstaff relied on props for the famous moment of exposure in his lie. In some performances he hid his face behind his shield in order to peep over it with 'By the lord, I knew ye as well as he that made ye' (2.4.258);

---

[1] John Cumberland's *British Theatre*, vol. 4, as performed at the Theatre-Royal, London (1826), 14.

[2] Charles Kemble at Covent Garden in 1824, cited by Sprague, *Shakespeare and the Actors*, 85.

on one occasion at least he rose from an armchair with its back to the audience, his face wreathed in smiles. His chair served him well throughout the tavern scene: a 'large oak arm chair' in one production provided a place for Peto to hang Falstaff's shield, and there are contemporary allusions to an 'elbow chair' or 'great chair'. The elaborate furnishings of the tavern on the nineteenth-century stage gave Falstaff and Hal everything they needed to conduct their mock interview in anticipation of Hal's appearance before his father. The arrival of the sheriff did not fluster Falstaff in Phelps's production: taking his hat from the table so as to leave no trace behind, he coolly made his exit.[1]

The second tavern scene (3.3) provided Phelps with an opportunity to triumph over the angry Hostess, putting her down with his laughter, and chuckling to the Prince as he succeeded in bringing her around. Stephen Kemble ended this scene not with an exit but by remaining in his chair and contemplating the arrival of breakfast until the scene shut him out. At Shrewsbury, when Falstaff is supposedly dead, Charles Kemble and other Falstaffs seem to have continued the eighteenth-century antics so deplored by Morgann, of raising or dodging the head from one side to the other, and making several attempts to get up but then ducking at the sound of drums.[2] One can understand Morgann's distaste for this sort of comic cowardice; nevertheless, it remained a central facet of stage tradition.

The twentieth century has seen a move away from the proscenium arch and the massive sets of the nineteenth century, towards a thrust stage, rapid movement from scene to scene, and freedom from reliance on painted scenery. *1 Henry IV* has usually been spared from period costuming in other than Elizabethan or medieval settings, for its historical particularity and Falstaff's colloquialisms do not lend themselves to the milieu of Edwardian England or the American West, for example. To the contrary, a major contribution to stage history in this century has been the presentation of Shakespeare's English history plays in their relation to one another. Frank Benson, a significant innovator in this as in other aspects of Shakespearian staging, presented a 'cycle' of history plays at Stratford between 1901 and 1906, moving W. B.

---

[1] Ibid., 85–6.

[2] Maurice Morgann, *An Essay on the Dramatic Character of Sir John Falstaff* (1777), 24–5.

Yeats to applaud the way in which 'play supports play'.[1] Benson omitted *1 Henry IV*, sad to say, evidently feeling that some major cutting was necessary, and that *2 Henry IV* provided a more necessary link to *Henry V*. *Part 2* continued to occupy a central place in the Benson Company's repertory at Stratford from 1894, when Benson first performed it, up to 1926. However, he did include both parts in a new cycle at Stratford in 1905, beginning with Marlowe's *Edward II*.

Yet to Sir Barry Jackson at the Birmingham Repertory Theatre belongs the credit of uniting both parts in performance on a single day, on Shakespeare's birthday (23 April) in 1921. Jackson employed the full text, with the proper sequence of scenes, that he had first staged on 11 October 1913. In 1932, Stratford celebrated Shakespeare's birthday in a similar fashion, with *Part 1* in the afternoon and *Part 2* in the evening, in honour of the opening of the New Memorial Theatre. Edward, Prince of Wales, flew in from Windsor in his private plane for the occasion.[2] A less happy attempt at unification was Orson Welles's *Five Kings*, produced in Philadelphia in 1939, which combined parts of *1* and *2 Henry IV* and *Henry V* into a single play, with readings from Holinshed to provide narrative transitions where material in Shakespeare had been omitted.[3] Ben Greet introduced *2 Henry IV* at the Old Vic in October 1917, and *1 Henry IV* in 1920.

The range and versatility of gesture on the modern stage, under the sharp eyes of directors looking for new theatrical approaches, can perhaps be illustrated with reference to ways of handling Hotspur's abrupt manner of speech. John Burrell's celebrated Old Vic production at the New Theatre in 1945–6 featured Laurence Olivier as Hotspur, with a slight speech impediment requiring him to hesitate before the letter *w*. The mannerism was especially affecting at the moment of Hotspur's death, when his unfinished sentence, 'No, Percy, thou art dust, | And food for—' had to be completed by the Prince: 'For worms, brave Percy' (5.4.84–6). Earlier actors had taken to stammering Hotspur's lines, perhaps because German actors had misinterpreted his 'speaking thick, which nature made his blemish' (see *2 Henry IV* 2.3.24) as a

[1] William Butler Yeats, 'At Stratford-on-Avon' (1901), in *Essays and Introductions* (1961), 97.

[2] Wilson, *NCS*, xliii.

[3] Sprague, *Shakespearian Players and Performances* (1953), 160.

stammer. Matheson Lang did so in Tree's production at His Majesty's in November 1914, though the theatrical idealist and visionary William Poel (who had established the Elizabethan Stage Society in 1894) protested with reason that there was 'no authority for it in the text'. Baliol Holloway in 1923 and Gyles Isham in 1931 (both at Stratford) were stammerers as well. Michael Redgrave chose instead a North-country accent with 'thick *rs*' in his performance of Hotspur at Stratford-upon-Avon in 1951. John Neville at the Old Vic in 1955 stammered on the letter *m*.[1]

Increasingly in the twentieth century, Shakespearian performance has become the director's or producer's creation, succeeding or failing in accordance with the quality of his or her vision. John Burrell's Old Vic production of 1945–6 assembled a brilliant cast (including Olivier as Hotspur, as we have seen) in whose acting the play might be seen in all its complexity rather than as a vehicle for the leading actor. As Falstaff, Ralph Richardson demonstrated how sensitivity and depth in the portrayal of Shakespeare's greatest comic creation need not be at the expense of the stage tradition of cowardice and lying. In the long tavern scene Richardson got completely carried away in the business of fabricating a good story, and was thus visibly jarred by Poins's and Hal's evidence confuting what he had said. He had to think his way out of this confrontation, not merely concocting a suitably outrageous excuse, but finding a way to recover his balance.[2] Frank Duncan offered an intelligent reading of Vernon, one that might have been lost in a production given over to the leading roles: he reluctantly agreed with Worcester not to reveal to Hotspur the King's 'liberal and kind offer' (5.2.2), but then, given an opportunity to describe the Prince's behaviour during the parley, offered a ringing tribute that in effect rebuked Worcester's cynicism. Burrell added to the depth of his casting with a number of new staging effects, including an off-stage march of Falstaff's ragamuffin recruits during his soliloquy describing abuses of the royal commission for recruitment.[3]

Directors of *1 Henry IV* in recent years have explored a wide range of possibilities, much like those studied in modern criticism.

---

[1] Sprague, *Shakespeare's Histories*, 57; Sprague and Trewin, *Shakespeare's Plays Today*, 102–3.

[2] A. J. A. Waldock, 'The Men in Buckram', *RES*, 23 (1947), 16–23.

[3] Sprague, *Shakespearian Players and Performances*, 171–2.

15. 'Prithee let her alone, and list to me' (3.3.93). Prince Hal (Richard Burton), Falstaff (Anthony Quayle), and Mistress Quickly (Rosalind Atkinson), watched by Bardolph (Michael Bates) and Gadshill (Edward Atienza), in the production directed by Quayle and John Kidd at Stratford-upon-Avon (1951)

The main thrust of interpretations has often been most apparent in the relationship between Hal and Falstaff. The Shakespeare Memorial Theatre's production at Stratford in 1951, as directed by Anthony Quayle and John Kidd, envisaged the break between Hal and his companion as inevitable from the start. Hal's denunciation of Falstaff (played by Quayle) began early in the tavern scene, and mounted to a violent climax on the series of accusatory questions beginning, 'Wherein is he good, but to taste sack and drink it?' (2.4.438 ff.) Richard Burton as Hal emphasized the dignity and resolve of the young man who was to become King Henry V, but made little attempt to suggest genuine merriment.[1]

Douglas Seale's production of *Parts 1* and *2* at the Old Vic in 1954–5 sought more of a balance between Prince Hal (Robert Hardy) and Falstaff (Paul Rogers). Although Hal's royal responsibilities were apparent from the start, and his eventual rift with Falstaff was foreseen, Hal was free of calculation and genuine in his enjoyment of Falstaff's company. The play-acting scene grew to a

[1] Sprague, *Shakespeare's Histories*, 60, 63.

climax of hilarity in Falstaff's defence of himself, but then suddenly became serious as Hal made plain his intention to banish his fat companion. After quietly pronouncing his unshakable resolution, 'I do, I will' (2.4.463), Hal jumped down from the table and tearfully embraced the old Falstaff in a gesture of love and farewell. During the interview with the sheriff, Hal's mind seemed preoccupied, and even the tavern reckonings found in Falstaff's pocket gave rise to no more than a fleeting smile. The succeeding tavern scene brought Hal and Falstaff together only to underline the distance that had come between them : Falstaff was by this time lachrymose and disreputable, while Hal was resolutely on his way to battle. Falstaff's capers at Shrewsbury merely confirmed by their tastelessness and poor timing the unbridgeable gulf between Hal and Falstaff.[1]

The historical scenes were played with an equal sensitivity. In the sad parting, Lady Mortimer (Virginia McKenna) expressed in Welsh her distress at her husband's departure, while Hotspur (John Neville) and Lady Percy (Ann Todd) covered their emotion with raillery. King Henry (Eric Porter) appeared cold and distant in his relationships with Hotspur and the seemingly profligate Hal, but came at last to reconciliation and fatherly pride. The overall balance and respect for the play's contrasting textures won high praise from the critics : the reviewer in *The Sunday Times*, for example, praised Seale for his 'masterly interweaving of tumult and reflection, of sophistication and simplicity, the clash of swords or tankards, great gusts of laughter and the quiet of prayer, the conflict of kingship, fellowship, and fatherhood'.[2]

Other directors have taken more emphatic lines of interpretation. Certainly the twentieth-century stage has not resisted the temptation to see Hal as heartless or priggish. The Royal Shakespeare Company's version of the Henry IV plays and *Henry V* at Stratford in 1964, directed by Peter Hall, John Barton, and Clifford Williams, showed the influence of Bertolt Brecht in the squalid tavern scenes and frightening renditions of battle, emphasizing throughout the contrast between a gargantuan capacity for life (embodied most of all in Hugh Griffith's ebullient Falstaff) and the

---

[1] Roger Wood and Mary Clarke, *Shakespeare at the Old Vic* (1956), vol. 2 (1954–5 season), 155–61; Sprague and Trewin, *Shakespeare's Plays Today*, 73.
[2] Wood and Clarke, *Shakespeare at the Old Vic*, 158.

emotionally sterile world of political struggle. Hal (Ian Holm) was cold-blooded, self-contained.

A more recent development has been to diminish Falstaff in order to stress the ties of father and son. The Royal Shakespeare Company's production in 1975 of *1* and *2 Henry IV* and *Henry V*, directed by Terry Hands, centred on the development of Hal (Alan Howard) and the carrying through of his role into *Henry V*. As a consequence, the relationship with a benevolent and gentlemanly Falstaff (Brewster Mason) was somewhat overshadowed. Hal's father (Emrys James) was an abrasive and domineering self-made man, one whom the Percy faction might well hate and to whom Prince Hal reacted with profound uneasiness; the emotional centre of the two-play sequence was the eventual reconciliation of father and son. Similarly, Peter Moss's Canadian Stratford production of *1 Henry IV* (1979) brought fresh approaches to the relationship between Hal and King Henry in the interview of 3.2 and the reconciliation on the field of battle in the fifth act.[1] Today the play is seldom the vehicle for a single star comic actor that it tended to be in the eighteenth and nineteenth centuries.

Trevor Nunn's production of *1* and *2 Henry IV*, with which the Royal Shakespeare Company celebrated its move to the Barbican Theatre in 1982, focused on a childishly defiant Hal, a young man fearful of growing up. As acted by Gerard Murphy, Hal was burly and physically unprepossessing, with a mop of greasy, straw-coloured hair and a fatuously toothy smile. Wholly under the spell of Falstaff (Joss Ackland) in their first scene together, Hal sat on the old man's knee, snuggled in Falstaff's arms, and even mopped up the mess his friend had made eating breakfast. In the long tavern scene he threw himself across Falstaff's chest like a child seeking assurance, even though he could also respond with ill temper and threats as he declared his intent to banish the old man. His first reconciliation with his father (Patrick Stewart) next morning at court proved to be a partial, angry gesture, and Hal ventured on to Shrewsbury field not at all reconciled to any sense of high duty. The duel with Hotspur (Timothy Dalton) was a protracted contest between two exhausted boys that ended in an unchivalrous dagger

[1] Samuel Crowl, 'The Long Goodbye: Welles and Falstaff', *SQ*, 31 (1980), 369–80; T. F. Wharton, *Henry the Fourth Parts 1 and 2: Text and Performance* (1983), 44–80.

thrust. Hal was thus portrayed as an awkward, madcap wild youth of deep emotional insecurity, with little intelligent agility or promise of the king he must become. Nunn, with his fondness for self-reflexive theatrical artifice, repeatedly staged the choices confronting Hal: Hotspur appeared in a spotlight during Hal's first soliloquy; Worcester was made visible during the tavern revels, as a reminder of a reckoning not yet made; various members of the cast emerged from nowhere to overhear Falstaff's disquisition on honour; and at Shrewsbury field Hal suddenly found himself caught between his stern father's appeal for affection and Falstaff's insistent call, 'Hal, if thou see me down in the battle....' (5.1.121).

The models offered to Hal were thus hard to assimilate: a father racked by guilt and remorse, a substitute father ready to gratify a longing for hugs and hair-ruffling and puppyish dependence, and a rival of blazing conviction. Behind the saintly mask of the ageing King lay rage and desperation; behind Falstaff's cultured, though decayed, gentility and warmth lay the harsh thrust of menace and quest for power. The Eastcheap tavern vibrated with Hogarthian vignettes of gaming and whoring, while John Napier's set continually reassembled its movable towers and platforms in an Elizabethan reminder of the Royal Shakespeare Company's *Nicholas Nickleby*.[1]

Conversely, in his BBC television production of *1 Henry IV* (1979), Cedric Messina chose to demystify Shakespeare in a generally sturdy, but unsurprising, interpretation, marred by low-budget naturalism and unconvincing studio filming techniques (especially in the battle sequence) but bolstered by the underplayed finesse of Anthony Quayle's Falstaff and by the camera's ability to focus on meaningful details such as the crown and King Henry's physical illness (as portrayed by Jon Finch).[2] The direction (by David Giles) was low-key, and the interpretation less insistent than that in the productions of Burrell, Seale, Hall, Hands, Nunn, and

[1] Reviews by J. C. Trewin in the *Birmingham Post*, 10 June 1982; John Barber in the *Daily Telegraph*, Irving Wardle in *The Times*, and Michael Billington in the *Guardian*, 11 June 1982; James Fenton in *The Sunday Times* and Robert Cushman in the *Observer*, 13 June 1982; and R. L. Smallwood in *Critical Quarterly*, 25 (1983), 15–20.

[2] Reviews by Nancy Banks-Smith in the *Guardian* and Richard Last in the *Daily Telegraph*, 10 December 1979; Russell Davies in *The Sunday Times* and Clive James in the *Observer*, 16 December 1979; Irving Wardle in *The Times*, 17 December 1979.

others. David Gwillim's Hal was boyishly attractive to outward appearances but in fact shallow, detached, and colourless.

Orson Welles's film *Chimes at Midnight* or (in the United States) *Falstaff* (1965–6) offers one more instance of directorial imprint. Film, even more than the modern stage, is the director's medium. Welles rearranges and cuts scenes with abandon in order to produce a single film from *1* and *2 Henry IV* (somewhat as he had done earlier in his *Five Kings*), enhancing his own role of Falstaff in the process. Inevitably some parts of the plays suffer, but in return we are given a remarkably sensitive reading of a fat comic who is at heart insecure and in need of affection. Falstaff's poverty and illness persist throughout the film; his relationship with Hal is always one that anticipates its termination. Falstaff is seldom off-camera; we see him framed in the Boar's Head entrance, slightly out of focus, looking quizzically at Hal during the latter's first soliloquy, and later with the same expression when Hal announces his intent to banish plump Jack and all the world (2.4.461–3). Beneath his joviality we sense the hurt in Falstaff's frightened eye, the predominant sadness that expresses itself in a series of farewells. To Welles, the film is a story 'all in dark colours', a 'lament' for Falstaff, and this reading is insistently maintained even in the film's most comic sequences. Falstaff's story is all the more poignant for being seen against the grim backdrop of history, like that of Jan Kott, one in which machiavellian and bloodless calculation overwhelms quixotic imprudence. Falstaff's perception of the sham in political rhetoric and in the mechanism of war arouses our sympathy for one who is to be sacrificed by the shrewdest survivor of all, Prince Henry.[1]

The text

In many respects the textual history of *1 Henry IV* is reasonably straightforward, and has clear implications for choice of a control text. The first extant complete quarto appeared in 1598, some time after the Stationers' Register entry of February, as printed by Peter Short for Andrew Wise. But there must have been an earlier quarto

[1] Jack Jorgens, *Shakespeare on Film* (Bloomington, Ind., 1977), 106–21; Daniel Seltzer, 'Shakespeare's Texts and Modern Productions', in *Reinterpretations of Elizabethan Drama*, ed. Norman Rabkin (New York, 1969), 89–115; Crowl, 'The Long Goodbye', *SQ*, 31 (1980), 369–80.

(Qo), dating also from 1598 and printed in the same shop, for a fragment of eight pages, or four leaves, was recovered by Halliwell 'some years' prior to 1867 from the binding of a copy of William Thomas's *Rules of the Italian Grammar* (1567). This fragment, sheet C, now in the Folger Shakespeare Library, extends from 1.3.201 to 2.2.105, and provides the best textual authority for this portion of the play, since Q1 was set from Qo. Both quartos were produced from the same distinctive stock of type, and they share many typographical and textual peculiarities, including errors not found in any other edition.[1]

Q1's omission of the word *fat* in the final line of 2.2, as printed in Qo, along with some crowding (Q1 has one line more to each page than Qo) and a few other small differences, confirms that Q1 was printed from Qo rather than the reverse. Otherwise the 250 or so variations between Q1 and Qo are almost entirely spelling and punctuation variants, or corrections of obvious typographical errors as at 1.3.238 and 296, indicating a different compositor or compositors—probably two—who used exemplary care in setting Q1. One corruption ('rogue' for 'fat rogue') in some 296 lines of text is a reasonable record of accuracy; at this same rate, the Q1 compositors would have introduced some ten errors into the play as a whole, in addition to any already in Qo. Since spelling practices and other typographical features indicate that the two compositors (if two were used) followed their copy closely in its lack of colloquial elision and other details throughout, we have good reason to believe that Q1 replicates Qo with acceptable fidelity.[2]

A comparison of the two quartos does suggest, to be sure, that the compositor(s) of Q1 were economizing on space by crowding prose speeches into the fewest possible lines, closing up space between scenes, and running some half-lines together (1.3.247–8, 1.3.300–2.1.0, 2.1.93–5, 2.2.29–31). Q1 ends with K4ᵛ, the last page of its tenth sheet; Qo must have run longer, necessitating at least half an eleventh sheet. The practice of crowding, observable also at 3.2.93, where a speech prefix and the beginning of a new speech occupy the second half of a single line of print, may have

[1] Charlton Hinman, ed., *Henry the Fourth Part 1 (1598)*, Shakespeare Quarto Facsimiles no. 14 (Oxford, 1966); Hemingway, 344–9.

[2] Hinman, ed., *Henry the Fourth Part 1*, ix; P. H. Davison, ed., *1 Henry IV*, New Penguin Shakespeare (1968), 250–2.

produced the misplacement of a speech prefix in the following lines as printed in the extant quarto and F1 texts:

> And is not this an honorable fpoile?
> A gallant prize?Ha coofen,is it not?   In faith it is.
>   *Weft*. A conqueft for a Prince to boaft of.
> *King.* Yea,there thou makft me fad, and makft me finne

$(1.1.74–7)^1$

Editors generally recognize the speech beginning 'In faith it is' as Westmorland's. The error may have been made in Q0, following a manuscript in which the speech 'In faith it is' was an authorial interlineation or marginal addition, but the preference of Q0, and especially Q1, for crowding half-lines has helped to perpetuate the error.

The two 1598 quartos of *1 Henry IV* are in any event among the cleanest and best-printed of all the Shakespeare quartos. A collation of the three surviving copies of Q1 reveals only four trifling corrections of typographical error (at 2.4.289 and 400, 3.1.45, and 4.3.72) during the press run,[2] and the number of uncorrected errors is small. Q0, moreover, was set from a manuscript of high textual authority. Shakespeare's company would not have turned over a successful play to the printer so soon without good reason, presumably that of setting the record straight on Old-castle–Falstaff, and the required change of names was of course included in the copy they submitted. Such a situation demanded a well-verified text.

What did the company submit: Shakespeare's foul papers, a fair copy thereof, or the prompt-book (either the original or a transcript)? The prompt-book was still of use in production, and in any case the text of Q0 and Q1 shows a casualness about entries and exits that a prompt-book would remedy. The absence of stage directions between 3.3 and 4.1 is so glaring that it probably represents an omission in setting the text from the manuscript, but

---

[1] Wilson, *NCS*, 103.

[2] Hinman, ed., *Henry the Fourth Part 1*, v, lists three variants but misses one at 3.1.45 recorded by Hemingway, 180.

other instances of vagueness sound authorial. Uncertainties as to comings and goings of the comic characters (especially Bardolph in 2.2 and Bardolph and the Hostess in 2.4) remain unresolved. If Blunt is intended to appear in 1.1, his movements are not clarified in the text. Servants tend to be overlooked in exits and entrances (2.3.62, 69, and 2.4.78, 82), and characters who might be expected to appear with their counterparts, like Vernon with Worcester at 5.1.8.2 and 114.1, are sometimes not named. Speech prefixes are occasionally imprecise, like the 'Car.' at 2.1.31 and 2.4.492 that does not specify which Carrier, or 'Travel.' at 2.2.74 for a speech that must have been assigned in the prompt-book to one player. 'Enter Glendower with the Ladies' at 3.1.186.1 is clear enough for the reader in context but too offhand for the prompter. Throughout, the stage directions read like the author's script before it received any attention from the book-keeper.

These characteristics of foul papers are offset to some extent by certain features of improvement not common to authorial manuscripts. An occasional formality of expression in Q1 seems out of keeping with the surrounding colloquialism, as in Hotspur's 'what do you call the place?' and 'A plague upon it' at 1.3.241–2, where the elided forms 'd'ye' and 'upon't' would seem more characteristic, or 'I smell it' at l. 275, 'he is . . . he is' at 3.1.226–7, and especially Falstaff's 'All is one for that' instead of 'All's one' at 2.4.149. The Folio text elides all but 'smell it' and the first 'he is' in these instances. Dover Wilson attributes these and other sedate expressions to a compositor or master-printer concerned with standards of orthography,[1] but they could be the work of a scribe preparing a fair copy. The speech prefixes are more regular than in texts such as *Romeo* Q2, printed from unimproved foul papers. To be sure, the character normally identified as 'Hot.', or occasionally as 'Hotsp.' is labelled 'Per.' in his first ten speeches of 4.1, but otherwise variation in speakers' names has been eliminated and speech prefixes generally brought into line with the names of characters as they appear in the stage directions.[2]

Minor variations in spelling or abbreviation are admittedly frequent: King, Kin.; Prince, Prin., Pri., Pr.; Falst., Fal., Fast. (in Qo); Poines, Poynes, Poin., Poi., Poy., Po.; Worst., Wor.; Hotsp., Hot.; North., Nor., Nort.; Gadshill, Gad., Ga.; Peto, Pet.; Trauel.,

[1] Wilson, *NCS*, 104.
[2] Alice Walker, 'The Folio Text of 1 *Henry IV*', *SB*, 6 (1954), 45–59.

Tra.; Lady, La.; Hostesse, Host., Ho.; Sher., She.; Glendow, Glen.; and P. Iohn, Ioh., John. Some of these speech-prefix forms may have been compositorial, although the inconsistencies in the Qo fragment suggest that many were authorial; Q1 differs at times from Qo, but generally in the direction of reducing anomalies. Stage directions reveal similar minor inconsistencies. Hotspur is 'Percy' at 5.2.25 and 5.4.75, and the character called 'Fran.' (i.e. Francis) in speech prefixes is 'Drawer' in the stage directions. 'Douglas' is abbreviated 'Doug.' in 4.3, though usually 'Douglas'; Vernon is introduced as 'Vernon' in 4.3 and 'sir Richard Vernon' in 5.2; 'Blunt' in 3.2 is expanded to 'sir Walter Blunt' in 4.3 and 5.3; the 'Earle of Westmerland' in 1.1 is 'Lord of Westmerland' in 4.2, and so on. These irregularities are less marked than in the Quarto of *2 Henry IV*, where, in 2.4 for example, Quickly is also 'Qui.', 'host.', and 'Ho.', and Doll is variously 'Tere.', 'Dorothy', 'Dol.', 'Teresh.', and 'Doro.'. At the same time they are more frequent than in *Julius Caesar*, the Folio text of which lacks prompt-book attention to matters of staging, and yet is so regular in the forms of its speech prefixes as to suggest that its source was a scribal fair copy.[1] Of course not every scribe regularized to the same extent, and a scribe copying *1 Henry IV* may simply have been less thorough in these matters.

The hypothesis of a fair copy for Qo remains problematic, therefore. Certainly Shakespeare and his company needed to alter the original version of the play to prepare it for publication, replacing Oldcastle's name with that of Falstaff. A fair copy would have facilitated clean printing, and as we have seen Qo and Q1 are probably the cleanest and best printed of all the Shakespeare quartos. The careful distinction between italics and roman in Hotspur's letter (2.3) may also point to a fair copy. On the other hand, the effort and expense of copying would hardly have been undertaken solely to effect the changes involving Oldcastle, Harvey, and Russell. One would expect, moreover, that the copyist, whether a scribe or the author himself, would at least attempt to get these controversial names right in the new draft, whereas in fact the names 'Haruey' and 'Rossill' still appear at 1.2.153 instead of 'Peto' and 'Bardolph' as substituted elsewhere, and *Ross.* stands as a speech-prefix three times at 2.4.167–73. The speech prefixes are

[1] Fredson Bowers, 'Establishing Shakespeare's Text: Poins and Peto in *1 Henry IV*', *SB*, 34 (1981), 189–98.

further confused in this passage: Q1 assigns to *Gad.* a speech (l. 166) that must be the Prince's, possibly because a correction in the manuscript replacing the three *Ross*'s with a single *Gads.* was mistaken by the compositor as a correction to the Prince's speech.[1] If so, the attempt at correction would appear to be an inconsistent one, for Bardolph (who elsewhere takes the place of 'Russell') is present and might well have been assigned the three speeches given to *Ross.* in Q1. In any event such a correction sounds more like a hasty alteration of an authorial draft than a fair copy. The jibe about 'my old lad of the castle' remains at 1.2.40–1, even though publication was presumably intended to establish the goodwill of Shakespeare's company toward Oldcastle's powerful descendants.

The possibility remains, then, that Shakespeare's foul papers were corrected by him or some other person for the press with a view to publication. This person might well have tidied up the speech prefixes and stage directions to some degree. Shakespeare's drafts were unusually free of blotted lines, to judge from the testimony of Heminges and Condell and Ben Jonson,[2] and served as printer's copy on several occasions. This theory does not explain, admittedly, why Qo and Q1 are cleaner than other quartos printed from foul papers, not does it explain the tidying up of colloquialisms, which might well be scribal. We appear to have in Qo and Q1 a text based either on Shakespeare's corrected papers, and hence close to his original, or on a scribal copy that imposed relatively few changes on its original. Humphreys argues that the punctuation shows signs of being Shakespeare's own; the unusual care in using elided forms of weak past verb forms (rightly eliding 168 verbs and rightly leaving unelided 33, while wrongly eliding 1 and wrongly failing to elide 10) may again be characteristically Shakespearian,[3] though the same consistency occurs in First Folio plays set from transcripts by Ralph Crane. In any case, Qo and Q1 give an impression of reliability. The text is unabridged, and only minimally revised to accommodate the Cobham family. If we had no texts other than these, we would lose little.

Does the First Folio text nevertheless show evidence of some

[1] Wilson, *NCS*, 149.

[2] 'To the Great Variety of Readers' in the Folio of 1623, and *Timber, or Discoveries*, in Jonson, viii. 583–4, ll. 647–61.

[3] Humphreys, lxviii, citing Hereward T. Price, 'The First Quarto of *Titus Andronicus*', *English Institute Essays 1947* (New York, 1948), 137–68.

'sprinklings of authority'[1] that would require serious consideration of a number of its readings? To be sure, a number of F1's
readings either merely perpetuate or introduce error. F1 was set
from an exemplar of Q5 (1613) that may have been selected, and
even prepared, as copy for the First Folio text before Q6 came on the
market in 1622. Q2 (1599), Q3 (1604), Q4 (1608), and Q5 had
been set up from the preceding edition in each case; the 'newly
corrected' on the title-page of Q2 does not point to any authority
behind the text even if some of its changes are plausible.[2] Qq2–5
show no certain signs of correction by reference to an authoritative
copy. Q5 thus stands at several removes from the original in the
accumulation of errors. The First Folio text does little to remove
this residue. Alice Walker concludes that F1 unsystematically cor-
rects a mere 26 of Q5's known errors, while retaining some 200
errors from Qq2–5.[3] Such evidence argues against any thorough
consultation of an earlier quarto or manuscript in the preparation
of Q5 as copy for the First Folio.

We need to consider whether the readings newly introduced by
F1 are the work of an 'editor' (such as Heminges or Condell) an-
notating a copy of Q5, or of the two compositors (B and a partner
traditionally called A, but tentatively identified by Gary Taylor as
J), who shared the task of setting the First Folio text.[4] Readings that
seem editorial raise in turn the question of their origin, such as the
prompt-book, a manuscript of some other kind, recollections of
theatrical practice, occasional consultation of an earlier quarto, or
simply the editor's own conjecture.

Act and scene divisions generally bear the mark of an editor, as
originator or annotator, and would perhaps have been his first
concern. For the most part the divisions are satisfactory, though
the editor has failed to mark a division at 5.3.0 because he did not
see the need for one, having been misled, evidently, by the absence
of 'Exeunt' in the Q5 stage directions. Action is virtually con-
tinuous during the battle sequence of Act 5, so that scene divisions
are literary conventions in any case. They are probably the work

---

[1] John Jowett and Gary Taylor, 'Sprinklings of Authority: The Folio Text of
Richard II', *SB*, 38 (1985), 151–200.

[2] Humphreys, 1xx–1xxi.

[3] Walker, 'Folio Text', *SB*, 6 (1954), 42.

[4] Gary Taylor, 'The Shrinking Compositor A of the Shakespeare First Folio', *SB*,
34 (1981), 96–117.

of the First Folio editor himself throughout *1 Henry IV*. The fact that the First Folio editor was misled in Act 5 by the absence of 'Exeunt' in his copy argues against the use of the prompt-book, though some other manuscript may have been consulted.

Alterations to the stage directions in F1 have generally been ascribed to the First Folio editor rather than to compositors A or J and B. Changes like the gratuitous addition of 'omnes' to 'Exeunt' appear at the end of 3.3 and 4.1, one on a page set by compositor B (f2), one on a page set by A or J (f2ᵛ).[1] Although such phraseology was perhaps not unknown in a prompt-book, it certainly required no prompt-book authority. The character called 'Pointz' is erroneously introduced at the beginning of 1.2 in F1, rather than (as in Q1) at l. 100.1, because Falstaff's exclamation on seeing him, 'Poins!', has been mistaken by the First Folio editor for a speech prefix, following the error in Qq4–6. The editor has even removed the entrance for Poins at l. 100.1 from his Q5 copy, evidently surmising from the dialogue as it mistakenly appeared in Q5 that Poins had been a part of the group from the start; the remarks in ll. 102–4 about hell and salvation by merit, if said by Poins, might well be taken to apply to Falstaff and the preceding conversation. The First Folio editor cannot have consulted the prompt-book, which would make no such error, nor Q1, which reports the matter correctly. The massing of names in a collective entrance at the start of the scene, as in the Crane texts, seems an unlikely explanation for the error, since it occurs nowhere else in this play, and since the First Folio editor has gone out of his way to remove Poins's entrance at l. 100.1 in Q5. The likeliest agent of such an error, then, is the First Folio editor, misreading the evidence of Q5 and acting on his own to rationalize it with a misplaced entry. A compositor would not have anticipated at the beginning of the scene the apparent presence of Poins at l. 100.1.

Similarly, the First Folio editor includes Westmorland in the opening stage direction for 5.1 (as in the quartos) though a prompt-book would surely have discovered that he cannot have been there. He follows the quarto texts in failing to distinguish a cleared stage at 5.3.0, and he does not clarify ambiguities about the arrivals and departures of Blunt in 1.1, of Bardolph in 2.2, or of the Hostess and Bardolph in 2.4. He retains from Qq2–5 the exits

[1] S. W. Reid, 'The Folio *1 Henry IV* and Its Copy', unpublished.

and entrances between 3.3 and 4.1 not found in Q1, and provides some plainly required exits at 2.1.94, 4.3.113, 5.3.60, AND 5.5.15.1 (most of them at the ends of scenes), together with one entrance for Douglas at 5.4.23.1, but conversely has omitted exits at 1.2.205, 1.3.21.1, 2.2.86.1 and 4.2.72 found in Q0 and Q1 along with helpful details such as 'and Falstalffe after a blow or two runs away' (2.2.97.2–3). The editor seems interested in rejecting anticipatory entries. His 'improvements' are literary, and in general fail to remedy those matters of practical stagecraft left unexplicit in the quartos. This evidence of failure to make corrections does not rule out occasional—and unsystematic—consultation of a manuscript, but it does seem of a piece with the First Folio editor's inability or unwillingness to provide any meaningful clarification of stage action.

Speech prefixes in F1 show the preference of both the compositors and the editor. Compositor A or J tends to prefer 'Falst.', 'Bard.', 'Hotsp.', and (sometimes) 'Prince', while compositor B tends to prefer 'Fal.', 'Bar.', 'Hot.', and 'Prin.' (except for folio f2, which seems partly contaminated by A or J's preferences).[1] *Poins* still appears in various forms: in 1.2 alone, set by compositor B, we have 'Pointz', 'Poines', 'Poin.', 'Poy.', and 'Poyn'. Some emendations and normalizations look like the work of the editor, as in the alterations from 'Gad.' to 'Prince' at 2.4.166 and 'Ross.' to 'Gad.' at ll. 167–73, or the substitution of 'Hot.' for Q1's 'Per.' throughout the first ninety lines of 4.1. The corrections in 2.4 suggest either a manuscript authority or the editor's knowledge of stage performance; those in 4.1 are easily explained as the editor's sporadic efforts to eliminate the most noticeable variations in the speech prefixes of his copy-text.

Excision of profanity in F1, though more thorough than for other plays, is inconsistent. 'O God' and 'would to God' become 'O heaven' and 'Would to heaven' in 5.4.50–68, for example, and even Falstaff is made to swear 'heaven reward him' (l. 158), but elsewhere in F1 we find 'God save the mark', 'God pardon it', 'Jesu [Q0: Iesus] bless us', 'By the mass', 'would to God', and a number of others.[2] The expressions ''sblood' and 'zounds', used with special frequency in this play, have disappeared entirely,

---

[1] Eric Rasmussen has helped me with this analysis.
[2] 1.3.56, 1.3.174, 2.2.78, 2.4.353, and 4.3.32.

sometimes lamely replaced with 'Yes', 'No', 'Away', and 'by this hand'. The excision is too pervasive to have been compositorial; it cuts across both compositors' stints, requires adjustments in scansion and lineation, and so on. Scholars are divided as to whether the excision was literary in nature or the result of theatrical influence. W. W. Greg argues for 'a purely literary tradition of expurgation' in various F1 texts, including *1 Henry IV*, whereas Dover Wilson argues for a scribe who was instructed to collate a copy of Q5 with the prompt-book, which had presumably been purged after the Act of 1606, and J. K. Walton sees no reason why a desultory collation may not have been made of the prompt-book.[1]

One argument in favour of literary excision is that the alterations of profanity in the F1 text of *1 Henry IV* sometimes seem quite untheatrical in character, vitiating exchanges between actors, and sounding like tone-deaf alterations for which actors would presumably have found more stageworthy substitutes. F1's removal of the Prince's 'wisdom cries out in the streets and no man regards it' at 1.2.84–5, for example, presumably in the interests of purging the play of indecorous citations of Scripture, makes theatrical nonsense of Falstaff's objection to 'damnable iteration' (l. 86).[2] The substitution of 'Yfaith' for ''Sblood' in Falstaff's impudent impersonation of Hal at 2.4.427 is also lame theatrically; Falstaff's use of strong profanity is necessary to make sense of Hal's retort, in the person of his father, 'Swearest thou, ungracious boy?' (l. 429). Hotspur's oath, 'Heart', is similarly needed to illustrate his point when he is urging Kate to use 'a good mouth-filling oath' at 3.1.242–51.

Yet there are persuasive reasons for doubting that 'literary' removal of profanity from printed texts was common. As Gary Taylor reminds us, the Act of 1606 against profanity applied to stage performances, not to published texts, so that compositors or scribes had no motive to remove profanity as part of their assignment. In other First Folio plays, excision of profanity is normally associated with the consultation of a manuscript of prompt-book

[1] W. W. Greg, *The Shakespeare First Folio* (Oxford, 1955), 149–52 and 264; Wilson, *NCS*, 105–7; J. K. Walton, *The Quarto Copy for the First Folio of Shakespeare* (Dublin, 1971), 235 ff.
[2] Humphreys, lxxiii.

authority perhaps reflecting either changes in performance after 1606, or anticipation of a stage revival. The F1 text of *1 Henry IV* may be theatrically inept in some of its excisions, but it does show more of an attempt to provide 'speakable' substitutions for omitted profanity than do several other texts. Possibly, then, a manuscript was consulted, one however that seems to have been too untheatrical in its removal of profanity to have been based on the prompt-book, and the nature of which is hard to determine.[1] Everything about the excision of profanity points to an editor somewhat inconsistently discharging his duties or relying on some manuscript other than the prompt-book.

F1's handling of colloquialisms, as of stage directions, is at the same time inconsistent (some are restored, others rejected) and spread indifferently across the pages of compositors A or J and B, suggesting once again the desultory and 'literary' efforts of the editor.[2] Changes in dialogue similarly offer only a few real improvements ('President' or 'precedent' for 'present' at 2.4.31, restoration of Q1's 'engross up' for Qq3–5's 'engrosse my' at 3.2.148, restoration of 'fat' for Qq2–5's 'faire' at 5.4.106) in the midst of many uncorrected errors carried over from Qq2–5.

Thus far, then, we can see that an editor like Heminges or Condell has provided act and scene divisions, altered stage directions largely as a matter of style, regularized some speech prefixes, and excised profanity, all without recourse to the prompt-book (unless the act divisions reflect a late stage revival and hence the inclusion of act divisions in King's Men's performances after about 1609), but possibly with reference to some other kind of manuscript or else to the editor's personal acquaintance with Shakespeare's acting company. In order to speculate more knowledgeably on his possible sources of information, we need to know in more detail what changes in F1 can be attributed to compositors A or J and B.

---

[1] Taylor, 'Zounds Revisited: Theatrical, Editorial, and Literary Expurgation', forthcoming. Alice Walker (*Textual Problems of the First Folio* (Cambridge, 1953), chapter on *2 Henry IV*) contends that the expurgation of the Folio text of *1 Henry IV* may have been in response to Sir George Buc's resignation as Master of the Revels in 1622, and the presumed expectation of greater stringency on the part of his successor; such an expurgation would certainly have been of editorial, rather than prompt-book, origin. Taylor points out, however, that Walker's conclusions are based upon bibliographical assumptions about dates of composition that have since been disproved.

[2] Reid, 'The Folio *1 Henry IV* and Its Copy.'

As a result of Alice Walker's investigations, compositor B's performance in setting his portion of *1 Henry IV* has until recently been regarded with deep suspicion. Assigning some fourteen and one-half pages (1.1–2.4.143, 3.3.108–4.1.19, and 4.4.27–end) to B and the remaining eleven pages to his partner (Walker's A, Taylor's J) on the basis of spelling characteristics, Walker saw a marked discrepancy between the two. In B's pages she found a far greater tendency to interpolate, omit, and alter words. B's total of 'errors' in this seemingly high-handed disregard for his copy came to 169, as against 20 for A. The imbalance in the distribution of errors suggested to Walker that most changes could not be editorial, for an editor would have had no reason to lose interest in the dialogue 'whenever compositor A chanced to become responsible for the Folio text'. She noted that the implications were disturbing for other plays set chiefly by B, including *King Lear*.[1] Her argument amounted to a clear warning to any modern editor of *1 Henry IV* to be wary of B's handling of his assignment.

Yet Walker's case against B rests solely on his setting of *1 Henry IV*. Paul Werstine has shown that when B worked from largely uncorrected copy in other First Folio plays, especially *A Midsummer Night's Dream*, *Love's Labour's Lost*, *The Merchant of Venice*, *Titus Andronicus*, and *Romeo and Juliet*, he achieved a perfectly respectable record of accuracy, the number of errors being not at all what we would anticipate from Walker's figures for *1 Henry IV*. B's record in those other plays is good in matters of omission and interpolation, whereas almost half of B's presumed errors in *1 Henry IV* are serious errors of this kind.[2]

The question becomes then, how are we to explain the anomalous pattern in *1 Henry IV*? One obvious possibility, that of hypothesizing a different compositor, yields inconclusive evidence in both directions. Certainly portions at least of B's supposed stint on *1 Henry IV* have been challenged.[3]

More conclusive is evidence that B was dealing with badly cast-

[1] Walker, 'Folio Text', *SB*, 6 (1954), 55. Her figures on error have been corrected by Werstine; see next note.

[2] Paul Werstine, 'Compositor B of the Shakespeare First Folio', *AEB*, 2 (1978), 241–63.

[3] Charlton Hinman, *The Printing and Proof-reading of the First Folio of Shakespeare* (Oxford, 1963), i. 373–4, suspects that d5–6^v and e1^v–2 may not be Compositor B's; see also S. W. Reid, 'Some Spellings of Compositor B in the Shakespeare First Folio', *SB*, 29 (1976), 102–38.

off copy on a page-by-page basis. Perhaps because of copyright difficulties, *1* and *2 Henry IV* were skipped for a time in the compositorial work on the First Folio. Only four quires (d through g), or 48 pages, were provisionally allotted for these two long plays and for the last third or more of *Richard II* that had not yet been set. Work began meanwhile on *Henry V* at quire h. When the inadequacy of the intervening allowance was discovered, a supplementary quire gg had to be allotted.[1] The compositors of *1 Henry IV* then found themselves with too much space for their copy. B set the first four pages of *1 Henry IV* in the reverse of reading order, dealing at various times with excess space and also, oddly enough, with crowding; the casting-off of individual pages appears to have been uneven, and compositor B was evidently unwilling to adjust the casting-off of his largely prose copy so as to make fuller pages less full and lean pages fuller. It is on pages with spacing difficulties that B's anomalous errors appear most frequently. Omissions and abbreviations are characteristic of crowded passages, interpolations of spare ones. Line justifications explain even more errors; B apparently often looked no further than the line he was setting in his attempt to conserve or fill space.[2]

These explanations notwithstanding, B's capability in setting other First Folio plays suggests that many of the 'errors' in his stint on *1 Henry IV* were in fact editorially introduced, either by one of the First Folio editors preparing a Q5 exemplar for the press or in the process of proof-reading. Because the printer's copy was cast off in large blocks, and was not (as Walker supposed) printed seriatim, B's stint may have differed significantly from that of A or J. Conceivably, argues Werstine, Jaggard provided each of his two compositors with a copy of Q5, one edited with a cursory consultation of Q1, the other more heavily annotated—the second having been acquired perhaps during the delay in printing the *Henry IV* plays owing to copyright difficulties.[3]

Both in kind and in number, the F1 variants in B's stint are not characteristic compositorial errors. Some are the result of proof-reading. Werstine shows that F1's correction of Prince Henry's

[1] Eleanor Prosser, *Shakespeare's Anonymous Editors* (Stanford, 1981), 73–5.

[2] Werstine, 'Compositor B', *AEB*, 2 (1978), 260.

[3] Werstine, 'Folio Editors, Folio Compositors, and the Folio Text of *King Lear*', in *The Division of the Kingdoms : Shakespeare's Two Versions of 'King Lear*', ed. Gary Taylor and Michael Warren (Oxford, 1983), 247–312 and 254.

'Yea but tis like' in Qq to 'I, but tis like' has resulted in twice as wide
a space after the speech-prefix as is usual in the column:

> ploit rhemſelues, which they ſhall haue no ſooner atchie-
> ued, but wee'l ſet vpon them.
>   *Prin.*   I, but tis like that they will know **vs** by our
> horſes,by our habits,and by euery other appointment to
> be our ſelues.
>   *Poy.* Tut our horſes they ſhall not ſee, Ile tye them in

(1.2.160–6)

Only the hypothesis of press correction and the subsequent need for
the compositor to insert a space to justify his prose line can account
for the anomalous spacing. Another uncharacteristically wide gap
at 2.1.13 seems to have been necessary to reset Q5's 'I thinke this
to be the most' to F1's 'I thinke this is the most':

>   1.*Car.* Poore fellow neuer ioy'd ſince the price of oats
> roſe, it was the death of him.
>   2. *Car.* I thinke this is the moſt villanous houſe in al
> London rode for Fleas: I am ſtung like a Tench.

(2.1.11–14)

Probably B set 'to be' (the reading of Q5) and then was instructed
to correct it to 'is', resulting in the need for a space. Conceivably
the person making the corrections was someone in Jaggard's shop;
close working relationships between individual compositors and
proof-readers were not uncommon, a fact that might explain a
preponderance of corrections in B's stint. On the other hand, as
Peter Blayney has shown, proofs were often read by authors or
editors rather than press correctors,[1] in which case the corrections
called for by the proof-reader may have had some kind of authority. Indeed, it is hard to explain why 'Yea' would be reset as 'I' or
'to be' as 'is', if there were no manuscript urging the corrected
reading.

Other F1 variants seem to have originated, however, not in the
course of proof-reading but in the preparation of press copy, and
some of these reveal the kind of 'literary' improvements we find in
the First Folio editor's work on stage directions and the like. Since
B does not add half-lines, verbs, adjectives, or expansions to his

---

[1] Peter Blayney, *The Texts of 'King Lear' and their Origins*, vol. 1 (Cambridge,
1982), 191–3.

copy elsewhere, interpolations of this sort at 1.3.211, 1.3.275, 5.2.93, and other places must be the work of the play's editor. The redundancy of such interpolations and their bungling attempts to repair metre suggest an editor's sporadic attempts to regularize what he views as stylistic imperfections in the text of Q5, rather than independent manuscript authority. The same is true of a tendency in F1 to interpolate words in such a way that characters repeat themselves exactly in prose speeches, and to impose formally balanced syntax upon colloquial and elliptical prose speech, as at 2.1.6 and 10.[1]

The evidence strongly points, then, to the involvement of both editor (perhaps annotator) and proof-reader in the text of F1, and their work accounts for many of the changes viewed by Walker as compositorial. On the crucial question of manuscript authority for such changes, however, the evidence is inconclusive and even contradictory. The First Folio editor seems to have proceeded on his own authority in correcting metrical irregularity, and may also have done so for act and scene divisions and the excision of profanity. Nevertheless, Heminges and Condell (or someone like them) did have a close working knowledge of Shakespeare's plays, and had access both to other members of Shakespeare's company and to playhouse documents in which subsequent changes to Shakespeare's play might have been recorded. If such alterations came about through repeated performance by actors who wished to change lines, we cannot assume that Shakespeare did not acquiesce; he may even have initiated some. The possibility remains that some of F1's variants may represent a fragment of an independent tradition, as Greg suggests. F1 readings cannot claim authority without some demonstration of plausibility in individual cases, but we have a ground at least for giving 'respectful consideration'.[2]

Some specific textual difficulties in *1 Henry IV* are explicable to varying degrees in terms of the textual history proposed here. F1's correction of speech prefixes for the Prince and Gadshill at 2.4.166–73, already referred to, has been adopted by many editors. Wilson's theory that 'Gad.' was written once for the 'Ross.' that occurs three times in the manuscript, and was then mistakenly used for the Prince's speech, is all the more plausible if

[1] Werstine, 'Folio Editors', 256–7.
[2] W. W. Greg, *Principles of Emendation in Shakespeare* (Oxford, 1928), 13.

we suppose that the corrector was emending Shakespeare's foul papers, attempting to get rid of the potentially offensive names 'Harvey' and 'Russell', but doing so in a manuscript that might then have been a little hard to read. Or the corrections in F1 could point to a better manuscript. Theatrical recollection by a company member might also explain the corrections, since anyone familiar with the play would recognize that 'Speak, sirs, how was it?' must be assigned to the Prince, but such a theory is hard to reconcile with the error made in 1.2 about 'Pointz' and with the cutting of helpful stage directions. Perhaps the F1 editor, after assigning this line to Hal on the basis of theatrical memory or common sense, might have given the response of 'Ross.' at random to one of the robbing crew, forgetting for the moment that 'Ross.' is elsewhere equivalent to Bardolph—an entirely plausible speaker for these three speeches. Familiarity with the play might have helped the editor in changing 'present' to 'President' ('precedent') at 2.4.31, and 'scantle' to 'cantle' at 3.1.97.

More complex is the matter of establishing the presence on stage at various times of Bardolph, Poins, Peto, and other figures whose entrances are sometimes omitted in the early texts. Bardolph is not named in the opening stage direction of 2.2 in QqF1, nor does he speak until after Gadshill enters at l. 44.1. At this point in QqF1, Poins recognizes Gadshill with 'O 'tis our setter, I knowe his voice', and goes on to inquire 'Bardoll [F1: Bardolfe], what newes', to which 'Bar.' responds with information about the approaching travellers. The least amendment of Qo is to suppose, as in Humphreys's Arden edition, that Bardolph enters with Gadshill. Yet many editions (including this one) see Bardolph as present from the start of the scene. The opening stage direction in Qo has '*Enter Prince, Poynes, and Peto &c*', and the '*&c*' would hardly seem to apply to Falstaff since he is given a specific entrance three lines later. We have seen that this kind of vagueness is common in Qo and Q1, owing to their derivation from foul papers. No one other than Bardolph is involved in the robbery to whom '*&c*' could apply. Moreover, Falstaff calls out imploringly to Poins, Hal, Bardolph, and Peto at ll. 19–20, assuming them all to be near. Gadshill appears to enter alone in Qo at l. 44, and to be recognized by Poins as a new and distinct arrival. The question that follows, 'what newes?', must surely be addressed to him, and the information given about the approaching victims of the robbery must surely derive from his function as 'setter'. Gadshill is the one who knows the number of the approaching victims at l. 60.

Can 'Bardoll' in Qo then be explained as the compositor's misinterpretation of a speech prefix? Although it is true that the presumed prefix 'Bar.' in the author's revised manuscript would not have provided the compositor with 'Bardoll' (Qo), the name had appeared already in that form at l. 20. If the printer's copy placed the two short speeches in ll. 47–9 on one line and wrote the speech prefixes in 'English' script like the rest, as Wilson surmises, the compositor may have guessed wrongly that 'Bardoll, what newes' was needed to fill out Poins's speech. The error, once made, would then prompt him to change 'Gad.' to 'Bar.' in l. 50. An alternative possibility, suggested by John Jowett, is that 'Bardoll, what newes' (l. 49) should read 'Gadshill, what newes', not as containing a mistaken speech prefix but as a continuation of Poins's speech addressed to the new arrival; Jowett finds evidence that the names of Gadshill and Bardolph were confused, and may originally have been conceived for one character.[1]

The Folio excision of '*&c*' in the opening stage direction looks like an error on the part of the F1 editor, who failed to correct Qq's misassignments of speeches at ll. 49–52 and may therefore have supposed Bardolph not to be on stage earlier. As we have seen, F1 elsewhere prunes stage directions ill-advisedly at 1.2.205, 1.3.21.1, 2.2.86.1, 2.2.97.2, 4.2.72, and 5.4.100.1. The F1 editor has provided no entrance at all for Bardolph to replace the excised '*&c*', even though Bardolph is addressed and, as in Qq, erroneously assigned one speech. These manifestly imperfect remedies do not suggest an editor who was familiar with the play, nor do they support the notion of an authoritative manuscript. They read like literary meddling, and, in this important detail at least, do not inspire confidence in F1's report of staging or assignment of speeches.

The essential problem may have been the author's manuscript. Bardolph is not yet a well-developed character—he is little more than one of the robbers—and Shakespeare may not yet have had him fully in mind. Bardolph is given no entrances or exits, though he is mentioned. He speaks only if one accepts the emendation of 'Bardoll, what newes', and then only briefly.

Moreover, the ambiguities of Qo leave us uncertain as to

[1] Wilson, *NCS*, 139; John Jowett, 'The Thieves in *1 Henry IV*', forthcoming.

whether Bardolph and Peto are in on the practical joking about Falstaff's horse. Poins and the Prince may be talking to one another in the opening speeches of the scene, and the Prince's 'Stand close' (l. 3) may apply chiefly to the two of them (as it does, for example, in the Dering manuscript adaptation of 1622, and in the Elliston–Macready performance of the early nineteenth century recorded in John Cumberland's *British Theatre*, vol. 4). It is the Prince who comes forward to torment Falstaff about his horse, and he presumably overhears with Poins the soliloquy of comic grumbling that Falstaff directs at them. Conventions of darkness on the Elizabethan stage allowed the audience to suppose that Falstaff could not see those who are teasing him and overhearing his complaint. The Qo stage direction 'They whistle' (ll. 26–7) may apply to the Prince and Poins, rather than to the whole gang. The Prince and Poins have already planned an elaborate practical joke in which Peto and Bardolph are to share with Falstaff the role of butt. Should Peto and Bardolph be partners in the fun about the horse? The text leaves us uncertain. Peto and Bardolph could well have exited during Falstaff's soliloquy, having entered at the start of the scene in highwaymen's garb merely to establish the scene as one of robbery; a good deal of movement on and off stage is likely during the early part of this scene. On the other hand, Peto and Bardolph may have been an appreciative audience for the Prince's and Poins's joke, remaining on stage in concealment to laugh at Falstaff's discomfiture. The choice is directorial. F1 leaves the matter unresolved, by bringing on Peto without Bardolph at l. 1, a halfway measure that suggests once again a lack of prompt-book input.

Are the early texts confused in the roles they assign to Poins and Peto in attending on Prince Hal? Dr Johnson and Dover Wilson are among those who find it strange that Poins, after his close association with Hal during the robbery, should disappear from the play altogether some time in 2.4, perhaps when the sheriff arrives at l. 486 (though Q1 provides no stage directions, and F1 vaguely specifies 'Exit' for an undetermined number of characters), and that Peto should then remain behind with the Prince. Poins is more deserving of Hal's promise that 'thy place shall be honourable' in the wars (l. 525); so the argument runs. Perhaps 'Po' and 'Pe' were confused in the copy.[1] But the Q1 speech prefixes specify

[1] Wilson, *NCS*, 157.

'Peto' or 'Pet.' at ll. 509, 514, and 530 (there is none at l. 516), and the Prince addresses Peto by name at l. 529. The problem recurs at 3.3.189, where Peto is again addressed by name. The 'honourable' place assigned to Peto (2.4.525) could well involve some personal service to Prince Hal; at 3.3.189–90 we learn that the Prince and Peto are to ride together to the battle. It is noteworthy that Peto is not promised a 'charge of foot', as is Falstaff (2.4.526). Instead, Falstaff refers in 4.2.8–9 to 'my lieutenant Peto', certainly an 'honourable' title for such a man, and comically not unlike that of 'Ancient Pistol' in *2 Henry IV* and *Henry V*. Peto addresses the Prince in 2.4 as 'my lord' or 'good my lord', and never as 'sweet Hal', 'my lad', 'sirrah', 'my good sweet honey lord', or other phrases of the sort used by Poins. (To be sure, Poins also addresses the Prince as 'my lord' three times in *2 Henry IV* 2.4.) Nor does Peto address Falstaff familiarly as 'Jack'. The Prince usually addresses Poins as 'Ned', but Peto is always called 'Peto' (e.g. 2.4.289). In *2 Henry IV* we again find the characteristic distinction: Poins is a companion to Hal at tennis and in practical joking, while Peto acts as servant and messenger.

Fredson Bowers, who agrees that the presence of Peto at the end of 2.4 and in 3.3 cannot be attributed to scribal or compositorial error, argues instead that the actor of Poins had to be withdrawn in the middle of 2.4 to prepare him for another role such as that of Glendower, but it seems doubtful that staging details worked out after the play had been written would have been marked in the author's foul papers, and the doubling could have been achieved by many other characters besides Poins.[1] The stage directions of QqF1 provide no entry for Peto in 3.3, but they provide none for Poins either, and Peto is addressed directly. The F1 editor sees nothing amiss with the role provided for Peto in the quartos, and even adds a speech prefix for Peto at 2.4.516, where it is generally agreed to be necessary. For other textual difficulties regarding the presence or absence of characters on stage, see the notes at 1.1.62–3 (Sir Walter Blunt), 2.4.463.1 (Bardolph and the Hostess), 5.1.8.2 (Vernon), and 5.4.0 (Blunt's body).

The lineation of the verse and distinguishing between verse and prose are at times problematic in *1 Henry IV*. Several factors may contribute to the difficulty: spacing constraints in the early texts,

[1] Bowers, 'Establishing Shakespeare's Text', *SB*, 34 (1981), 189–98; Jowett, 'The Thieves in *1 Henry IV*'.

the predilection of compositor A or J for realigning long verse lines, the F1 editor's attempts to correct passages where his Q5 copy seemed erroneous (possibly with reference to some manuscript), and Shakespeare's own flexible idiom in this mature play. Spacing problems are not uncommon. The compositors of Q1, as we have seen, were under constraint to reproduce in ten sheets an earlier quarto (Q0) that must have run at least a half-sheet longer. The compression, visible several times in the eight pages common to Q0 and Q1, no doubt encouraged the Q1 compositors to run verse as prose when ambiguity in their copy could justify their doing so.

The F1 compositors were under a different sort of constraint, owing as we have seen to a large error in casting-off that invited them to waste space but also (owing to a reluctance to redistribute their copy from page to page) to crowd on certain occasions. The effect on choosing between prose and verse is evident on f2, for example, where compositor B, faced with an abundance of room, versifies the prose exchanges of Falstaff and Hal at 3.3.164–71. Perhaps the Prince's verse ending to the scene a few lines later, characteristic of many comic scenes in this play, was thought to offer a precedent. In any case, the odds favour compositorial, rather than editorial, revision. On the same page compositor B twice divides a single verse into two at 4.1.15–16. On f3^{v}, another sparsely set page, compositor A or J realigns three verses as four, breaking at punctuation in mid-line (4.4.3–5). Compositor A or J is sufficiently inclined to relineation of long verse lines by dividing them at the caesura that he does so even when he is under no pressures to eke out his copy.

These compositorial changes are easy to identify and emend. More difficult are passages in which Shakespeare's own idiom may have shifted between prose and verse, especially when Hotspur is on stage. In 2.3 at ll. 67–85, Q1 prints as fourteen lines of closely set prose what modern editions generally perceive to be nineteen lines of dialogue between Hotspur and Kate, most but not all of it in verse. F1 follows the example of Qq, taking sixteen lines in a visibly crowded column (compositor B's e3b) because of narrower column width than Q1. F1 shortens Kate's speech at ll. 82–5, perhaps to fit it into three lines. A similar shift from verse to prose saved the compositor of Q1 some two lines in the opening eighteen lines of 3.1, where Hotspur squares off against Glendower, though some of Glendower's clearly metrical speech is left versified. Hotspur's lines at ll. 16–18 are so hypermetrical that lineation remains uncertain; Shakespeare's manuscript must have been ambiguous in passages of this sort. Compositor A or J of the First Folio text, working with too little copy for his page, expanded 3.1.1–18 to twenty-one lines, five more than in Q1, in verse that is so plainly defective and so plainly occasioned by the need to use up space that the corrections cannot be regarded as authoritative. At l. 23 F1 breaks into two short verse lines what Q1 prints as a plausible, if rough, single verse line. In the same scene, at ll. 104–7, Q1 prints what seem to be four lines of verse (though beginning hypermetrically) in three lines of prose, whereas compositor A or J, on a loosely set page of F1 (e6), unconvincingly produces four lines of verse by breaking at punctuation. Still later in 3.1, the badinage of Hotspur and Kate moves repeatedly back and forth between prose and verse, leading to uncertainties at ll. 222–3, 242–5, and (in Glendower's speech) at 193–4. Compositor A or J of the First Folio again lines these passages as verse to use up space; the results at 242–5 are more plausible than elsewhere.

A few similar ambiguities are found in scenes not involving Hotspur. At the end of 2.4, the transition from the prose of this comic scene to verse for the serious exchange between Prince Hal and the sheriff is seemingly not recognized at first by the Q1 compositor, for he sets as prose the sheriff's first two speeches (488–92) before settling down into blank verse, and F1 copies him. The sheriff's first speech is formed metrically of two regular blank verse lines, but the second is not, suggesting that the manuscript's intent may not have been clear. In Blunt's first speech of 5.3, Q1 misaligns the verse, perhaps to save space, and compositor B in a tightly set column follows copy; at l. 42, Q1 prints the Prince's hypermetric, though clearly verse speech as prose (F1 treats it as a long verse line) in a passage in which the Prince's verse is contrasted with Falstaff's prose as a way of underlining the distance that has come between them.

Though difficulties remain, the pattern seems clear. Especially with Hotspur, whose impatient starts and professed dislike of poetry lend themselves to hypermetric effects even in lines accepted by QqF1 as verse (e.g. 1.3.218, 223, and 246), Shakespeare evidently composed with a freedom that makes exact reconstruction problematic. Half-lines cannot always be neatly matched to produce pentameter verse lines, as in the three-line sequence of half-lines at 3.1.113–15. Passages of verse are interrupted by short lines, often two or more in succession, as at 1.3.247–8, 3.1.49, 3.1.233–9, and 3.1.252–3. Hotspur speaks in all these passages.

Shakespeare also explores the boundary between verse and prose at the ends of the largely prose comic scenes, allowing Hal to soliloquize in blank verse at the end of 1.2, or to comment in verse on the absurd cowardly retreat of the robbers at the end of 2.2. (The latter passage is set as prose in QqF1, even though it has been recognized as metrical since Pope, suggesting that the intentions of Shakespeare's manuscript with regard to distinctions between prose and verse were not always apparent to the Q compositors.) The arrival of the sheriff towards the end of 2.4 calls for serious talk in verse, though the very end of the scene appropriately reverts to prose for the business of Falstaff's tavern reckonings. The blend of verse and prose in 3.1 nicely catches the ambivalent mood of sorrow and playfulness at the moment of parting, and the contrast in characterization between Hotspur and Mortimer. The second tavern scene (3.3) ends in verse on the serious note of Hal's departure for war, so ringingly patriotic that it even inspires a concluding verse couplet (not without its mocking effect) from Falstaff. In the battle scenes, the comic prose of Falstaff is insistently contrasted with the verse of the warriors, and Hal, after two brief exchanges with Falstaff over the ragged recruits and the coming battle (4.2.46–72, 5.1.123–6), speaks only in verse, even when in Falstaff's presence.[1] These patterns serve as no more than guidelines for determining whether Shakespeare intended verse or prose at any given moment, but cumulatively they do indeed give perspective on Q1's tendency to make verse into prose to save space, and F1's tendency on most pages to lineate uncertain passages in short lines of defective verse in order to fill up space.

The last textual question to be considered here is in some ways the most important, as well as the most problematic. Scholars are virtually certain, from evidence cited at the start of this Introduction, that Shakespeare originally called the chief comic character of *1 Henry IV* not 'Falstaff' but 'Oldcastle'. The name appeared as such in his manuscript, and made its way into production, as contemporary references indicate. As we have seen, the earlier

[1] Milton Crane, *Shakespeare's Prose* (Chicago, 1951).

name has left its trace in 'My old lad of the castle' (1.2.40–1), in a defective line of verse (2.2.102), and in a speech prefix in *2 Henry IV* (1.2.114), as well as in the designations 'Harvey' and 'Russell' (1.2.153, 2.4.167–73) in *Part 1*. Is it not the editor's duty to restore what Shakespeare wrote until he was obliged by censorship to back down? Gary Taylor argues that it is, and that restoration clarifies Shakespeare's changing conception of the role. A similar restoration in *Part 2* is impossible, he points out, because by the time Shakespeare wrote it he had been forced to change his idea of the character; as a result, the historical figure of Oldcastle is of little importance to this play. In *Part 1*, on the other hand, Shakespeare clearly had the historical Oldcastle in mind. Oldcastle was in fact a soldier and proto-Protestant 'martyr' or 'rebel'. To retain his name is to see that Shakespeare at once softens the rejection (the historical Oldcastle was probably burned alive) and accepts its necessity (King Henry V's hand was forced by Oldcastle's treachery). When obliged to change the name, Shakespeare did so perfunctorily, *pace* Dover Wilson's unsubstantiated claim of extensive revision. Taylor sees the chief arguments against restoration to be a wish to avoid inconsistency in Shakespeare's tetralogy (though inconsistency remains in any event) and sheer weight of tradition, as evidenced by the silence of editors on this important point. If we retain the profanity of Q0 and Q1 excised from the First Folio in the name of censorship, Taylor asks, ought we not to restore 'Oldcastle' as well?[1]

To this strongly reasoned argument one can raise questions about the purposes of an edition, and what it should preserve. Heminges and Condell, the editors of the First Folio, seem to have had no hesitation in retaining 'Falstaff'. Even though they may have had reasons to do so other than a presumed regard for Shakespeare's own intentions, and even though they elsewhere overlooked some apparent blunders, their choice (or their failure to consider any other choice) requires some consideration. They evidently felt that the issue of names, once settled, should remain so.

Were they merely allowing discretion to be the better part of valour in 1623, or were they respecting what they took to be their author's wishes? Shakespeare must have acceded to the decision to use 'Falstalffe' (as it appears throughout the dialogue and many of

[1] Gary Taylor, 'The Fortunes of Oldcastle', *ShS* 38 (1985), 85–100.

the stage directions) in the quartos of 1598. However much the result of pressure from the Cobham family, the decision, once made, must have seemed irreversible, and Shakespeare kept the name of 'Falstaff' for *2 Henry IV* and *Henry V*. He wrote *The Merry Wives of Windsor* for a very different Falstaff, but one whose comic appeal depended in good part on the audience's recognition of a familiar character and on the use of a familiar name, albeit in a new context. 'Falstaff' had become a fictional entity, requiring a single name. Since that name could no longer be 'Oldcastle', it had to be 'Falstaff', in *1 Henry IV* as in the later plays.

1 Henry IV is a separate play, to be sure, and was produced as such, but it introduces characters and situations that continue into the subsequent plays in a historical, or purportedly historical, succession of events. Characters do occasionally change names, but not in the way that is here proposed for Falstaff. Prince Henry is the Prince until he is King, Hotspur is remembered as Hotspur, and so on. Bardolph and Peto remain Bardolph and Peto, unless we restore 'Russell' and 'Harvey' (and 'Russell' is still present in the quarto of *2 Henry IV* at 2.2, so he would presumably have to be restored in both plays). To be sure, 'York' in *Henry V* is the same character historically as 'Aumerle' in *Richard II*, and 'Bedford' in *Henry V* (and *1 Henry VI*) is to be identified with 'Prince John of Lancaster' in *1* and *2 Henry IV*, but these are merely alterations of aristocratic title. Such changes occur within the fictional narrative, and do not interfere with the audience's perception of continuity and single identity. Gary Taylor's solution, by contrast, involves a shift of names that does not represent the fictional narrative. The solution loses sight of what a character's name is *for*. It destroys an understood correspondence between a fictional character and the verbal sign used to signify that character. It obtrudes the literary and textual work of editors into the fictional space of Shakespeare's plays, where a character's name must exist primarily as a contract between dramatist and audience on the identity of the character in question.

Surely we can assume that Shakespeare intended to use one name throughout. When he finished *1 Henry IV*, he planned to continue to use the name 'Oldcastle' in *Part 2*. In some important ways, of course, the character in *2 Henry IV* was not to be 'the same' as that in *1 Henry IV*: he would have to be older, more infirm, more pitiable. But this kind of change is common in fiction and does not express itself through a change of names forced on the author by non-literary considerations. Indeed, continuity of name is needed to understand the change of personality and fortune. A central joke in *Merry Wives*, for example, is to see a character called 'Falstaff' fall in love; the rich portrayal of this character in the earlier plays, including *1 Henry IV*, is needed to appreciate the comical incongruity of Prince Hal's fat and rascally companion penning identical love-notes to two women, and suffering the indignities of satirical exposure. Shakespeare could have used some other label to identify this character, and indeed began in *1 Henry IV* with 'Oldcastle'. He clearly planned to use one name, but then had to abandon the name he had originally chosen. However much he may have preferred it, however much its loss may have obscured his original artistic intent in *1 Henry IV*, we can see that Shakespeare accepted the logic of the new name 'Falstaff', for *1 Henry IV* as well as for the subsequent plays.

It is true enough that retention of 'Oldcastle' insists on the integrity of the play as written and performed before censorship obtruded. It preserves the original 'contract' between dramatist and audience, one that illuminates the relationship between the dramatic character and the original historical figure. Censorship broke that contract, and an editor must see the attraction of re-establishing it—especially since Shakespeare may not have conceived of *1* and *2 Henry IV* as a closely knit unit when he was working on *Part 1*. Anomalies remain no matter what an editor chooses to do. Still, the greater anomaly is that of ignoring the need for a single name throughout. That is why the restoration of 'Oldcastle' for *1 Henry IV* alone differs from the retention of censored profanity. We can reintroduce excised oaths without distortion —indeed they are present in our Q1 copy-text—but we cannot go back to 'Oldcastle' without creating the very anomaly that Shakespeare and his editors avoided. The label 'Falstaff' is a compromise, but it is the one settled on at the time, the one used in stage directions and speech prefixes as well as in dialogue. Above all, the character had to have the same name from play to play.

No evidence suggests that Heminges and Condell were under any constraint from the Cobham family in 1623. Their decision, if they deliberated about it at all, was to set down the only 'final intention' of their author that was possible—not solely for reasons of political restraint, but because by 1623 no other name would serve as an adequate label for the character in his appearance in four separate plays. Because the label is a compromise, any modern editor must point out the contemporary meanings that 'Oldcastle' would have conveyed, but he must also honour Shakespeare's very evident wish that the character be given one name. Editors have sound editorial reasons, besides sentiment and tradition, for resisting this latest 'rejection' of Falstaff, one in which his very identity is (in Pistol's fine phrase from *Henry V*) 'fracted and corroborate'.

EDITORIAL PROCEDURES

THIS edition is based on Qo and QI for reasons given in the Introduction. The First Folio text provides some readings for which it may have had independent manuscript authority or knowledge of playhouse practice. The Dering manuscript provides three useful readings that may derive from acquaintance with Shakespeare's play on stage.

Substantive departures from Qo and QI are listed in the collation. These include instances in which alterations in punctuation affect meaning. The lemma records the word or phrase as it appears in the present modernized text, followed usually by the authority in which the preferred reading was first adopted, and then by the rejected reading of Qo or QI. For example, '1.1.62 a dear] Q4 *corr.*; deere QI' means that the reading of Q4 as corrected, 'a dear', is adopted in this edition in place of QI's 'deere'. The collation does not attempt to give a detailed textual history of the early quartos and folios other than Qo, QI, and FI, but it indicates readings in editions after QI that deserve consideration; also, because the First Folio's readings have a potential claim to authority, the collation lists substantive variants (other than manifest errors, some minor relineation, and excisions of profanity) that originate in the First Folio. For example, '1.2.177 lives] QI; lyes Q2–6, FI' means that the QI reading, 'lives', has been retained, but that 'lyes' in Q2–6 and FI has appealed to a number of more recent editors, even though Q2 has no independent authority. Where this edition considers the adopted reading to be simply the modernization of a variant form, rather than an emendation, collation is as follows: '4.2.11 soused] QI (souct)', meaning that the Q reading is retained but is modernized from its obsolete form 'souct' to 'soused'. For the most part, however, the collation ignores minor variations in proper names and details of spelling, italicization, hyphenation, and capitalization.

The collation lists all substantive changes to stage directions, such as the entries of characters not mentioned in Qo or QI, as well as stylistic additions of 'the' and 'and' that do not affect the sense of the original. Normalizations of stage directions, as in 'Enter Lady Percy' at 2.3.32.1 for QI's 'Enter his Lady', or 'Enter Glendower with Lady Percy and Lady Mortimer' at 3.1.186.1 (Q1 refers simply to 'the Ladies'), are noted in the collation but are not marked by bracketing in the text. These are alterations in form merely, intended to bring stage directions and speech prefixes in line with one another and to provide consistency throughout. Nor does this edition bracket added stage directions that are unambiguously called for by the dialogue, such as Falstaff's exit at 1.2.150, even though they are absent from Q0 and Q1; where their accuracy is virtually certain and has been endorsed by editors from an early date, a note in the collation seems sufficient notice to the reader.

Parentheses mark off stage directions within a speech, such as (*to Northumberland*) or (*within*); the collation indicates whether or not they appear in Q0 or Q1. All indications of speaking aside or to another character or within are in fact editorial, but they are collated to distinguish them from other directions like (*They whistle*) or (*He drinketh*) that appear in the original. Parentheses do not then imply additions to the original texts; they contain observations about stage action that are either marked in Q0 and Q1 or seem plainly indicated by the dialogue.

Broken square brackets, on the other hand, indicate uncertainty about the placement, or even the veracity, of an added stage direction, as at 2.4.486.1 (⌈*Exeunt all except the Prince and Peto*⌉), where we cannot be sure precisely when everyone leaves, and whether it is Peto or Poins who remains, or at 2.4.463.1–2 (⌈*A knocking heard. Exeunt Hostess, Francis, and Bardolph*⌉), where the delay necessary for Bardolph's re-entry and speaking of the next line of dialogue raises the very real possibility that he and perhaps others have left the stage earlier. Such brackets are thus reserved for instances of genuine puzzlement about stage action.

This edition silently normalizes speech prefixes throughout, while bracketing and collating all substantive alterations. Speech prefixes appear on a separate line above verse passages but on the same line as prose passages. Where one speaker completes the verse line of the preceding speaker, as at 1.3.22, the second part-line is indented, and the verse is counted as one line in the line numbering, a convention not found in the early quartos or folios. This edition follows editorial tradition in all instances except those noted. On the other hand, unassimilated part-lines or part-lines that could form a complete line of verse with either the previous or the following line, as at 3.1.113–15, are here treated neutrally without indentation. At 4.3.15 and 5.5.24–5, dramatic logic and metre assist in making a choice.

Act and scene divisions are not recorded in the collation, and indications of locale are confined to the commentary. Like most modern editions, this one follows the First Folio text in its act and scene divisions, except for the provision of a new scene at 5.3. No new scene is provided at 2.2.86.1 because the Prince and Poins may come forward from hiding (see commentary on this line). The marking of scenes during the fluid movement of a battle sequence, as in Act 5, is essentially a matter of literary convention. Thus, the First Folio seems justified in not prescribing a new scene at 5.3.29, since Blunt's body remains on-stage. At 5.4.0, on the other hand, the situation is ambiguous; no stage direction informs us that Blunt's body has been removed, but the First Folio marking of a new scene may itself possess some authority. Thus the First Folio markings, as modified in editorial tradition, seem plausible, and serve as a generally accepted basis.

With regard to spelling, this edition adheres generally to Stanley Wells's criteria for vigorous and thorough modernization. The attempt is to avoid, on the one hand, eccentric preservation of archaic or obsolete spellings, and on the other, an 'insensitive levelling' that might obscure special effects of word-play, scansion, and rhyme (*Modernizing*, 5). Semantically indifferent variants are given in their modern form, as in the following: *strands (stronds), buckram (buckrom), holler (hollow), Weald (Wild), beholden (beholding), grip (gripe), rites (rights), square (squire), manège (mannage), keech (catch), talon (talent), mettle (mettall), northern (Northren), bonds (bands), owe (ought), jostling (justling), doffed (daft), cuisses (cushes), lief (lieve), tattered (tottered), feazed (fazd), southern (Southren), bosky (busky), alarum (alarme),* and *wardrobe (wardrop)* (see notes to these words in the commentary). The uninflected form in *recreation sake, safety sake,* and the like, though common in Elizabethan English, is no longer in use, and has been modernized to *recreation's sake* and *safety's sake. Mo* occurs only once in *1 Henry IV, more* sixty-one times, and since no distinction is apparent in the single use of *mo,* it has been modernized. *An,* meaning 'if', is substituted for *and* in order to avoid confusion with the copulative *and* (*Modernizing,* 16). *1 Henry IV* make no use of *a* as a clipped form of 'he'. Where *a* is used in *a clocke, a Thursday,* and so on, it has been modernized to *o'clock* and *o' Thursday*. Alternative Elizabethan spellings such as *then / than*, *to / too*, and *lose / loose* have been regularized according to modern usage.

Semantically significant variants require preservation of the original form. *Loaden* at 1.1.37 means much the same as 'laden', but is a strong past participle of the verb 'load', whereas 'laden' is the strong past participle of 'lade'; the forms are similar but historically distinct. *Afeard* at 2.4.355 is used interchangeably with *afraid*, but the first is from *afear*, 'in fear', the second from *affray*, 'to startle'. Shakespeare's texts use the word *ancient* to indicate a standard-bearer, and generally prefer *ensign* for the standard itself; see 4.2.23, 30, and notes. *Receipt* at 2.1.83 means 'recipe', but is historically distinct. *Task* 4.1.9 means 'tax' in the sense of 'test', and may be derived by metathesis from the Latin *taxare*, but the words are distinct. So too with *prune* at 1.1.97, meaning 'preen'. Rhyme can dictate the preservation of an older form that might otherwise be modernized, as with *corse* ('corpse') at 4.1.124, paired with *horse* in the preceding line. *Parmacety* at 1.3.58 is a standard spelling of the obsolete word *parmacetie*, described in the *OED* as 'a popular corruption of spermaceti', and hence a form that Hotspur might use without any particular flavour (*Modernizing*, 14). *Estridges* at 4.1.98 probably means 'ostriches', and is a variant of that word, but preservation of the original form allows for other possible meanings such as 'goshawk'.

Proper names can present difficulties. Some modernizations are easy, as with *Westmorland* (*Westmerland*), *Falstaff* (*Falstalffe* in Qo and Q1's dialogue and many stage directions, *Falstaffe* generally in the First Folio), *Michael* (*Mighell*), *Bristol* (*Bristow*), *Canterbury* (*Canturburie*), and *Trojans* (*Troyans*). The modern form simplifies recognition in *Atholl* (*Athol*), *Shirley* (*Sherly*), *Scrope* (*Scroope*), *Saint Albans* (*S. Albones*), and *Daventry* (*Dauintry*). *Bolingbroke* no doubt distorts the pronunciation of Q1's *Bullingbrooke*, or *Bullenbrooke*, but the use of older spellings as a possible key to Shakespeare's pronunciation is something that an edition using modern spelling attempts at the certain cost of inconsistency and sporadic archaism.

On the other hand, metrical considerations demand the disyllabic *Holmedon*, as it consistently appears in Q1, in preference to the modern *Homildon* or *Humbleton* (*Modernizing*, 29). The *Complete Oxford Shakespeare* intends to use the standard modern Welsh form

Glendŵr, but this edition prefers the original *Glendower* as familiar and well suited to the uncertain or varying stress indicated in different verses. For the same reason, the original *Murrey* is rendered *Murray* instead of the modern Scottish county name *Moray*. Shakespeare's *Mordake* is presumably equivalent to *Murdoch*, but whether Shakespeare made this connection is not clear; he took the proper name as he found it in Holinshed. *Gawsey* (*Gausell* in Holinshed) is best left alone, rather than being changed to the modern *Goushill*. Colloquialism can be a reason for retaining an original form. Falstaff's *Co'fil'* (4.2.3) is a plausible rendition of Q1's 'cop-hill', probably reflecting Shakespeare's spelling 'Cophil', whereas the modern form *Coldfield* loses what may have been a colloquial flavour. Francis the Drawer's *Pomgarnet* (2.4.36) signifies *Pomegranate*, of which it is a variant form, and is perhaps characteristic of Francis's vocabulary. *Bardolph* is the commonest form in the First Folio of a name that Q0 and Q1 spell *Bardol* or *Bardoll*; F1's spelling may be authoritative, is phonetically equivalent to *Bardolf(e)* in the Quarto of *2 Henry IV*, and is also the spelling most familiar today.

This edition follows Q0 and Q1 in using the elided form in prose for the second person singular in such words (most of them modal verbs) as *canst, couldst, wouldst, shouldst, hadst, didst,* and *sayst,* that are regularly spelled this way for the modern reader. In the case of verbs to which we would add an apostrophe for the second person singular, on the other hand—for example, *camst, standst, hearst,* and *dreamst*—this edition gives the contracted forms *cam'st, stand'st, hear'st,* and *dream'st,* following the preferences of Q0 and Q1 with regard to elided and unelided forms in both prose and verse. The quartos are generally sensitive to metrical requirements in verse, as in *mak'st*, 1.1.77.

Treatment of the final *-ed* in the weak past tense of verbs also observes a distinction between prose and verse, but, necessarily, by a different convention. In prose, verbs like *dic't* and *cal'd* appear as *diced* and *called*. In verse, forms such as *loved* and *slandered* indicate elided pronunciation, whereas *armèd* and *butcherèd* indicate the metrical need for a sounded *-ed* syllable. The Q0 and Q1 texts of *1 Henry IV* are careful in their use of the elided form in verse and require little emendation.

Elision within words, as in *wand'ring* (1.2.14), is ignored in prose as metrically immaterial, and, conversely, is retained in verse when metrically necessary. Q0 and Q1 are the guides here, and no attempt has been made to give such internal elisions when the metre might seem to call for them.

This edition follows Q0 and Q1 conservatively in colloquial or metrical elision of such forms as *I'll, upon't,* and *what's.* A number of elisions that appear in the later quartos and the First Folio seem attractively in keeping with the speech habits of Falstaff and Hotspur especially. Q0 and Q1 are at times oddly formal, as noted above, and metre sometimes urges an expanded or contracted form in preference to what is printed in Q0 or Q1. Yet subsequent efforts in Q2–5 and F1 or later to restore colloquialisms or to emend metre are manifestly sporadic, and it would be impossible to follow such proposed emendations without introducing some inauthentic readings along with some presumed restorations. We cannot be sure that the efforts of the First Folio editors or compositors have any more authority than the attempts at regularization of Pope and Capell. Fortunately, the matter is not all that important, since the actor or reader can readily perceive the clipped cadence in Hotspur's 'what do you call the place?' or 'A plague upon it' (1.3.241–2). Q0 and Q1 are such carefully prepared texts that they require little assistance here.

Punctuation adheres to that of Q0 and Q1 insofar as is practicable, but with allowance as required by a modernized text for present-day conventions. Although Q0 and Q1 are probably based on Shakespeare's own manuscript, or a transcript thereof, the punctuation may well be compositorial, and indeed a collation of Q0 with the comparable portion of Q1 reveals many minor changes in punctuation. Certainly the interpretative effect of punctuation needs to be considered in every departure from the copytext. Quotation marks and apostrophes in possessive forms (*Harry's, devil's*), both singular and plural, are always editorial. So, in general, are apostrophes marking elision, as in *'tis, 'sblood, i'faith, is't.*

Abbreviations and References

In addition to the abbreviations for editions and scholarly works listed below, this edition employs the standard abbreviations found in the *Oxford English Dictionary (OED)* such as *v.* (verb), *sb.* (substantive), and *int.* (interjection). Abbreviations of the titles of

Shakespeare's plays in the commentary are those of the Oxford English Texts series and are reasonably self-explanatory. References to plays by Shakespeare other than *1 Henry IV* are keyed to individual volumes of the new Oxford Shakespeare where available (*Henry V, Troilus, Taming, Caesar, Titus*), otherwise to Peter Alexander's edition of 1951. Biblical citations are from the Bishops' Bible (1568) unless otherwise noted. Page references to Holinshed are to Geoffrey Bullough's *Narrative and Dramatic Sources of Shakespeare*, volume 4, except for an occasional quotation not included there, in which case reference, by volume and page (e.g. iii. 520), is keyed to the original edition of 1587. Line references to *The Famous Victories of Henry the Fifth* are to Bullough, volume 4. Quotations in the commentary and Introduction from early texts including Holinshed and the Elizabethan dramatists have been modernized except in cases where the original spelling is pertinent.

The following abbreviations are used in the collation, commentary, and notes. The place of publication is London unless otherwise specified.

EDITIONS OF SHAKESPEARE

Q0	(1598) sig. C1–C4^{v} only
Q1	*The History of Henry the Fourth* (1598)
Q2	(1599)
Q3	(1604)
Q4	(1608)
Q5	(1613)
Q6	(1622)
F1	The First Folio, 1623
F2	The Second Folio, 1632
F3	The Third Folio, 1663
F4	The Fourth Folio, 1685
Alexander	Peter Alexander, ed., *William Shakespeare : The Complete Works* (1951)
Cambridge	William George Clark, John Glover, and William Aldis Wright, eds., *The Works of William Shakespeare*, The Cambridge Shakespeare, 9 vols. (Cambridge, 1863–6)

Capell	Edward Capell, ed., *Mr William Shakespeare His Comedies, Histories, and Tragedies*, 10 vols. (1767–8)
Collier	John Payne Collier, ed., *The Works of Shakespeare*, first edition, 8 vols. (1842–4); third edition, 8 vols. (1877–8)
Cowl and Morgan	R. P. Cowl and A. E. Morgan, eds., *The First Part of King Henry the Fourth*, The Arden Shakespeare, fourth edition (1930)
Davison	P. H. Davison, ed., *The First Part of King Henry the Fourth*, New Penguin Shakespeare (Harmondsworth, 1968)
Dering MS	George Walton Williams and Gwynne Blakemore Evans, eds., *William Shakespeare, 'The History of King Henry the Fourth', As Revised by Sir Edward Dering, Bart.* (Charlottesville, Va., 1974)
Dyce	Alexander Dyce, ed., *The Works of William Shakespeare*, 6 vols. (1857)
Elton	O. Elton, ed., *The First Part of King Henry the Fourth* (1889)
Evans (*Suppl.*)	G. Blakemore Evans, 'Supplement to *Henry IV, Part 1*, A New Variorum Edition of Shakespeare', *SQ*, 7.3 (1956), 1–121
Halliwell	J. O. Halliwell-Phillipps, ed., *The Works of William Shakespeare*, 16 vols. (1853–65)
Hanmer	Thomas Hanmer, ed., *The Works of Mr William Shakespear*, 6 vols. (Oxford, 1743–4)
Hemingway	Samuel Burdett Hemingway, ed., *Henry the Fourth, Part 1*, A New Variorum Edition of Shakespeare (Philadelphia, 1936)
Hinman	Charlton Hinman, ed., *Henry the Fourth, Part 1*, Shakespeare Quarto Facsimiles no. 14 (Oxford, 1966)
Humphreys	A. R. Humphreys, ed., *The First Part of King Henry IV*, The Arden Shakespeare (1960)
Johnson	Samuel Johnson, ed., *The Plays of William Shakespeare*, 8 vols. (1765)
Johnson, T.	T. Johnson, pub., *The Works of Mr William Shakespear*, first edition (1710), second edition (1721)
Kittredge	George Lyman Kittredge, ed., *Sixteen Plays of Shakespeare* (Boston, 1946)
Malone	Edmond Malone, ed., *The Plays and Poems of William Shakespeare*, 10 vols. (1790)

Oxford	Stanley Wells and Gary Taylor, eds., *The Complete Oxford Shakespeare* (forthcoming)
Pope	Alexander Pope, ed., *The Works of Mr William Shakespeare*, 6 vols. (1723–5)
Riverside	G. Blakemore Evans, textual editor, *The Riverside Shakespeare* (Boston, 1974)
Rowe	Nicholas Rowe, ed., *The Works of Mr William Shakespear*, 7 vols. (1709), third edition, 8 vols. (1714)
Singer	S. W. Singer, ed., *The Dramatic Works of William Shakespeare*, 10 vols. (Chiswick, 1826)
Steevens	*The Plays of William Shakespeare*, notes by Samuel Johnson and George Steevens, 10 vols. (1773), known as the Johnson–Steevens Variorum; second edition, 10 vols. (1778); third edition, 10 vols. (1785); fourth edition, 15 vols. (1793); and ed. Isaac Reed, 21 vols. (1803)
Theobald	Lewis Theobald, ed., *The Works of Shakespeare*, 7 vols. (1733)
Warburton	William Warburton, ed., *The Works of Shakespear*, 8 vols. (1747)
White	R. G. White, ed., *Mr William Shakespeare's Comedies, Histories, Tragedies, and Poems* (Boston, 1859)
Wilson, *NCS*	J. Dover Wilson, ed. *The First Part of the History of Henry IV*, New Cambridge Shakespeare (1946)
Wright	W. A. Wright, ed., *The First Part of King Henry IV*, Clarendon Press Series (1897)

OTHER WORKS

Abbott	E. A. Abbott, *A Shakespearian Grammar*, third edition (1870)
Adams	Joseph Q. Adams, ed., *Chief Pre-Shakespearean Dramas* (Boston, 1924)
AEB	*Analytical and Enumerative Bibliography*
Bailey	Nathaniel Bailey, *Dictionary of Cant Words*, added to *The New Universal English Dictionary*, fourth edition (1759)
Bamborough	J. B. Bamborough, *The Little World of Man* (1952)
Beaumont and Fletcher	Fredson Bowers, ed., *The Dramatic Works in the Beaumont and Fletcher Canon* (Cambridge, 1966–)

Brooke	C. F. Tucker Brooke, ed., *The Shakespeare Apocrypha* (Oxford, 1918)
Bullough	Geoffrey Bullough, ed., *Narrative and Dramatic Sources of Shakespeare*, 8 vols. (1957–75), especially vol. 4 (1966)
Cercignani	Fausto Cercignani, *Shakespeare's Works and Elizabethan Pronunciation* (Oxford, 1981)
Chambers	E. K. Chambers, *William Shakespeare: A Study of Facts and Problems*, 2 vols. (Oxford, 1930)
Cotgrave	Randle Cotgrave, *A Dictionary of the French and English Tongues* (1611)
CritQ	*Critical Quarterly*
Daniel	Samuel Daniel, *The First Four Books of the Civil Wars* (1595), excerpted in Bullough, iv. 208–15
Dekker (Bowers)	Fredson Bowers, ed., *The Dramatic Works of Thomas Dekker*, 4 vols. (Cambridge, 1953–61)
Dekker (Grosart)	A. B. Grosart, ed., *The Non-Dramatic Works of Thomas Dekker*, 5 vols. (1884–6)
Dent	R. W. Dent, *Shakespeare's Proverbial Language : An Index* (Berkeley, 1981)
Dent *PLED*	R. W. Dent, *Proverbial Language in English Drama Excluding Shakespeare, 1495–1616 : An Index* (Berkeley, 1984)
DNB	*Dictionary of National Biography*
EETS	Early English Text Society
ELR	*English Literary Renaissance*
Famous Victories	*The Famous Victories of Henry the Fifth*, reprinted in Adams and in Bullough iv. 299–343
Greene	A. B. Grosart, ed., *Life and Complete Works of Robert Greene*, 15 vols. (1881–6)
Hakluyt	Richard Hakluyt, *The Principal Navigations, Voyages, Traffics, and Discoveries of the English Nation*, second edition, 1598–1600, 12 vols. (Glasgow, 1903–5)
Hall	Edward Hall, *The Union of the Two Noble and Illustre Families of Lancaster and York* (1548)
Hardyng	Henry Ellis, ed., *The Chronicle of John Hardyng* (1812)
Harvey	A. B. Grosart, ed., *The Works of Gabriel Harvey*, 3 vols. (1884–5)
Heywood	*The Dramatic Works of Thomas Heywood*, Pearson Reprint, 6 vols. (1874)

Holinshed	Raphael Holinshed, *The Chronicles of England, Scotland, and Ireland*, 3 vols. (1587). Portions reprinted in Bullough iv. 180–96
JEGP	*Journal of English and Germanic Philology*
Jonson	Ben Jonson, *Works*, ed. C. H. Herford and P. and E. Simpson, 11 vols. (Oxford, 1925–52)
Joseph	Sister Miriam Joseph, *Shakespeare's Use of the Arts of Language* (New York, 1947)
Linthicum	M. Channing Linthicum, *Costume in the Drama of Shakespeare and His Contemporaries* (Oxford, 1936)
Long	John H. Long, *Shakespeare's Use of Music : The Histories and Tragedies* (Gainesville, Fla., 1971)
Lyly	R. Warwick Bond, ed., *The Complete Works of John Lyly*, 3 vols. (Oxford, 1902)
Madden	D. H. Madden, *The Diary of Master William Silence* (1897)
Mahood	M. M. Mahood, *Shakespeare's Wordplay* (1957)
Marlowe	Fredson Bowers, ed., *The Complete Works of Christopher Marlowe*, 2 vols. (Cambridge, 1973)
Marston	H. Harvey Wood, ed., *The Plays of John Marston*, 3 vols. (1934)
Milward	Peter Milward, *Shakespeare's Religious Background* (1973)
Minsheu	John Minsheu, *Ductor in Linguas, The Guide into the Tongues* (1617)
MLN	*Modern Language Notes*
MLR	*Modern Language Review*
Modernizing	Stanley Wells and Gary Taylor, *Modernizing Shakespeare's Spelling* (Oxford, 1979)
Nashe	R. B. McKerrow, ed., *The Works of Thomas Nashe* (1904–10), with supplementary notes by F. P. Wilson, 5 vols. (Oxford, 1958)
Naylor	Edward W. Naylor, *Shakespeare and Music* (1931)
Noble	Richmond Noble, *Shakespeare's Biblical Knowledge and Use of the Book of Common Prayer* (1935)
Odell	George C. D. Odell, *Shakespeare from Betterton to Irving*, 2 vols. (1920, reprinted New York, 1963)
OED	*Oxford English Dictionary*
Onions	C. T. Onions, *A Shakespeare Glossary*, second edition (Oxford, 1919)

PQ	*Philological Quarterly*
Partridge	Eric Partridge, *Shakespeare's Bawdy* (1947)
RES	*Review of English Studies*
SB	*Studies in Bibliography*
Schäfer	Jürgen Schäfer, *Documentation in the O.E.D. : Shakespeare and Nashe as Test Cases* (Oxford, 1980)
ShakS	*Shakespeare Studies*
ShS	*Shakespeare Survey*
Sisson	C. J. Sisson, *New Readings in Shakespeare*, 2 vols. (Cambridge, 1956)
SP	*Studies in Philology*
SQ	*Shakespeare Quarterly*
SR	*Stationers' Register, A Transcript of the Registers of the Company of Stationers of London 1554–1640 A.D.*, ed. Edward Arber, 5 vols. (1875)
Stow, *Annals*	John Stow, *The Annals of England* (1592)
Stow, *Chronicles*	John Stow, *The Chronicles of England* (1580)
Tilley	M. P. Tilley, *A Dictionary of the Proverbs in England in the Sixteenth and Seventeenth Centuries* (Ann Arbor, 1950)
TLS	*Times Literary Supplement* (London)
TSL	*Tennessee Studies in Literature*
TSLL	*Texas Studies in Literature and Language*
UTSE	*University of Texas Studies in English*
West	Gilian West, '"Titan", "Onyers", and Other Difficulties in the Text of *1 Henry IV*', *SQ*, 34 (1983), 330–3
Wilson, *Fortunes*	J. Dover Wilson, *The Fortunes of Falstaff* (Cambridge, 1943)

The History of King Henry the Fourth,
Part 1

THE PERSONS OF THE PLAY

KING HENRY THE FOURTH, also called King Harry and Bolingbroke

PRINCE HENRY, Prince of Wales, also called Hal and Harry, King Henry's eldest son and heir

LORD JOHN OF LANCASTER, also called Prince John of Lancaster, a younger son of the King

EARL OF WESTMORLAND
SIR WALTER BLUNT
} loyal to the King

EARL OF NORTHUMBERLAND, Henry Percy

EARL OF WORCESTER, Thomas Percy, Northumberland's younger brother

Sir Henry (or Harry) Percy, known as HOTSPUR, Northumberland's son and heir

LORD MORTIMER, Edmund Mortimer, Hotspur's brother-in-law, also referred to as the Earl of March

OWEN GLENDOWER, a Welsh lord, Mortimer's father-in-law

EARL OF DOUGLAS, Archibald Douglas, a Scottish lord

SIR RICHARD VERNON, an English knight

ARCHBISHOP OF YORK, Richard le Scrope

SIR MICHAEL, a priest or knight in the Archbishop's household

} rebels against the King

LADY PERCY, also called Kate, Hotspur's wife and Mortimer's sister

LADY MORTIMER, Glendower's daughter and Mortimer's wife

SIR JOHN FALSTAFF

Edward POINS, also called Ned and Yedward

BARDOLPH
PETO
} followers of Falstaff

GADSHILL, setter for the highway robbery

HOSTESS of the tavern (Mistress Quickly)

FRANCIS, a drawer, or tapster ⎫
                                ⎬ at the tavern
VINTNER, or tavern-keeper   ⎭

FIRST CARRIER, or transporter of produce ⎫
                                          |
SECOND CARRIER |
                                          ⎬ at an inn near Gad's Hill
OSTLER or stable groom |
                                          |
CHAMBERLAIN, or room servant   ⎭

FIRST TRAVELLER

SHERIFF

SERVANT to Hotspur

MESSENGER

SECOND MESSENGER

Soldiers, Travellers at Gad's Hill, others attending

THE CHARACTERS OF THE PLAY] ROWE *is the first to provide such a list*

126

Henry IV, Part 1

1.1 *Enter the King, Lord John of Lancaster, the Earl of* ⟨2/20⟩
Westmorland, ⌈*Sir Walter Blunt,*⌉ *with others*

KING HENRY

So shaken as we are, so wan with care,
Find we a time for frighted peace to pant,
And breathe short-winded accents of new broils
To be commenced in strands afar remote.
No more the thirsty entrance of this soil
Shall daub her lips with her own children's blood;
No more shall trenching war channel her fields,
Nor bruise her flow'rets with the armèd hoofs
Of hostile paces. Those opposèd eyes

The History of King Henry the Fourth, Part 1] Q1   (THE HISTORY OF HENRIE THE FOVRTH;
With the battell at Shrewsburie, *betweene the King and Lord* Henry Percy, surnamed Henrie
Hotspur of the North. *With the humorous conceits of Sir* Iohn Falstalffe); The First Part of Henry
the Fourth, with the Life and Death of HENRY Sirnamed HOT-SPVRRE. F1
1.1.0.1 *the Earl*] Q1 (*Earle*)   0.2 *Sir Walter Blunt*] DERING MS, CAPELL; *not in* Q1

1.1 Like many scenes in Shakespeare, this one is not precisely localized, but evidently takes place at court: King Henry refers to 'this seat of ours', l. 65.

0.1 Lord John of Lancaster Prince Hal's younger brother appears on-stage as a member of the King's entourage, both here and in Act 5, but has no lines until the last two scenes of the play. See Appendix for historical information.

1 shaken . . . wan See Appendix for Holinshed's commentary.

2 Find we let us find
frighted affected with fright. *OED* wrongly gives the earliest date as 1647. It appears in *Lucrece* 1149.

3 breathe speak, give forth audible sound
accents words, speech, language. Commonly used this way in Shakespeare, as, for example, in *K. John* 5.6.13–15: 'pardon me | That any accent breaking from thy tongue | Should scape the true acquaintance of mine ear'. Henry's thought is that the time has come, after civil strife, to speak briefly and simply (because we are *short-winded*, out of breath from the effort of conflict) of a new and different kind of fighting (*broils*), a crusade to the Holy Land.

4 strands i.e. the shore of the Holy Land, to which, in *Richard II* (5.6.49), King Henry vowed a crusade. 'Stronds', the QqF1 spelling, is a phonetic variant.

5 thirsty entrance i.e. parched mouth. The earth of England is personified as a ravenous mouth devouring its young. The image may have been prompted, as Malone suggests, by the story of Cain and Abel in Genesis 4, to which Shakespeare refers in *Richard II* (1.1.104, 5.6.43). God tells Cain that he is 'cursed from the earth, which hath opened her mouth to receive thy brother's blood from thy hand' (cited by Humphreys).

6 daub coat, smear, suggesting both 'befoul' and 'bedeck'

7 trenching cutting, severing, ploughing, as though opening up the *thirsty entrance* of l. 5

8 armèd i.e. plated with tough covering, tipped, shod. *Henry V* speaks similarly of 'wounded steeds' that 'Jerk out their armèd heels at their dead masters' in the aftermath of a battle (4.7.73–5). Perhaps by metonymy we are to imagine armed horses as well.

9 paces horses' tread

Which, like the meteors of a troubled heaven,   10
All of one nature, of one substance bred,
Did lately meet in the intestine shock
And furious close of civil butchery,
Shall now in mutual well-beseeming ranks
March all one way, and be no more opposed
Against acquaintance, kindred, and allies.
The edge of war, like an ill-sheathèd knife,
No more shall cut his master. Therefore, friends,
As far as to the sepulchre of Christ—
Whose soldier now, under whose blessed cross   20
We are impressèd and engaged to fight—
Forthwith a power of English shall we levy,
Whose arms were moulded in their mother's womb
To chase these pagans in those holy fields
Over whose acres walked those blessed feet
Which fourteen hundred years ago were nailed
For our advantage on the bitter cross.
But this our purpose now is twelve month old,
And bootless 'tis to tell you we will go.

---

26 fourteen hundred] Q1 (1400.)   28 now is twelve month] Q1 ; is a tweluemonth F1

---

10 **meteors** bright lights in the sky that suddenly appear and move, especially shooting stars, thought to belong to a middle region of the air below that of the stars and planets, and hence prophetic of disorders in earthly affairs; they might be 'exhaled' as vapours from the earth, or dragged from a celestial course. At 5.1.19, King Henry speaks of the Earl of Worcester as an 'exhaled meteor', i.e. a disobedient subject.

11 **one** one and the same

12 **intestine** internal, domestic, civil (the original and literal meaning in English)

13 **close** coming together or closing in fight; a grapple
   civil as in 'civil war', but gaining vigour from the rejected reading, 'polite' (Mahood, 26)

14 **well-beseeming** attractively arranged, well-ordered

17–18 **like . . . master** A common comparison, found in *Winter's Tale* 1.2.156–8, and Chaucer's *Merchant's Tale* (E. 1839–40): 'A man may do no

synne with his wyf, | Ne hurte hymselven with his owene knyf.' (Ann Thompson, *Shakespeare's Chaucer* (Liverpool, 1978), 62)

18 **his** its

19–22 **As far . . . levy** See Appendix for historical context.

20 **Whose . . . cross** under whose blessed cross, I being his soldier now

21 **impressèd** conscripted. Compare *Macbeth* 4.1.95–6: 'Who can impress the forest, bid the tree | Unfix his earth-bound root?' King Henry speaks of himself in the royal 'we' as conscripted, or *engaged*, pledged by his vow.

22 **power** army

23 **their mother's** i.e. England's, as at ll. 5–6

24 **fields** (a) battlefields (b) terrain

27 **For . . . cross** Compare the Prayer of Consecration from the Communion Service in the Book of Common Prayer: 'to suffer death upon the cross for our redemption' (Noble, 169).

29 **bootless** useless

Therefor we meet not now. Then let me hear　　　30
Of you, my gentle cousin Westmorland,
What yesternight our council did decree
In forwarding this dear expedience.

WESTMORLAND

My liege, this haste was hot in question,
And many limits of the charge set down
But yesternight, when all athwart there came
A post from Wales, loaden with heavy news,
Whose worst was that the noble Mortimer,
Leading the men of Herefordshire to fight
Against the irregular and wild Glendower,　　　40
Was by the rude hands of that Welshman taken,
A thousand of his people butcherèd—
Upon whose dead corpse there was such misuse,
Such beastly shameless transformation
By those Welshwomen done as may not be
Without much shame retold or spoken of.

KING HENRY

It seems then that the tidings of this broil
Brake off our business for the Holy Land.

WESTMORLAND

This matched with other did, my gracious lord,

30 Therefor] Q1 (Therefore)　　39 Herefordshire] Q1 (Herdforshire)　　42 A] Q1; And a F1
43 corpse] Q1 (corpes)

30 **Therefor we meet not now** that is not the
　reason for our present meeting
31 **Of** from
　gentle cousin See Appendix for historical
　information.
33 **dear expedience** urgent and highly
　valued enterprise or expedition requiring
　speed. Westmorland answers in the next
　line to the primary sense of 'haste' in *ex-
　pedience*.
34 **hot in question** being hotly debated
35 **limits of the charge** particular assign-
　ments and restrictions as to expense and
　responsibility; the specifying of com-
　missions. Compare *Richard III* 5.3.25:
　'Limit each leader to his several charge.'
36 **athwart** in opposition to the proper or
　expected course
37 **post** messenger
　loaden laden
38 **Whose worst** the worst of which

Mortimer See Appendix for historical in-
　formation and for Shakespeare's confla-
　tion of Sir Edmund de Mortimer with his
　nephew, the fifth Earl of March.
40 **the irregular and wild Glendower** See
　Appendix for historical information.
　Metrically this line appears to call for an
　accent on the second syllable of
　Glendower, as also in 1.3 at ll. 83, 101,
　and 114, but elsewhere in this play the
　accent is either indeterminate or thrown
　to the first syllable as in the modern stan-
　dard Welsh form *Owain Glyndwr*.
41 **rude** uncivilized
43 **corpse** corpses. In the French *cors* or *corps*
　(the *p* is mute), the plural is the same as
　the singular; similarly in English, *corps*,
　corpse, and *corpes* are plural forms as late
　as 1750.
43-6 **Upon . . . spoken of** See Appendix for
　Holinshed's report of this incident.

For more uneven and unwelcome news   50
Came from the north, and thus it did import:
On Holy Rood Day the gallant Hotspur there,
Young Harry Percy, and brave Archibald,
That ever-valiant and approvèd Scot,
At Holmedon met, where they did spend
A sad and bloody hour,
As by discharge of their artillery
And shape of likelihood the news was told;
For he that brought them in the very heat
And pride of their contention did take horse,   60
Uncertain of the issue any way.

KING HENRY

Here is a dear, a true industrious friend,
Sir Walter Blunt, new lighted from his horse,
Stained with the variation of each soil
Betwixt that Holmedon and this seat of ours;
And he hath brought us smooth and welcome news.

62 a dear] Q4 *corr.*; deere Q1   64 Stained] Q1 (Staind); Strain'd F1

50 **uneven** not smooth, and hence distress-
ing. Contrast *uneven and unwelcome* with
smooth and welcome in l. 66.
52 **Holy Rood Day** 14 September, the day
dedicated to the Holy Cross. See Appendix
for historical information.
52–3 **Hotspur . . . Percy** See Appendix for
historical information.
53 **Archibald** See Appendix for historical information.
54 **approvèd** proved by experience (as in
Much Ado 4.1.43: 'to knit my soul to an
approvèd wanton')
55 **Holmedon** Humbleton (the usual modern
form), also variously spelled Humbledon,
Homildon, or Homildoun Hill, in Northumberland, near Wooler, where a Scottish invasion of 1402 was stopped by the
Percys.
    met joined battle
57 **by discharge of their artillery** The severity
of the fighting has been estimated from
intelligence reports of the firing (*discharge*)
of both sides. See Appendix for
Holinshed's apparent reference to
discharge of archery rather than guns.
58 **shape of likelihood** likely outcome
59 **them** i.e. the news
60 **pride** height, intensity, as in *heat* (l. 59)

62 **true industrious** zealous in the loyal performance of duty
62–3 **Here . . . Blunt** Blunt's presence on-
stage in this scene, or the point at which
he enters if present, is uncertain. Possibly
he is to enter now, for his news resolves
the uncertainty voiced by Westmorland,
and the way his appearance is described
suggests hasty arrival. Yet Blunt is given
no lines that would seem appropriate to a
messenger arriving in mid-scene, and he
is spoken of in the third person in l. 69 as
though unable to testify in person. If he is
on-stage from the beginning of the scene,
entering as one of the 'others' mentioned
in the opening stage direction, why is his
urgent dispatch not brought up earlier?
Possibly the King simply wishes to receive
a report of his council before he announces the good news of which he is already
assured. *Here is* could then mean 'There is
at court'.
63 **Sir Walter Blunt** Historically spelled
Blount (d. 1403). Shakespeare has mag-
nified his role; see Introduction and Appendix 4.3.29.2.
64 **with . . . soil** with every kind of soil
66 **smooth** agreeable

The Earl of Douglas is discomfited;
Ten thousand bold Scots, two-and-twenty knights,
Balked in their own blood did Sir Walter see
On Holmedon's plains. Of prisoners, Hotspur took   70
Mordake, Earl of Fife and eldest son
To beaten Douglas, and the Earl of Atholl,
Of Murray, Angus, and Menteith.
And is not this an honourable spoil?
A gallant prize? Ha, cousin, is it not?

WESTMORLAND

In faith, it is a conquest for a prince to boast of.

KING HENRY

Yea, there thou mak'st me sad, and mak'st me sin
In envy that my lord Northumberland
Should be the father to so blest a son—
A son who is the theme of honour's tongue,   80
Amongst a grove the very straightest plant,
Who is sweet Fortune's minion and her pride—
Whilst I, by looking on the praise of him,
See riot and dishonour stain the brow
Of my young Harry. O that it could be proved
That some night-tripping fairy had exchanged
In cradle-clothes our children where they lay,
And called mine Percy, his Plantagenet!

69 blood did] Q5; bloud. Did Q1   70 plains. Of] Q5 (plaines: of) plaines, of Q1–4   76 WEST-
MORLAND In . . . of] *as one line* This edition; [KING] In faith it is. | WEST. A conquest for a Prince
to boast of Q1; WEST. In faith, | It . . . of STEEVENS

67 **The Earl of Douglas** the *brave Archibald* of
  l. 53
68 **two-and-twenty** See Appendix for Holinshed.
69 **Balked** lying in heaps, as in 'balks', or
  ridges, between furrows; with connotation also of 'foiled', 'checked', 'halted'
71–2 **Mordake . . . Douglas** See Appendix
  for Shakespeare's misreading of Holinshed
  in calling Mordake a son of Douglas.
72–3 **Atholl . . . Menteith** See Appendix for
  Shakespeare's error in regarding Menteith as a separate person, rather than
  recognizing the name as a title of 'Mordake'. The name *Murray* is that of the
  earls of Moray, as in the present-day Scottish county.
77 **there** (emphatic): 'by using that word

prince' (Kittredge)
78 **my lord Northumberland** See Appendix
  for historical information.
81 **plant** i.e. young tree
82 **minion** favourite
84 **riot** debauchery. The word is used again
  of Prince Hal in *2 Henry IV* at 4.4.62,
  4.5.135–6 and 5.5.63.
86 **had exchanged** 'Ugly and deformed infants were often thought to be "changelings"—impish creatures left by the
  fairies in exchange for the babies they had
  stolen and carried off to fairyland. Cf.
  Midsummer Night's Dream, ii,1,23'
  (Kittredge).
88 **Plantagenet** This surname is traditionally attached to the English royal family,
  beginning with the reign of Henry II

Then would I have his Harry, and he mine.
But let him from my thoughts. What think you, coz,   90
Of this young Percy's pride? The prisoners
Which he in this adventure hath surprised
To his own use he keeps, and sends me word
I shall have none but Mordake, Earl of Fife.

WESTMORLAND

This is his uncle's teaching, this is Worcester,
Malevolent to you in all aspects,
Which makes him prune himself, and bristle up
The crest of youth against your dignity.

KING HENRY

But I have sent for him to answer this;
And for this cause awhile we must neglect   100
Our holy purpose to Jerusalem.
Cousin, on Wednesday next our council we
Will hold at Windsor; so inform the lords.
But come yourself with speed to us again,
For more is to be said and to be done
Than out of anger can be utterèd.

WESTMORLAND   I will, my liege.   *Exeunt*

102–3 we | Will hold at] T. JOHNSON (1721); we wil hold | At Q1   103 so] Q1; and so F1

(1154–89), whose father, Geoffrey, was thus nicknamed, but it was not until the time of Richard Duke of York, father of Edward IV and Richard III, that the name was formally adopted; it is thus used in the *Henry VI* plays.

90 **coz** cousin, kinsman (a familiar form)

92 **adventure** hazardous undertaking
   surprised captured through sudden assault

93 **use** i.e. to obtain ransom. The law of arms (referred to by Shakespeare in *Henry V* 4.7.2) expressly gave to the capturer the right of demanding ransom, except for prisoners of princely rank; see next note.

94 **I shall . . . Fife** Mordake, or Murdoch, Stewart (as in ll. 71–2 above) was of royal blood, being grandson to Robert II of Scotland, and hence could not be claimed by Hotspur as his prisoner according to the law of arms. See Appendix for Holinshed.

95 **Worcester** See Appendix for historical information.

96 **Malevolent . . . aspects** See Appendix for Holinshed. *Malevolent* and *aspects* are also astrological terms, suggesting metaphorically that Worcester, as a baleful planet in the courtly orbit of King Henry, is ominous at all times and in every position as seen from earth.
   aspects (accent on second syllable)

97 **Which . . . himself** i.e. which teaching encourages Hotspur to preen himself like a falcon trimming its feathers with its beak. To 'bristle up | The crest of youth' (ll. 97–8) continues the image of a bird of prey trained to display its temper in preparation for attack. So *Henry V* 2.3.4–5: 'Boy, bristle | Thy courage up.' The modern word *preen* apparently has its origin as a variant of *prune*.

99–103 **I have sent . . . Windsor** See Appendix for Holinshed.

105–6 **For . . . utterèd** Compare the proverb 'Nothing is well said or done in a passion (in anger)' (Tilley N307).

I.2   *Enter the Prince of Wales and Sir John Falstaff*   2/20

FALSTAFF Now, Hal, what time of day is it, lad?

PRINCE HENRY Thou art so fat-witted with drinking of old
sack, and unbuttoning thee after supper, and sleeping
upon benches after noon, that thou hast forgotten to
demand that truly which thou wouldst truly know. What
a devil hast thou to do with the time of the day? Unless
hours were cups of sack, and minutes capons, and clocks
the tongues of bawds, and dials the signs of leaping-
houses, and the blessed sun himself a fair hot wench in
flame-coloured taffeta, I see no reason why thou shouldst   10
be so superfluous to demand the time of the day.

FALSTAFF Indeed, you come near me now, Hal, for we that
take purses go by the moon and the seven stars, and not

1.2.0 the] *not in* Q1; *Henry* F1   *and Sir John Falstaff*] Q1; *Sir Iohn Falstaffe, and Pointz* F14
after noon] Q1; *in the afternoone* F1

1.2 Shakespeare does not specify the location of the scene in detail; editors have
generally supposed Hal to be in his royal
apartments. See Appendix for Holinshed's
reference to gatherings of companions at
the Prince's 'house'.

0.1 *Enter . . . Falstaff* Wilson (*Fortunes*, 37)
conjectures that the scene begins with
stertorous snoring issuing from behind
the curtain at the back of the stage,
whereupon the entering Prince lifts the
curtain to discover Falstaff asleep on a
bench. Other ways in which actors have
sought to give point to Falstaff's opening
words are discussed by Sprague and
Trewin, *Shakespeare's Plays Today*, 28.

2 **fat-witted** thick-witted

3 **sack** general name for a class of white
wines, imported from Spain and the
Canary Islands. Falstaff seems to drink it
with sugar (l. 107 below and 2.4.453).
This wine is mentioned twenty-one times
in the play, always in association with
Falstaff or (on one occasion) Bardolph.
The pattern continues in *2 Henry IV*, and
in *Henry V* we learn of Falstaff that in his
last hours on earth 'he cried out of sack'
(2.3.25).

4 **forgotten** forgotten how

5 **truly . . . truly** in fact . . . legitimately,
rightfully

7 **capons** castrated cocks, regarded as suc-
culent fare, especially by Falstaff (l. 110
below, and 2.4.439–516). Like sack,
capon is associated with Falstaff more

frequently than with any other Shakespearian character. In *As You Like It*
2.7.154, the 'fair round belly with good
capon lined' is again suggestive of gluttony and advancing years.

8–9 **leaping-houses** brothels

9 **sun** The humorous word-play on 'son' is
a standard joke. Later too, at 2.4.393–4,
Falstaff's reference to 'the blessed sun of
heaven' invokes an ironic comparison
with Christ.

10 **taffeta** silken material commonly used by
prostitutes for their gowns or petticoats,
as in *All's Well* 2.2.20: 'your French
crown for your taffety punk.' Elsewhere
Shakespeare associates it with over-
dressed flamboyance, as in the 'Taffeta
phrases, silken terms precise' of *LLL*
5.2.406.

11 **superfluous** (a) unnecessarily inquisitive
(b) extravagant, exceeding all bounds, in-
dulging in the luxury. In *Lear* 4.1.68, the
word similarly suggests luxuriousness.

12 **you come near me now** you've come
near the mark, have scored a point. A
common expression (Dent N56.1), as in
Romeo 1.5.18 and *Twelfth Night* 3.4.61.

13 **go by** (a) direct our course by the light of
(b) tell time by
   seven stars the Pleiades. Compare *2
Henry IV* 2.4.176: 'What, we have seen
the seven stars', and the common expression: 'The (sun), moon, and seven
stars (are against us)' (Dent, *PLED*
S982.11).

133

by Phoebus, he, 'that wandering knight so fair'. And I
prithee, sweet wag, when thou art king, as, God save thy
grace—majesty I should say, for grace thou wilt have
none—

PRINCE HENRY What, none?

FALSTAFF No, by my troth, not so much as will serve to be
prologue to an egg and butter.   20

PRINCE HENRY Well, how then? Come, roundly, roundly.

FALSTAFF Marry, then, sweet wag, when thou art king, let
not us that are squires of the night's body be called thieves
of the day's beauty. Let us be Diana's foresters, gentlemen
of the shade, minions of the moon; and let men say we be
men of good government, being governed, as the sea is,
by our noble and chaste mistress the moon, under whose
countenance we steal.

15 king] Q2; a king Q1

14 **Phoebus . . . fair** The wandering knight,
and the pleonastic use of *he* coupled with
the proper name, have suggested to War-
burton and others a ballad source. No
such ballad of the knight of the sun has
been found, but 'The Knight of the Sun is
the hero of a chivalric romance popular in
Shakespeare's day' (Kittredge). Wilson,
NCS, cites *The Mirror of Knighthood* by
Ortuñez de Calahorra, translated in 1578
by Margaret Tyler, in which the Knight of
the Sun is a leading character, and *The
Voyage of the Wandering Knight* by Jean de
Cartigny, translated by William Goodyear
in 1581. Compare the 'Knight of the
Burning Lamp' in 3.3.25–6. The sun was
a planet, hence *wandering*, in Ptolemaic
astronomy.

15 **wag** The term of endearment suggests
both a mischievous boy and a habitual
joker.

16 **grace** (a) royal highness (b) spiritual
grace (c) 'grace' or blessing before a meal

20 **prologue to an egg and butter** grace
before a scanty repast, suitable for fasting
on Friday or in Lent, though the 'eggs and
butter' called for at 2.1.57 are probably
standard breakfast fare

21 **roundly** without circumlocution or concealment, to the point (and perhaps, in
view of Falstaff's girth, 'rotundly'). Hal
still wants an answer to his first question,
why Falstaff should ask about something
so irrelevant to him as the time of day.

22 **Marry** a mild oath, originally an oath by
the Virgin Mary

22–4 **let not . . . beauty** Falstaff responds to
Hal's questions, and to the wit at the expense of his fleshliness and sloth, by urging that those who perform service by
night should not be criticized for squan-
dering the hours of daylight in inaction.
He plays upon the idea of 'squires of the
body', or squires of the household, officers
charged with personal attendance on a
sovereign or person of rank, suggesting a
pun on *night's* and *knight's* (despite the
Elizabethan tendency to pronounce the *k*
in *knight*; there is a similar pun at 5.4.22
in *2 Henry IV*). *Beauty* suggests 'booty'.

24 **Let us be Diana's foresters** let us be called
those who follow the goddess of the moon
and the hunt, ranging about at night—in
this case in search of booty

24–5 **gentlemen of the shade** The phrasing
jocosely parallels such honorific titles as
gentlemen of the (King's) chamber and
gentlemen of the Chapel Royal, and
means something like *squires of the . . .
body* at l. 23, again with comic mis-
application.

25 **minions** favourites

26 **government** (a) conduct (b) commonwealth

28 **countenance** (a) visage (b) protection,
maintenance, as at l. 147 below
    steal (a) go stealthily (b) rob

PRINCE HENRY Thou sayst well, and it holds well too, for the
fortune of us that are the moon's men doth ebb and flow   30
like the sea, being governed as the sea is by the moon. As
for proof now : a purse of gold most resolutely snatched on
Monday night and most dissolutely spent on Tuesday
morning ; got with swearing 'Lay by', and spent with crying 'Bring in'; now in as low an ebb as the foot of the
ladder, and by and by in as high a flow as the ridge of the
gallows.

FALSTAFF By the Lord, thou sayst true, lad. And is not my
hostess of the tavern a most sweet wench ?

PRINCE HENRY As the honey of Hybla, my old lad of the   40
castle. And is not a buff jerkin a most sweet robe of
durance ?

---

32 proof now :] ROWE; proofe. Now Q1   40 As the honey of Hybla] Q1 ; As is the hony F1

---

29 **it holds well** the comparison is apt

30–1 **ebb . . . sea** A common comparison
(Dent S182.1).

32–3 **snatched . . . spent** Compare the
proverb 'Soon gotten soon spent' (Tilley
G91).

34 **Lay by** A highwayman's cry, evidently
counselling victims either to lay aside
(drop) weapons and luggage or to stand
and deliver.

35 **Bring in** An order given to a waiter in a
tavern to bring food and drink.

35–7 **low . . . gallows** Compare the proverb
'He that is at a low ebb at Newgate may
soon be afloat at Tyburn' (Dent E56; see
also F378 and S182.1).

36 **ladder** The image here is of a ladder on a
pier reaching down to the water at low
tide, but it suggests also the ladder to the
gallows.
ridge horizontal crossbar at the top

39 **hostess of the tavern** In *Famous Victories*,
Hal and his robbing companions talk
about 'our old hostess | At Feversham'
and 'the old tavern in Eastcheap' where
'There is good wine; besides, there is a
pretty wench | That can talk well'
(ll. 83–9). See Introduction, p. 20.
Similarly, the talk of highway robbing
leads Falstaff to consider how the stolen
money might be spent—a pleasanter
train of thought than the gallows to
which Hal has just been referring.

40 **Hybla** a town in Sicily celebrated for the

honey produced on neighbouring hills.
'As sweet as honey' is a common comparison (Dent H544).

40–1 **old lad of the castle** (a) i.e. Sir John
Oldcastle (see Introduction, p. 3–8), Falstaff's counterpart in the original version
of *1 Henry IV* (b) a roisterer, one who
might frequent brothels like The Castle in
Southwark, or taverns, known in medieval homiletic literature as the devil's
castles (G. R. Owst, *Literature and Pulpit in
Medieval England* (Oxford, 1961), 438,
cited by Humphreys). Dent (C124.1)
cites familiar and colloquial uses in
Renaissance literature.

41 **buff jerkin** leather jacket worn by an arresting officer, like the fellow 'in a suit of
buff' in *Errors* 4.2.45. As Ian Donaldson
observes in a note (*SQ*, 37 (1986),
100–1), *buff* could also refer to human
skin (especially of the female anatomy),
and may well introduce a sexual joke that
continues in *sweet robe*; compare *bona
roba*, a term for a well-dressed wench, in *2
Henry IV* 3.2.200.

42 **durance** (a) durability (b) a stout durable
cloth (*OED*, 3) (c) incarceration. Hal
returns to the theme of punishment and
imprisonment for robbery and extravagance, from which Falstaff has
attempted to sidetrack him, and hints at
sexual indulgence also (see previous
note).

FALSTAFF How now, how now, mad wag, what, in thy
quips and thy quiddities? What a plague have I to do with
a buff jerkin?

PRINCE HENRY Why, what a pox have I to do with my hostess of the tavern?

FALSTAFF Well, thou hast called her to a reckoning many a
time and oft.

PRINCE HENRY Did I ever call for thee to pay thy part?   50

FALSTAFF No, I'll give thee thy due, thou hast paid all there.

PRINCE HENRY Yea, and elsewhere, so far as my coin would
stretch, and where it would not I have used my credit.

FALSTAFF Yea, and so used it that were it not here apparent
that thou art heir apparent—but I prithee, sweet wag,
shall there be gallows standing in England when thou art
king? And resolution thus fubbed as it is with the rusty
curb of old Father Antic the law? Do not thou, when thou
art king, hang a thief.

PRINCE HENRY No, thou shalt.   60

FALSTAFF Shall I? O rare! By the Lord, I'll be a brave judge.

---

54 were it not] Q1; were it F1   58 law?] F1; ~ , Q1–2; ~ : Q3–6

43 **wag** habitual joker (as at l. 15)
44 **quiddities** subtleties of speech, quibbles
46 **what a pox** Hal's exclamation echoes Falstaff's *What a plague* in l. 44, since *pox* ('pocks') can mean 'plague', but its suggestion of venereal disease is also pertinent to the matter of relations with a hostess of a tavern.
48 **reckoning** (a) account of behaviour (b) settlement of a tavern bill (c) rendezvous in which a tavern wench is to show her worth, as hinted at in ll. 38–9 above and continued in the following lines in *pay thy part*, *paid all*, and *my coin would stretch*. *Coin* often plays on the idea of engendering, coining a child. The proverbial wisdom that 'oft counting makes good friends' (Dent C706) is here varied into a jest. *Reckoning* later assumes a darker meaning of judgement to come, the *due* that must be *paid* to God and the devil; see ll. 116–7 below and 5.1.126–9.
54 **so used it** Compare the proverb 'He that has lost his credit is dead to the world' (Dent C817). Hal has so overused his credit (both moral and financial) by his prodigalities, Falstaff suggests, that a person of lesser name than Prince of Wales might find himself quite discredited.

54–5 **here . . . heir** The nearness of sound in Elizabethan English permits a play on words, reinforcing the implied warning that recklessness and dissipation will land Hal in trouble.
56–8 **shall . . . law** In *Famous Victories*, it is the Prince who insists to Oldcastle and his mates that 'when I am King, we will have no such things [as prisons, hanging, etc.], but, my lads, if the old king my father were dead, we would be all kings' (ll. 455–7). See Introduction, p. 20.
57 **resolution** courage, being resolute
    fubbed cheated
58 **Antic** buffoon, grotesque (ironically appropriate to Falstaff himself)
59 **hang a thief** order the hanging of a thief; but Hal's answer at l. 60 suggests the sense of 'be hanged as a thief'.
61 **I'll . . . judge** in *Famous Victories*, the Prince says to Ned that 'thou shalt be my Lord Chief Justice of England', to which Ned replies, 'Shall I be Lord Chief Justice?| By God's wounds, I'll be the bravest Lord Chief Justice | That ever was in England' (ll. 461–4).
    brave excellent; but Hal's answer also plays on 'courageous'.

PRINCE HENRY Thou judgest false already. I mean thou shalt have the hanging of the thieves, and so become a rare hangman.

FALSTAFF Well, Hal, well; and in some sort it jumps with my humour as well as waiting in the court, I can tell you.

PRINCE HENRY For obtaining of suits?

FALSTAFF Yea, for obtaining of suits, whereof the hangman hath no lean wardrobe. 'Sblood, I am as melancholy as a gib cat or a lugged bear.   70

PRINCE HENRY Or an old lion, or a lover's lute.

FALSTAFF Yea, or the drone of a Lincolnshire bagpipe.

PRINCE HENRY What sayst thou to a hare, or the melancholy of Moorditch?

---

62 **Thou judgest** (a) you pass sentence (b) you apprehend

62–3 **thou shalt . . . thieves** (a) you will be in charge of hanging thieves; compare Dent T119: 'The great thieves hang the little ones' (b) as Chief Justice you will protect the condemned from hanging (c) you will hang like other thieves, be your own hangman

63 **rare** (a) rarely used (b) excellent, unusual

65 **Well . . . well** Compare the saying 'Well, well is a word of malice' (Dent W269).

65–6 **jumps with my humour** agrees with my temperament

66 **waiting in the court** being in attendance at the royal court; but with a suggestion also of a law court

67 **suits** petitions, preferment; but the word reminds Falstaff of a condemned man's suit of clothes, to which the executioner was entitled.

69 **no lean wardrobe** (because hangings are plentiful)
    'Sblood Like *Zounds* (l. 95 below), this colourful oath, literally meaning 'by his (Christ's) blood', occurs more frequently in this than in other Shakespeare plays. This is its earliest citation in the *OED*.

70 **gib cat** tomcat or castrated male, proverbially melancholy, perhaps because of its association with night and howling (Dent C129). In *Hamlet*, *gib* is linked to the *paddock* ('toad') and *bat* (3.4.190). *Gib* (a diminutive of Gilbert) is a common name for a cat, as in *Gammer Gurton's Needle* 1.5.15 and elsewhere.
    lugged baited

71 **old lion** Elsewhere in Shakespeare

(*Richard II* 5.1.29–31, *2 Henry IV* 4.1.218), ageing or fangless lions suggest royal might fallen into powerlessness and neglect.
lover's lute The association of lutes and lovers' music with melancholy is found, for example, in the changed behaviour of Benedick as lover in *Much Ado*; Claudio notes 'his jesting spirit, which is now crept into a lute-string, and now governed by stops' (3.2.53–4).

72 **bagpipe** The wailing sound of the bagpipe as it 'sings i'th' nose' (*Merchant* 4.1.49) was popularly regarded as melancholic (Dent B35); anyone who could manage to 'laugh like parrots at a bagpiper' (*Merchant* 1.1.53) would be regarded as of an unusually cheerful disposition.

73 **hare** Proverbially timorous as well as melancholic, and often contrasted with the lion in its full vigour, but here (l. 71) compared with an ageing lion. Hare's flesh was thought to engender melancholy in those who ate it (Dent H151).

74 **Moorditch** a foul ditch draining Moorfields, a marshy area running north between Bishopsgate and Cripplegate north of the city. Stow's *Annals* describes the field as until 1606 'a most noisome and offensive place, being a general laystall . . . burrowed and crossed with deep stinking ditches and noisome common sewers' (E. Howe's 1631 edition, 1021). Lepers and mad folk (with whom melancholy was associated) were allowed to beg there, as Jonson observes in *The Alchemist* 1.4.20.

FALSTAFF Thou hast the most unsavory similes, and art indeed the most comparative, rascalliest, sweet young prince. But Hal, I prithee trouble me no more with vanity. I would to God thou and I knew where a commodity of good names were to be bought. An old lord of the Council 80 rated me the other day in the street about you, sir, but I marked him not; and yet he talked very wisely, but I regarded him not; and yet he talked wisely, and in the street too.

PRINCE HENRY Thou didst well, for wisdom cries out in the streets and no man regards it.

FALSTAFF O, thou hast damnable iteration, and art indeed able to corrupt a saint. Thou hast done much harm upon me, Hal, God forgive thee for it. Before I knew thee, Hal, I knew nothing; and now am I, if a man should speak 90 truly, little better than one of the wicked. I must give over this life, and I will give it over. By the Lord, an I do not, I am a villain. I'll be damned for never a king's son in Christendom.

PRINCE HENRY Where shall we take a purse tomorrow, Jack?

75 similes] Q5; smiles Q1–4, Q6, F1   89 am I] Q1; I am F1

76 **comparative** adept at (abusive) comparisons. King Henry IV uses the word substantively in 3.2.67 to mean one who deals in insulting comparisons.
77 **vanity** A word repeatedly associated with Falstaff as Hal's companion, in 2.4.438, 5.3.33, 5.4.105, and *2 Henry IV* 4.5.120 and 5.2.130. Here it suggests futile frivolity, worldly idleness. Falstaff mockingly adopts the stance of a Puritan zealot.
78 **commodity** supply, as in 4.2.17: 'such a commodity of warm slaves'
79 **names** reputations
79–83 **An old . . . street too** Falstaff flavours his parody of religious cant by using the figure of *homiologia*, tedious and inane repetition.
80 **rated** scolded
84–5 **wisdom . . . it** Hal, responding to Falstaff's religious cant, paraphrases Proverbs 1 : 20; 'Wisdom crieth without, and putteth forth her voice in the streets', and 1 : 24; 'Because I have called, and ye

refused, I have stretched out my hand, and no man regarded.' Shakespeare's language is closer to the Bishops' Bible (cited here) than to the Geneva (Noble, 74).
86 **damnable iteration** a soul-endangering way of twisting Scripture out of its sacred context. Falstaff suggests with mock piety that both he and Hal are on their way to damnation.
87 **saint** Puritan term for one of the godly
89 **nothing** i.e. no evil
90 **little . . . wicked** Puritan cant, echoed for example in Marston's *Dutch Courtesan* (1603–4), 1.2.19: 'I am none of the wicked that eat fish o' Fridays.' Dent (W333.1) cites other examples after Shakespeare.
91–2 **I am a villain** A common expression of opprobrium, suggesting low birth and baseness of mind, as well as lack of principle (Dent J49.1). Similar phrasing occurs at l. 96 and 2.1.28–9, 2.2.22–3, 2.4.145–6, 165, and 199, and 3.3.156.

FALSTAFF Zounds, where thou wilt, lad, I'll make one. An I
do not, call me villain and baffle me.

PRINCE HENRY I see a good amendment of life in thee—from
praying to purse-taking.

FALSTAFF Why, Hal, 'tis my vocation, Hal, 'tis no sin for a
man to labour in his vocation.   100

Enter Poins

Poins! Now shall we know if Gadshill have set a match. O,
if men were to be saved by merit, what hole in hell were
hot enough for him? This is the most omnipotent villain
that ever cried 'Stand!' to a true man.

100.1 *Enter Poins*] Q1 ; *not in* F1   101 Poins! Now] THEOBALD ; Poynes nowe Q1 ; Poynes, now
Q2–3 ; *Poines*. Now Q4–6 (*taking* Poines *as a speech prefix*)   match] Q1 ; Watch F1

95 **Zounds** literally, by his (Christ's)
wounds. A particularly strong oath; see
Frances Shirley, *Swearing and Perjury in
Shakespeare's Plays* (1979). Compare l. 69
note on '*Sblood*.
  make one take part, be present (also at
l. 129 below)
  An if
96 **baffle** vilify, disgrace, especially to de-
grade a perjured knight with infamy by
trumpeting his dishonour and hanging
him or his image with the heels upward
(e.g. in Spenser, *Faerie Queene*, VI. vii.
27). Shakespeare's use is in general more
metaphorical than this. The idea of disgrace lends to *villain* its root sense of 'low-
born base-minded rustic' (*OED, sb.* 1), in
addition to its more general opprobrious
sense.
97 **amendment of life** Milward, 106–7, cites
the Litany of the Anglican liturgy: 'That
it may please thee to give us true repentance . . . to amend our lives according to
thy holy word', and the exhortation
before Communion to 'confess yourselves
to Almighty God with full purpose of
amendment of life'. Noble (61) cites parallel phrases in Luke 15: 7, Matthew 3: 2
and 3: 8, Acts 26: 20, and the Homily on
Repentance in the Book of Common
Prayer.
99 **vocation** 'the particular function or sta-
tion to which a person is called by God'
(*OED*, 2). Protestant divines often cited
the Geneva version of 1 Corinthians
7: 20—'let every man abide in the same
vocation wherein he was called'—as
textual authority for hard work and con-
tentment with one's place in the social

hierarchy. (The Bishops' Bible reads 'calling'.) A similar point is made in r
pag1402 Thessalonians 3: 10, Ephesians
4: 1, the Catechism and the Homily
against Idleness, Erasmus's *Adagia* (II. ii.
82: *Quam quisque norit artem in hac se
exerceat*), Cicero's *Tusculan Disputations* (i.
41), and elsewhere; see Dent C23 and
Charles G. Smith, *Shakespeare's Proverb
Lore* (Cambridge, Mass., 1963), para.
320. Falstaff comically misapplies, as does
Nashe (*Christ's Tears*, ii. 64), a favourite
Puritan text by using it to justify thievery.
101 **Gadshill** The thief Cutbert Cutter in
Famous Victories is nicknamed 'Gad's Hill'
because he is known as 'a taking fellow |
Upon Gad's Hill in Kent' (ll. 165–6). See
note to l. 119 and Introduction, p. 21.
Shakespeare adopts the nickname as the
character's only name. This edition
arbitrarily uses the form *Gadshill* (as do
other editions) to distinguish the character from the place.
  set a match Thieves' cant for arranging a
meeting between highwaymen and their
victims, i.e. a robbery. In 2.2.47–8 Gadshill is called 'our setter'.
102 **by merit** according to one's deserving
earned through good works, rather than
by God's grace alone as stressed in
Lutheran and Calvinist theology. Romans
3: 28 was often cited: 'We hold that a
man is justified by faith, without the deeds
of the law.'
103 **omnipotent** unparalleled, almighty
(applied humorously)
104 **'Stand'** 'Stand and deliver', the cry of
the highwayman to his victims
  true honest

PRINCE HENRY Good morrow, Ned.

POINS Good morrow, sweet Hal. What says Monsieur
Remorse? What says Sir John, Sack-and-Sugar Jack?
How agrees the devil and thee about thy soul that thou
soldest him on Good Friday last for a cup of Madeira and
a cold capon's leg?   110

PRINCE HENRY Sir John stands to his word, the devil shall
have his bargain, for he was never yet a breaker of
proverbs; he will give the devil his due.

POINS Then art thou damned for keeping thy word with the
devil.

PRINCE HENRY Else he had been damned for cozening the
devil.

POINS But my lads, my lads, tomorrow morning by four o'clock
early at Gad's Hill there are pilgrims going to Canterbury
with rich offerings, and traders riding to London with fat   120

107 John ... Jack] Q1–4 (Iohn Sacke, and Sugar Iacke?); Sacke and Sugar, Iacke? Q5–6; Iohn
Sacke and Sugar: Iacke? F1; John Sack-and-Sugar? Jack! ROWE   116 been] Q1; *not in* F1

107 **Remorse** Although Poins has not heard
the previous conversation, he continues
the note of Puritan piety mockingly sounded in *vanity* (l. 77) and *amendment of life*
(l. 97). Poins has heard such cant from
Falstaff before.
  Sir John, Sack-and-Sugar Jack Most
editors consider *Jack* to be said in direct
address, at the beginning of the next sentence, but the Q1 punctuation—'Sir John
Sacke, and Sugar Jacke?'—invites interpretation of *Jack* in the quibbling sense of
'drinking vessel' or 'tankard' (*OED,*
sb.² 2). *Jack* also suggests 'knave', and
Sack may hint at the sackcloth of
penitence; see previous note. On Falstaff's preference for sugared wine, see
note at l. 3 above.
109 **Good Friday** In his determination to
gormandize on even this most strict of fast
days, Falstaff resembles the supposed
epicure in *Measure* who 'would eat mut-
ton on Fridays' (3.2.168).
112–13 **breaker of proverbs** (in itself a
proverbial idea; Dent P615.1)
113 **he ... due** This proverbial saying (Dent
D273) sounds the motif of the judgement
to come, anticipated in ll. 48–51 above
and echoed in 5.1.126–9. The word *devil*
occurs more often in *1 Henry IV* than in

any other Shakespeare play. Prince Hal
jests that Falstaff will go to hell in any
case, will pay to the devil the soul that he
owes him.
114–15 **Then ... devil** 'It is an odd thing,
says Poins, to be damned for keeping
faith, even with the Devil; to which the
P[rince] replies that it matters little as he
would be damned in any case' (Wilson,
NCS).
116 **cozening** cheating
119 **Gad's Hill** a location near Rochester on
the road from London to Canterbury,
noted as a place of danger from highwaymen. Compare *Westward Ho* (1604) by
Dekker and Webster, 2.2.226: 'the way
lies over Gad's Hill, very dangerous'
(Dekker, ed. Bowers, ii. 343). The robbery
of 'a poor carrier' in *Famous Victories*
takes place at Gad's Hill in Kent (l. 166);
see note to l. 101 above.
  pilgrims The London–Canterbury road
through Gad's Hill was a main route for
pilgrims going to the shrine of St Thomas
of Canterbury, as in Chaucer's *Canterbury
Tales*. In *Famous Victories* (l. 10 ff.) it is the
King's receivers who are set upon by
Prince Hal and his companions, not innocent pilgrims or private 'traders' (see next
line). See Introduction, pp. 21–2.

purses. I have vizards for you all; you have horses for
yourselves. Gadshill lies tonight in Rochester. I have be-
spoke supper tomorrow night in Eastcheap. We may do it
as secure as sleep. If you will go, I will stuff your purses full
of crowns; if you will not, tarry at home and be hanged.

FALSTAFF Hear ye, Yedward, if I tarry at home and go not,
I'll hang you for going.

POINS You will, chops?

FALSTAFF Hal, wilt thou make one?

PRINCE HENRY Who, I rob? I a thief? Not I, by my faith.   130

FALSTAFF There's neither honesty, manhood, nor good
fellowship in thee, nor thou camest not of the blood royal,
if thou darest not stand for ten shillings.

PRINCE HENRY Well then, once in my days I'll be a madcap.

FALSTAFF Why, that's well said.

PRINCE HENRY Well, come what will, I'll tarry at home.

FALSTAFF By the Lord, I'll be a traitor then, when thou art
king.

PRINCE HENRY I care not.

POINS Sir John, I prithee leave the Prince and me alone. I   140
will lay him down such reasons for this adventure that he
shall go.

---

123 night] Q1 ; *not in* F1   128 chops?] Q7 ; ~. Q1-6, F1

---

121 **vizards** masks. See Appendix for Stow's
account.

123 **Eastcheap** an area of London: literally,
East Market. This is the first of three
references to Eastcheap in this scene; see
also ll. 148 and 180. In *Famous Victories*,
Hal plans to gather with his merry
companions at a tavern in Eastcheap
(ll. 87–8); see 1.2.39 and Introduction,
p. 20. Similarly, Shakespeare's tavern
scene takes place in Eastcheap (2.4.14
and 425). See Appendix for Stow.

126 **Yedward** Edward (dialectal)

127 **hang you** have you hanged. At 2.2.42,
Falstaff again comically threatens to turn
state's evidence.

128 **chops** fat cheeks (*OED, sb.* 2)

131 **honesty** honour. Compare the pro-

verbs 'There's honour among thieves'
and 'Thieves are never rogues among
themselves' (Dent ?T121a).

133 **stand for ten shillings** (a) stand and fight
for booty; compare *stand* at 2.2.45 (b) be
worth 10s., the value of the gold coin
known as the royal, with a play on *blood
royal* (l. 132)

134 **once . . . madcap** A proverbial idea
(Dent D121.1). In Stow's *Annals*, 547,
and in *Famous Victories*, Prince Hal is
reportedly involved in robbing ex-
peditions. In l. 94 above, Hal talks to Falstaff as though to a thieving companion.
madcap one acting on wild impulses (as
also at 4.1.95)

136 **come what will** A common expression
(Dent C529).

FALSTAFF Well, God give thee the spirit of persuasion and
him the ears of profiting, that what thou speakest may
move and what he hears may be believed, that the true
prince may, for recreation's sake, prove a false thief; for
the poor abuses of the time want countenance. Farewell.
You shall find me in Eastcheap.

PRINCE HENRY Farewell, thou latter spring; farewell, All-
hallown summer.   *Exit Falstaff*   150

POINS Now, my good sweet honey lord, ride with us tomorrow. I have a jest to execute that I cannot manage alone.
Falstaff, Peto, Bardolph, and Gadshill shall rob those men
that we have already waylaid; yourself and I will not be
there; and when they have the booty, if you and I do not
rob them, cut this head off from my shoulders.

PRINCE HENRY How shall we part with them in setting forth?

POINS Why, we will set forth before or after them, and ap-
point them a place of meeting, wherein it is at our
pleasure to fail; and then will they adventure upon the   160

---

146 recreation's] Q1 (recreation)   149 thou] POPE; the Q1   150 *Exit Falstaff*] F2; *not in*
Q1   153 Peto, Bardolph] This edition *(following John Jowett)*; Haruey, Rossill Q1; Bardolph,
Peto THEOBALD *and other editors*   157 How] Q1; But how F1

143–5 **Well . . . believed** Another humorous
jab at the Puritan reformers for their insistence on acting only in accordance with
the *spirit* of God, a spirit able to *move* and
to be *believed*. As Milward observes
(107–8), a prayer in the form of a collect
is here put into Falstaff's mouth. This
collect is of a type appropriate to the close
of a service (Noble, 171), and thus serves
as an exit line for Falstaff. See Introduction, p. 33.

146 **recreation's sake** Here modernized from
'recreation sake' in QqF1. *Sake* is preceded
by an uninflected noun instead of a
possessive in other texts of *1 Henry
IV* 2.1.68 and 70, 5.1.65, *Merry Wives*
3.1.39, *Errors* 5.1.33, etc.

  prove a false thief D. J. Palmer (*CritQ*, 12
(1970), 267–83), points out that Prince
Hal, 'for recreation's sake', is indeed
going to 'prove a false thief' in the sense of
exposing Falstaff as a liar.

147 **want countenance** lack sponsorship (by
men of noble rank); compare *countenance*
at l. 28 above. At the end of *2 Henry IV*,
Falstaff still asks his friends to 'mark the
countenance' (face, demeanour, protec-

tion) that King Henry V will bestow on
him (5.5.7). Here he parodies the common complaint that the nobility failed to
encourage worthy causes, and also
Puritan fulminations against the abuses
of the time (Kittredge; Wilson, *NCS*).

149–50 **All-hallown summer** a season of
clement weather around All Saints' Day,
1 November; hence, the Indian summer
of old age. Compare *latter spring*, l. 149.

153 **Peto, Bardolph** For what appear to have
been the original names of these characters, namely Harvey and Sir John Russil,
or Rossill, who have left traces of their
original identity here, as well as at
2.4.166–73, and in *2 Henry IV* 2.2.0, see
Introduction, pp. 5, 89. The names are
not found in *Famous Victories*. Editors
since Theobald have changed Harvey to
Bardolph and Russil to Peto, but, as John
Jowett observes, the fossil name *sir Iohn
Russel* in the Quarto of *2 Henry IV* 2.2.0 is
changed in F1 to *Bardolfe*, and it is Bardolph who in fact enters in that same
scene.

154 **waylaid** set an ambush for
160 **pleasure** discretion, choice

142

exploit themselves, which they shall have no sooner
achieved but we'll set upon them.

PRINCE HENRY Yea, but 'tis like that they will know us by
our horses, by our habits, and by every other appointment, to be ourselves.

POINS Tut, our horses they shall not see— I'll tie them in
the wood; our vizards we will change after we leave
them; and, sirrah, I have cases of buckram for the nonce,
to immask our noted outward garments.

PRINCE HENRY Yea, but I doubt they will be too hard for us.   170

POINS Well, for two of them, I know them to be as true-bred
cowards as ever turned back; and for the third, if he fight
longer than he sees reason, I'll forswear arms. The virtue
of this jest will be the incomprehensible lies that this same
fat rogue will tell us when we meet at supper—how thirty
at least he fought with, what wards, what blows, what
extremities he endured; and in the reproof of this lives the
jest.

PRINCE HENRY Well, I'll go with thee. Provide us all things
necessary, and meet me tomorrow night in Eastcheap.   180
There I'll sup. Farewell.

POINS Farewell, my lord.   *Exit Poins*

PRINCE HENRY

I know you all, and will awhile uphold
The unyoked humour of your idleness.

---

163 Yea, but] Q1 ; I, but F1   170 Yea, but] Q1 ; But F1   177 lives] Q1 ; lyes Q2–6, F1

163 **like** likely
164 **habits** garments
164–5 **appointment** accoutrement
168 **sirrah** a form of *sir* usually addressed to
inferiors and children, often in reprimand
or contempt, but here expressing familiarity (as later in 2.4.6 and 85).
cases . . . for the nonce suits of coarse
(and often stiffened) cloth for the occasion
169 **immask** cover with a mask (the only
recorded occurrence in *OED*)
noted known
170 **doubt** fear
too hard for us more than we can
manage
172 **turned back** i.e. turned their backs, ran
away (as distinguished from 'went back',

'returned')
174 **incomprehensible** boundless, that
which cannot be contained or 'com-
prehended'
176 **wards** parrying postures. Falstaff demonstrates his 'old ward' at 2.4.187–8,
just as Poins here predicts.
177 **reproof** disproof
lives is active, lies, inheres. Qq2–5F1
read 'lyes' and many editors follow; but
'lives' occurs in a similar sense at 4.1.56
and 5.2.20.
180 **tomorrow night** i.e. at supper time
(though they will meet before that in the
morning at Gad's Hill)
184 **unyoked . . . idleness** unrestrained inclination of your frivolity

143

Yet herein will I imitate the sun,
Who doth permit the base contagious clouds
To smother up his beauty from the world,
That, when he please again to be himself,
Being wanted he may be more wondered at
By breaking through the foul and ugly mists   190
Of vapours that did seem to strangle him.
If all the year were playing holidays,
To sport would be as tedious as to work;
But when they seldom come, they wished-for come,
And nothing pleaseth but rare accidents.
So when this loose behaviour I throw off
And pay the debt I never promisèd,
By how much better than my word I am,
By so much shall I falsify men's hopes;
And like bright metal on a sullen ground,   200
My reformation, glitt'ring o'er my fault,
Shall show more goodly and attract more eyes
Than that which hath no foil to set it off.
I'll so offend to make offence a skill,
Redeeming time when men think least I will.   *Exit*

205 *Exit*] Q1; *not in* F1

185 **sun** This symbol of royalty often plays upon 'son', as at l. 9 above and at 2.4.394 and 3.2.79. Compare the proverb 'The sun shines brightest after rain' (Dent, *PLED* S984.11).

186 **contagious** noxious. The concept of contagion as generated and spread by fogs and clouds was widespread; e.g. 'contagious fogs' (*Dream* 2.1.90), 'filthy and contagious clouds' (*Henry V* 3.3.111), and 'foul contagious darkness in the air' (*2 Henry VI* 4.1.7).

189 **wanted** missed

192 **If . . . holidays** Dent D68 (see also S548) cites the proverb 'Every day is not holiday', but with no examples before Shakespeare.

195 **nothing . . . accidents** Proverbial: 'The thing which is rare is dear' (Dent T145).
  but rare accidents as much as exceptional events

199 **hopes** expectations

200 **sullen ground** dull or sombre background serving as a foil, as in l. 203

203 **foil** thin leaf (Latin *folium*) of hammered metal placed under a jewel to set off its lustre; compare *Richard II* 1.3.265–7: 'The sullen passage of thy weary steps | Esteem as foil wherein thou art to set | The precious jewel of thy home return.'

204 **to** as to
  skill piece of good policy, art, science

205 **Redeeming time** buying back time, as in redeeming a debt (compare 'pay the debt' in l. 197); saving time from being lost, making amends for lost time (*OED*, 8 and 9). Dent T340.3 cites *Edward III* 3.2.16–19 among examples of proverbial use. St Paul commands: 'Walk in wisdom toward them that are without, redeeming the time' (Colossians 4: 5), and 'Walk circumspectly, not as unwise, but as wise, | Redeeming the time, because the days are evil' (Ephesians 5: 15–16). The theme is continued in *2 Henry IV* 2.2.134 and 2.4.348ff. See also note on *redeem* at 1.3.206.

1.3 *Enter the King, Northumberland, Worcester, Hotspur,* 2|20
Sir Walter Blunt, with others

KING HENRY

My blood hath been too cold and temperate,
Unapt to stir at these indignities,
And you have found me, for accordingly
You tread upon my patience. But be sure
I will from henceforth rather be myself,
Mighty and to be feared, than my condition,
Which hath been smooth as oil, soft as young down,
And therefore lost that title of respect
Which the proud soul ne'er pays but to the proud.

WORCESTER

Our house, my sovereign liege, little deserves   10
The scourge of greatness to be used on it—
And that same greatness too which our own hands
Have holp to make so portly.

NORTHUMBERLAND   My lord—

KING HENRY

Worcester, get thee gone, for I do see
Danger and disobedience in thine eye.
O sir, your presence is too bold and peremptory,
And majesty might never yet endure
The moody frontier of a servant brow.
You have good leave to leave us. When we need   20

1.3.0.2 *with others*] Q1 ; *and others* F1

1.3 According to Holinshed, this confrontation between King Henry and the Percys
took place at Windsor, and Shakespeare,
in Scene 1, seems to anticipate such a
meeting-place; see 1.1.103 and Appendix. The scene itself gives no mention of
place, however, and in the theatre we are
simply presented with a throne scene suggesting a royal residence.
3 **found me** found me so
5 **myself** i.e. my royal self, as at 3.2.92–3.
Dent's examples of the familiar phrase 'to
not be (or be) oneself' (O64.1) all post-
date Shakespeare.
6 **condition** inherent disposition (in this
case, towards mildness)
7 **smooth . . . down** Traditional similes,
found for example in Lyly's *Euphues*

(i. 224) and in Marlowe's *Tamburlaine,
Part 2* 1.3.25 (Dent O25 and D576.1).
10 **Our house** i.e. the Percy family
12–13 **which . . . portly** Refers to events in
Richard II 2.1, 2.3, 3.1–3, etc.
13 **holp** helped
portly majestic, stately (with suggestion
of 'over-prosperous')
16 **Danger** menace
17 **peremptory** obstinate, imperious
19 **The moody . . . brow** the subject's brow
frowning in angry defiance. A *frontier* is a
rampart or fortification, as in Hotspur's
talk of 'palisadoes, frontiers, parapets'
(2.3.49), here visualized as an angry jut-
ting brow.
20 **good leave** full permission.

Your use and counsel, we shall send for you.

                                        Exit Worcester

(*To Northumberland*) You were about to speak.

NORTHUMBERLAND   Yea, my good lord.

Those prisoners in your highness' name demanded,

Which Harry Percy here at Holmedon took,

Were, as he says, not with such strength denied

As is delivered to your majesty.

Either envy, therefore, or misprision

Is guilty of this fault, and not my son.

HOTSPUR

My liege, I did deny no prisoners.

But I remember when the fight was done,   30

When I was dry with rage and extreme toil,

Breathless and faint, leaning upon my sword,

Came there a certain lord, neat and trimly dressed,

Fresh as a bridegroom, and his chin new reaped

Showed like a stubble-land at harvest-home.

He was perfumèd like a milliner,

And 'twixt his finger and his thumb he held

A pouncet-box, which ever and anon

He gave his nose and took't away again,

Who therewith angry, when it next came there,   40

Took it in snuff; and still he smiled and talked;

21.1 *Exit Worcester*] Q1 ; *not in* F1   22 *To Northumberland*] ROWE ; *not in* Q1   26 is] Q1 ; he Q5 ;
was F1   27 Either envy, therefore] Q1 ; Who either through enuy F1   28 Is] Q1 ; Was F1

21 **use and counsel** 'advice. Lit. ''to use you
   in counsel''' (Wilson, NCS).
26 **delivered** reported, as at 5.2.26 below:
   'Deliver what you will; I'll say 'tis so.'
27 **envy** malice (as also at 5.2.66)
   misprision misunderstanding, error on
   the part of one's informant
31 **rage** fervour of battle
   extreme (accented on first syllable)
34 **Fresh as a bridegroom** A common simile,
   as in Spenser's *Faerie Queene*, I. v. 2 (Dent
   B664.1).
   new reaped recently shaved (in contrast
   to rough soldiers' beards)
35 **Showed** looked
   harvest-home time of bringing home the
   last of the harvest, when the stubble is cut
   back
36 **milliner** dealer in bonnets, gloves, and
   finery, such as were imported from Milan.
   Gloves at that time were often scented or

   perfumed; see *Much Ado* 3.4.54–5 and
   Marlowe, *Massacre at Paris* (1592), Scene
   3, line 170. Compare *Winter's Tale*
   4.4.189; 'no milliner can so fit his customers with gloves.'
38 **pouncet-box** small perfume box with per-
   forated lid. To *pounce* is to emboss or ornament by perforating. (Not recorded before
   Shakespeare in *OED*.)
40 **Who** i.e. the nose. For *who* meaning
   which, see also 1.2.186 and 1.3.104.
41 **Took it in snuff** (a) inhaled it (b) took offence; with a suggestion of sneezing to
   expel the offensive matter. To draw in the
   breath sharply through the nostrils is a
   characteristic gesture of anger. The
   meaning of *to take in snuff* is connected
   with the offensive smell of a *snuff* or smoking candle-end (*OED*, *sb.*¹ 4). The practice
   of taking powdered tobacco as snuff
   appears to have become fashionable

And, as the soldiers bore dead bodies by,
He called them untaught knaves, unmannerly,
To bring a slovenly unhandsome corpse
Betwixt the wind and his nobility.
With many holiday and lady terms
He questioned me, amongst the rest demanded
My prisoners in your majesty's behalf.
I then, all smarting with my wounds being cold,
To be so pestered with a popinjay,   50
Out of my grief and my impatience
Answered neglectingly I know not what,
He should, or he should not; for he made me mad
To see him shine so brisk, and smell so sweet,
And talk so like a waiting-gentlewoman
Of guns and drums and wounds— God save the
        mark!—
And telling me the sovereignest thing on earth
Was parmacety for an inward bruise,
And that it was great pity, so it was,
This villainous saltpetre should be digged   60
Out of the bowels of the harmless earth,
Which many a good tall fellow had destroyed

53 or he] Q1 ; or F1   60 This] Q1 ; That F1

about 1680, though earlier, around
1650, in Ireland and Scotland (*OED,*
*sb.*¹ 1), but the snuffing of various roots,
barks, leaves, etc., is much older.
still always
44 **slovenly** (a) nasty (b) base
46 **holiday** elegant, dainty, not the ordinary
workaday sort suited to soldiers
47 **questioned** (a) conversed with (*Lucrece*
122: 'after supper, long he questioned |
With modest Lucrece') (b) put questions
to, challenged
50 **popinjay** parrot, taken as a type of
prattling and of gaudy plumage. Compare
Spanish *papagayo,* or Papageno and
Papagena in Mozart's *The Magic Flute*;
also *starling,* 1.3.223, and *paraquito,*
2.3.82.
51 **grief** pain, bodily affliction. So 5.1.132:
'Or take away the grief of a wound'
52 **neglectingly** negligently (the earliest of
only two citations in *OED*)

56 **God save the mark** A common formula
(Dent G179.1) perhaps originally used to
ward off evil by invoking God's blessing
on the mark of the cross, as in *Romeo*
3.2.52–3 : 'I saw the wound, I saw it with
mine eyes—God save the mark!—here
on his manly breast', and sometimes used
apologetically or deprecatorily, but here
an expression of indignant impatience, as
also in *Othello* 1.1.33.
57 **sovereignest** most efficacious, as in *Antony* 5.1.41: 'With tears as sovereign as
the blood of hearts'
58 **parmacety** spermaceti, a fatty substance
from the sperm whale used medicinally
60 **saltpetre** This chief ingredient of gunpowder was also used medicinally; hence
there is a play of antithesis between *parmacety* (l. 58) and *saltpetre.*
62 **Which** i.e. saltpetre. (The subject of *had
destroyed.*)
tall brave

147

So cowardly, and but for these vile guns
He would himself have been a soldier.
This bald unjointed chat of his, my lord,
I answered indirectly, as I said,
And I beseech you, let not his report
Come current for an accusation
Betwixt my love and your high majesty.

BLUNT

The circumstance considered, good my lord,   70
Whate'er Lord Harry Percy then had said
To such a person and in such a place,
At such a time, with all the rest retold,
May reasonably die, and never rise
To do him wrong, or any way impeach
What then he said, so he unsay it now.

KING HENRY

Why, yet he doth deny his prisoners,
But with proviso and exception
That we at our own charge shall ransom straight
His brother-in-law, the foolish Mortimer,   80
Who, on my soul, hath wilfully betrayed
The lives of those that he did lead to fight
Against that great magician, damned Glendower,
Whose daughter, as we hear, that Earl of March
Hath lately married. Shall our coffers then
Be emptied to redeem a traitor home?

66 I answered] Q1 ; Made me to answer F1   71 Whate'er Lord] Q1 ; Whate're Q2 ; What euer
F1   84 that] Q1 ; the Q2–5, F1

65 **bald** bare of meaning, trivial, as in *Errors* 2.2.107: 'I knew 'twould be a bald conclusion'
66 **indirectly** not to the point, evasively. Compare *neglectingly* at l. 52.
68 **Come current** (a) be taken at face value, like sterling coin, as in *Richard III* 1.3.257: 'Your fire-new stamp of honour is scarce current' (b) come rushing in, like a swift current
71 **had said** may have said
74 **die** i.e. be forgotten
75 **impeach** call in question as disloyal
76 **so** provided that
77 **yet** (emphatic) i.e. even now, when all is said and done
  deny his prisoners refuse to surrender to me his prisoners

78 **But** except
  proviso and exception (synonymous terms)
79 **we** The royal *we*, as at l. 20.
  straight straightway
80 **His brother-in-law** Hotspur's wife, Kate (historically, Elizabeth), was elder sister to Sir Edmund de Mortimer, captured by Glendower.
83 **great magician** See Appendix for Holinshed.
85–6 **Shall . . . home** On Shakespeare's confusion (following Daniel and Holinshed) of Hotspur's brother-in-law with the Earl of March and on King Henry's unwillingness to rescue one with so well known a claim to the throne, see Appendix 1.1.38.

Shall we buy treason, and indent with fears
When they have lost and forfeited themselves?
No, on the barren mountains let him starve;
For I shall never hold that man my friend   90
Whose tongue shall ask me for one penny cost
To ransom home revolted Mortimer.

HOTSPUR   Revolted Mortimer!
He never did fall off, my sovereign liege,
But by the chance of war. To prove that true
Needs no more but one tongue for all those wounds,
Those mouthèd wounds, which valiantly he took
When on the gentle Severn's sedgy bank,
In single opposition, hand to hand,
He did confound the best part of an hour   100
In changing hardiment with great Glendower.
Three times they breathed, and three times did they
    drink,
Upon agreement, of swift Severn's flood,
Who then, affrighted with their bloody looks,
Ran fearfully among the trembling reeds
And hid his crisp head in the hollow bank,
Bloodstainèd with these valiant combatants.
Never did bare and rotten policy
Colour her working with such deadly wounds,

95 war.] Q2–6, FI (~ ;); ~, QI   96 tongue_A] HANMER; ~ : QI–6; ~. FI   108 bare] QI ;
base FI

87 **indent with fears** enter into an agreement
with cowards and traitors, persons we
have reason to fear. To *indent* literally is to
sever the two halves of a document by a
tooth-like, notched, or zigzag line, thereby providing subsequent means of matching the two parts of the agreement.
Compare the sealed *indentures tripartite* at
3.1.77. The *fears*, both abstract (in ap-
position to *treason*) and concrete, suggest
at once Mortimer's cowardly surrender
and his threat to the Lancastrian throne.
89 **mountains** (of Wales)
92 **revolted** rebellious
94 **fall off** change his allegiance
95 **the chance of war** A recollection of the
proverb 'The chance of war is uncertain'
(Dent C223).
97 **mouthèd** (a) gaping, as in 'mouthèd
graves', *Sonnets* 77.6 (b) eloquent (compare *Caesar* 3.2.221–2: 'and put a

tongue | In every wound of Caesar')
98 **sedgy** bordered with reeds and rushes
100 **confound** consume, waste
101 **changing hardiment** exchanging bold
thrusts, matching valour
102 **breathed** paused for breath. So 5.4.14:
'We breathe too long', also 5.3.44,
5.4.46, and 2.4.241.
103 **of** from
flood river. On *Severn*, see 3.1.70–6,
note.
106 **crisp head** rippled surface, compared to
the curled wavy hair of the personified
river deity
108 **bare** paltry, worthless. So also at
3.2.13: 'Such poor, such bare, such
lewd, such mean attempts', and 4.2.66.
policy stratagem, cunning
109 **Colour** disguise, render specious; also,
make coloured (with blood)

Nor never could the noble Mortimer   110
Receive so many, and all willingly.
Then let not him be slandered with revolt.

KING HENRY

Thou dost belie him, Percy, thou dost belie him.
He never did encounter with Glendower.
I tell thee,
He durst as well have met the devil alone
As Owen Glendower for an enemy.
Art thou not ashamed? But, sirrah, henceforth
Let me not hear you speak of Mortimer.
Send me your prisoners with the speediest means,   120
Or you shall hear in such a kind from me
As will displease you. My lord Northumberland,
We license your departure with your son.
Send us your prisoners, or you will hear of it.

Exit King with Blunt and attendants

HOTSPUR

An if the devil come and roar for them
I will not send them. I will after straight
And tell him so, for I will ease my heart,
Albeit I make a hazard of my head.

NORTHUMBERLAND

What, drunk with choler? Stay, and pause awhile.

---

112 not him] Q1 ; him not Q6, F1   115–161 I . . . alone] STEEVENS (1793); *as one line,* Q1   122
you] Q1 ; ye F1   124 you will] Q1 ; you'l F1   124.1 *with Blunt and attendants*] CAPELL (*subs.*);
not in Q1   128 Albeit I make a] Q1 ; Although it be with F1

---

112 **with revolt** by an accusation of having
revolted against his allegiance to Henry
(echoing ll. 92–3)

113 **belie** misrepresent

116 **devil** (pronounced in one syllable)
alone in single combat

118 **sirrah** Used scornfully here; contrast
the usage at 1.2.168 and note.

119 **speak** (emphatic) i.e. so much as speak.
Hotspur picks this meaning up at ll.
130–1 below.

125 **devil . . . roar** 1 Peter 5 : 8 speaks of the
devil as a 'roaring lion' who 'walketh
about, seeking whom he may devour'.
The roaring devil is commonplace in
Tudor moralities; the Boy in *Henry V*
4.4.64 refers to Pistol as 'this roaring

devil i'th' old play'.

126 **will after straight** will go after him immediately

128 **Albeit . . . head** (a) even if I risk
execution for disobeying (b) even if I risk
allowing my emotions (*heart*) to sway my
reason (*head*)

129 **choler** anger. The dominance of bile in
Hotspur's temperament, suggested literally here by the idea of an intoxicating
excess of it in him, helps explain not only
his valour, rashness, and arrogance, but
also his vivid imagination (Bamborough,
93–4). The relationship between physi-
ology and the emotions is suggested again
at 2.3.75; see note there on *spleen*.

Here comes your uncle.
    Enter Worcester
HOTSPUR   Speak of Mortimer?   130
Zounds, I will speak of him; and let my soul
Want mercy if I do not join with him.
Yea, on his part I'll empty all these veins
And shed my dear blood drop by drop in the dust
But I will lift the downtrod Mortimer
As high in the air as this unthankful king,
As this ingrate and cankered Bolingbroke.
NORTHUMBERLAND
Brother, the King hath made your nephew mad.
WORCESTER
Who struck this heat up after I was gone?
HOTSPUR
He will forsooth have all my prisoners;   140
And when I urged the ransom once again
Of my wife's brother, then his cheek looked pale,
And on my face he turned an eye of death,
Trembling even at the name of Mortimer.
WORCESTER
I cannot blame him. Was not he proclaimed
By Richard, that dead is, the next of blood?
NORTHUMBERLAND
He was; I heard the proclamation.

---

133 Yea, on his part] Q1; In his behalfe F1   135 downtrod] Q1; downfall F1   137 Boling-
broke] Q1 (Bullingbrooke)   145 not he] Q1; he not F1

---

132 **Want mercy** lack mercy, be damned
133 **on his part** i.e. fighting on his (Mor-
    timer's) side
135 **But** but that—i.e. if that is the only way
    to do it
137 **ingrate** ungrateful
    cankered infected and corrupt, as though
    by a canker-worm; malignant
    Bolingbroke Hotspur's use of the cog-
    nomen pointedly refuses to acknowledge
    Henry's royal authority. The spellings in
    Holinshed and in QqF1—*Bullenbrooke*,
    Bollinbrook, and the like—indicate a
    pronunciation that drops the *g* and
    rhymes with *look* as in *Richard II*
    3.4.98–9. See Cercignani, 135.

143 **an eye of death** a look that is deathlike,
    fearful. The context does not seem to
    allow the sense of menace that the phrase
    might suggest.
145–6 **Was . . . blood** Richard named Ed-
    mund de Mortimer, fifth Earl of March, as
    heir presumptive to the throne in 1398,
    after the death of Edward's father Roger,
    the fourth Earl. Holinshed explains the
    royal lineage that substantiated this
    designation of the fifth Earl of March as
    heir presumptive: 'Edmund was son to
    Roger Earl of March, son to the lady
    Philip, daughter of Lionel Duke of
    Clarence, the third son of King Edward the
    third' (184). See Appendix, 1.1.38.

And then it was when the unhappy king—
Whose wrongs in us God pardon!—did set forth
Upon his Irish expedition;   150
From whence he intercepted did return
To be deposed and shortly murderèd.

WORCESTER

And for whose death we in the world's wide mouth
Live scandalized and foully spoken of.

HOTSPUR

But soft, I pray you, did King Richard then
Proclaim my brother Edmund Mortimer
Heir to the crown?

NORTHUMBERLAND   He did; myself did hear it.

HOTSPUR

Nay, then I cannot blame his cousin king,
That wished him on the barren mountains starve.
But shall it be that you, that set the crown   160
Upon the head of this forgetful man,
And for his sake wear the detested blot
Of murderous subornation—shall it be
That you a world of curses undergo,
Being the agents, or base second means,
The cords, the ladder, or the hangman rather?
O, pardon me that I descend so low
To show the line and the predicament
Wherein you range under this subtle king!

159 starve] Q1 ; staru'd F1   162 wear] Q1 wore F1

148–50 **And then ... expedition** See Appendix for Holinshed.
148 **unhappy** unfortunate
149 **in us** done by us, of which we are guilty. The *wrongs* here referred to are the rebellious acts committed against Richard by the Percys.
151 **intercepted** interrupted (by the return of Bolingbroke). So *Titus* 2.3.80: 'And, being intercepted in your sport'.
152 **shortly** soon afterwards
154 **scandalized** disgraced
155 **soft** wait a minute (also at 2.1.34, 5.3.31, 5.4.128)
156 **brother** i.e. brother-in-law; see Appendix, 1.1.38
158 **cousin** (with a quibble on *cozen*, cheat)
162 **detested** detestable
163 **murderous subornation** giving aid and support to murder
164 **world of curses** i.e. because treason against the King was treason against God
165 **second means** agents
166 **cords ... ladder** means of ascent by rope ladder, but also, as Hotspur sardonically notes, instruments of the hangman. In helping Bolingbroke to rise, the Percys have become his hated hatchet men.
168 **line** rank, status, degree (*OED*, 18), but continuing also the suggestion of hangman's cord, as at l. 166
  predicament (a) in logic, a category or class about which certain predications or assertions are made (b) dangerous situation
169 **range** (a) are ranked (b) stray
  subtle cunning, insidious

Shall it for shame be spoken in these days,   170
Or fill up chronicles in time to come,
That men of your nobility and power
Did gage them both in an unjust behalf,
As both of you—God pardon it!—have done,
To put down Richard, that sweet lovely rose,
And plant this thorn, this canker, Bolingbroke?
And shall it in more shame be further spoken
That you are fooled, discarded, and shook off
By him for whom these shames ye underwent?
No. Yet time serves wherein you may redeem   180
Your banished honours, and restore yourselves
Into the good thoughts of the world again;
Revenge the jeering and disdained contempt
Of this proud king, who studies day and night
To answer all the debt he owes to you
Even with the bloody payment of your deaths.
Therefore I say—
WORCESTER   Peace, cousin, say no more.
And now I will unclasp a secret book,
And to your quick-conceiving discontents
I'll read you matter deep and dangerous,   190
As full of peril and adventurous spirit
As to o'erwalk a current roaring loud
On the unsteadfast footing of a spear.

185 to] Q1; *not in* Q5; vnto F1

173 **gage them both** (a) engage, pledge both
of themselves (l. 174) (b) pledge their
nobility and power (l. 172). A *gage* is often
a glove thrown on the ground as a pledge
or challenge, as in *Richard II* 1.1.69–186
and 4.1.25–106.
  behalf interest, cause
176 **canker** wild and inferior kind of rose,
the dog rose, with suggestion also of
'ulcer' and 'canker-worm', recalling
cankered at l. 137
183 **Revenge** Parallel to *redeem* at l. 180;
'wherein you may revenge' is understood.
  disdained disdainful. Onions (374),
Humphreys, and Kittredge cite other instances such as *bearded* and *short-winded*
in which the *-ed* form is equivalent to *-ful*,

-ing, and the like, meaning 'furnished
with' or 'characterized by'.
185 **answer** satisfy, repay
186 **deaths** Despite the warning of Cercignani, 328–9, that the *th* was pronounced
fully in *death*, the phrase 'payment of your
deaths' suggests a pun on *debts* in the
previous line. Falstaff's word-play on a
death not due yet, in 5.1.126–7, seems
even more irresistible.
189 **quick-conceiving** grasping quickly,
conceiving that which is alive, or 'quick'.
Discontent has made the mind more
alacritous.
193 **of a spear** i.e. of a spear laid across as a
bridge, like the sword bridges in such
medieval romances as the *Mabinogion* and
Erec and Enid (Humphreys)

HOTSPUR

   If he fall in, good night, or sink or swim!
   Send danger from the east unto the west,
   So honour cross it from the north to south,
   And let them grapple. O, the blood more stirs
   To rouse a lion than to start a hare!

NORTHUMBERLAND

   Imagination of some great exploit
   Drives him beyond the bounds of patience.   200

HOTSPUR

   By heaven, methinks it were an easy leap
   To pluck bright honour from the pale-faced moon,
   Or dive into the bottom of the deep,
   Where fathom-line could never touch the ground,
   And pluck up drownèd honour by the locks,
   So he that doth redeem her thence might wear
   Without corrival all her dignities;
   But out upon this half-faced fellowship!

201 HOTSPUR] Q5; *not in* Q0

194 **If . . . swim** Such a man, if he fall into the roaring current, will find himself facing a life-or-death challenge. The phrase *good night* suggests that it may be 'curtains' for him. *Sink or swim* is proverbial for dire choice (Dent S485).

195 **from . . . west** A common expression of vast distance, as in Spenser, *Faerie Queene*, III. vii. 42: 'He . . . reeled to and fro from east to west' (Dent E43.1).

196 **So** provided that (also at l. 206)
   cross it cross its path

198 **rouse . . . start** Hunting terms, differentiated according to the kind of beast. John Taylor, the Water Poet, says that woodsmanship employs 'divers and sundry terms of art . . . as you must say, rouse a buck, start a hare, and unkennel a fox' (*Armado, Works*, 1630, i. 92–3; other citations under *rouse, OED, v.* 2, and Humphreys). In *Titus* (2.2.21) it is said that Marcus's dogs 'Will rouse the proudest panther in the chase'. *Start* is applied to Hotspur (perhaps ironically) at l. 216 below. Lions and hares have already been implicitly contrasted at 1.2.71–3.

199 **Imagination** Worcester (as S. K. Heninger, jun., has pointed out to me) manipulates Hotspur's thinking by implanting an image in his mind's eye. See note on l. 209 below.

201 The text, from this line to the end of 2.2, is based on Q0.

206 **redeem** rescue. The word is central to King Henry and Hotspur at ll. 86 and 180. It is no less important for Hal at 1.2.205, 3.2.132, and 5.4.47.

207 **corrival** (a) one having equal claims (b) a rival in affection (*OED, sb.* 1b). *Honour* is personified as a mistress with flowing *locks* (l. 205), in need of chivalrous rescue.
   dignities favours

208 **out . . . fellowship** away with the ignoble suggestion of sharing glory with others; *half-faced* because, like a profile on a coin, one can enjoy only part. Shakespeare's image may be of a pair (*fellowship*) of half-faces on a coin, as on 'Philip and Marys' coined in Mary's reign and still common in the 1590s (West, 330). No one has spoken of sharing honour; the idea comes from Hotspur's innate hostility towards rivals.

WORCESTER

He apprehends a world of figures here,

But not the form of what he should attend.—   210

Good cousin, give me audience for a while.

HOTSPUR

I cry you mercy.

WORCESTER   Those same noble Scots

That are your prisoners—

HOTSPUR   I'll keep them all.

By God, he shall not have a Scot of them,

No, if a scot would save his soul, he shall not!

I'll keep them, by this hand.

WORCESTER   You start away

And lend no ear unto my purposes.

Those prisoners you shall keep.

HOTSPUR   Nay I will, that's flat.

He said he would not ransom Mortimer,

Forbade my tongue to speak of Mortimer,   220

But I will find him when he lies asleep,

And in his ear I'll holler 'Mortimer!'

Nay, I'll have a starling shall be taught to speak

Nothing but 'Mortimer', and give it him

To keep his anger still in motion.

WORCESTER Hear you, cousin, a word.

HOTSPUR

All studies here I solemnly defy

---

211 a while] QO; a-while, | And list to me F1   212–13 Those . . . prisoners] F1; *as one line*, QO
222 holler] QO (hollow)

209 **apprehends** snatches at (Davison).
Compare *Dream* 5.1.5, and Theseus'
whole speech there on imagination.
  figures (a) shapes of the imagination (b)
rhetorical figures of speech. Hotspur's
world of figures is an imagined world of
men in action.
210 **form** essential principle, Greek ἰδέα,
matter at hand (*OED*, *sb.* 4 and 5)
  attend direct his mind to
212 **cry you mercy** ask your pardon (as at
4.2.49)
214–15 **Scot . . . scot** Scotsman . . . trifling
amount; literally, small payment of local
tax or tavern reckoning. Hotspur quibbles
that he would not pay a scot-penny to
save Henry's soul. Compare Falstaff's
word-play involving 'scot and lot' at

5.4.113, meaning final settlement.
216 **by this hand** A conventional oath.
  start See note at l. 198 above.
217 **my purposes** the purport of my conversation
218 **that's flat** A familiar tag (Dent F345):
that's for certain. So also at 4.2.37.
222 **And . . . 'Mortimer'** Malone cites Mortimer junior in Marlowe's *Edward II*
2.2.127–9: 'an if he will not ransom
him, | I'll thunder such a plea into his ears
| As never subject did unto his King.'
  holler A modern dialectal form of QqF1's
'hollow', 'hollo', and 'holla'.
225 **still** continually
227 **studies** pursuits
  defy renounce

Save how to gall and pinch this Bolingbroke,
And that same sword-and-buckler Prince of Wales.
But that I think his father loves him not,   230
And would be glad he met with some mischance,
I would have him poisoned with a pot of ale.

WORCESTER
Farewell, kinsman, I'll talk to you
When you are better tempered to attend.

NORTHUMBERLAND (*to Hotspur*)
Why, what a wasp-stung and impatient fool
Art thou to break into this woman's mood,
Tying thine ear to no tongue but thine own?

HOTSPUR
Why, look you, I am whipped and scourged with rods,
Nettled and stung with pismires, when I hear
Of this vile politician, Bolingbroke.   240
In Richard's time—what do you call the place?
A plague upon it, it is in Gloucestershire;
'Twas where the madcap Duke his uncle kept,
His uncle York; where I first bowed my knee
Unto this king of smiles, this Bolingbroke—

229–31 Wales. | But . . . mischance,] Q5 ; Wales, | But . . . mischance: Q0   232 him poisoned]
Q0 ; poyson'd him F1   235 *to Hotspur*] This edition ; *not in* Q0   wasp-stung] Q0 ; waspe-tongue
Q2 ; Waspe-tongu'd F1   238 Why, look you,] Q1 (Why looke you,); Why looke you?
Q0   whipped] Q1 (whipt); whip Q0   241 do you] Q0 ; de'ye F1   242 upon it] Q0 vpon't F1

228 **pinch** torture, afflict, as in *Tempest*
    5.1.74, and *Merry Wives* 4.4.56.
229 **sword-and-buckler** blustering, swash-
    buckling. Compare Porter, *Two Angry
    Women of Abington* (1599): 'I . . . put on
    my fellow Dick's sword-and-buckler voice
    and his swounds and sblood words'
    (Malone Society edn., 1912, ll. 2202–3;
    cited in *OED*, *sword, sb.* 5d). Even as early
    as 1570, Florio's *First Fruits* (17b) calls
    the buckler or small round shield 'a clown-
    ish dastardly weapon' (*OED*, *buckler, sb.*²
    1). Falstaff brags of his feats with sword
    and buckler at Gad's Hill in 2.4.161–2.
    Gentlemen of Shakespeare's day gener-
    ally preferred the rapier and dagger, leav-
    ing the sword and small round shield to
    servants and swaggerers. Humphreys
    cites *Two Angry Women*, ll. 729–30:
    'Where's your blue coat, your sword and
    buckler, sir? | Get you such like habit for a
    servingman.'

232 **pot of ale** Another contemptuous glance
    at Hal's reputation for lower-class
    manners and habits.
239 **Nettled** (a) stung with nettles (b) vexed
    pismires ants. Compare Proverbs 6 : 6
    (Geneva Bible): 'Go to the pismire, O
    sluggard.' Thought to derive from the
    urinous smell of an anthill. To be whipped
    with nettles is also proverbial (Dent
    N135.1).
240 **politician** shrewd schemer, deceitful
    opportunist. Compare *Lear* 4.6.171–2:
    'like a scurvy politician, seem | To see the
    things thou dost not'.
243 **madcap Duke** See Appendix for histori-
    cal background.
    kept dwelled
244–5 **bowed . . . Bolingbroke** Shakespeare
    dramatizes this encounter and Boling-
    broke's fair speaking of the Percys in
    Richard II 2.3.1–50.

'Sblood, when you and he came back from Ravenspurgh—

NORTHUMBERLAND At Berkeley Castle.

HOTSPUR You say true.

Why, what a candy deal of courtesy
This fawning greyhound then did proffer me!   250
'Look when his infant fortune came to age',
And 'gentle Harry Percy', and 'kind cousin'—
O, the devil take such cozeners!—God forgive me,
Good uncle, tell your tale, I have done.

WORCESTER

Nay, if you have not, to it again;
We will stay your leisure.

HOTSPUR   I have done, i'faith.

WORCESTER

Then once more to your Scottish prisoners.
Deliver them up without their ransom straight,
And make the Douglas' son your only mean
For powers in Scotland, which for divers reasons   260
Which I shall send you written, be assured
Will easily be granted. (*To Northumberland*) You, my lord,

254 I] QO; for I FI   255 to it] QO; too't FI   256 We will] QO; Wee'l FI   262 granted …
lord,] HANMER; granted you my Lord. QO–1; granted you, my Lord. Q2–3, Q5–6, FI   *To
Northumberland*] THEOBALD; *not in* QO

246 **Ravenspurgh** Bolingbroke's landing-
place on his return from exile in 1399 (see
Richard II 2.2.51 and 2.3.31–5, and *1
Henry IV* 3.2.95 and 4.3.77), a busy
Yorkshire seaport on the River Humber,
since then submerged by the sea. The
hypermetric irregularity of this line and of
the two short lines that follow (as lineated
in Q1; FI smooths the verse by excising
the profanity) well conveys Hotspur's impatience with his faulty memory.

247 **Berkeley Castle** castle near Bristol; see
Richard II 2.2.119–2.3.51

249 **candy** sugary, flattering, as in *Hamlet*
3.2.58: 'let the candied tongue lick
absurd pomp'

250 **greyhound** Compare *Coriolanus* 1.6.38:
'Like a fawning greyhound in the leash'.

251 **Look when** when, as soon as. A common locution, as in *look what* ('whatever'), *look how* ('however'), *look as* ('just
as'), *look how many* ('however many'),
etc. There are verbal echoes in ll. 251–2
of *Richard II* 2.3.45 and 66.

253 **cozeners** cheats (with play on *cousin*,
l. 252, making explicit the pun suggested

earlier at l. 158). Compare the proverb
'Call me cousin but cozen me not' (Dent
C739).

256 **stay** await

258 **Deliver them up** free them (in order to
further an alliance with Scotland against
Henry)
    straight straightway

259 **the Douglas' son** Mordake, Earl of Fife,
wrongly supposed by Shakespeare to be
son of the Earl of Douglas; see Appendix,
1.1.71–2. Prefixing *the* to a title or proper
name is a formula normally employed to
designate the head of a noble Scottish
family, as in *the Douglas*, 2.3.24, 4.1.3,
5.4.25, 5.5.23 and 27, but see also 'The
Douglas and the Hotspur' in 5.1.116,
where the untitled Hotspur is similarly
honoured (as he is in the ballad of 'The
Battle of Otterburn'). *OED* (*the*, 10c) explains *the* before names and titles of men
as a corruption of the French *de*. See also
2.4.99–100, 'the Hotspur of the North'.
    mean means

260 **For powers** for raising an army

Your son in Scotland being thus employed,
Shall secretly into the bosom creep
Of that same noble prelate well beloved,
The Archbishop.
HOTSPUR Of York, is it not?
WORCESTER True, who bears hard
His brother's death at Bristol, the Lord Scrope.
I speak not this in estimation,   270
As what I think might be, but what I know
Is ruminated, plotted, and set down,
And only stays but to behold the face
Of that occasion that shall bring it on.
HOTSPUR
I smell it. Upon my life, it will do well.
NORTHUMBERLAND
Before the game is afoot thou still lett'st slip.
HOTSPUR
Why, it cannot choose but be a noble plot.
And then the power of Scotland and of York
To join with Mortimer, ha?
WORCESTER   And so they shall.
HOTSPUR
In faith, it is exceedingly well aimed.   280
WORCESTER
And 'tis no little reason bids us speed,
To save our heads by raising of a head;
For, bear ourselves as even as we can,
The King will always think him in our debt,
And think we think ourselves unsatisfied
Till he hath found a time to pay us home.

267 is it] QO; is't F1   275 I . . . well] QO; I smell it : | Vpon my life, it will do wond'rous well F1

263 **in Scotland** with the Scots
264 **into the bosom creep** insinuate himself
  into the confidence. A familiar expression
  (Dent B546).
266 **The Archbishop** Richard Scroop, or
  Scrope (1350?–1405), Archbishop of
  York, who appears in 4.4 as an ally of the
  rebellious Percys
268 **bears hard** begrudges
269 **the Lord Scrope** See Appendix for
  Holinshed.
270 **estimation** guessing
273 **but** (reinforces sense of *only*)

274 **occasion** opportunity
276 **Before . . . slip** you're always letting
  loose the dogs, 'jumping the gun'. Antony in *Caesar* 3.1.273 invokes Ate to 'let
  slip the dogs of war'.
277 **cannot choose but be** cannot help being
282 **head** army of insurrection (with play on
  heads)
283 **even** carefully
286 **pay us home** (a) completely discharge
  his debt to us (b) requite us to the very
  heart (with the suggestion of a fatal
  thrust)

And see already how he doth begin
To make us strangers to his looks of love.

HOTSPUR

He does, he does. We'll be revenged on him.

WORCESTER

Cousin, farewell. No further go in this   290
Than I by letters shall direct your course.
When time is ripe, which will be suddenly,
I'll steal to Glendower and Lord Mortimer,
Where you and Douglas and our powers at once,
As I will fashion it, shall happily meet
To bear our fortunes in our own strong arms,
Which now we hold at much uncertainty.

NORTHUMBERLAND

Farewell, good brother. We shall thrive, I trust.

HOTSPUR

Uncle, adieu. O, let the hours be short
Till fields and blows and groans applaud our sport!   300

Exeunt

2.1   *Enter a Carrier with a lantern in his hand*
FIRST CARRIER Heigh-ho! An it be not four by the day, I'll be
hanged. Charles's Wain is over the new chimney, and yet
our horse not packed. What, ostler!

291 course.] F4 (~ ;); ~ ₐ QO   296 bear our] Q1; beare out QO   300.1 *Exeunt*] QO; *exit*
F1   2.1.1 An it] QO; an't F1

292 **suddenly** immediately
294 **our powers at once** all our forces together
295 **happily** fortunately
296 **arms** (with word-play on idea of 'armed might')
300 **fields** battlefields
2.1 The scene, clearly taking place in an inn-yard on the London–Canterbury road, is plausibly located by Theobald and subsequent editors in Rochester because of its proximity (two and one-half miles) to Gad's Hill, and because we learn in 1.2.122 that 'Gadshill lies tonight in Rochester', but Rochester is not mentioned in this scene.
0.1 *Carrier* one who hauls farm produce to the London area in his *pannier*, or basket

(l. 25), by means of a pack-horse (ll. 3–9). The *lantern* is a conventional signal of night-time on the daylit Elizabethan stage.
1 **by the day** in the morning
2 **Charles's Wain** the constellation of the Plough, or Great Bear, or Big Dipper (Latin, *plaustrum*, wagon). Literally, Charlemagne's wagon, because it appears to move through the sky ahead of the bright star Arcturus, associated with King Arthur. Charlemagne and Arthur were paired in medieval legend.
3 **horse** horses. The nominative plural was originally the same as the singular, as with *sheep*, *swine*, and *deer*.
   ostler stableman, groom; originally a *hosteler*, or innkeeper

159

OSTLER (*within*) Anon, anon.

FIRST CARRIER I prithee, Tom, beat cut's saddle, put a few
 flocks in the point. Poor jade is wrung in the withers out
 of all cess.

  Enter another Carrier

SECOND CARRIER Peas and beans are as dank here as a dog,
 and that is the next way to give poor jades the bots. This
 house is turned upside-down since Robin ostler died.   10

FIRST CARRIER Poor fellow never joyed since the price of oats
 rose. It was the death of him.

SECOND CARRIER I think this be the most villainous house in
 all London road for fleas. I am stung like a tench.

FIRST CARRIER Like a tench? By the mass, there is ne'er a

---

4 *within*] THEOBALD; *not in* QO   5 cut's] QO (Cuts)   6 Poor] QO; the poore FI   9 that] QO; this
FI   10 Robin] QO; *Robin* the FI   13 be] QO; to be Q5; is FI

---

4 **Anon** I'll be there in a minute
5 **Tom** the name of either the ostler (compare *Robin ostler* in l. 10) or the Second
  Carrier. The instructions about the horse
  are appropriate to an ostler, but the first-
  name familiarity and the sharing of ad-
  versities on the road seem better suited to
  the Second Carrier, who is coming to join
  his fellow carrier at this point, and who
  later seems to address the First Carrier as
  neighbour Mugs (l. 42).
  beat cut's saddle soften up the pack-
  saddle by pounding out the lumps. *Cut* is
  a term for a common labouring horse,
  suggesting either that it is dock-tailed or a
  gelding. Probably the First Carrier simply
  omits *the* before the noun as in ll. 6 and 11
  (see also l. 10), but he may also use *cut* as
  the horse's name, like 'Gib our cat' in
  Gammer Gurton's Needle, 1.1.15.
6 **flocks** tufts (of wool)
  point pommel of the saddle
  Poor jade the poor nag. Omission of the
  definite article characterizes rustic
  speech, as with *Robin ostler* in l. 10 and
  poor fellow in l. 11.
  wrung in the withers saddle-chafed in the
  ridge between his shoulder-blades. So in
  Hamlet 3.2.236: 'Let the galled jade
  wince, our withers are unwrung.'
6–7 **out of all cess** beyond all estimate, ex-
  cessively
8 **Peas and beans** (used for horse fodder)
  dank . . . as a dog damp as can be. *Dog* is

used similarly as an intensifier in dog-
drunk, dog-cheap, dog-tired (cf. *Shrew*
4.2.60), etc. (*OED, dog, sb.* 17d).
9 **next** nearest, quickest, as in 3.1.254
  bots parasitical intestinal maggots,
  hatched from eggs clinging to leaves of
  horse fodder. *Shrew* 3.2.53 characterizes
  an inferior horse as 'spoiled with the
  staggers, begnawn with the bots'.
10 **house** inn
  turned upside-down A common phrase
  (Dent T165) of biblical origin (Psalm 146:
  9, Isaiah 24: 1, etc.), connoting social
  disorder.
  Robin ostler i.e. 'Robin the ostler', omitting the definite article as in ll. 6 and 11,
  though he may well have been called
  'Robin ostler' as if that were his proper
  name. This ostler was a keeper of inns, not
  a mere stable groom, for he purchased
  oats for provender and was ruined by an
  inflation in costs that outpaced his
  revenue. The price of oats more than
  doubled between 1593 and 1596–7,
  after which it again fell (see Hemingway,
  89; Humphreys, 38).
14 **tench** carp-like fish whose spotted markings, or parasitic incrustations, may have
  been thought to resemble flea-bites. See
  *OED, fish, sb.*¹ 7, 'fish-louse'. A bit of stage
  business is sometimes provided for the
  actor: '*Catches fleas, and examines them by
  the light of his lantern.*'

king christen could be better bit than I have been since
the first cock.

SECOND CARRIER Why, they will allow us ne'er a jordan, and
then we leak in your chimney, and your chamber-lye
breeds fleas like a loach.   20

FIRST CARRIER What, ostler! Come away and be hanged!
Come away.

SECOND CARRIER I have a gammon of bacon, and two races
of ginger, to be delivered as far as Charing Cross.

FIRST CARRIER God's body, the turkeys in my pannier are
quite starved. What, ostler! A plague on thee, hast thou
never an eye in thy head? Canst not hear? An 'twere not
as good deed as drink to break the pate on thee, I am a
very villain. Come, and be hanged! Hast no faith in thee?
          Enter Gadshill

GADSHILL Good morrow, carriers, what's o'clock?   30
FIRST CARRIER I think it be two o'clock.

---

16 christen] QO; in Christendome F1   31 FIRST CARRIER] HANMER; *Car*: QO

16 **king christen** king in Christendom, accustomed to 'have the best of everything'
(Kittredge)
17 **first cock** i.e. midnight, as in *Dream*
2.1.267. The second cock (*Romeo* 4.4.3)
conventionally crowed at 3 a.m., and
the third, or 'morning cock' (*Hamlet*
1.2.218), an hour before sunrise
(Kittredge)
18 **jordan** chamber-pot
19 **leak** urinate
   your chimney the fireplace. For *your*,
   meaning 'that you know of' (also in *your*
   chamber-lye), compare *Hamlet* 5.1.166:
   'Your water is a sore decayer of your
   whoreson dead body.'
   chamber-lye urine. The image is not of a
   substance that might *lie* about in an un-
   sanitary chamber (QO spelling is *lie*) but of
   an alkaline solution like *lye* commonly
   used in washing clothes or wounds.
20 **loach** another fish like the tench (l. 14,
   note) evidently thought to breed vermin
21 **Come away** come along
   and be hanged A common tag (Dent
   H130.1) here and at l. 29.
23 **gammon of bacon** ham
   races roots; compare *radish*, from Latin
   radix, *radicum*. Derick, a robbed carrier in

Famous Victories, complains to the Chief
Justice of the thief Cutbert Cutter that he
'hath taken the great rase of ginger, that
bouncing Bess with the jolly buttocks
should have had' (ll. 302–4). See
Introduction, p. 22.
24 **Charing Cross** market between London
and Westminster, on the opposite side of
London from Rochester
26–7 **hast . . . head** A common colloquial
expression (Dent E248.1), also in
Coriolanus 4.5.11.
27 **never** (emphatic for 'not')
28 **as good deed as drink** This colloquial expression (Dent D183.1) recurs in 2.2.21
and *Twelfth Night* 2.3.118.
   to break the pate on thee to crack your
   skull. Not a fracture, but enough of a blow
   to break the skin and cause blood to flow,
   as when Jack of 'Jack and Jill' fell down
   and 'broke his crown'.
28–9 **I am a very villain** See note at 1.2.
91–2. *Very* means 'true'.
29 **faith** trustworthiness
31 **two o'clock** The First Carrier knows that
it is four o'clock (l. 1), but answers
evasively to a stranger who seems sus-
piciously curious about the time of their
departure.

GADSHILL I prithee lend me thy lantern, to see my gelding in the stable.

FIRST CARRIER Nay, by God, soft. I know a trick worth two of that, i'faith.

GADSHILL I pray thee, lend me thine.

SECOND CARRIER Ay, when, canst tell? Lend me thy lantern, quoth he! Marry, I'll see thee hanged first.

GADSHILL Sirrah carrier, what time do you mean to come to London?   40

SECOND CARRIER Time enough to go to bed with a candle, I warrant thee. Come, neighbour Mugs, we'll call up the gentlemen. They will along with company, for they have great charge.   *Exeunt Carriers*

GADSHILL What ho! Chamberlain!
        Enter the Chamberlain

CHAMBERLAIN At hand, quoth pickpurse.

GADSHILL That's even as fair as 'at hand, quoth the chamberlain'; for thou variest no more from picking of purses than giving direction doth from labouring; thou layest the plot how.   50

CHAMBERLAIN Good morrow, Master Gadshill. It holds current that I told you yesternight: there's a franklin in the

38 he] QO; a FI   44 *Carriers*] ROWE; *not in* QO   45.1 *Enter the Chamberlain*] KITTREDGE; *after l. 44* QO (*Enter Chamberlaine*)

34 **soft** wait a minute (as at 1.3.155)
34–5 **I know . . . of that** A common expression (Dent T518) signifying wariness of being taken for a fool.
37 **Ay, when, canst tell?** Colloquial retort (Dent T88) used to turn aside a question; roughly equivalent to 'You must be joking' or 'Not bloody likely'.
38 **quoth he** A way of expressing scorn in repeating what another person has said.
41 **Time . . . candle** Again, wary evasion in reply to questions about the carriers' itinerary.
    Time enough in time
42 **warrant** assure
43–4 **They . . . charge** The gentlemen wish to travel with others because they take with them a heavy load of valuables or cargo. No carriers are specifically mentioned during the robbery in 2.2, though they may be part of the group referred to as 'travellers'; one carrier later enters with the sheriff at 2.4.486 as part of the

'hue and cry' pursuing Falstaff, and the victim of the Gad's Hill robbery in *Famous Victories* is a carrier (Wilson, *NCS*).
45 **Chamberlain** attendant at an inn responsible for the bedchambers (and therefore able to overhear news about the occupants' wealth and travel plans)
46 **At hand, quoth pickpurse** i.e. (a) at your disposal (b) within easy reach. A popular tag (Dent H65), joking on the notion that a pickpocket is quickly by one's side.
47 **even as fair as** just as good as saying
48–9 **thou variest . . . labouring** you are no more different from an actual pickpocket than an overseer is from a common workman
50 **plot** (a) overseer's plan of work (b) robbery plot (Wilson, *NCS*)
51–2 **holds current that** holds true still what
52 **a franklin** one who possesses his own land, ranking next below the gentry; a well-to-do yeoman

Weald of Kent hath brought three hundred marks with him in gold. I heard him tell it to one of his company last night at supper—a kind of auditor, one that hath abundance of charge too, God knows what. They are up already, and call for eggs and butter. They will away presently.

GADSHILL Sirrah, if they meet not with Saint Nicholas' clerks, I'll give thee this neck.   60

CHAMBERLAIN No, I'll none of it. I pray thee, keep that for the hangman, for I know thou worshippest Saint Nicholas as truly as a man of falsehood may.

GADSHILL What talkest thou to me of the hangman? If I hang, I'll make a fat pair of gallows; for if I hang, old Sir John hangs with me, and thou knowest he is no starveling. Tut, there are other Trojans that thou dream'st not of, the which for sport's sake are content to do the profession some grace, that would, if matters should be looked into, for their own credit's sake make all whole. I   70

---

53 Weald] QO (wild)   66 he is] QO; hee's FI   68 sport's] QO (sport)   70 credit's] QO (credit)

53 **Weald** (of which QO's 'wild' is a variant spelling), a wooded or open tract of country; specifically the formerly wooded plain between the North and South Downs
 marks valued at 13s. 4d. or two nobles, two-thirds of the pound sterling; not a coin
55 **auditor** a royal official charged with receiving and examining accounts of money of receivers, sheriffs, etc. In 2.2.50–2, Gadshill notes: 'There's money . . . going to the King's Exchequer.'
57 **eggs and butter** See note at 1.2.20.
58 **presently** at once
59–60 **Saint Nicholas' clerks** highwaymen. St Nicholas was patron saint of, among others, children and scholars (as in *Two Gentlemen* 3.1.292–3) and those who travelled. In a medieval play for St Nicholas's day the saint miraculously restores to life three slain clerics; in another, he obliges robbers to restore the treasure they have stolen (Adams, 55–62). His attribute, three balls or purses of gold, may have contributed to the popular tradition of regarding him as the patron of robbers (Hemingway; Wilson, NCS). 'Nick' may also have suggested 'to nick', to cut a purse, or to cheat and

defraud (*OED*, v.² 11, from 1595), and 'old Nick', the devil.
60 **neck** (with a pun on *Nick*)
61 **I'll none** I want none
63 **truly . . . falsehood** The antithesis of *true* (suggesting both 'faithful' and 'honest') and *false* ('faithless' and 'dishonest') continues at ll. 89–91 below and at 2.2.21–2 and 87.
64 **What** why, as at 2.4.77
67 **Trojans** (QO's *Troyans* is only a variant spelling): merry or roistering fellows, boon companions, as in Will Kempe, *Nine Days' Wonder* (1600), C ii: 'He was a kind good fellow, a true Troyan' (*OED*, 2). The term is one of several cant phrases in Shakespeare for fellowship, including *Corinthian* (2.4.11), *Ephesian* (*2 Henry IV* 2.2.143 and *Merry Wives* 4.5.16), and *Greek* (*Troilus* 4.4.55). Gadshill is alluding to Prince Hal.
68 **the which** who
68, 70 **sport's, credit's** On the omission of the possessive form in QO's 'sport' and 'credit', see note at 1.2.146.
68–9 **do . . . grace** do honour to robbery, set it in a good light
70 **for . . . whole** for the sake of their personal reputation, will insure that all goes well

am joined with no foot-land-rakers, no long-staff sixpenny strikers, none of these mad mustachio purple-
hued malt-worms, but with nobility and tranquillity,
burgomasters and great oneyers, such as can hold in,
such as will strike sooner than speak, and speak sooner
than drink, and drink sooner than pray. And yet, zounds,
I lie, for they pray continually to their saint, the commonwealth, or rather not pray to her but prey on her, for they
ride up and down on her and make her their boots.

CHAMBERLAIN What, the commonwealth their boots? Will   80
she hold out water in foul way?

---

74 oneyers] QQ (Oneyers); Moneyers THEOBALD (*conj*.HARDINGE); owners HANMER; mynheers
CAPELL; 'oyez'-ers (OXFORD)   in,] Q7, F1; ~ ∧ QQ   77 to] QQ; vnto F1   78 not pray] QQ; not
to pray F1

71 **foot-land-rakers** those who *rake*, or roam
on foot, for prey. The point is presumably
that they can't afford a horse.

71–2 **long-staff sixpenny strikers** robbers
who would use long pikes with iron hooks
in the end to knock down their victims or
pull them from their horses, for a paltry
sixpence (Bailey)

72–3 **mad . . . malt-worms** rowdy drunkards with fierce-looking moustaches and
purple faces. The braggart Spaniard Don
Armado in *LLL* sports just such a 'mustachio' (5.1.89), and Bardolph a purple
face; 'his face', says Falstaff, 'is Lucifer's
privy-kitchen, where he doth nothing
but roast malt-worms' (*2 Henry IV*
2.4.321–2). *Malt-worms* are weevils that
infest malt, and hence drunkards who
love liquor made from malt.

73 **tranquillity** the well-to-do, who lead easy
lives. Gadshill seems grandly to coin such
a comically far-fetched title by analogy
with *nobility*. *Tranquillity* was a familiar
word by Shakespeare's time in the sense
of 'serenity', but not as a designation for a
social class.

74 **oneyers** Origin and meaning uncertain
(*OED*). Many emendations have been
proposed. Jowett (Oxford) suggests '*oyez*'-
ers, criers of 'Oyez', perhaps suggesting
court officials rather than public criers. A
possible legal meaning has been suggested by Malone, based on *O.Ni*
as an abbreviation for the Latin
phrase *oneratur, nisi habeat sufficientem
exonerationem*, meaning 'he is charged, or
legally responsible unless he have a suf-

ficient discharge', suggesting a sheriff of
the King or public accountant possessed
of large sums of money belonging to the
state. One attractive possibility is that
Gadshill is grandiloquently pairing
oneyers with *burgomasters* as he did *tranquillity* with *nobility*, coining a word by
appending an impressive-sounding suffix.
Great oneyers would then be a neologism
for 'great ones', as Dr Johnson suggests.
The chink in the near-rhyme is unmistak-
able. Other suggestions include *moneyers*
(officers of the mint), *owners*, *mynheers*,
wonners (dwellers), and *younkers*.

   hold in (a) 'keep in', keep a secret (*OED*,
hold, *v*. 38b) (b) stay with it, continue to
pursue the task or the quarry (Madden,
54)

75–6 **strike . . . drink** knock down a victim
(compare *strikers* at l. 72) without a word,
or go highway robbing and cry 'Lay by'
(1.2.34) even sooner than drink

76 **zounds** by his (Christ's) wounds, as at
1.2.95

79 **ride** (with a suggestion of mounting the
commonwealth as though she were a
female; *OED*, 3)
   boots booty, with a play in the following lines on 'footwear'. In *Henry V*
1.2.194–5, bees 'Make boot upon the
summer's velvet buds, | Which pillage
they with merry march bring home'. Perhaps there is a play too on *boot*, 'remedy',
though the plural makes this problematic.

80–1 **Will . . . way** will she let you go dry-
footed in muddy roads, i.e. will she shelter
you in a difficult spot

GADSHILL She will, she will. Justice hath liquored her. We steal as in a castle, cocksure. We have the receipt of fern-seed, we walk invisible.

CHAMBERLAIN Nay, by my faith, I think you are more beholden to the night than to fern-seed for your walking invisible.

GADSHILL Give me thy hand. Thou shalt have a share in our purchase, as I am a true man.

CHAMBERLAIN Nay, rather let me have it as you are a false 90 thief.

GADSHILL Go to; *homo* is a common name to all men. Bid the ostler bring my gelding out of the stable. Farewell, you muddy knave.   *Exeunt severally*

2.2   *Enter the Prince, Poins, Peto, ⌈and Bardolph⌉*
POINS Come, shelter, shelter! I have removed Falstaff's horse, and he frets like a gummed velvet.

---

85 by ... think] QO; I thinke rather FI   86 beholden] QO (beholding)   than to] QO; than to the FI   89 purchase] QO; purpose FI   93 my] QO; the FI   94 *Exeunt severally*] *not in* QO; *Exeunt* FI   2.2.0 *the*] *not in* QO   *Peto, and Bardolph*] *and Peto &c*. QO–6; *and Peto*. FI

---

82 **Justice hath liquored her** the authorities have (a) 'greased' her as with waterproof dressing, thereby affording protection from the law (b) made her drunk and hence ineffectual

83 **as in a castle** The familiar comparison 'as safe as in a castle' (Dent C122.1) may here contain an echo of 'Oldcastle' (Kittredge).

83–4 **receipt of fern-seed** formula or recipe for fern-seed, supposed invisible (the mode of reproduction of ferns by minute spores was not yet understood), and hence capable of bestowing invisibility on those who possessed it

86 **beholden** obligated (QO 'beholding' is a variant spelling)

89 **purchase** i.e. booty
true honest (but a play on words follows)

92 **homo ... men** the Latin name for 'man' applies to all sorts, including the false thief (ll. 90–1); hence, says Gadshill, his phrase 'as I am a true man' (l. 89) applies

to him, for he is *homo*, a man. He alludes to a well-known definition from Lily and Colet's *Short Introduction of Grammar* (1549): 'A noun substantive either is proper . . . or else is common . . . as *homo* is a common name to all men' (Humphreys).

94 **muddy** dull or muddled

2.2 Location is the highway near Gad's Hill.

0.1 ***Bardolph*** Not named in the stage directions of QqFI (see collation), but the '*&c*' in QO and QI can apply to no one else, and Falstaff calls out imploringly to Poins, Hal, Bardolph, and Peto at ll. 19–20, assuming them all to be near. See Introduction, p. 102, as to whether Peto and Bardolph are in on the practical joke about Falstaff's horse.

2 **frets** (a) chafes, is vexed (b) rubs and frays like *gummed velvet*, velvet made glossy with a stiffening gum, and hence liable to *fret* or wear; a familiar comparison (Dent T8)

PRINCE HENRY Stand close.

> *They step aside.*
>
> *Enter Falstaff*

FALSTAFF Poins! Poins, and be hanged! Poins!

PRINCE HENRY (*coming forward*) Peace, ye fat-kidneyed
rascal! What a brawling dost thou keep?

FALSTAFF Where's Poins, Hal?

PRINCE HENRY He is walked up to the top of the hill. I'll go
seek him.

> *He steps aside*

FALSTAFF I am accursed to rob in that thief's company. The   10
rascal hath removed my horse, and tied him I know not
where. If I travel but four foot by the square further afoot,
I shall break my wind. Well, I doubt not but to die a fair
death for all this, if I scape hanging for killing that rogue.
I have forsworn his company hourly any time this two-
and-twenty years, and yet I am bewitched with the
rogue's company. If the rascal have not given me
medicines to make me love him, I'll be hanged. It could
not be else—I have drunk medicines. Poins! Hal! A plague
upon you both! Bardolph! Peto! I'll starve ere I'll rob a   20

3.1 *They step aside*] DYCE (*subs.*); *not in* QO   5 *coming forward*] DYCE; *not in* QO   9.1 *He steps aside*
DYCE (*subs.*); *not in* QO   10 The] QO; *that* F1   12 square] QO (squire)   15–16 two-and-
twenty] F1; xxii QO   20 Bardolph] DERING MS (Bardolfe), F1 (Bardolph); Bardol QO; Bardoll
Q1–6 (*throughout*)   I'll rob] QO; I rob F1

3 **close** concealed, as at ll. 71 and 91 below,
and 2.4.523. The Prince may be speaking
to Poins alone, or to Bardolph and Peto as
well; see Introduction, p. 102.

6 **keep** keep up

10–14 **The rascal . . . that rogue** It is Poins
who has removed Falstaff's horse; but
much of what Falstaff says in ll. 10–19
about the rascal's bewitching company
applies no less aptly to Hal. Falstaff wishes
'a plague' on both Poins and Hal (l. 19),
and comically considers leaving them
both, for he perceives that Hal is one of the
'stony-hearted villains' (ll. 24–5) that
know how uncomfortable Falstaff is afoot.

12 **by the square** precisely. A *square* (Qo,
'squire', is an obsolete form) is a measur-
ing tool. In *Winter's Tale* 4.4.331, dancers
are said to be able to jump 'twelve foot and
a half by th' square'.

13 **break my wind** 'pant and wheeze like a
wind-broken horse' (Kittredge); but *OED*
also lists sixteenth-century usages of the

phrase meaning 'to discharge flatus from
the stomach or bowels' (*break, v.* 47; *wind,
sb.* 10). Nashe's *Pierce Penniless* (1592)
describes how the Roman censors made a
practice of taking away the horse of a corpulent man to chastise a carcass 'so puffed
up with gluttony or idleness' (i. 201, cited
in Wilson, *NCS*).

13–14 **die . . . this** die peacefully after all this
suffering, or despite all this practical
joking. The image of martyrdom is
appropriate to Oldcastle.

13 **fair** exemplary, noble

18 **medicines** potions

20 **Bardolph** On the significance of Falstaff's
assumption that Bardolph is within hearing, see head-note to this scene and
Introduction, p. 100.

starve The original meaning is simply to
die, as in *Coriolanus* 2.3.110: 'Better it is to
die, better to starve', but, coming from Falstaff, the word here surely means to 'die of
starvation'.

foot further. An 'twere not as good a deed as drink to turn
true man and to leave these rogues, I am the veriest varlet
that ever chewed with a tooth. Eight yards of uneven
ground is threescore-and-ten miles afoot with me, and
the stony-hearted villains know it well enough. A plague
upon it when thieves cannot be true one to another. (*They
whistle*) Whew! A plague upon you all! Give me my
horse, you rogues, give me my horse, and be hanged!

PRINCE HENRY (*coming forward*) Peace, ye fat-guts! Lie down.
Lay thine ear close to the ground and list if thou canst   30
hear the tread of travellers.

FALSTAFF Have you any levers to lift me up again, being
down? 'Sblood, I'll not bear my own flesh so far afoot
again for all the coin in thy father's exchequer. What a
plague mean ye to colt me thus?

PRINCE HENRY Thou liest. Thou art not colted, thou art un-
colted.

FALSTAFF I prithee, good Prince Hal, help me to my horse,
good king's son.

PRINCE HENRY Out, ye rogue, shall I be your ostler?   40

FALSTAFF Hang thyself in thine own heir-apparent garters!

---

21 as drink] Q0; as to drinke F1   26 upon it] Q0; vpon it F1   27 upon] Q0; light vpon
F1   me] Q0; *not in* F1   29 *coming forward*] DYCE; *not in* Q0   33 my] Q0; mine Q1–5, F1   41
Hang] Q0; Go hang Q3–5, F1

---

21 **as good a deed as drink** See note at
2.1.28 for this colloquial comparison.

21–2 **turn true man** reform, with anticipation also of turning informer (as at l. 42
below)

25–6 **A plague . . . another** 'What is the
world coming to, when not even thieves
can trust one another?' Falstaff gives a
comic twist to the proverb 'Thieves are
never rogues among themselves' (Dent
T121a). He himself hints more than once
at turning informer (ll. 21–2, 42).

27 **Whew** An interjection expressing Falstaff's disgust or relief (*OED*, *int.*), or perhaps the actual sound of whistling indicated in the stage directions. Wilson
(*NCS*) suggests that Falstaff 'mocks at the

whistling' of the others. Another comic
possibility is that he tries vainly (because
out of breath) to respond to the whistling
of Hal and Poins (Davison).

35 **colt** cheat, trick (followed by obvious
pun)

38 **help me to my horse** Falstaff means 'help
me to find my horse', but the Prince punningly takes it to mean 'help me to mount
my horse' as an ostler would do by holding the stirrup.

41 **Hang . . . garters** Falstaff modifies the
saying 'He may go hang himself in his
own garters' (Dent G42) by applying it to
Hal's position as heir apparent and as a
member of the Order of the Garter.

If I be ta'en, I'll peach for this. An I have not ballads made
on you all and sung to filthy tunes, let a cup of sack be my
poison. When a jest is so forward, and afoot too! I hate it.
        Enter Gadshill

GADSHILL Stand.

FALSTAFF So I do, against my will.

POINS (*coming forward with Bardolph and Peto*) O, 'tis our
setter. I know his voice.

⌈BARDOLPH⌉ What news?

⌈GADSHILL⌉ Case ye, case ye, on with your vizards. There's   50
money of the King's coming down the hill; 'tis going to
the King's Exchequer.

---

47 *coming ... Peto*] DYCE; *not in* QO   49 BARDOLPH What news?] JOHNSON; Bardoll, what newes.
(*continuing Poins's speech on the same line*) QO; *Bardolfe*, what newes? (*on a separate line*) F1
50 GADSHILL] JOHNSON; *Bar.* QO

---

42 **peach** appeach, inform, inform against ac-
complices, turn informer (suggested at
ll. 21–2 above)
  An if
  ballads The use of especially composed
ballads to castigate deplorable behaviour
was common. Helena, in *All's Well*, risks
'Tax of impudence, | A strumpet's bold-
ness, a divulgèd shame | Traduced by
odious ballads' if she fails to cure the King
(2.1.169–71). One could hire a ballad-
writer to accuse one's enemies thus, as is
proposed in Jonson's *Bartholomew Fair*
2.2.15–17. Such ballads were set to
familiar and appropriate tunes.

44 **When a jest is so forward** (a) when our
robbery plot is so well advanced (b) when
a practical joke is so presumptuous
  and afoot (a) on the move, well advanced; synonymous with *forward* (b) on
one's own feet as opposed to on horse-
back; continuing the sense of *forward* as
presumptuous practical joking

44.1 **Enter Gadshill** Some editors argue that
Bardolph enters here with Gadshill, but
see head-note to this scene and Introduction, p. 100.

45–6 **Stand . . . So I do** Gadshill's *Stand*
means to stay put, as in 'Stand and
deliver'; Falstaff plays on the sense of
standing erect on one's feet. Gadshill jestingly challenges them as though he were
about to rob them.

48 **setter** Thieves' cant for one who gathers

information and 'sets' the 'match', or encounter, between highwaymen and their
victims; see 1.2.101 and note. *OED*, 7a,
cites Greene, *Notable Discovery of Cozenage*
(1591), A4: 'There be requisite effectu-
ally to act the art of coney-catching three
several parties, the setter, the verser, and
the barnacle. The nature of the setter is to
draw any person familiarly to drink with
him', etc. (ed. Grosart, x. 15).
  I know his voice Gadshill is probably
masked, and Elizabethan stage conventions of darkness (as at 2.1.0.1 *lantern*
and note) further enable the spectators to
suppose him unrecognized at first by
Poins and the others.

49 BARDOLPH In QqF1 (see collation) Poins
is given the speech 'Bardoll [F1 : Bardolfe]
what newes', and the reply in ll. 50–2 is
assigned to '*Bar.*'; but surely Gadshill as
setter is the one to whom the question is
put and by whom the answer is supplied.
For a possible explanation of how the
compositor may have mistaken '*Bar.*' in
his copy for a form of address and then
compounded his error by changing '*Gad.*'
at l. 50 to '*Bar.*', see Introduction, p. 101.

50 **Case ye** Synonymous with 'on with your
vizards', or on with your masks.

52 **Exchequer** Revenue collected by sheriffs
and other officers (as distinguished from
pilgrims and franklins) would be paid into
the Exchequer (Cowl and Morgan); see
2.1.55 and note.

FALSTAFF You lie, ye rogue, 'tis going to the King's Tavern.

GADSHILL There's enough to make us all.

FALSTAFF To be hanged.

PRINCE HENRY Sirs, you four shall front them in the narrow
lane; Ned Poins and I will walk lower. If they scape from
your encounter, then they light on us.

PETO How many be there of them?

GADSHILL Some eight or ten.   60

FALSTAFF Zounds, will they not rob us?

PRINCE HENRY What, a coward, Sir John Paunch?

FALSTAFF Indeed, I am not John of Gaunt, your grandfather, but yet no coward, Hal.

PRINCE HENRY Well, we leave that to the proof.

POINS Sirrah Jack, thy horse stands behind the hedge.
When thou need'st him, there thou shalt find him.
Farewell, and stand fast.

FALSTAFF Now cannot I strike him, if I should be hanged.

PRINCE HENRY (*to Poins*) Ned, where are our disguises?   70

POINS (*to Prince Henry*) Here, hard by. Stand close.

⌐*Exeunt Prince and Poins*⌐

FALSTAFF Now, my masters, happy man be his dole, say I.
Every man to his business.

---

53 'tis] Q1; *scarcely present in* Q0   57 Poins] Q0; *not in* F1   65 Well] Q0; *not in* F1   we] Q0;
weele Q3   70 *to Poins*] COLLIER (*subs.*); *not in* Q0   71 *to Prince Henry*] DYCE (*subs.*); *not in*
Q0   71.1 *Exeunt Prince and Poins*] MALONE; *not in* Q0

---

53 **King's Tavern** On tavern names in this
play, see head-note to 2.4.

54 **make us all** make our fortunes (but Falstaff takes *make* in the sense of 'cause')

56 **front** confront

57 **lower** lower down

60 **eight or ten** Hal later recalls having seen
'four set on four' (2.4.245).

63 **Gaunt** i.e. Ghent, the birthplace of Henry
IV's father, with a familiar pun on *gaunt*,
thin, as in *Richard II* 2.1.73–84: 'Old
Gaunt indeed, and gaunt in being old',
and 2 *Henry IV* 3.2.312. Falstaff here
glances at Hal's thinness as well, as later
in 2.4.237–40 (Kittredge).

65 **proof** test

69 **Now . . . hanged** Falstaff laments that
Poins is too quick for him to repay the

practical joking with a blow.

71 **Stand close** QqF1 have no *Exeunt Prince
and Poins* at this juncture (see collation),
and, although such omissions of exits are
common elsewhere in QqF1, it is possible
that the Prince and Poins conceal themselves somewhere on-stage. QqF1 do
specify that the two *enter* at l. 86, but see
note at l. 91.2–3.

72 **happy man be his dole** A familiar
colloquial expression (Dent M158) meaning may each person's *dole*, or portion in
life, be that of a happy man. So in *Merry
Wives* 3.4.63, *Shrew* 1.1.137, and *Winter's Tale* 1.2.163.

73 **Every man to his business** Varying the
common phrase 'Every man as his business lies' (Dent M104).

Enter the Travellers

⌐FIRST TRAVELLER⌐ Come, neighbour. The boy shall lead our
   horses down the hill; we'll walk afoot awhile and ease our
   legs.

THIEVES Stand!

TRAVELLERS Jesus bless us!

FALSTAFF Strike! Down with them! Cut the villains'
   throats! Ah, whoreson caterpillars, bacon-fed knaves!   80
   They hate us youth. Down with them, fleece them!

TRAVELLERS O, we are undone, both we and ours for ever!

FALSTAFF Hang, ye gorbellied knaves, are ye undone? No,
   ye fat chuffs, I would your store were here! On, bacons,
   on! What, ye knaves, young men must live. You are
   grandjurors, are ye? We'll jure ye, 'faith.

Here they rob them and bind them. Exeunt.
Enter the Prince and Poins in buckram

PRINCE HENRY The thieves have bound the true men. Now
   could thou and I rob the thieves and go merrily to London, it would be argument for a week, laughter for a
   month, and a good jest for ever.   90

73.1 *the*] QO; *not in* FI   74 FIRST TRAVELLER] CAPELL; *Trauel.* QO   78 Jesus] QO; Iesu F
80 Ah,] QO (a‸)   83 are ye] QO; are you FI   86.1 *Exeunt*] QO; *not in* Q4–5, FI   86.2 *in
buckram*] HALLIWELL 1859 (*subs.*); *not in* QO

73.1 *Travellers* Evidently there should be
   four in number; at 2.4.245 Prince Henry
   recalls seeing four robbers set upon four
   travellers and bind them.
80 **whoreson** i.e. abominable, 'scurvy',
   'bloody'
   caterpillars parasites feeding on the commonwealth, a conventional metaphor
   found in *Richard II* 2.3.166 and 3.4.47,
   2 Henry VI 3.1.90 and 4.4.37, etc.; here
   suggesting the rapacity of the King's
   receivers. Most of Falstaff's terms 'are
   applicable to himself' (Wilson, *NCS*).
   bacon-fed knaves i.e. overfed, fat country
   bumpkins, as in *bacons*, l. 84
81 **us youth** The claim is comically absurd
   on the face of it, and yet Falstaff's sanguine temperament is associated with
   heat and moisture, the qualities of youth;
   see note at 2.4.234–5 and note on *stockfish* at 2.4.238.
83 **gorbellied** fat-bellied
84 **chuffs** i.e. coarse churlish persons, misers
   (compare *knaves*, ll. 80 and 83)
   store total wealth
86 **grandjurors** Only the 'good and lawful

man of a county' (*OED*) who owned land,
such as the *franklin* of 2.1.52 (see note),
might sit on a grand jury.
   jure ye A play on words common in
comic or threatening retort. Wright cites
Merry Wives 4.2.160–1: 'MRS. PAGE
Come, Mother Prat, come, give me your
hand. FORD I'll prat her!' Similarly in
Coriolanus 2.1.121, Menenius says: 'I
would not have been so fidiused [i.e.
beaten as Aufidius deserves] for all the
chests in Corioles.'
86.2 *Enter . . . buckram* The Prince and
Poins may come forward from hiding, as
suggested at l. 71 above and 91.2–3
below. Hence this edition does not mark a
new scene.
87 **thieves . . . true men** Continuing the
antithesis at ll. 21–2 above and 2.1.63
(see note), with a glance at the proverb
'One true man is too hard for two thieves'
(Dent T119.1).
89 **argument** a subject of conversation. See
2.4.271 and *Timon* 3.3.20: 'So it may
prove an argument of laughter.'

POINS Stand close. I hear them coming.
        They stand aside.
        Enter the thieves (Falstaff, Bardolph, Peto and
        Gadshill) again
FALSTAFF Come, my masters, let us share, and then to horse
    before day. An the Prince and Poins be not two arrant
    cowards, there's no equity stirring. There's no more
    valour in that Poins than in a wild duck.
        The thieves begin to share the booty
PRINCE HENRY *(coming forward)* Your money!
POINS Villains!
        As they are sharing, the Prince and Poins set upon
        them. They all run away, and Falstaff, after a blow or
        two, runs away too, leaving the booty behind them
PRINCE HENRY
    Got with much ease. Now merrily to horse.
    The thieves are all scattered and possessed with fear
    So strongly that they dare not meet each other;   100
    Each takes his fellow for an officer.
    Away, good Ned. Falstaff sweats to death,
    And lards the lean earth as he walks along.
    Were't not for laughing, I should pity him.
POINS How the fat rogue roared!   *Exeunt*

91.1 *They stand aside*] DYCE *(subs.)*; *not in* QO   91.2 *the*] QO; *not in* F1   *(Falstaff, Bardolph, Peto,*
and Gadshill)] DYCE; *not in* QO   95.1 *The thieves begin to share the booty*] This edition; *not in*
QO   96 *coming forward*] CAPELL *(subs.)*; *not in* QO   97.2–3 *and . . . too*] QO; *not in*
F1   98–104 Got . . . him] *as verse*, POPE; *as prose*, QO

91.2–3 *Enter the thieves . . . again* We need
    not suppose that Falstaff and his com-
    panions return to share the booty on the
    spot where they assaulted the travellers.
    The entering of the Prince and Poins at
    l. 86 after the exeunt of the thieves does
    not necessarily call for an empty stage,
    since the Prince can later report that 'We
    two saw you four set on four and bound
    them' (2.4.245–6), and in the present
    scene the Prince similarly observes that
    'The thieves have bound the true men';
    yet the fluid conventions of evoking locale
    on the Elizabethan stage permit us to
    imagine the Prince and Poins lying in
    wait for the thieves along their
    subsequent path. We are not told what is

    done with the victims of the robbery.
94 **no equity stirring** no discerning judge-
    ment anywhere to be found
98–104 **Got . . . him** Printed as prose in
    QqF1 (see collation); but Shakespeare's
    intention to end a comic prose scene with
    a metrical speech by Hal, thereby re-
    inforcing his royal status, as in 1.2 and 3.3
    (see also 5.3.39–54), seems evident. Most
    editors have followed Pope's arrangement
    of the lines.
101 **Each . . . officer** Varying the proverbial
    phrase 'The thief does fear each bush an
    officer' (Dent T112).
103 **lards** (as though his sweat were fat
    melted out of his body by exercise; a com-
    mon view)

2.3   *Enter Hotspur solus, reading a letter*   2/22

HOTSPUR 'But, for mine own part, my lord, I could be well
     contented to be there, in respect of the love I bear your
     house.' He could be contented; why is he not, then? In
     respect of the love he bears our house! He shows in this,
     he loves his own barn better than he loves our house. Let
     me see some more. 'The purpose you undertake is dan-
     gerous'—why, that's certain. 'Tis dangerous to take a
     cold, to sleep, to drink; but I tell you, my lord fool, out of
     this nettle, danger, we pluck this flower, safety. 'The
     purpose you undertake is dangerous, the friends you have   10
     named uncertain, the time itself unsorted, and your
     whole plot too light for the counterpoise of so great an
     opposition.' Say you so, say you so? I say unto you again,
     you are a shallow, cowardly hind, and you lie. What a
     lack-brain is this! By the Lord, our plot is a good plot as
     ever was laid, our friends true and constant; a good plot,
     good friends, and full of expectation; an excellent plot,
     very good friends. What a frosty-spirited rogue is this!
     Why, my lord of York commends the plot and the general
     course of the action. Zounds, an I were now by this rascal,   20
     I could brain him with his lady's fan. Is there not my
     father, my uncle, and myself? Lord Edmund Mortimer,
     my lord of York, and Owen Glendower? Is there not
     besides the Douglas? Have I not all their letters to meet me
     in arms by the ninth of the next month, and are they not
     some of them set forward already? What a pagan rascal

2.3.3.4 In respect] F1; in the respect Q1   15 a good] Q1; as good a F1   20 Zounds, an] Q1
(Zoundes and); By this hand, if F1

2.3 The traditional location of this scene (by
     Capell) at Warkworth Castle in Northum-
     berland, principal seat of the Percy family,
     is historically plausible. In the theatre we
     know only that Hotspur is at home, and
     on the verge of departure.
  1 For the remainder of the play, the text is
     based on Q1.
  1–13 **But . . . opposition** See Appendix for
     Holinshed.
  3 **house** family (but Hotspur plays on the
     sense of a dwelling, as distinguished from
     a *barn* (l. 5)
  8–9 **out . . . safety** Varying the proverbial
     sayings 'Danger itself the best remedy for

     danger' (Dent D30), 'To pluck a flower
     from among nettles' (F388.1), and 'Dan-
     ger and delight grow both upon one stalk'
     (Tilley D28).
  11 **unsorted** unsuitable
  12 **for the counterpoise of** to counterbalance
  14 **hind** menial, rustic
  17 **expectation** promise, prospects
  19–20 **my lord . . . action** See Appendix for
     Holinshed.
  21 **fan** (made of feathers at this time and
     hence very light; or else the handle of the
     fan)
  24 **all their** from them all
  26 **pagan** infidel, unbelieving

is this, an infidel! Ha, you shall see now in very sincerity
of fear and cold heart will he to the King and lay open all
our proceedings. O, I could divide myself and go to buffets
for moving such a dish of skim milk with so honourable   30
an action. Hang him, let him tell the King, we are
prepared. I will set forward tonight.

    Enter Lady Percy

How now, Kate? I must leave you within these two hours.

LADY PERCY

O my good lord, why are you thus alone?
For what offence have I this fortnight been
A banished woman from my Harry's bed?
Tell me, sweet lord, what is't that takes from thee
Thy stomach, pleasure, and thy golden sleep?
Why dost thou bend thine eyes upon the earth,
And start so often when thou sitt'st alone?   40
Why hast thou lost the fresh blood in thy cheeks,
And given my treasures and my rights of thee
To thick-eyed musing and cursed melancholy?
In thy faint slumbers I by thee have watched,
And heard thee murmur tales of iron wars,
Speak terms of *manège* to thy bounding steed,
Cry, 'Courage! To the field!' And thou hast talked
Of sallies and retires, of trenches, tents,

---

30 skim milk] Q1; skim'd Milk F1   32 forward] Q1; forwards F1   32.1 *Enter Lady Percy*]
ROWE; *Enter his Lady* Q1   45 thee] Q2; the Q1   46 *manège*] Q1 (mannage)

---

29 **divide . . . buffets** divide myself in two,
  each part cuffing the other
30 **moving** urging
  skim milk (first recorded use in *OED*)
33 **Kate** Lady Percy was historically Elizabeth
  Mortimer (1371?–1444), elder sister of
  Sir Edmund de Mortimer (who married
  Glendower's daughter) and aunt of the
  fifth Earl of March. See Appendix, 1.1.38.
  Her name seems to have caused confusion,
  for Holinshed calls her 'Elianor' (184) as
  does Hall.
34 **why are you thus alone** In *Caesar* 2.1,
  Brutus is similarly implored by his anxious
  wife not to remain alone, melancholically
  preoccupied with cares, but to share his
  troubles with a courageous and noble wife.
  This present scene differs, however, in
  using witty comedy to define the relationship of husband and wife.
38 **stomach** appetite
  golden precious
42 **given . . . thee** abandoned my precious
  rights as a wife to have some of your time
  and attention (Wilson, *NCS*)
43 **thick-eyed** characterized by vacant star-
  ing
  cursed bad-tempered
44 **faint** light, restless
  watched lain awake
46 *manège* (Q1, 'mannage', is a variant
  spelling) horsemanship
48 **retires** retreats, i.e. the recalling of a pursuing force, or giving ground before the
  enemy

Of palisadoes, frontiers, parapets,
Of basilisks, of cannon, culverin,   50
Of prisoners' ransom, and of soldiers slain,
And all the currents of a heady fight.
Thy spirit within thee hath been so at war,
And thus hath so bestirred thee in thy sleep,
That beads of sweat have stood upon thy brow
Like bubbles in a late-disturbèd stream,
And in thy face strange motions have appeared,
Such as we see when men restrain their breath
On some great sudden hest. O, what portents are these?
Some heavy business hath my lord in hand,   60
And I must know it, else he loves me not.
HOTSPUR
    What ho!
            Enter a Servant
            Is Gilliams with the packet gone?
SERVANT He is, my lord, an hour ago.
HOTSPUR
    Hath Butler brought those horses from the sheriff?
SERVANT
    One horse, my lord, he brought even now.

---

51 prisoners' ransom] Q1 (prisoners ransome); prisoners ransom'd DYCE 1864 *(conj.*
CAPELL)   62 *Enter a Servant*] DERING MS *(after l. 61); as here,* CAPELL; *not in* Q1   63 ago] Q1;
agone F1

49 **palisadoes** defences made of stakes fixed
   in the ground
   frontiers ramparts, fortifications, as at
   1.3.19 (see note)
50 **basilisks** large cannon, named for the
   fabulous serpent whose breath and look
   were considered fatal
   culverin a smaller cannon, originally a
   firearm, later a long cannon; also named
   for a serpent (French *coulevrine*, from
   couleuvre; compare Latin *colubrinus*, of the
   nature of a snake)
51 **prisoners' ransom** See collation. Capell
   conjectures that 'prisoners ransome' in
   QqF1 is an error for 'prisoners ransom'd'
   (the common 'e/d' misprint), and hence a
   parallel to 'soldiers slain' (Humphreys).
52 **currents** eddies, movements
   heady headlong

56 **late-disturbèd stream** water recently
   stirred up
57 **motions** (a) facial gestures (b) emotions
   (Kittredge)
59 **hest** behest, command (as in all other
   uses in Shakespeare; compare *Tempest*
   1.2.274, 3.1.37, and 4.1.65), but possibly meaning 'purpose, determination'
   (*OED*, 3, suggested by Cowl and Morgan).
   West, 331, proposes 'heft', heaving.
   portents (stress on second syllable)
60 **heavy** weighty and sorrowful
62 **packet** letter, dispatch, essential to the
   conspiracy; see 1.3.291 and 2.3.24.
64 **sheriff** a shire official (not a policeman)
   whose peace-keeping responsibilities might
   include those of bailiff or overseer
65 **even** just

HOTSPUR

What horse? Roan, a crop-ear, is it not?

SERVANT

It is, my lord.

HOTSPUR   That roan shall be my throne.

Well, I will back him straight. O Esperance!

Bid Butler lead him forth into the park.   *Exit Servant*

LADY PERCY But hear you, my lord.   70

HOTSPUR What sayst thou, my lady?

LADY PERCY What is it carries you away?

HOTSPUR Why, my horse, my love, my horse.

LADY PERCY Out, you mad-headed ape!

A weasel hath not such a deal of spleen

As you are tossed with. In faith,

I'll know your business, Harry, that I will.

I fear my brother Mortimer doth stir

About his title, and hath sent for you

To line his enterprise; but if you go—   80

---

66 Roan,] Q1–2 (Roane?); a roane? Q3   68–9 Well . . . park] *as verse, POPE; as prose, continuing from previous line,* Q1   69 *Exit Servant*] DERING MS; *not in* Q1   74–85 Out . . . true] *as verse,* CAPELL; *as prose,* Q1

66 **roan** a horse of roan colour, one in which the prevailing colour (bay, sorrel, chestnut) is thickly interspersed with white or grey. Compare *Henry V* 3.7.18: 'He's of the colour of the nutmeg.' Richard II's horse is 'roan Barbary' (5.5.78). Hotspur's roan horse is mentioned again at 2.4.104. Shakespeare's fondness for roan horses is discussed in Madden, 260–2. Q3's improvement of the metre (see collation), in a quarto with no independent authority and in a passage of mixed prose and occasionally uneven verse, must be questioned.

67–85 **It is . . . true** See collation. QqF1 render this entire passage in prose, perhaps to conserve space; see Introduction, p. 104.

68 **O Esperance!** The Percy motto was *Esperance*, 'hope', or *Esperance ma comforte*. See 5.2.96 and note (Humphreys).

72 **carries you away** Lady Percy means 'transports you beyond the bounds of reason and judgement', but Hotspur replies punningly in the literal sense.

75 **weasel** 'As angry (etc.) as a weasel' is a common comparison (Dent W211.1). See *Cymbeline* 3.4.158: 'As quarrelous as the weasel'.

spleen This notion of a governing humour in Hotspur recurs in 5.2.19: 'A hare-brained Hotspur governed by a spleen'. The spleen was often regarded by Shakespeare and his contemporaries as the seat of sudden impulse and laughter (e.g. *Shrew*, Induction 1.134), but the idea of caprice (*Venus* 907) also lent itself to nervous excitability and arrogance (Bamborough, 60). Prince Hal, too, is associated with spleen, at 3.2.125. On Hotspur's *choler*, see 1.3.129 and note.

78 **my brother Mortimer** Lady Percy was indeed elder sister to Sir Edmund de Mortimer, but the fifth Earl of March, whom Richard II named as heir presumptive to the throne, was her nephew; see 3.1.191 where Mortimer calls her his 'Aunt Percy'. On Shakespeare's conflating of these two Edmunds, following Daniel and Holinshed, see Appendix 1.1.38.

80 **line** strengthen, reinforce with a second layer as one lines a garment, as in *Henry V* 2.4.7: 'To line and new-repair our towns of war'.

go She means 'depart', but he again replies quibblingly, in the sense of 'walk'; compare l. 72 and note.

HOTSPUR

So far afoot I shall be weary, love.

LADY PERCY

Come, come, you paraquito, answer me
Directly unto this question that I ask.
In faith, I'll break thy little finger, Harry,
An if thou wilt not tell me all things true.

HOTSPUR

Away, away, you trifler! Love? I love thee not;
I care not for thee, Kate. This is no world
To play with mammets and to tilt with lips.
We must have bloody noses and cracked crowns,
And pass them current too. Gods me, my horse!   90
What sayst thou, Kate? What wouldst thou have with
    me?

LADY PERCY

Do you not love me? Do you not indeed?
Well, do not then, for since you love me not
I will not love myself. Do you not love me?
Nay, tell me if you speak in jest or no.

HOTSPUR Come, wilt thou see me ride?
And when I am a-horseback, I will swear

---

85 An ... true] Q1 ; if thou wilt not tel me true F1   92 you ... you] Q1 ; ye ... ye F1   95 you
speak] Q1 ; thou speak'st F1

---

82 **paraquito** little parrot; a term of endearment, but recalling the *popinjay* of 1.3.50
(see note) and the *starling* of 1.3.223,
both incessant talkers like Hotspur.

84 **break thy little finger** A lover's pinch, or
wringing. Compare *How a Man May
Choose a Good Wife from a Bad*, 1602 (ed.
A. E. Swaen, Louvain, 1912, l. 405):
'And still my love I by the finger wrung'.

85 **An if** if

86 **Love** Hotspur returns at length to the
question posed by Lady Percy at l. 61.

88 **mammets** dolls or puppets, originally
false gods or idols; from Mahomet, or
Mohammed. Compare *Romeo* 3.5.185:
'A whining mammet, in her fortune's
tender'. Partridge's conjecture of a play
on the Latin *mamma*, a familiar term in
Shakespeare's time for a woman's breast
(*OED, mamma, sb.* 2), is strengthened by
Hotspur's insistent jesting about child-
hood games. This is no time to play with

dolls or nubile girls, he jokes, nor is it time
to kiss them or banter with them in the
delightful war of the sexes.
  tilt contend in kissing or arguing, as in a
tournament

89 **crowns** (a) heads (b) coins valued at 5s.
French crowns, the original coin, were
still current in sixteenth-century England. See *Henry V* 4.1.216–17: 'It is no
English treason to cut French crowns.'

90 **pass them current** (a) use them freely,
crack heads often (b) pass off cracked
coins as sterling. Hotspur, wryly continuing the metaphor of boyhood games, says
that boys turned men in battle must expect the equivalent of boys' bloody noses
and cracked heads, i.e. the serious
wounds of warfare, and must give as good
as they get, thereby keeping *cracked
crowns* (l. 89) in currency.
  Gods me God save me

I love thee infinitely. But hark you, Kate,
I must not have you henceforth question me
Whither I go, nor reason whereabout.   100
Whither I must, I must; and, to conclude,
This evening must I leave you, gentle Kate.
I know you wise, but yet no farther wise
Than Harry Percy's wife; constant you are,
But yet a woman; and for secrecy
No lady closer, for I well believe
Thou wilt not utter what thou dost not know,
And so far will I trust thee, gentle Kate.

LADY PERCY How, so far?

HOTSPUR

Not an inch further. But hark you, Kate: 110
Whither I go, thither shall you go too.
Today will I set forth, tomorrow you.
Will this content you, Kate?

LADY PERCY   It must of force.   *Exeunt*

2.4   *Enter the Prince and Poins*

PRINCE HENRY Ned, prithee come out of that fat room, and
lend me thy hand to laugh a little.

---

102 you] Q1; thee F1   103 farther] Q1; further F1   2.4.0 *the*] *not in* Q1

---

100 **reason whereabout** question what my
business is

107 **Thou... know** Compare the proverb 'A
woman conceals what she knows not'
(Dent W649, and similar formulations in
S196 and W706.1). The jest is at least as
old as the elder Seneca's *Controversiae*
(Humphreys).

110 **Not an inch** A common comparison
(Dent I 52).

111 **Whither...too** Hotspur echoes (though
from a male point of view) Ruth's vow to
Naomi in Ruth 1: 16: 'Whither thou
goest, I will go also' (Davison).

113 **of force** perforce

2.4 Location: This scene takes place in
Eastcheap; see ll. 14 and 425, anticipated
by 1.2.123, 148, and 180, and *Famous
Victories*, where Hal and his companions
frequent 'the old tavern in Eastcheap'
(l. 87). The gathering-place for Hal and
Falstaff's merriment is repeatedly called a

'tavern' (see 1.2.39, 47, 2.2.53, 3.3.41
and 3.3.198), and tables and chairs are
required as props for this scene. Falstaff
speaks in 2.2.53 as though the place were
called the 'King's Tavern', for it is there
that the stolen money is to be taken; but
perhaps the phrase derives from a play on
'King's Exchequer' (2.2.52). Tradition
identifies the tavern as the Boar's Head,
and points to *2 Henry IV* 2.2.140 where,
in response to Hal's question 'Doth the old
boar feed in the old frank', Bardolph
replies: 'At the old place, my lord, in
Eastcheap'. The Boar's Head was a well-
known tavern on the north side of Great
Eastcheap.

1 **fat** Possible meanings include 'vat' (as in
*OED, fat, sb.*¹ 2 and in *Antony* 2.7.113:
'In thy fats our cares be drowned'), or
well-stocked (*OED, a.* and *sb.*² 10), or
stuffy, close, thick, greasy.

POINS Where hast been, Hal?

PRINCE HENRY With three or four loggerheads amongst
three or four score hogsheads. I have sounded the very
bass string of humility. Sirrah, I am sworn brother to a
leash of drawers, and can call them all by their Christian
names, as Tom, Dick, and Francis. They take it already
upon their salvation that, though I be but Prince of
Wales, yet I am the king of courtesy, and tell me flatly I   10
am no proud Jack like Falstaff, but a Corinthian, a lad of
mettle, a 'good boy'—by the Lord, so they call me!—and
when I am king of England I shall command all the good
lads in Eastcheap. They call drinking deep, dyeing scarlet;
and when you breathe in your watering they cry 'hem!'

7 them all] Q1; them F1   Christian] Q1 (christen); *not in* F1   10 and tell] Q1; telling F1
15 they] Q1; then they F1

4 **loggerheads** blockheads; a *logger* is a
block of wood used to hobble horses
5 **hogsheads** Hal has been in the wine
cellar with the *drawers*, or tapsters (l. 7).
Dekker, in *Gull's Horn-Book* (1609),
mockingly urges gallants to 'accept of the
courtesy of the cellar when 'tis offered you
by the drawers' (ed. Grosart, ii. 260, cited
by Hemingway), implying that to do so is
ungentlemanly.
6 **humility** baseness, low condition (not
humbleness of mind)
  sworn brother intimate friend, from the
oath taken by two companions in arms to
share good and bad fortune
7 **leash** a set of three—usually hounds,
hawks, foxes, etc. (a sporting term)
7–8 **Christian names** Dekker, *Gull's Horn-
Book* (ii. 256), sardonically instructs the
tavern-frequenting gallant (see note at
l. 5 above): 'Your first compliment shall
be to grow most inwardly acquainted
with the drawers, to learn their names, as
Jack, and Will, and Tom.'
8 **Tom, Dick, and Francis** Perhaps an
intentional and comic variation on the
phrase 'Tom, Dick, and Harry' conventionally used to refer to any men taken at
random from the common run. The substitution of 'Francis' for 'Harry' may be
funny because the Prince's own name is
Harry. *OED* does not cite any use of 'Tom,
Dick, and Harry' before 1815, but in the
final song of *LLL*, 'Dick the shepherd' and
'Tom' bearing logs are presented as men
having conventional names, and Eric
Rasmussen has pointed out to me that in

The First Part of the Contention (1594), the
writer/reporter introduces two characters
to accompany 'Dicke the Butcher' named
'Harry' and 'Tom' (4.2.27 ff.).
8–9 **take...salvation** already maintain it as
they hope to be saved (Wright)
10 **king** nonpareil (Dent K65.1)
11 **Jack** (a) Jack Falstaff (b) fellow, knave, as
in *Richard III* 1.3.71–2: 'Since every Jack
became a gentleman, | There's many a
gentle person made a Jack'
  Corinthian jolly companion (from the
proverbial luxury and licentiousness of
ancient Corinth). A cant term like *Trojans*
(see 2.1.67 and note) and *Ephesians* (*2
Henry IV* 2.2.143, *Merry Wives* 4.5.16).
11–12 **lad of mettle** A familiar expression
after Shakespeare (Dent M908.1).
14 **dyeing scarlet** Perhaps said thus because
drinking reddens the complexion; compare the 'purple-hued malt-worms' of
2.1.72–3 and Bardolph's fiery complexion at 2.4.302–15 and elsewhere.
Drinking deep also produced urine (as in
Macbeth 2.3.29), and the use of urine in
the fixing of dyes suggests another possible meaning. Wilson (*NCS*) cites authority for the belief that 'Topers' urine was
supposed to make the best scarlet dye'.
Seemingly a familiar expression after
Shakespeare (Dent D659.1).
15 **breathe . . . 'hem!'** pause for breath in
your drinking—a lack of expertise in
toping that evokes an admonitory 'hem!'.
Compare Shallow in *2 Henry IV* 3.2.212:
'Our watchword was "Hem boys!"'—
i.e. 'down the hatch'. *Watering* is a term

and bid you play it off. To conclude, I am so good a
proficient in one quarter of an hour that I can drink with
any tinker in his own language during my life. I tell thee,
Ned, thou hast lost much honour that thou wert not with
me in this action. But, sweet Ned—to sweeten which   20
name of Ned, I give thee this pennyworth of sugar,
clapped even now into my hand by an under-skinker, one
that never spake other English in his life than 'Eight shillings and sixpence', and 'You are welcome', with this
shrill addition, 'Anon, anon, sir! Score a pint of bastard in
the Half-moon', or so—but Ned, to drive away the time
till Falstaff come, I prithee do thou stand in some by-
room, while I question my puny drawer to what end he
gave me the sugar; and do thou never leave calling 'Francis', that his tale to me may be nothing but 'Anon'. Step   30
aside and I'll show thee a precedent.   ⌜*Exit Poins*⌝

31 precedent] F1 (Prefident); prefent Q1   *Exit Poins*] THEOBALD (*subs.*); *not in* Q1

usually applied to animals' drinking (*OED*, 6). Or it may mean 'urinating', and *breathe* may mean 'break wind', make audible sound (*OED*, 7; Davison).
16 **play it off** finish, drink up; or discharge, let off (*OED*, *v.* 6c)
18 **tinker** Tinkers were noted both for drinking and for cant speech, like Christopher Sly in *Shrew*, Induction 2.19 and 71, a drunkard and 'by present profession a tinker'.
20 **action** engagement, as with an enemy; hence the *honour* that Poins has lost for not being there. At 3.3.2 Falstaff speaks of the Gad's Hill robbery as an *action*.
21 **sugar** Used to sweeten wine, as noted at 1.2.3, 1.2.107, and 2.4.453. Hemingway cites Dekker, *Gull's Horn-Book*: 'Inquire what gallants sup in the next room, and, if they be any of your acquaintance, do not you (after the city fashion) send them in a pottle of wine; and your name, sweetened in two pitiful papers of sugar, with some filthy apology crammed into the mouth of a drawer' (ed. Grosart, ii. 258–9).
22 **under-skinker** A *skinker* is one who draws, pours, and serves liquor; a tapster, as in Thomas Heywood, *2 Fair Maid of the West* (1631), Act 4: 'I'll see an I can be entertained to my old trade of drawing wine; if't be but an under skinker, I care

not' (Pearson reprint, ii. 354). First recorded use in *OED*.
25 **Anon** right away, coming, as at 2.1.4. Compare Nashe, *Summer's Last Will and Testament* (1592): 'Why, friend, I am no tapster to say anon, anon, sir' (ll. 822–3), and citations from *The Unfortunate Traveller* (1594) in Wilson, *NCS*, 193.
   Score tally as a tavern reckoning. (Said to the vintner, who is distributing drinks and keeping track of the amounts.)
   bastard a sweet Spanish wine, considered a mongrel, or adulterated, wine, as at l. 70 below
26 **Half-moon** i.e. a room in the inn, like *Pomgarnet* at l. 36
27–8 **by-room** side room (first recorded use in *OED*)
28 **puny** raw, inexperienced; compare young Talbot's 'puny sword' in *1 Henry VI* 4.7.36. A phonetic spelling of *puisne*, junior, applied to the younger-born and to new students, hence here to an *under-skinker* (l. 22).
31 **precedent** i.e. a jest that will set the tune for what follows
   Exit Poins Q1 indicates a re-entry for Poins after the jest with Francis is completed (l. 83.1). He probably exits here at l. 31, but could exit at l. 34 or might simply retire backstage without a complete exit.

POINS (*within*) Francis!

PRINCE HENRY Thou art perfect.

POINS (*within*) Francis!

    Enter Francis, a Drawer

FRANCIS Anon, anon, sir. (*Calling*) Look down into the
    Pomgarnet, Ralph.

PRINCE HENRY Come hither, Francis.

FRANCIS My lord?

PRINCE HENRY How long hast thou to serve, Francis?

FRANCIS Forsooth, five years, and as much as to—   40

POINS (*within*) Francis!

FRANCIS Anon, anon, sir.

PRINCE HENRY Five year! By'r lady, a long lease for the
    clinking of pewter. But Francis, darest thou be so valiant
    as to play the coward with thy indenture and show it a
    fair pair of heels and run from it?

FRANCIS O Lord, sir, I'll be sworn upon all the books in
    England, I could find in my heart—

POINS (*within*) Francis!

FRANCIS Anon, sir.   50

PRINCE HENRY How old art thou, Francis?

FRANCIS Let me see: about Michaelmas next I shall be—

POINS (*within*) Francis!

FRANCIS Anon, sir. Pray stay a little, my lord.

32, 34 *within*] DYCE; *not in* Q1   34 POINS] Q4; *Prin.* Q1   34.1 *Francis, a*] ROWE (*subs.*); *not in*
Q1   35 *Calling*] This edition; *not in* Q1   41, 49, 53, 60, 74 *within*] CAPELL; *not in* Q1
50 Anon] Q1; Anon, anon F1

---

33 **Thou art perfect** you have learned your
    part

35 **Look down into** go down and look into

36 **Pomgarnet** An old form of *Pomegranate*,
    here the name of a room, like *Half-moon* in
    l. 26.

39 **serve** i.e. serve out an apprenticeship,
    normally of seven years. If Francis has
    served two years, he is presumably four-
    teen or sixteen (Wilson, *NCS*).

43 **By'r lady** by Our Lady
    lease term of contract

45 **indenture** contract (here, of appren-
    ticeship). See 1.3.87 and note for the
    word's literal meaning, and for a passage
    in which indenture is associated (as here)
    with cowardice.

45–6 **show . . . heels** A familiar expression
    (Dent P31), as in *Henry V* 3.5.34. Hal's
    joke is to tantalize the drawer with the
    prospect of a situation in the Prince's
    household, and then to arrange matters
    with Poins so that Francis repeatedly
    interrupts the impending offer with his
    parrot-like response of 'Anon' (Wilson,
    NCS). See Introduction p. 60–1.

47 **books** Bibles, as in *Merry Wives* 1.4.130:
    'I'll be sworn on a book she loves you'

48 **find in my heart** Francis seems on the
    verge of agreeing eagerly.

52 **Michaelmas** the Feast of Michael the
    Archangel, 29 September

54 **stay a little** wait a moment, be patient

PRINCE HENRY Nay, but hark you, Francis: for the sugar
   thou gavest me, 'twas a pennyworth, was't not?
FRANCIS O Lord, I would it had been two!
PRINCE HENRY I will give thee for it a thousand pound. Ask
   me when thou wilt, and thou shalt have it.
POINS (*within*) Francis!   60
FRANCIS Anon, anon.
PRINCE HENRY Anon, Francis? No, Francis; but tomorrow,
   Francis, or, Francis, o' Thursday, or indeed, Francis,
   when thou wilt. But, Francis—
FRANCIS My lord?
PRINCE HENRY Wilt thou rob this leathern-jerkin, crystal-
   button, not-pated, agate-ring, puke-stocking, caddis-
   garter, smooth-tongue, Spanish-pouch—
FRANCIS O Lord, sir, who do you mean?
PRINCE HENRY Why then your brown bastard is your only   70
   drink; for look you, Francis, your white canvas doublet
   will sully. In Barbary, sir, it cannot come to so much.
FRANCIS What, sir?
POINS (*within*) Francis!
PRINCE HENRY Away, you rogue, dost thou not hear them
   call?
         Here they both call him; the Drawer stands amazed,
         not knowing which way to go.

57 O Lord] Q1 ; O Lord sir F1   75 not hear] Q1 ; heare F1   76.3 *the] not in* Q1

66 **rob** i.e. rob your master of your services,
   by breaking your indenture
66–68 **leathern-jerkin . . . Spanish-pouch**
   Hal satirically composes the 'character' of
   a London citizen, one who wears a close-
   fitting jacket with crystal buttons, goes
   not-pated (i.e. with close-cropped hair
   (*OED, not, a.* 1)), wears rings mounted
   with agates carved in small figures for
   seals, has stockings of *puke* (i.e. heavy and
   superior woollen cloth in bluish grey),
   secures his stockings with *caddis* (i.e.
   worsted tape garters), speaks in the
   flattering and ingratiating manner of a
   small entrepreneur, and has a Spanish-
   leather wallet at his side.
70–2 **Why . . . much** Hal bewilders the poor
   Francis with a mystifying speech of non-

sense, but he may also imply that Francis,
having passed up in return for a
pennyworth of sugar an offer that could
not be matched even in Barbary in
Northern Africa from which so much
sugar comes (Wilson, *NCS*), is doomed by
his lack of resolution to endure this tavern
world of brown bastard wine in which his
white canvas jacket will look more and
more stained. Alternatively, Hal may be
consoling Francis with the thought that
he is better off in the tavern, for his canvas
doublet would be out of place in a wan-
derer's life.
70–1 **your . . . drink** this sweet wine that
   people talk about is the only drink worth
   mentioning. On *your* see 2.1.19 and note.
76.1 *amazed* in a maze, dumbfounded

Enter the Vintner

VINTNER What stand'st thou still and hear'st such a calling? Look to the guests within.   *Exit Francis*
My lord, old Sir John, with half a dozen more, are at the
door. Shall I let them in?   80
PRINCE HENRY Let them alone awhile, and then open the
door.   *Exit Vintner*
Poins!

Enter Poins

POINS Anon, anon, sir.
PRINCE HENRY Sirrah, Falstaff and the rest of the thieves are
at the door. Shall we be merry?
POINS As merry as crickets, my lad. But hark ye, what cun-
ning match have you made with this jest of the drawer?
Come, what's the issue?
PRINCE HENRY I am now of all humours that have showed   90
themselves humours since the old days of Goodman
Adam to the pupil age of this present twelve o'clock at
midnight.

Enter Francis, hurrying across the stage with wine
What's o'clock, Francis?
FRANCIS Anon, anon, sir.   ⌈*Exit*⌉
PRINCE HENRY That ever this fellow should have fewer
words than a parrot, and yet the son of a woman! His
industry is upstairs and downstairs, his eloquence the

78 *Exit Francis*] JOHNSON (*Exit Drawer*); *not in* Q1   82 *Exit Vintner*] THEOBALD (*subs., placed at
l. 83*); *not in* Q1   93.1 *Enter ... wine*] CAPELL (*Re-enter Drawer, with Bottles*); DERING MS *has
Francis speak from within*; *not in* Q1   95 *Exit*] COLLIER; *not in* Q1

76.3 **Vintner** i.e. innkeeper or landlord
(literally wine dealer)
77 **What** why, as at 2.1.64. The comma
added in Q2–5F1 and by subsequent early
editors (excepting those of F3–4) is lacking in authority, and unnecessary.
87 **As merry as crickets** A familiar comparison (Dent C825).
88 **match** contest
89 **the issue** the point of it all. The *issue* of a
match would be its outcome.
90–3 **I am ... midnight** My present mood or
humour embraces all states of mind and
temperament and all capricious inclina-

tions (*humours*) that have formed any part
of human experience on this earth. Hal
responds elliptically to Poins's query
about the point of the jest by insisting that
he is ready for any sort of fun.
91 **Goodman** yeoman (referring perhaps to
the saying 'When Adam delved and Eve
span who was then the gentleman?' Dent
A30), head of household; vague title of
dignity
92 **pupil** infant (as contrasted with *the old
days*)
98 **upstairs and downstairs** (first recorded
uses in *OED*)

parcel of a reckoning. I am not yet of Percy's mind, the
Hotspur of the north, he that kills me some six or seven   100
dozen of Scots at a breakfast, washes his hands, and says
to his wife, 'Fie upon this quiet life, I want work.' 'O my
sweet Harry,' says she, 'how many hast thou killed
today?' 'Give my roan horse a drench,' says he, and
answers, 'Some fourteen,' an hour after, 'a trifle, a trifle.'
I prithee call in Falstaff. I'll play Percy, and that damned
brawn shall play Dame Mortimer his wife. 'Rivo!' says
the drunkard. Call in ribs, call in tallow.

    Enter Falstaff, Gadshill, Bardolph, and Peto;
    Francis following with wine

POINS Welcome, Jack. Where hast thou been?
FALSTAFF A plague of all cowards, I say, and a vengeance   110
too! Marry and amen! Give me a cup of sack, boy. Ere I
lead this life long, I'll sew netherstocks, and mend them

108.1 *Gadshill, Bardolph, and Peto*] THEOBALD; *not in* Q1   108.2 *Francis . . . wine*] *in the* DERING
MS *Dering has added* and Francis; *not in* Q1

99 **parcel of a reckoning** items of a tavern bill
99–100 **I am . . . north** This seemingly
abrupt interjection of Hotspur follows
from what has just been said at ll. 90–3.
Hal has professed himself ready for any
merriment—but, he now adds, unlike
Hotspur, 'who thinks all the time lost that
is not spent in bloodshed, forgets decency
and civility, and has nothing but the barren talk of a brutal soldier' (Dr Johnson).
Hotspur of the north is thus seen as the
antithesis of Hal's merriment, sociability,
and idleness. Perhaps, too, this thought of
Hotspur is prompted by Francis's feverish
activity, or his limitation of ideas. Both
Hotspur and Francis make a career of
calling other men to a *reckoning* (West,
331), and both are associated with a
parrot or starling. The word *scot* elsewhere (1.3.215, 5.4.113) conveys the
sense of reckoning'. See Introduction,
pp. 60–1.
100 **kills me** kills. The dative *me*, sometimes
called the dative of indirect interest, or
ethical dative, is seen also at ll. 194 and
209 below, 3.1.95 and 104, 4.2.14,
4.3.75, etc. It is used here chiefly to give
a colloquial tone.
104 **drench** draught (sometimes of medi-
cine)
    says he Hotspur addresses a groom. The
preoccupation and tardy response to Lady

Percy nicely caricature what we are
shown in 2.3.
106 **I'll play Percy** Three skits are proposed
in the course of this scene: Hotspur with
his wife, Falstaff running away, and King
Henry IV confronting his son. Play-acting
serves not only as a frequent entertainment for Hal and Falstaff but also as a way
of gaining perspective on those with
whom Hal must come to terms; see
Introduction, p. 51.
107 **brawn** a boar fattened for the table, and
hence well provided with fleshly limbs. As
Wilson (*Fortunes*) points out, this and comparable terms like *ribs* and *tallow* (l. 108),
i.e. drippings, deal in the stock-in-trade
of Eastcheap butchers and victuallers.
    Rivo A cry of uncertain origin used at
revels or bouts of drinking. *OED* cites Marlowe's *Jew of Malta* (*c.*1589), 4.4.10:
'Hey, *Rivo Castiliano*, a man's a man', and
other Elizabethan plays.
108 **ribs . . . tallow** rib roast and suet or
drippings
110 **of** on
112 **netherstocks** stockings, as distinguished from *upper stocks*, or breeches.
The resolution to sew stockings is a part of
Falstaff's comic pose of pious virtue; at
l. 127 below, he similarly associates
weaving with psalm-singing and the
renunciation of a 'bad world'.

and foot them too. A plague of all cowards. Give me a cup
of sack, rogue. Is there no virtue extant?
      He drinketh

PRINCE HENRY Didst thou never see Titan kiss a dish of
butter—pitiful-hearted Titan—that melted at the sweet
tale of the sun's? If thou didst, then behold that compound.

FALSTAFF You rogue, here's lime in this sack too. There is
nothing but roguery to be found in villainous man, yet a   120
coward is worse than a cup of sack with lime in it. A
villainous coward! Go thy ways, old Jack, die when thou
wilt; if manhood, good manhood, be not forgot upon the
face of the earth, then am I a shotten herring. There lives
not three good men unhanged in England, and one of
them is fat and grows old, God help the while! A bad

---

113 and foot them] Q1 ; *not in* F1

---

113 **foot** make new feet for (*OED, v.* 8). Falstaff gloomily envisages an increasingly
dire set of menial tasks forced upon those
who must trudge afoot (as he has been
forced to do), from making of stockings to
darning to replacement of worn-out soles.
114 **virtue** manliness
115–18 **Titan . . . compound** Titan is the
sun; this particular mythological name
also hints at gigantic size. Falstaff's corpulent and ruddy features, as he addresses
himself greedily to a cup of sack, suggest
to Hal both the sun overpowering a dish of
butter and the sun-god compassionately
melting the resolve of the earthly lover
whom he wishes amorously to devour.
The *compound*, or mixture of elements
thus produced (antedating *OED*'s earliest
illustrations of this meaning), playfully
contains the Ovidian idea of metamorphosis. *That* in l. 116 must refer to the
butter, though the passage has been
much emended; the second 'Titan'
(l. 116) could be an erroneous repetition
of the first. Theobald proposes 'Butter' in
place of the second 'Titan'; Cowl and
Morgan propose 'creature'. 'To melt like
butter before the sun' is a familiar comparison (Dent B780).
119 **lime** Taverners who doctored their wine
with lime to make it dry and sparkling

were the subject of much complaint. *OED,
sb.*[1] 3, cites Richard Hawkins, *Voyage into
the South Sea*, 1593 (1622), section 43,
p. 103: 'Since the Spanish sacks have
been common in our taverns, which (for
conservation) is mingled with lime in its
making, our nation complains of calen-
turas, of the stone', etc.
120 **nothing . . . man** Compare the saying
'There is no faith (trust, honesty) in man'
(Dent F34).
122 **Go thy ways** away with you, be on your
way
124 **a shotten herring** a herring that has
spawned or shot its roe and is especially
thin and emaciated. The familiar comparison 'As lean (lank) as a shotten herring' (Dent H447) is comically applied.
Wilson, *Fortunes* (31), notes that Falstaff
habitually contrasts himself with thin or
meagre fare from food shops—for example 'a bunch of radish' (2.4.179), 'a
rabbit-sucker' (l. 421), 'a poulter's hare'
(l. 421), 'a peppercorn' (3.3.8), 'a soused
gurnet' (4.2.11–12), and 'a carbonado',
or rasher of bacon (5.3.57). Contrast
Hal's terms for Falstaff, such as brawn,
ribs, and tallow (see ll. 107–8 and notes).
See Introduction, pp. 28–9.
125 **good** (a) brave (b) virtuous
126 **the while** i.e. these bad times we live in

world, I say. I would I were a weaver. I could sing psalms
or anything. A plague of all cowards, I say still.

PRINCE HENRY How now, woolsack, what mutter you?

FALSTAFF A king's son! If I do not beat thee out of thy   130
kingdom with a dagger of lath, and drive all thy subjects
afore thee like a flock of wild geese, I'll never wear hair on
my face more. You, Prince of Wales!

PRINCE HENRY Why, you whoreson round man, what's the
matter?

FALSTAFF Are not you a coward? Answer me to that. And
Poins there?

POINS Zounds, ye fat paunch, an ye call me coward, by the
Lord, I'll stab thee.

FALSTAFF I call thee coward? I'll see thee damned ere I call   140
thee coward, but I would give a thousand pound I could
run as fast as thou canst. You are straight enough in the
shoulders, you care not who sees your back. Call you that
backing of your friends? A plague upon such backing!
Give me them that will face me. Give me a cup of sack. I
am a rogue if I drunk today.

127–8 psalms or anything] Q1 ; all manner of songs F1

127 **weaver** Weavers, many of them Protestant immigrants from the Low Countries,
were often noted for their singing of
hymns and psalms, as in *Twelfth Night*
2.3.57, where Sir Toby proposes a rous-
ing catch 'that will draw three souls out of
one weaver'. Falstaff continues the note of
pious renunciation sounded in *netherstocks* (l. 112 above).

129 **woolsack** a large bale of wool, suggested by the talk about weaving, and
applied jocularly to the corpulent Falstaff;
with possible reference to the seats used
for judges who were summoned to attend
Parliament, and hence to the issue of Falstaff as false judge (1.2.61–4). The term
was thus in use by 1577 (*OED*, 2). Perhaps there is also a play on *wool* as a
material worn next to the skin in a
gesture of repentance—compare *LLL*,
5.2.697–8: 'I go woolward for penance'
—and on *sack*, as in sackcloth and as
drink.

131 **dagger of lath** a stage property of the
Vice in morality plays, with whom Falstaff is also compared at l. 437 below:

'that reverend Vice, that grey iniquity'.
The Vice's dagger is similarly mentioned
in *Twelfth Night* 4.2.120–7, *Henry V*
4.4.64–5, *2 Henry IV* 3.2.307, and Jonson's *The Devil is an Ass* (1616), 1.1.85.
The dagger was a comic weapon in morality plays, often brandished by the Vice
against his craven associates (in *Like Will
to Like* and *Enough Is as Good as a Feast*, for
example, and it is perhaps this sort of
absurd combat to which Falstaff alludes.
As a figure of both comic hilarity and evil,
the Vice could beguile audiences with his
inventive theatrics and also alarm them
with his roaring, much as Falstaff comically proposes to frighten Hal's subjects
like a flock of wild geese. See Introduction,
pp. 24–6.

134 **round** stout, large, perhaps with a suggestion of 'not mincing words' (*OED*, 13)

141 **a thousand pound** A common formula
of hyperbole (Dent T248.1), but the sum
is significantly repeated in l. 153 below.

144 **backing** Falstaff plays on the ideas of (a)
supporting, seconding (b) turning the
back in flight.

PRINCE HENRY O villain, thy lips are scarce wiped since thou
    drunk'st last.

FALSTAFF All is one for that. (*He drinketh*) A plague of all
    cowards, still say I.   150

PRINCE HENRY What's the matter?

FALSTAFF What's the matter? There be four of us here have
    ta'en a thousand pound this day morning.

PRINCE HENRY Where is it, Jack, where is it?

FALSTAFF Where is it? Taken from us it is. A hundred upon
    poor four of us.

PRINCE HENRY What, a hundred, man?

FALSTAFF I am a rogue if I were not at half-sword with a
    dozen of them two hours together. I have scaped by mir-
    acle. I am eight times thrust through the doublet, four   160
    through the hose, my buckler cut through and through,
    my sword hacked like a handsaw—*ecce signum*! I never
    dealt better since I was a man. All would not do. A plague
    of all cowards! Let them speak. If they speak more or less
    than truth, they are villains and the sons of darkness.

149 All is] Q1 ; All's Q3

147–8 **thy lips . . . last** Compare the saying
    'You licked not your lips since you lied
    last' (Dent L329, Appendix C).
149 **All is one for that** i.e. no matter
153 **a thousand pound** a sum also named
    in *Famous Victories* (l. 86), though
    elsewhere in this play (2.1.53 and
    2.4.501) the sum is 300 marks, or 200
    pounds. The inflated figure here is
    appropriate to Falstaff's hyperbole, as in
    l. 141 above (see note).
    this day morning this morning
158 **at half-sword** fighting at close quarters
    with swords (*OED*, 2), or, possibly, with
    short swords (*OED*, 1)
161–2 **buckler, sword** As Hotspur has sug-
    gested earlier in his contemptuous epithet
    'sword-and-buckler Prince of Wales'
    (1.3.229), in the late sixteenth century
    these weapons were considered more suit-
    able for servants and roisterers than for
    gentlemen. A conservative opinion, on
    the other hand, still lamented the passage
    of an older style of fighting equated with

'good manhood' (l. 123 above), and
    deplored 'this poking fight of rapier and
    dagger' as unsportsmanlike; see Porter,
    Two Angry Women of Abington, 1599
    (Malone Society ed., 1912, ll. 1339—44,
    cited by Humphreys). Falstaff has a
    dagger too (l. 295), and in *2 Henry IV* a
    rapier (2.4.191). The *buckler* is a small
    round shield.
162 *ecce signum* behold the sign, or proof.
    Falstaff displays his hacked sword, quot-
    ing a familiar saying (Dent S443) that
    echoes the language of the Mass.
163 **All would not do** i.e. all my bravery was
    of no avail
164–5 **more or less than truth** A familiar
    expression (Dent T590).
165 **sons of darkness** Another biblical echo
    favoured by the Puritans; compare 1
    Thessalonians 5 : 5 : 'Ye are all the child-
    ren of light . . . we are not of the night,
    neither of darkness' (quoted by Hum-
    phreys). Falstaff returns to the phrase at
    3.3.35.

⌈PRINCE HENRY⌉ Speak, sirs, how was it?

⌈GADSHILL⌉ We four set upon some dozen—

FALSTAFF Sixteen at least, my lord.

⌈GADSHILL⌉ And bound them.

PETO No, no, they were not bound.　　　　170

FALSTAFF You rogue, they were bound, every man of them,
or I am a Jew else, an Hebrew Jew.

⌈GADSHILL⌉ As we were sharing, some six or seven fresh
men set upon us—

FALSTAFF And unbound the rest, and then come in the
other.

PRINCE HENRY What, fought you with them all?

FALSTAFF All? I know not what you call all, but if I fought
not with fifty of them, I am a bunch of radish. If there were
not two- or three-and-fifty upon poor old Jack, then am　　　180
I no two-legged creature.

PRINCE HENRY Pray God you have not murdered some of
them.

FALSTAFF Nay, that's past praying for. I have peppered two
of them. Two I am sure I have paid, two rogues in buckram suits. I tell thee what, Hal, if I tell thee a lie, spit in my

---

166 PRINCE HENRY] DERING MS, F1 ; *Gad* Q1   167, 169, 173 GADSHILL] F1 ; *Ross.* Q1

166 **PRINCE HENRY** See Introduction, pp.
99–100, for a possible explanation of Qq's
seeming misassignment of this line to
'Gad.' and the three speeches at ll. 167,
169, and 173–4 to 'Ross.', the original
name of Bardolph (as at 1.2.153). Most
editions, including this one, follow F1
here, which may reflect independent textual authority, or at least theatrical
recollection.

172 **Hebrew Jew** i.e. forsworn. This intensi-
fying comic pleonasm appears also in *Two
Gentlemen* 2.5.45–6 : 'if not, thou art an
Hebrew, a Jew, and not worth the name of
a Christian.' Shakespeare's characters
sometimes use the opprobrious term *Jew*
to connote ingratitude, lack of charity or
tenderness, and blasphemy; see *Two
Gentlemen* 2.3.9, *Much Ado* 2.3.239,
Macbeth 4.1.26.

176 **other** others

179 **a bunch of radish** See l. 124 and note on
images of emaciation with which Falstaff

is contrasted. In *2 Henry IV*, Shallow's
extraordinary leanness puts Falstaff in
mind of a 'forked radish, with a head fan-
tastically carved upon it with a knife'
(3.2.309–11). As with many herbal
remedies, the physical appearance was
thought to suggest its medical effect as
well; Wilson (*NCS*) quotes Sir Thomas
Elyot, *Castle of Health* (1541), ii. chap. 16,
p. 28b: 'Radish roots have the virtue to
extenuate or make thin.' A radish is also
appropriately red on the outside, but
white (the colour of cowardice) within.

180 **three-and-fifty** G. R. Stewart (*PQ*, 14
(1935), 274–5) notes that in the popular
accounts by Ralegh, Markham, and
others of the fight of the *Revenge* against
the Spanish fleet in 1591, the number of
Spanish vessels is always listed as three-
and-fifty. See Introduction, p. 28.

184 **peppered** made it hot for, slain (*OED*,
pepper, v. 5a and b)

185 **paid** settled with, slain

face, call me horse. Thou knowest my old ward. Here I
lay, and thus I bore my point. Four rogues in buckram
let drive at me—

PRINCE HENRY What, four? Thou saidst but two even now.   190

FALSTAFF Four, Hal, I told thee four.

POINS Ay, ay, he said four.

FALSTAFF These four came all afront, and mainly thrust at
me. I made me no more ado but took all their seven points
in my target, thus.

PRINCE HENRY Seven? Why, there were but four even now.

FALSTAFF In buckram?

POINS Ay, four, in buckram suits.

FALSTAFF Seven, by these hilts, or I am a villain else.

PRINCE HENRY (*to Poins*) Prithee let him alone. We shall   200
have more anon.

FALSTAFF Dost thou hear me, Hal?

PRINCE HENRY Ay, and mark thee too, Jack.

FALSTAFF Do so, for it is worth the listening to. These nine
in buckram that I told thee of—

PRINCE HENRY So, two more already.

FALSTAFF Their points being broken—

POINS Down fell their hose.

FALSTAFF Began to give me ground; but I followed me close,

---

190 What,] Q2; ~ ₐ Q1   200 *to Poins*] WHITE (*subs.*); *not in* Q1   203 too, Jack] Q2; to iacke
Q1

---

187 **call me horse** Compare 'call me cut', or
curtal horse (*Twelfth Night* 2.3.176, Dent
C940), and 'write me down an ass' (*Much
Ado* 4.2.70); a popular formula. Compare
also the saying 'Spit in his mouth and
make him a mastiff' (Dent M1259).
  ward a defensive posture or movement,
parry

187–8 **Here . . . point** this is the defensive
posture I assumed, and this is how I
pointed my sword. (The actor gestures to
demonstrate.)

190 **even** just

193 **afront** abreast
  mainly mightily

194 **I made me** The ethical dative, as in
l. 100 and note, l. 209, etc.; still idio-
matically acceptable in some speech.

195 **target** light round shield, synonymous

with the *buckler* in l. 161 (*OED, sb.*[1] 1)

199 **hilts** Shakespeare often uses the plural
hilts as a singular ('sword hilt'), as in
Richard III 1.4.151: 'Take him on the costard with the hilts of thy sword', *Henry V*
2.1.61, *Caesar* 5.3.43, and elsewhere.
The hilts formed a cross with the sword,
making it a suitable object on which to
swear an oath, as in *Hamlet* 1.5.147.

203 **mark** (a) pay heed (b) keep count (Wilson, *NCS*)

204 **it is . . . to** A common expression (Dent
H300).

207 **points** sword's points. But Poins takes
up the meaning of a tagged lace or cord
used to attach the hose to the doublet.

209 **followed me** followed; see l. 100 and
note on the dative *me*.

came in foot and hand; and with a thought seven of the   210
eleven I paid.

PRINCE HENRY O monstrous! Eleven buckram men grown
out of two!

FALSTAFF But, as the devil would have it, three misbegotten
knaves in Kendal green came at my back, and let drive at
me, for it was so dark, Hal, that thou couldst not see thy
hand.

PRINCE HENRY These lies are like their father that begets
them, gross as a mountain, open, palpable. Why, thou
clay-brained guts, thou knotty-pated fool, thou whore-   220
son, obscene, greasy tallow-keech—

FALSTAFF What, art thou mad? Art thou mad? Is not the
truth the truth?

PRINCE HENRY Why, how couldst thou know these men in
Kendal green, when it was so dark thou couldst not see
thy hand? Come, tell us your reason. What sayst thou to
this?

POINS Come, your reason, Jack, your reason.

---

221 tallow-keech] Q1 (tallow-catch); tallow-ketch HANMER; tallow-cake COWL AND MORGAN

---

210 **came . . . hand** pursued them closely
and ready to do service (see *OED, foot, sb.*
3ob, and the common saying 'to wait
upon one hand and foot')
   with a thought quick as thought. A common expression (Dent T240).

214 **as the devil would have it** A common
expression (Dent D221.1).

215 **Kendal** a town in Westmorland (now
Cumbria) noted since the thirteenth century for its cloth manufacture. Falstaff is
perhaps taking a dig at Hal by portraying
the imaginary attackers as clothed in a
coarse cloth worn by woodsmen and
associated with outlaws (Linthicum,
79); compare the coarse buckram that
Hal and Poins have in fact used for their
disguise.

216–7 **it was . . . hand** A common expression (Dent *PLED* D40.11).

218 **their father** Falstaff is compared to the
devil as the proverbial father of lies (John
8 : 44, Dent D241.1 and F92).

219 **gross as a mountain** The comparison
describes both the obviousness of the lies
and Falstaff's huge size. Compare 'huge
hill of flesh' at l. 236 below.

220 **clay-brained** dull clod-pated (*OED, clay,
sb.* 9)
   knotty-pated blockheaded. *OED* (*knotty*,
5) suggests a possible association with
'not-pated' (2.4.67 and note). See also
loggerheads (2.4.4 and note).

221 **obscene** loathsome
   tallow-keech The spelling of QqF1, 'tallow-catch', might possibly suggest a pan
to catch the dripping tallow of cooking
meat, or a tub to receive and hold butchers'
tallow, but the more likely interpretation
is as a variant spelling of *tallow-keech*, a
lump of congealed fat, or the rolled-up fat
of a slaughtered animal. *OED* lists
'katche', 'keche', 'ketch', etc., as variant
spellings of *catch*. Under *keech, sb.* 1, *OED*
cites *2 Henry IV* 2.1.89: 'Did not good-
wife Keech, the butcher's wife, come in
then?', and *Henry VIII* 1.1.54–6 apropos
of Wolsey: 'I wonder | That such a keech
can with his very bulk | Take up the rays
o' th' beneficial sun.' Dr Johnson notes
that 'in some parts of the kingdom, a *cake*,
or *mass*, of wax or tallow is called a *keech*'.

222–3 **Is not the truth the truth?** A proverbial saying (Dent T581).

FALSTAFF What, upon compulsion? Zounds, an I were at
the strappado, or all the racks in the world, I would not   230
tell you on compulsion. Give you a reason on compul-
sion? If reasons were as plentiful as blackberries, I would
give no man a reason upon compulsion, I.

PRINCE HENRY I'll be no longer guilty of this sin. This sanguine coward, this bed-presser, this horse-backbreaker,
this huge hill of flesh—

FALSTAFF 'Sblood, you starveling, you eel-skin, you dried
neat's tongue, you bull's pizzle, you stockfish! O for

---

229 Zounds, an I were] Q1 (Zoundes, and I were); No: were I F1   237 eel-skin] HANMER;
elſskin Q1–2; elfskin Q3–6, F1

---

230 **strappado** (Italian *strappato*, from *strap-pare*, 'to drag' or 'to snatch'), a method of torture used to extract confessions, in which the victim was lifted off the ground by means of ropes attached to his hands tied behind his back. In the more cruel form of the torture he was then let down half-way with a jerk.

232 **reasons . . . blackberries** Falstaff's pun, based on the similarity of pronunciation of *reason* and *raisin*, seems intentional (see Cercignani, 235). 'As plentiful as black-berries' is a familiar comparison (Dent B442). Wilson (*NCS*) notes that '"Reasons" or opinions were in that age commonly extracted by the "compulsion" of torture'.

234 **this sin** i.e. concealment of a lie, complicity

234–5 **sanguine coward** Hal's oxymoronic jest is that Falstaff's ruddy complexion and corpulence, the signs of a sanguine temperament, are at odds with cowardice, in which the blood withdraws to the heart and leaves the features pale (Bamborough, 120–2). A sanguine person was expected to be high-spirited and brave.

237 **starveling** The comic contrast between Hal's thinness and Falstaff's corpulence in this series of epithets is reinforced by repetition, for Gadshill observed in 2.1.66–7 that Falstaff 'is no starveling'.
eel-skin See collation. Q1–2 read elſskin, i.e. elsskin; Q3–5F1 rationalize to *elfskin*, *Elfe-skin*, a typographically plausible emendation. The Q3–5F1 reading can be defended, since Shakespeare elsewhere equates 'elf' with fairy spirits and other diminutive creatures, and *elf-skin* could

mean a skin in which an elf wraps himself. Yet the emendation proposed by Hanmer, *eel-skin*, is more attractive because of its closeness to the Q1–2 reading (the unusual ſs in 'elſskin' may result in part from the compositor's wish to avoid a kerning problem if he were to put his long s, ſ, before *k*), and because Shakespeare elsewhere uses *eel-skin* to suggest a comically exaggerated thinness (in 2 *Henry IV* 3.2.313 and *K. John* 1.1.141). In *Dream* as well, the snake's 'enamelled skin' that is 'Weed wide enough to wrap a fairy in' (2.1.255–6) suggests eel-skin rather than elf-skin. The reading proposed by Evans (*Supplement*), *elshin* or *elsin*, 'awl', seems less apposite to the idea of thinness, and *OED*'s few citations are not encouraging.

238 **neat's** ox's
bull's pizzle A dried bull's pizzle, or penis (compare *dried neat's tongue*), could serve as a whip. *OED*, *bull*, *sb.* 11b, cites Hakluyt, *Voyages* (1599), II. i. 187: 'The boatswain . . . walked abaft the mast, and his mate afore the mast, and each of them a bull's pizzle dried in their hands' (v. 301).
stockfish dried cod. The dryness emphasized in Falstaff's comparisons would produce not only emaciation but a temperament opposite to sanguinity with its heat and moisture—the qualities of youth. Falstaff's images repeatedly suggest genital emaciation or insufficiency (see Partridge under *pizzle, cod, eel, fish, yard, tongue*, and, in the following lines (239–40), notes on *tailor's yard, sheath, bow-case*, and *standing tuck*).

breath to utter what is like thee, you tailor's yard, you
sheath, you bow-case, you vile standing tuck—   240
PRINCE HENRY Well, breathe awhile, and then to it again,
and when thou hast tired thyself in base comparisons,
hear me speak but this.
POINS Mark, Jack.
PRINCE HENRY We two saw you four set on four and bound
them, and were masters of their wealth. Mark now how
a plain tale shall put you down. Then did we two set on
you four, and, with a word, outfaced you from your prize,
and have it, yea, and can show it you here in the house.
And, Falstaff, you carried your guts away as nimbly,   250
with as quick dexterity, and roared for mercy, and still
run and roared, as ever I heard bull-calf. What a slave art
thou, to hack thy sword as thou hast done, and then say
it was in fight! What trick, what device, what starting-
hole canst thou now find out to hide thee from this open
and apparent shame?
POINS Come, let's hear, Jack. What trick hast thou now?
FALSTAFF By the Lord, I knew ye as well as he that made ye.
Why, hear you, my masters, was it for me to kill the heir
apparent? Should I turn upon the true prince? Why, thou   260

241 to it] QI ; to't FI   249 here] QI ; *not in* FI   252 run] QI ; ranne FI   259 you] QI ; ye FI

239 **tailor's yard** yardstick. Tailors were
often accused of being thin and lacking in
virility, and *yard* suggests a quibble on
'penis' (Partridge). The tailor in *Dream* is
called Robin Starveling (compare l. 237
above and note), and Francis Feeble, the
woman's tailor in *2 Henry IV* (3.2.146
ff.), is expected to be 'as valiant as the
wrathful dove or most magnanimous
mouse'.
240 **sheath** empty case, suggestive of both
the female sexual anatomy and the fore-
skin
 bow-case a long, thin case for unstrung
bows, with the suggestion once again of
female anatomy and male insufficiency;
frequently applied to a lean starveling
 standing tuck (a) a rapier standing on its
point, or up-ended (b) one that has lost its
pliancy (OED, 8; Cowl and Morgan).
Another withering genital comparison.
245-6 **set ... bound ... were** On the shift of
mood to the indicative past, compare
4.1.105–8: 'I saw young Harry ... Rise

from the ground ... And vaulted' (Humphreys).
248 **with a word** (a) in a word (b) with only
a brief shout (Humphreys)
 outfaced you from confronted you and
forced you away from
251-2 **roared ... bull-calf** A familiar comparison (Dent B715).
254-5 **starting-hole** bolt-hole in which a
hunted animal takes refuge; from *start*
(OED, *v.* 6) meaning 'to escape'. Both
Thomas Wilson's *The Rule of Reason*
(1563), fol. 61^v (misnumbered fol. 90),
and Abraham Fraunce's *The Lawyer's
Logic* (1588), fol. 101^v, warn of ways in
which the answerer 'will seek starting
holes to escape' (Joseph, 376–8).
256 **apparent** manifest; but Falstaff plays on
the sense of *heir apparent* (ll. 259–60),
and thereby finds his 'starting-hole'.
258 **I knew ... made ye** A familiar expression (Dent K170.1), here with possible ironic reference to Hal's own father.

knowest I am as valiant as Hercules, but beware instinct. The lion will not touch the true prince. Instinct is a great matter. I was now a coward on instinct. I shall think the better of myself and thee during my life—I for a valiant lion, and thou for a true prince. But by the Lord, lads, I am glad you have the money. Hostess, clap to the doors! Watch tonight, pray tomorrow. Gallants, lads, boys, hearts of gold, all the titles of good fellowship come to you! What, shall we be merry? Shall we have a play extempore?   270

PRINCE HENRY Content; and the argument shall be thy running away.

FALSTAFF Ah, no more of that, Hal, an thou lovest me!
    Enter Hostess Quickly

HOSTESS O Jesu, my lord the Prince!

PRINCE HENRY How now, my lady the hostess, what sayst thou to me?

HOSTESS Marry, my lord, there is a nobleman of the court at door would speak with you. He says he comes from your father.

268 titles of good fellowship] Q1 ; good Titles of Fellowship F1   273.1 *Quickly*] *not in* Q1

262 **The lion . . . prince** As 'king of beasts' (*Richard II* 5.1.34), the lion was fabled to hold a particular veneration for princes.

263–4 **I shall . . . life** A popular expression (Dent PLED T219.11).

265 **thou for a true prince** Falstaff's sly suggestion is that he will now at last have a reason to consider Hal a legitimate prince (H. N. Hudson, *Shakespeare: His Life, Art, and Characters* (Boston, 1872), ii. 86, cited by Wilson, *NCS*).

267 **Watch** (a) keep a wakeful vigil (b) spend the night in revelry
    pray (a) make application to God (b) prey, pillage. Thus Falstaff turns to his own witty use the biblical injunction to 'Watch and pray that ye enter not into temptation' (Matthew 26 : 41).

268 **hearts of gold** Compare *Henry V* 4.1.45 : 'The King's a bawcock and a heart-of-gold.'

269–70 **play extempore** See Humphreys for examples of extempore plays as a common feature of tavern life.

271 **the argument** the plot of the play; see 2.2.89 and note.

273 **no more . . . lovest me** A familiar tag

(Dent M1154.1).

273.1 *Enter Hostess Quickly* Falstaff and Prince Hal refer twice to 'my hostess of the tavern' in 1.2.38–47 (compare *Famous Victories*, ll. 83–4) as a familiar acquaintance. She is addressed and referred to regularly as 'my hostess' or 'hostess', or, with a mock politeness, 'my lady the hostess', in 1 and 2 *Henry IV* and *Henry V*; see 1 *Henry IV* 2.4.266 and 275 and 3.3.57, 126, 164 and 197. The Hostess is further identified as 'Mistress Quickly' in 3.3.90, and as 'Nell' in *Henry V* 2.1.29. In 1 *Henry IV* she is married (3.3.54, 115, 165), though in 2 *Henry IV* she is 'a poor widow of Eastcheap' (2.1.67, 79), and in *Merry Wives* she is not hostess of a tavern at all, but servant to Dr Caius.

277–81 **a nobleman, a royal man** Familiar punning on the value of coin ; a noble was worth 6s. 8d., a royal 10s. Compare 2 *Henry IV* 1.2.19: 'his face is a face-royal', and *Richard III* 1.3.79–81: 'great promotions | Are daily given to ennoble those | That scarce some two days since were worth a noble.'

PRINCE HENRY Give him as much as will make him a royal   280
  man, and send him back again to my mother.

FALSTAFF What manner of man is he?

HOSTESS An old man.

FALSTAFF What doth gravity out of his bed at midnight?
  Shall I give him his answer?

PRINCE HENRY Prithee, do, Jack.

FALSTAFF Faith, and I'll send him packing.   *Exit*

PRINCE HENRY Now, sirs, by'r lady, you fought fair; so did
  you, Peto; so did you, Bardolph. You are lions too, you
  ran away upon instinct, you will not touch the true   290
  prince; no, fie!

BARDOLPH Faith, I ran when I saw others run.

PRINCE HENRY Faith, tell me now in earnest, how came
  Falstaff's sword so hacked?

PETO Why, he hacked it with his dagger, and said he would
  swear truth out of England but he would make you
  believe it was done in fight, and persuaded us to do the
  like.

BARDOLPH Yea, and to tickle our noses with spear-grass to
  make them bleed, and then to beslubber our garments   300
  with it and swear it was the blood of true men. I did that
  I did not this seven year before: I blushed to hear his
  monstrous devices.

PRINCE HENRY O villain, thou stolest a cup of sack eighteen
  years ago, and wert taken with the manner, and ever

289 Bardolph] DERING MS (Bardolffe), ROWE; Bardol Q1   lions too,] Q1 *corr.* (lions to,) (*Huntington Library, Bunbury–Devonshire copy*); lions, to Q1 *uncorr.* (*British Museum and Trinity College Cambridge copies*)

296 **swear truth out of England** 'swear so
  many false oaths that Truth would flee
  the country in horror' (Kittredge)
  but he would if he did not
299 **tickle our noses with spear-grass** In
  Famous Victories, Derick tells how he gave
  the impression of being wounded in
  action in France: 'Every day when I went
  into the field, | I would take a straw and
  thrust it into my nose | And make my nose
  bleed, and then I would go into the field, |
  And when the captain saw me he would
  say, | "Peace! A bloody soldier", and bid
  me stand aside' (ll. 1426–30). The trick of
  feigning wounds is a staple of the *miles*

gloriosus, or boastful soldier, as with
  Parolles in *All's Well* 4.1.33–56 and
  Pistol in *Henry V* 5.1.80–2 (also indebted
  to *Famous Victories*).
300 **beslubber** daub
301 **that** something
302 **this seven year** A familiar reckoning of
  time (Dent Y25).
305 **taken with the manner** caught in the
  act. A familiar expression (Dent M633).
  'It signifieth in the common law when a
  thief hath stolen, and is followed with hue
  and cry, and taken with the manner, that
  is, having the thing stolen about him, that
  is called the Mainour' (Minsheu, entry

since thou hast blushed extempore. Thou hadst fire and
sword on thy side, and yet thou rann'st away. What
instinct hadst thou for it?

BARDOLPH My lord, do you see these meteors? Do you
behold these exhalations? 310

PRINCE HENRY I do.

BARDOLPH What think you they portend?

PRINCE HENRY Hot livers and cold purses.

BARDOLPH Choler, my lord, if rightly taken.

PRINCE HENRY No, if rightly taken, halter.

> *Enter Falstaff*

Here comes lean Jack, here comes bare-bone. How now,
my sweet creature of bombast? How long is't ago, Jack,
since thou sawest thine own knee?

FALSTAFF My own knee? When I was about thy years, Hal,
I was not an eagle's talon in the waist; I could have crept 320

315.1 *Enter Falstaff*] F1 ; *after l.* 314 Q1   320 talon] Q1 (talent)

---

under *Mainour*). From old French
maneuvre, literally 'hand-work'. In *LLL*
1.1.199, Costard is 'taken with the
manner'—that is, with Jaquenetta. Hal
jests that Bardolph, having stolen a cup of
sack, was found with the evidence on him
in the form of his red complexion (compare
the expression 'taken red-handed').

306 **extempore** i.e. without needing an
occasion
  fire i.e. a fiery complexion caused by
  drink. To have fire and sword on one's
  side is to be invincible; Henry V has
  'famine, sword, and fire' at his heels
  crouching for employment (*Henry V*, 1
  Prol. 7–8).

309–10 **meteors . . . exhalations** Meteors
were sometimes thought to be exhaled as
vapours from the earth, and to *portend*
(l. 312) disorders on earth (see 1.1.10
and note). Bardolph is here comically a
microcosm; fiery eruptions in the face of
heaven signify strife in the elements
below.

313 **Hot livers and cold purses** The liver,
chief seat of such passions as love and
courage, could be fired with wine; Falstaff, in *2 Henry IV* 4.3.98–102, explains
how sherry warms the liver, previously
white and pale, 'which is the badge of
pusillanimity and cowardice', and causes
warmth to 'course from the inwards to

the parts extremes'. Earlier he complains
of the incurable 'consumption of the
purse' caused by drinking and revelling
(1.2.223). An empty purse is a cold purse
in *Winter's Tale* 4.3.114 and *Timon*
3.4.15.

314 **Choler** A choleric, or bilious, temperament tended to produce anger in which
the blood boiled in the heart and ascended
to the brain (Bamborough, 122–5),
producing fiery features that (in Bardolph's wishful thought) might resemble
the reddening effects of drinking too
much.
  if rightly taken if correctly understood;
  but Hal, in the next speech, punningly
  suggests 'if justly arrested'.

315 **No . . . halter** Both a correct interpretation and a just arrest, Hal wittily
proposes, would substitute for Bardolph's
choler a *halter* or 'collar', a hangman's
noose. Hal may be playfully varying the
proverb 'After a collar comes a halter'
(Dent C513).

315.1 *Enter Falstaff* Bardolph may leave at
this point; see note at l. 463.1.

317 **bombast** (a) cotton padding (b) fustian
speech

320 **talon** The spelling of QqF1, 'talent',
represents a common corruption in which
-ant is confused and assimilated with the
final *-an*, as in 'truan[t]', 'peasan[t]', etc.

into any alderman's thumb-ring. A plague of sighing and
grief, it blows a man up like a bladder. There's villainous
news abroad. Here was Sir John Bracy from your father;
you must to the court in the morning. That same mad
fellow of the north, Percy, and he of Wales that gave
Amamon the bastinado and made Lucifer cuckold and
swore the devil his true liegeman upon the cross of a
Welsh hook—what a plague call you him?

POINS Owen Glendower.

FALSTAFF Owen, Owen, the same; and his son-in-law Mor-   330
timer, and old Northumberland, and that sprightly Scot
of Scots, Douglas, that runs a-horseback up a hill perpen-
dicular—

PRINCE HENRY He that rides at high speed, and with his
pistol kills a sparrow flying.

FALSTAFF You have hit it.

PRINCE HENRY So did he never the sparrow.

FALSTAFF Well, that rascal hath good mettle in him; he will
not run.

329 Owen] DERING MS; O QI

321 **alderman's thumb-ring** Compare the
agate-stone worn 'On the forefinger of an
alderman' in *Romeo* 1.4.55–6, and the
'agate-ring' attributed to the innkeeper in
2.4.67 above. First recorded use in *OED*.

322 **it . . . bladder** Falstaff's theory about
grief and sighing is comically at variance
with the view generally prevailing. In
grief, the heart supposedly contracted,
withdrawing heat and blood from the rest
of the body and producing paleness,
goose-flesh, and the like (Bamborough,
122). On the other hand Kittredge quotes
Greene's *Mamillia*, Pt. II, 1593 (ed.
Grosart, ii. 243): 'blown up with sighs'.
Falstaff again invokes his pose as Monsieur Remorse (see ll. 111–28,
1.2.106–7), but his girth is hardly the
result of worldly renunciation. Compare
also 4.2.46: 'blown Jack'.

323 **Bracy** Nothing is known from the
chronicles about such a man.

326 **Amamon** the name of a demon.
Reginald Scot, *Discovery of Witchcraft*,
1584, Book xv, chap.3, p. 393, cites
'Amaymon, king of the east', and at xv,
chap. 29, 'king Baell, or Amoimon,
which are spirits reigning in the furthest

regions of the east' (Humphreys). Cited
again in *Merry Wives* 2.2.262.
  bastinado cudgelling, especially on the
soles of the feet; from Italian and Spanish
baston, 'stick'
  cuckold The devil, like cuckolded men,
wore horns.

327 **swore . . . liegeman** made the devil
swear allegiance as a true vassal, or subject

328 **Welsh hook** bill-hook, heavy weapon
with a hooked end, hence without the
cross-shape of a sword on which such
oaths were customarily sworn; a weapon
suited only to a rustic soldier

329 **Owen** QI has 'O' without punctuation,
Qq2–5F1 'O' followed by a comma, and
the Dering MS 'Owen' (see collation).
Falstaff's reply seems to suggest that the
'O' assigned to Poins in QI is an abbreviation, and the Dering MS may reflect
theatrical practice.

336 **hit it** hit the nail on the head. But Hal
puns on the literal sense.

338 **mettle** the 'stuff' of which a person is
made; a variant spelling of *metal* and
originally a figurative meaning of that
word. Compare QqF1, *mettall*. Having

PRINCE HENRY Why, what a rascal art thou then, to praise   340
him so for running?

FALSTAFF A-horseback, ye cuckoo; but afoot he will not
budge a foot.

PRINCE HENRY Yes, Jack, upon instinct.

FALSTAFF I grant ye, upon instinct. Well, he is there too,
and one Mordake, and a thousand blue-caps more. Worcester is stolen away tonight. Thy father's beard is turned
white with the news. You may buy land now as cheap as
stinking mackerel.

PRINCE HENRY Why, then, it is like, if there come a hot June   350
and this civil buffeting hold, we shall buy maidenheads as
they buy hobnails, by the hundreds.

FALSTAFF By the mass, lad, thou sayst true; it is like we shall
have good trading that way. But tell me, Hal, art not thou

good 'metal' in him, jests Falstaff, the
Douglas will not easily 'run', or melt,
away. Falstaff implies a contrast between
this *rascal* Douglas (the word's original
meaning suggests low birth) and the well-
born Prince of Wales who did run away
from the robbery (l. 142 above).

341 **running** Hal plays upon the idea of (a)
fleeing in fear, Falstaff's meaning in the
previous speech (b) riding at high speed,
as in Falstaff's speech at ll. 332–3.

342 **ye cuckoo** Falstaff chides Hal for mind-
lessly repeating Falstaff's words *rascal*
and *running*, like a cuckoo, without dif-
ferentiating the meaning. Shakespeare
usually associates the cuckoo with
cuckoldry, but the idea of incessant
repetition (derived from the monotonous
iteration of its call) was also current
(*OED*, 3).

  afoot Falstaff means 'in hand to hand
combat', and quibbles in l. 343 on *a foot*
in the sense of 'a short distance'.

344 **upon instinct** i.e. (ironically), don't for-
get what instinct will do even to brave
men. Hal parries the implication of cowardice in ll. 338–9 by reminding Falstaff of
his discomfiture at Gad's Hill and his
cowardice when he fled *afoot* and *upon
instinct*.

345 **there** i.e. in the list of names, or at some
supposed place of assembly

346 **Mordake** The Earl of Fife, captured at
Holmedon, was prisoner in England until
1415; but see Appendix, 1.1.71–2, on

Shakespeare's confusion of this Mordake
with the son of Douglas.

  blue-caps Scots soldiers in their caps of
blue, blue-bonnets (first recorded use in
OED)

348–9 **You . . . mackerel** Land may be cheap
because of quick sales to raise revenues for
war, as in *Henry V*, 2 Chor. 5: 'They sell
the pasture now to buy the horse', or
more generally because of economic uncertainty and fear of dislocation in time of
civil strife. *Mackerel* is cheap even when
fresh.

350 **like** likely
  hot warm, angry, lustful

351 **civil buffeting** the strife of civil war, but
with a suggestion of amorous contending
(in anticipation of the jest about *maidenheads*)
  hold takes place, continues

351–2 **we shall . . . hobnails** maidenheads
will be cheaply obtained—an image, perhaps, of disorder in time of military conflict, when soldiers rape and pillage. Compare *Henry V* 3.3.93–4: 'mowing like
grass | Your fresh fair virgins and your
flow'ring infants'. In such a time,
maidenheads will corrupt like *stinking
mackerel* (ll. 348–9) in a *hot June* (l. 350),
since heat promotes lechery.

354 **trading** commerce, or 'intercourse', in
flesh. Compare *Pericles* 4.6.66: 'pretty
one, how long have you been at this
trade?'

horrible afeard? Thou being heir apparent, could the
world pick thee out three such enemies again as that fiend
Douglas, that spirit Percy, and that devil Glendower? Art
thou not horribly afraid? Doth not thy blood thrill at it?
PRINCE HENRY Not a whit, i'faith. I lack some of thy instinct.
FALSTAFF Well, thou wilt be horribly chid tomorrow when   360
thou comest to thy father. If thou love me, practise an
answer.
PRINCE HENRY Do thou stand for my father and examine me
upon the particulars of my life.
FALSTAFF Shall I? Content. This chair shall be my state, this
dagger my sceptre, and this cushion my crown.
     He sits
PRINCE HENRY Thy state is taken for a joint-stool, thy golden
sceptre for a leaden dagger, and thy precious rich crown
for a pitiful bald crown.
FALSTAFF Well, an the fire of grace be not quite out of thee,   370
now shalt thou be moved. Give me a cup of sack to make
my eyes look red, that it may be thought I have wept; for
I must speak in passion, and I will do it in King Cambyses'
vein.

366.1 *He sits*] This edition; *not in* Q1

355 **horrible** Adjectives are freely used as adverbs; compare ' 'Tis noble spoken', in
Antony 2.2.102 (Abbott, 1). The familiar
adverbial form *horribly* is also used, as at
ll. 358 and 360.
 afeard From *afear*, in fear, plus *-ed*, a form
used interchangeably by Shakespeare
with *afraid*, as at l. 358 (originally the past
participle of *affray*, 'to startle'); rapidly
becoming obsolete in literature in the
seventeenth century, though continuing
in popular speech.
357 **spirit** i.e. fiend, devil. In Milton's *Paradise
Lost*, i. 423–4, Baalam and Ashtaroth are
called 'spirits', able when they please to
assume 'either sex . . . or both'.
358 **thrill** shudder, as in cold fear. Compare
Romeo 4.3.15: 'I have a faint cold fear
thrills through my veins.'
365 **state** throne, chair of state, i.e. of splendour and greatness. Compare *Henry VIII*
1.2.8.1: 'the King riseth from his state'.
Normally placed on a dais beneath a canopy, as in *Henry VIII* 1.4.0.1.
367 **taken for** seen to be reckoned as (*OED*,
take, 48b)

joint-stool stool well fitted together by a
joiner, as distinguished from one of more
clumsy workmanship (*OED*)
368 **leaden** i.e. of base or soft quality, ineffectual. *OED*, 1b, cites William Fulke,
Heskins' Parliament (1579), 396: 'He
heweth at it with his leaden sword.' As an
actual stage property in this scene, Falstaff's leaden dagger accentuates role-
playing, and perhaps recalls the Vice's
dagger of lath at l. 131 (see note). Falstaff's weapons (sword and buckler,
sword hacked with his own dagger, a
bottle of sack in his pistol case) are
repeatedly comic.
370 **fire of grace** A Puritan idiom.
371–2 **to make my eyes look red** Bloodshot
eyes, induced by heavy drinking, are
also conventionally a sign of weeping.
373 **in passion** with strong emotion (also at
l. 401)
373–4 **King Cambyses' vein** Thomas Pres-
ton's *Lamentable Tragedy, Mixed Full of
Pleasant Mirth, Containing the Life of
Cambyses, King of Persia* (1569) was a
stock joke by the 1590s, as indicated by

PRINCE HENRY *(bowing)* Well, here is my leg.

FALSTAFF And here is my speech. Stand aside, nobility.

HOSTESS O Jesu, this is excellent sport, i'faith!

FALSTAFF

Weep not, sweet queen, for trickling tears are vain.

HOSTESS O, the Father, how he holds his countenance!

FALSTAFF

For God's sake, lords, convey my tristful queen,   380

For tears do stop the floodgates of her eyes.

HOSTESS O Jesu, he doth it as like one of these harlotry
players as ever I see!

FALSTAFF Peace, good pint-pot; peace, good tickle-brain.
—Harry, I do not only marvel where thou spendest thy
time, but also how thou art accompanied; for though the
camomile, the more it is trodden on, the faster it grows,

---

375 *bowing*] This edition; *not in* Q1   379 Father] Q1 (father)   380 tristful] DERING MS;
trustfull Q1

Shakespeare's seeming parody of the title
in 'A tedious brief scene of young
Pyramus | And his love Thisby; very tragi-
cal mirth' (*Dream* 5.1.56–7), and by
other humorous references (see M. P.
Tilley, *MLN*, 24 (1909), 244–7).
Cambyses was probably performed by the
Earl of Leicester's Men, who in 1572 included in the roster James Burbage, father
of Richard; in 1576 they established
themselves at The Theatre, built by Burbage, and were thus a leading troupe of
the adult commercial theatrical world to
which Shakespeare later devoted his services. Shakespeare here uses *Cambyses'*
vein as a general label for old-fashioned
theatrical bombast, rather than as an ex-
clusive model, since he seems more
interested in pillorying the euphuistic
style of John Lyly and his imitators such as
Robert Greene; see ll. 378, 386–8 below
and notes.

375 **my leg** my bow (in which one leg is
drawn back and the other bent at the
knee)

378 **Weep . . . vain** Humphreys, Wilson
(*NCS*), Cowl and Morgan, etc., cite
analogues from *Cambyses*, Greene's
Alphonsus, *A Mirror for Magistrates*, and
Kyd's *Spanish Tragedy*, of which the
closest perhaps are 'Then, dainty damsel,
stint these trickling tears' (*Alphonsus*,
l. 2001) and King Cambyses' query to his

weeping queen 'What dost thou mean,
my spouse, to weep for loss of any prize?'
(*Cambyses*, l. 1031).

379 **the Father** i.e. in God's name; or possibly referring to Falstaff's play-acting
role as the father, Henry IV

holds his countenance keeps a straight
face

380 **convey** escort away

tristful (see collation) sorrowful

381 **stop** fill

382 **harlotry** scurvy, vagabond; often, as
here, a term of playful, and even affec-
tionate, contempt

384 **tickle-brain** Cant name for a potent
liquor, here transferred, like *pint-pot*, to
the person who supplies it. *OED* (*tickle, v.*
10) cites Robert Davenport, *A New Trick to
Cheat the Devil* (1639), 3.1, sig. E1ᵛ: 'A
cup of nipsitate [good ale or liquor], brisk
and neat; | The drawers call it tickle-
brain.'

386–8 **the camomile . . . wears** A proverbial,
sententious simile (Dent C34), popular in
the sixteenth century, based upon
camomile's ability to propagate itself by
means of runners. Shakespeare surely has
in mind Lyly's *Euphues* (ed. Bond, i. 196)
—'Though the camomile, the more it is
trodden and pressed down, the more it
spreadeth, yet the violet, the oftener it is
handled and touched, the sooner it
withereth and decayeth'—for Falstaff

yet youth, the more it is wasted, the sooner it wears. That
thou art my son I have partly thy mother's word, partly
my own opinion, but chiefly a villainous trick of thine eye   390
and a foolish hanging of thy nether lip that doth warrant
me. If then thou be son to me, here lies the point: why,
being son to me, art thou so pointed at? Shall the blessed
sun of heaven prove a micher and eat blackberries? A
question not to be asked. Shall the son of England prove
a thief and take purses? A question to be asked. There is
a thing, Harry, which thou hast often heard of, and it is
known to many in our land by the name of pitch. This
pitch, as ancient writers do report, doth defile; so doth the

388 yet] Q3; so Q1

nicely catches the alliteration, the
elaborately balanced antitheses, the
parison (even balance in the grammatical
members of a sentence), the *isocolon*
(equal length of two sentences or clauses),
paramoion (equal sound), and the similes
drawn from exotic or fabulous 'natural
history' that were the staple devices
(along with affectation of abstruse learning from ancient history or mythology
and the use of apophthegms from ancient
writers) of euphuistic style. Lyly's
mannerisms were fashionable in the
1580s, but were becoming outdated by
1597.

389 **thy mother's word** Compare the saying
'Ask the mother if the child be like his
father' (Dent M1193).

390 **trick** trait, as at 5.2.11 and *All's Well*
1.1.90

391 **foolish** Cowl and Morgan and Humphreys suggest 'wanton, roguish', and
offer cogent citations to show that the
hanging lower lip was regarded as a sign
of beauty and wantonness; but the common pejorative meaning of 'foolish' (indicative of ridiculous folly and trifling)
was dominant in the sixteenth century,
and is surely present in Falstaff's comic
insult.

    warrant assure

392 **here lies the point** this is the crux of the
matter; but with a play in the next line on
pointed at, i.e. pointed at in derision

393-4 **Shall . . . blackberries** A series of
rhetorical questions, elegantly balanced,
is another favourite stylistic device of
Lyly, as in *Campaspe* (2.2.31–76), when
Alexander's warlike adviser Hephaestion

questions the emperor's fall from royal
greatness into wanton embracements:
'What, is the son of Philip, King of
Macedon, become the subject of Campaspe, the captive of Thebes? . . . Will
you handle the spindle with Hercules,
when you should shake the spear with
Achilles? . . . Beauty is like the blackberry,
which seemeth red when it is not ripe,
resembling precious stones that are
polished with honey, which the smoother
they look the sooner they break', etc.
(Arnold Davenport, *Notes and Queries*,
199 (1954), 19).

394 **micher** truant. The meaning and
derivation of this word blend with
moocher, one who 'plays truant from
school, especially in order to gather
strawberries' (*OED, moocher*, 2). See Lyly,
Mother Bombie, 1.3.190–1: 'How like a
micher he stands, as though he had
truanted from honesty!' (*OED, micher, sb.*
3). *Micher* can also mean 'petty thief' and
'one who pretends to poverty' (first cited
by *OED* in 1611).

398-9 **This pitch . . . defile** Falstaff's mock-
learned citation of authorities points to
both Ecclesiasticus 13: 1: 'Whoso
toucheth pitch shall be defiled withal',
and Lyly's *Euphues to Philautus* (ed. Bond,
i. 250) and *Euphues to his Friend Livia* (i.
320), in which the biblical quotation is
employed in a euphuistically rhetorical
style (Humphreys). The sententiously
proverbial saying serves an ironic function here, in view of Euphues' warning to
'have no fellowship with one that is
mightier and richer than thyself'.

company thou keepest. For, Harry, now I do not speak to　400
thee in drink, but in tears; not in pleasure, but in passion;
not in words only, but in woes also. And yet there is a
virtuous man whom I have often noted in thy company,
but I know not his name.

PRINCE HENRY　What manner of man, an it like your
majesty?

FALSTAFF　A goodly portly man, i'faith, and a corpulent; of
a cheerful look, a pleasing eye, and a most noble carriage;
and, as I think, his age some fifty, or, by'r lady, inclining
to threescore; and now I remember me, his name is Fal-　410
staff. If that man should be lewdly given, he deceiveth me;
for, Harry, I see virtue in his looks. If then the tree may be
known by the fruit, as the fruit by the tree, then, peremptorily I speak it, there is virtue in that Falstaff. Him keep
with, the rest banish. And tell me now, thou naughty
varlet, tell me, where hast thou been this month?

PRINCE HENRY　Dost thou speak like a king? Do thou stand
for me, and I'll play my father.

---

400 Harry, now] Q1 *corr.* (Harrie, now) (*Huntington Library, Bunbury–Devonshire copy*); Harrie
now, Q1 *uncorr.* (*British Museum and Trinity College Cambridge copies*)

400–2 **now . . . woes also** The balanced
antitheses, alliteration, *parison, isocolon,*
and so on are again the marks of euphuism, as at ll. 386–8.

407 **portly** stately, as in 1.3.13 (see note),
but surely also synonymous here with
corpulent, as in *Merry Wives* 1.3.58–9:
'Sometimes the beam of her view gilded
my foot, sometimes my portly belly.'
　corpulent Kittredge rightly points to a
primary meaning of 'full-bodied', but to
insist that the word does not incorporate
'the modern sense of "extremely stout"'
is to discount citations from *OED,* 2
(Fabyan, *Chronicle,* 1494, Part VI, chap.
clviii. 158: 'Bernelphus' knights were fat,
corpulent, and shortbreathed', and
others) and to miss the humour of the
situation on-stage. Falstaff, as play-king,
chooses decorous terms to describe his
own girth, which are funny in part
because they seem offered as a kind of
litotes, or understatement, and yet confirm what is vividly true. He tries again by
boasting of his *noble carriage* (i.e. distin-

guished manner of carrying his body) and
by understating his age, but his auditors
will not let him get away with it.

411 **lewdly** wickedly and lasciviously
　given inclined, as in 3.3.13

412–3 **If . . . by the tree** Like many proverbial similes based on Scripture (Matthew
12 : 33: 'The tree is known by his fruit',
and Luke 6 : 44; see Dent T497), this one
could have been found in Lyly's *Euphues*
(ed. Bond, i. 207): 'No, no, the tree is
known by his fruit, the gold by his touch,
the son by the sire.'

413–4 **peremptorily** decisively (from Latin
peremptor, destroyer; hence that which
puts an end to all debate). Compare *Henry
V* 5.2.81–2: 'We will suddenly | Pass our
accept and peremptory answer.'

415–6 **naughty varlet** 'bad boy. Falstaff
suddenly drops the elaborate preaching
style and speaks like an ordinary father
scolding a youngster who has mis-
behaved' (Kittredge). Hal's reply responds
to this last sentence.

FALSTAFF Depose me? If thou dost it half so gravely, so
  majestically, both in word and matter, hang me up by the   420
  heels for a rabbit-sucker or a poulter's hare.
    They exchange places
PRINCE HENRY Well, here I am set.
FALSTAFF And here I stand. Judge, my masters.
PRINCE HENRY Now, Harry, whence come you?
FALSTAFF My noble lord, from Eastcheap.
PRINCE HENRY The complaints I hear of thee are grievous.
FALSTAFF 'Sblood, my lord, they are false.—Nay, I'll tickle
  ye for a young prince, i'faith.
PRINCE HENRY Swearest thou, ungracious boy? Henceforth
  ne'er look on me. Thou art violently carried away from   430
  grace. There is a devil haunts thee in the likeness of an old
  fat man; a tun of man is thy companion. Why dost thou
  converse with that trunk of humours, that bolting-hutch
  of beastliness, that swollen parcel of dropsies, that huge
  bombard of sack, that stuffed cloak-bag of guts, that

421.1 *They exchange places*] This edition; *not in* Q1

421 **rabbit-sucker** young rabbit, as in Lyly,
  Endymion (5.2.30): 'I prefer an old cony
  before a rabbit-sucker'
    poulter's hare hare hanging in a poul-
  terer's (poultry dealer's) shop. For other
  comic contrasts with emaciated animals
  and foodstuffs in the shops, see l. 124
  above and note. Beaumont and Fletcher's *Philaster* (1608–10), 5.4.36–7
  (ed. Bowers, i. 473): 'I could . . . hang
  you up cross-legg'd, | Like a hare at a
  poulter's', may be a recollection of
  Shakespeare's line.
422 **set** seated
427–8 **tickle ye for** amuse you in the role of.
  (Spoken in an aside to Falstaff's tavern
  audience.)
429 **ungracious** devoid of grace, profane. A
  response to *'Sblood* (by Christ's blood)
  which after all is Falstaff's choice of
  words, not Hal's. That the reproof of
  'ungracious boy' is partly directed at Falstaff, beneath the raillery of play-acting, is
  reinforced by a suggestion of the banishment of Falstaff in 'Henceforth ne'er look
  on me' (ll. 429–30). King Henry does not
  banish his son, or threaten to do so.
432 **tun** (a) large barrel, especially for wine
  or beer (b) ton. The words *tun* and *ton* are
  identical in origin, and have been dif-

ferentiated in spelling only from about
1688.
433 **converse** associate
    trunk (a) the visceral part of Falstaff's
  body that is so corpulent (b) chest or container, like a *tun*
    humours Falstaff's *trunk* is stuffed with
  morbid bodily fluids such as bile, phlegm,
  choler, and blood, which account for his
  beastliness.
    bolting-hutch sifting-bin used to separate
  bran, or coarse meal, and hence another
  container laden with impurities (compare
  tun and *trunk*, as well as *parcel*
  ('package'), *bombard*, and *cloak-bag* in the
  following lines)
435 **bombard** a leather jug or bottle for
  wine; compare the black cloud in *Tempest*
  2.2.20–1 that, in Trinculo's imagination, 'looks like a foul bombard that
  would shed his liquor'.
    cloak-bag a portmanteau for clothing of
  any sort, as in *Cymbeline* 3.4.168–9, con-
  taining 'doublet, hat, hose, all | That
  answer to them'. *OED* cites a similar
  figurative use in *2 Return from Parnassus*
  (1602), 4.2: 'You that are a plague
  stuffed cloak-bag of all iniquity'
  (ll. 1698–9).

roasted Manningtree ox with the pudding in his belly,
that reverend Vice, that grey iniquity, that father ruffian,
that vanity in years? Wherein is he good, but to taste sack
and drink it? Wherein neat and cleanly, but to carve a
capon and eat it? Wherein cunning, but in craft?   440
Wherein crafty, but in villainy? Wherein villainous, but
in all things? Wherein worthy, but in nothing?

FALSTAFF I would your grace would take me with you.
Whom means your grace?

PRINCE HENRY That villainous abominable misleader of
youth, Falstaff, that old white-bearded Satan.

FALSTAFF My lord, the man I know.

PRINCE HENRY I know thou dost.

FALSTAFF But to say I know more harm in him than in
myself, were to say more than I know. That he is old, the   450
more the pity, his white hairs do witness it; but that he is,
saving your reverence, a whoremaster, that I utterly

436 **roasted Manningtree ox** Manningtree,
a town in Essex, was known both for its
plays, including moralities (see next two
lines and note), and its fair, which may
well have featured ox-roasts. Dekker, *The
Seven Deadly Sins of London*, 1606 (ed.
Grosart, ii. 73), mentions 'the old Morals
at Manningtree' acted by 'tradesmen',
and Nashe, *The Choice of Valentines* (ed.
McKerrow, iii. 404), tells of 'a play of
strange morality | Shown by bachelry of
Manningtree', along with 'cream and
cakes and such good cheer'; quoted by
Malone, Kittredge, and others.
  pudding entrails stuffed with minced
meat, oatmeal, seasoning, etc., as a kind
of sausage

437–8 **reverend . . . years** See l. 131 and
note on the Vice's dagger of lath. Hal uses
the device of oxymoron to accentuate the
contrast between Falstaff's beguilingly
genial appearance and his assumption of
personified roles from the morality play.
Grey, 'grey-headed', ought to be
synonymous with *reverend* and *father*,
since old age ought to be dignified and
worthy of respect. Instead, Falstaff plays
the part of *Iniquity*, the deceiving Vice (as
in *Richard III* 3.1.82: 'the formal Vice,
Iniquity'), or *Ruffian* the swaggerer, or
Vanity the foppish gallant. His deceptive
outward appearance is like the Vice's, too,

for in a morality play such as *The Longer
Thou Livest the More Fool Thou Art*, Idleness disguises himself as Pastime, Wrath
as Manhood, Incontinency as Pleasure,
etc. See Introduction, pp. 24–6.

439 **neat and cleanly** A set phrase (see *Winter's Tale* 1.2.123) that should mean
'pure and innocent', but here is reduced
to 'cleverly executed and deft'.

440 **cunning** skilful, but in Falstaff perverted
to 'crafty'

440–1 **craft . . . crafty** Hal, in his turn at
playing king, uses rhetorical figures no
less formally and artfully than does Falstaff. *Climax* here is a series in which each
proposition rises above the preceding,
beginning with a key word in the former
phrase (craft–crafty, villainy–villainous).
Anaphora repeats a word (*Wherein*) at the
beginning of two or more successive
clauses. On *parison* and *isocolon*, etc., see
note at ll. 386–8.

443 **take me with you** i.e. let me keep pace
with your meaning. A common tag (Dent
T28.1), as in *Romeo* 3.5.141; we should
probably not read into it a plea that Falstaff be taken along by Hal in his role as
future king.

452 **saving your reverence** An apologetic
phrase, introducing a potentially critical
or offensive remark. A common expression (Dent R93 and citations).

deny. If sack-and-sugar be a fault, God help the wicked!
If to be old and merry be a sin, then many an old host that
I know is damned. If to be fat be to be hated, then
Pharaoh's lean kine are to be loved. No, my good lord,
banish Peto, banish Bardolph, banish Poins; but for
sweet Jack Falstaff, kind Jack Falstaff, true Jack Falstaff,
valiant Jack Falstaff, and therefore more valiant being as
he is old Jack Falstaff, banish not him thy Harry's com-   460
pany, banish not him thy Harry's company—banish
plump Jack, and banish all the world.
PRINCE HENRY I do, I will.

> ⌈*A knocking heard. Exeunt Hostess, Francis, and
> Bardolph.*⌉
> *Enter Bardolph, running*

BARDOLPH O, my lord, my lord, the sheriff with a most monstrous watch is at the door.
FALSTAFF Out, ye rogue, play out the play. I have much to
say in the behalf of that Falstaff.

> *Enter the Hostess*

HOSTESS O Jesu, my lord, my lord!
PRINCE HENRY Heigh, heigh! The devil rides upon a fiddlestick. What's the matter?   470
HOSTESS The sheriff and all the watch are at the door. They
are come to search the house. Shall I let them in?

---

456 lean] Q2; lane QI   457 Bardolph] DERING MS (Bardolffe), FI (Bardolph); Bardoll
QI   463.1–2 *A knocking ... Bardolph*] MALONE; *not in* QI   463.3 *Bardolph*] FI; Bardoll
QI   464 most] QI; most most F

---

453 **sack-and-sugar** A recollection of
Poins's name for Falstaff, 'Sir John, Sack-
and-Sugar Jack' (1.2.107).
454 **host** innkeeper
456 **Pharaoh's lean kine** In Genesis 41,
Joseph interprets the seven lean kine who
devour seven fat kine in Pharaoh's dream
as seven years of famine that are to follow
seven years of plenty.
463.1–3 *A knocking . . . Bardolph* QQF1
provide no exits for these characters (see
collation), specifying only that Bardolph
must enter 'running' in the next line and
the Hostess at l. 467. The pause required
for exits and Bardolph's re-entrance at
this point has struck some editors and
critics (e.g. Sisson and Wilson) as awkward, and we cannot be certain that the

characters are not intended to slip out at
l. 383 or at some unspecified point. Bardolph might leave at l. 315 as Falstaff
enters, perhaps in a huff. Are we to take
literally Falstaff's lofty command as king:
'For God's sake, lords, convey my tristful
queen' (l. 380)? Still, one must doubt that
the Hostess and Bardolph would want to
miss the fun, and some confused running
around in response to a knocking at the
door at l. 463 would punctuate the conclusion of the late-night revelry.
465 **watch** posse of watchmen
469–70 **The devil rides upon a fiddlestick** i.e.
here's much ado about nothing. Conceivably this proverbial-sounding phrase
originated with Shakespeare (Dent
D263).

FALSTAFF Dost thou hear, Hal? Never call a true piece of
    gold a counterfeit. Thou art essentially made without
    seeming so.
PRINCE HENRY And thou a natural coward without instinct.
FALSTAFF I deny your major. If you will deny the sheriff, so;
    if not, let him enter. If I become not a cart as well as
    another man, a plague on my bringing up! I hope I shall
    as soon be strangled with a halter as another.   480
PRINCE HENRY Go hide thee behind the arras. The rest walk

474 made] Q1; mad F3

473–7 **Never . . . major** A difficult passage,
all the more so because of a crux; F3 substitutes 'mad' for 'made' in QqF1–2
(though perhaps the change is no more
than a spelling variant), and has been
followed by many editors, including
Malone, the Globe editors, and Wilson
(*NCS*). If 'mad' is adopted as the reading,
then Falstaff may be urging Hal to acknowledge, beneath all their play-acting,
that Hal is genuinely the 'madcap' he
professed to be in 1.2.134 (Hotspur, too,
calls him 'madcap Prince of Wales' at
4.1.95), that he truly shares the fellowship of the tavern, and that, accordingly,
Hal should be able to recognize Falstaff's
true worth instead of turning him over to
the authorities as a counterfeit. If we
retain the original reading of 'made', on
the other hand, then perhaps Falstaff may
be said to address Hal as follows: Bear in
mind that, despite all our raillery about
cowardice and friendship, I am in fact true
gold and should not be turned over to the
sheriff as a counterfeit. You too are the
real thing (essentially made), i.e. a true
prince, although your actions don't seem
to show it.
    With this quip, Falstaff hearkens back
to their previous conversation, in which
he professed instinctively to recognize
Hal's princeliness beneath the buckram
disguise of a highwayman, and so played
the coward on instinct. Hal parries this
sally of wit as follows: If we are to
drop the pretence of play-acting, then I
insist that you are a natural coward, not
the 'coward on instinct' you invented
as your excuse. This accusation sounds
paradoxically like the conclusion to a
false syllogism, for how can an action be
'natural' if it is lacking in instinct? The
contradiction in terms, however, does
not prevent Falstaff from rejoinder in

order to deny Hal's 'major', or 'major
premise', namely that Falstaff was (and
is) a genuine coward. The implied syllogism would then go as follows: (a) Major
premise: Falstaff's cowardice 'on instinct' is merely one of the pretences with
which we have entertained ourselves. (b)
Minor premise: we have agreed to drop all
pretences. (c) Conclusion: Then we must
agree that Falstaff is a natural coward.
Major may also quibble on 'Mayor' (compare QqF 'Maior'), suggesting a parallel
between 'mayor' and 'sheriff', both of
them denied.
477 **deny the sheriff** In *Famous Victories*,
when a follower of Prince Henry robs a
poor carrier on Gad's Hill, the Prince undertakes to 'save the base villain's life' (l.
27) by intervening with the Chief Justice.
See Introduction, p. 20.
    deny . . . deny (a) refuse to concede (b)
refuse entrance to
478 **become** befit, adorn
    cart hangman's cart proceeding to the
gallows. Falstaff insists again that he
lacks the 'natural' coward's fear of death,
and so can play the part of the condemned
prisoner on his way to execution as bravely as any man.
479 **bringing up** (a) upbringing (b) being
brought before the authorities and up the
gallows
480 **as soon be strangled** etc. 'His weight
would ensure that' (Wilson, *NCS*). There
is a pun on *as soon*: (a) as willingly or
readily (b) as quickly.
481 **arras** a wall-hanging behind which one
might gain concealment, as with
Claudius's and Polonius's concealments
'behind the arras' in *Hamlet* (2.2.162,
also 3.3.28) and similar concealments in
Merry Wives 3.3.79, *Much Ado* 1.3.53,
and *K. John* 4.1.2. In Shakespeare's
theatre, the arras might be hung before a

up above. Now, my masters, for a true face and good
conscience.

FALSTAFF Both which I have had, but their date is out, and
therefore I'll hide me.

  He hides behind the arras

PRINCE HENRY Call in the sheriff.

                                ⌈*Exeunt all except the Prince and Peto*⌉
                Enter Sheriff and the Carrier

Now, Master Sheriff, what is your will with me?

SHERIFF

First, pardon me, my lord. A hue and cry
Hath followed certain men unto this house.

PRINCE HENRY What men?   490

SHERIFF

One of them is well known, my gracious lord,
A gross fat man.

CARRIER   As fat as butter.

PRINCE HENRY

The man, I do assure you, is not here,
For I myself at this time have employed him.
And, sheriff, I will engage my word to thee
That I will, by tomorrow dinner-time,
Send him to answer thee or any man

485.1 *He . . . arras*] F1 (*Exit*); *not in* Q1   486.1 *Exeunt . . . Peto*] COWL AND MORGAN; *not in*
Q1   488–9 First . . . house] *as verse*, POPE; *as prose*, Q1   491–2 One . . . butter] *as verse*, POPE;
as prose, Q1

door or 'discovery space' in the tiring-
house, facilitating an unobtrusive departure backstage at the very end of a scene.
Presumably Peto 'discovers' Falstaff to
view at l. 509 by lifting aside the arras; he
then searches his pockets, and leaves him
there asleep. At the end of the scene the
actor of Falstaff, concealed again by the
arras, withdraws into the tiring-house.

481–2 **walk up above** go upstairs (in the
tavern, to avoid being seen; not visibly in
the theatre)

484 **date is out** lease has run out. A common
expression (Dent D42.1).

486.1 *Exeunt . . . Peto* These directions are
not provided in Qq (see collation), and F1
provides only an *Exit* in the previous line.

Whether Peto in fact remains, or whether
Poins should instead accompany the
Prince, is controversial, though QqF1 are
unambiguous on Peto's presence at
ll. 509ff. See Introduction, pp. 102–3.

488–9 **First . . . house** On QqF1's failure to
recognize these two lines as verse (see
collation), see Introduction, p. 105.

488 **hue and cry** a muster of citizens to pursue a felon. In *Famous Victories*, 'the town
of Deptford is risen | With hue and cry
after your man | Which . . . robbed a poor
carrier' (ll. 19–22).

492 **As fat as butter** A familiar comparison
(Dent B767).

495 **engage** pledge

496 **dinner-time** i.e. around noon

For anything he shall be charged withal;
And so let me entreat you leave the house.

SHERIFF

I will, my lord. There are two gentlemen   500
Have in this robbery lost three hundred marks.

PRINCE HENRY

It may be so. If he have robbed these men
He shall be answerable; and so farewell.

SHERIFF Good night, my noble lord.

PRINCE HENRY

I think it is good morrow, is it not?

SHERIFF

Indeed, my lord, I think it be two o'clock.

                                     Exit with the Carrier

PRINCE HENRY This oily rascal is known as well as Paul's. Go
call him forth.

PETO Falstaff!—Fast asleep behind the arras, and snorting
like a horse.   510

PRINCE HENRY Hark how hard he fetches breath. Search his
pockets.

> *Peto searcheth Falstaff's pocket, and findeth certain*
> *papers*

What hast thou found?

PETO Nothing but papers, my lord.

PRINCE HENRY Let's see what they be. Read them.

PETO (*reads*) 'Item, a capon, ... 2*s*. 2*d*.
    Item, sauce, ... 4*d*.
    Item, sack, two gallons, ... 5*s*. 8*d*.
    Item, anchovies and sack after supper, ... 2*s*. 6*d*.
    Item, bread, ... *ob*.'   520

501 three hundred] Q1 (300.)   504 Good] Q3; God Q1   505 good] Q4; god Q1   506.1 *with
the carrier*] HANMER (*subs.*); *not in* Q1   512.1 *Peto searcheth Falstaff's pocket*] This edition; *He
searcheth his pocket* Q1   516 PETO (*reads*)] F1 (*Peto.*); *not in* Q1

501 **three hundred marks** See notes at
    2.1.53 and 2.4.153.
505 **morrow** morning (since it is after
    midnight). Wilson (*Fortunes*, 58–9)
    speculates that Falstaff's snoring may
    have become audible by now.
507 **Paul's** St Paul's Cathedral, as vast as it
    was famous
516 **PETO** The omission of a speech prefix
    (see collation) before some quoted docu-
    ment to be read or proclaimed is not
    unusual; compare *1 Henry VI* 1.3.74.

519 **anchovies** a delicacy used to increase
    thirst, and to enhance the taste of wine
    (first recorded use in *OED*). Compare
    Tobias Venner, *Via Recta ad Vitam Longam*
    (1637), 103: 'Anchova's, the famous
    meat of drunkards, and of them that
    desire to have their drink oblectate
    [delight] the palate' (*OED*).
520 *ob*. obolus (originally a small Greek
    coin), halfpenny. Compare *d*. (*denarius*)
    for penny, and £ (*libra*) for pound.

PRINCE HENRY O monstrous! But one half-pennyworth of
bread to this intolerable deal of sack? What there is else,
keep close; we'll read it at more advantage. There let him
sleep till day. I'll to the court in the morning. We must all
to the wars, and thy place shall be honourable. I'll
procure this fat rogue a charge of foot, and I know his
death will be a march of twelve score. The money shall be
paid back again with advantage. Be with me betimes in
the morning; and so, good morrow, Peto.

PETO Good morrow, good my lord.   *Exeunt*   530

3.1   *Enter Hotspur, Worcester, Lord Mortimer, and Owen
          Glendower*

MORTIMER
   These promises are fair, the parties sure,
   And our induction full of prosperous hope.
HOTSPUR
   Lord Mortimer, and cousin Glendower,

521 PRINCE HENRY] F1 (*Prince.*); *not in* Q1

3.1.0 *and*] *not in* Q1   3–10 Lord ... heaven] SINGER (1856) *for ll.* 3–5, ROWE *for* 6–10; *as
verse*, F1, *ending* Glendower, | downe? | vpon it, | Mappe. | it is: | *Hotspurre*: | of you, | sigh, |
Heauen; *as prose* Q1

522 **intolerable** excessive
523 **close** hidden
     advantage favourable opportunity
525 **thy ... honourable** Dr Johnson and
     others find it odd that Peto, not Poins,
     should be offered a place in the war befit-
     ting a gentleman, but perhaps we see here
     a reflection of the comic convention
     through which Bardolph becomes (like
     Peto) a lieutenant, Pistol an ensign and a
     lieutenant, and Falstaff himself both a
     knight and a captain. See Introduction,
     pp. 102–3.
526 **charge of foot** command of an infantry
     company. In 3.3.179 the Prince makes
     good his promise.
526–7 **his death ... twelve score** it will be
     the death of him to march as far as 240
     yards or paces. The jest about Falstaff's
     walking recalls 2.2.12–25.
527–8 **The money ... advantage** See Ap-
     pendix for Stow's account.
528 **advantage** interest
     betimes early

530 *Exeunt* Falstaff is evidently able to
     depart rear-stage without being visible to
     the audience; see l. 481 and note.
3.1 Location: See Appendix for Holinshed's
     report of a meeting among deputies of the
     three lords at the house of the Arch-
     deacon of Bangor in north-west Wales. In
     Shakespeare's unhistorical meeting of the
     three lords themselves, the Archdeacon is
     mentioned (l. 69) but is not present, and
     Glendower appears to be entertaining his
     two allies at his home.
   2 **induction** beginning, as in the introduc-
     tory scene before the play's main action.
     The theatrical sense is found also in
     Richard III 1.1.32, and 4.4.5: 'A dire in-
     duction am I witness to.'
     prosperous hope hope of prospering
3–11 Qq print as prose (see collation),
     whereas F1's lineation seems generated
     by the compositor's need to use up space;
     see Introduction, pp. 104–5. F1 similarly
     breaks l. 23 into two defective short lines.

Will you sit down? And uncle Worcester—
A plague upon it, I have forgot the map.

GLENDOWER (*showing the map*)

No, here it is. Sit, cousin Percy,
Sit, good cousin Hotspur—for by that name
As oft as Lancaster doth speak of you
His cheek looks pale, and with a rising sigh
He wisheth you in heaven.

HOTSPUR   And you in hell,   10
As oft as he hears Owen Glendower spoke of.

GLENDOWER

I cannot blame him. At my nativity
The front of heaven was full of fiery shapes,
Of burning cressets, and at my birth
The frame and huge foundation of the earth
Shaked like a coward.

HOTSPUR   Why, so it would have done
At the same season, if your mother's cat
Had but kittened, though yourself had never been born.

GLENDOWER

I say the earth did shake when I was born.

HOTSPUR

And I say the earth was not of my mind,   20
If you suppose as fearing you it shook.

GLENDOWER

The heavens were all on fire, the earth did tremble.

HOTSPUR

O, then the earth shook to see the heavens on fire,
And not in fear of your nativity.
Diseasèd nature oftentimes breaks forth

---

6 *showing the map*] This edition; *not in* Q1   9 cheek looks] Q1; Cheekes looke F1   10–11 And
... spoke of] COLLIER; *as prose*, Q1   16–18 Why ... born] POPE; *as prose*, Q1

---

8 **Lancaster** Glendower speaks of King
Henry IV by his ducal, rather than his
royal, title. At l. 61 Glendower calls the
King 'Henry Bolingbroke'. See also Hotspur's use of *Bolingbroke* at 1.3.137 and
note.

12–16 **At my nativity . . . coward** See Appendix for Shakespeare's apparent mis-

reading of Holinshed.

13 **front** forehead, hence face

14 **cressets** small metal fire-baskets, filled
with combustibles and lighted as a torch,
usually swinging from pivots attached to
the end of a pole or suspended from a ceil-
ing; hence, blazing heavenly bodies

25 **Diseasèd** (a) disturbed, disordered (b) sick

208

In strange eruptions; oft the teeming earth
Is with a kind of colic pinched and vexed
By the imprisoning of unruly wind
Within her womb, which, for enlargement striving,
Shakes the old beldam earth and topples down   30
Steeples and moss-grown towers. At your birth
Our grandam earth, having this distemperature,
In passion shook.
GLENDOWER   Cousin, of many men
I do not bear these crossings. Give me leave
To tell you once again that at my birth
The front of heaven was full of fiery shapes,
The goats ran from the mountains, and the herds
Were strangely clamorous to the frighted fields.
These signs have marked me extraordinary,
And all the courses of my life do show   40
I am not in the roll of common men.
Where is he living, clipped in with the sea
That chides the banks of England, Scotland, Wales,
Which calls me pupil or hath read to me?

30 topples] Q1 ; tombles F1

26 **eruptions** (a) astronomical and geophysical outbreaks (b) burstings forth of disease
26–31 **oft...towers** Hemingway and others cite Gabriel Harvey's *Pleasant ... Discourse of the Earthquake in April Last*, 1580 (ed. Grosart, i. 52): 'The material cause of earthquakes (as . . . is sufficiently proved by Aristotle in the second book of his *Meteors*) is no doubt great abundance of wind, or store of gross and dry vapours and spirits fast shut up, and as a man would say imprisoned in the caves and dungeons of the earth: which wind or vapours, seeking to be set at liberty . . . violently rush out ... which forcible eruption, and strong breath, causeth an earthquake.' A similar view is found in Pliny, *Natural History*, II. lxxii; is parodied in Aristophanes's *The Clouds*; and recurs in Marlowe's *Tamburlaine Part I*, 1.2. 49–51: 'shall make the mountains quake, | Even as when windy exhalations | Fighting for passage, tilt within the earth'.
29 **enlargement** release from confinement. 'Hotspur hints that Grandam Earth brought forth a windbag' (Wilson, *NCS*, citing Isaiah 26: 17–18: 'we have been with child, and suffered pain, as though we had brought forth wind'). This *unruly wind*, generated by *colic* and released from within earth's *womb* or bowels (ll. 27–9), might well be intended to suggest a fart.
30 **beldam** Synonymous with *grandam*, 'grandmother', at l. 32.
32 **distemperature** a disordered condition of the air or elements not properly tempered for human well-being, as in *Dream* 2.1.106–7: 'And thorough this distemperature we see | The seasons alter', or of the bodily humours, as in *Romeo* 2.3.40: 'Thou art uproused with some distemperature.'
33 **passion** suffering
     of from
34 **crossings** thwartings, interruptions
36 **front of heaven** brow or face of heaven, the sky
42 **he** anyone
     clipped in with encircled by
43 **chides** chafes against, contends angrily with, thunders upon
     banks shores
44 **Which** who
     read to lectured, instructed

And bring him out that is but woman's son
Can trace me in the tedious ways of art
And hold me pace in deep experiments.

HOTSPUR

I think there's no man speaks better Welsh.
I'll to dinner.

MORTIMER

Peace, cousin Percy; you will make him mad.   50

GLENDOWER

I can call spirits from the vasty deep.

HOTSPUR

Why, so can I, or so can any man;
But will they come when you do call for them?

GLENDOWER

Why, I can teach you, cousin, to command the devil.

HOTSPUR

And I can teach thee, coz, to shame the devil
By telling truth. Tell truth and shame the devil.
If thou have power to raise him, bring him hither,
And I'll be sworn I have power to shame him hence.
O, while you live, tell truth and shame the devil.

MORTIMER

Come, come, no more of this unprofitable chat.   60

GLENDOWER

Three times hath Henry Bolingbroke made head
Against my power; thrice from the banks of Wye

---

45 son] Q1 *corr.* (sonne,) (*British Museum copy*); sonne? Q1 *uncorr.* (*Trinity College Cambridge and Huntington Library, Bunbury–Devonshire copies*)   55 coz] Q1 (coose)

45 **bring him out** produce any man
46 **Can . . . art** who can follow my tracks in the time-consuming and laborious ways of magic art
47 **hold me pace** keep pace with me
48–9 **I . . . dinner** Metrical irregularity catches the tone of Hotspur's impatience.
48 **Welsh** Hotspur drily suggests that Glendower's proficiency amounts to little more than command of a barbaric provincial tongue that was synonymous with thrasonical boasting, unintelligibility (see l. 116), and converse with devils (l. 225). *OED*, 2b, cites Thomas Fuller, *Worthies of England* (1661), under Denbighshire: 'Amelcorne. This English word (which I find in the English

Camden) is Welsh to me.'
51 **call** convene, summon into presence. (But Hotspur quibbles on the sense of 'cry aloud to' without any necessary response.)
   vasty deep lower world, 'the abyss or depth of space' (*OED*, *deep*, *sb.* 3c). Compare *2 Henry IV* 2.4.149: 'to th' infernal deep, with Erebus and tortures vile also', and Milton, *Paradise Lost*, vii. 166–9. *Vasty* is a word coined by Shakespeare.
56 **Tell . . . devil** Proverbial (Dent T566).
61 **Three times** See Appendix for historical background.
   made head raised a force
62 **power** army, as at 1.1.22.

And sandy-bottomed Severn have I sent him
Bootless home and weather-beaten back.

HOTSPUR

Home without boots, and in foul weather too!
How scapes he agues, in the devil's name?

GLENDOWER

Come, here is the map. Shall we divide our right
According to our threefold order ta'en?

MORTIMER

The Archdeacon hath divided it
Into three limits very equally: 70
England, from Trent and Severn hitherto,
By south and east is to my part assigned;
All westward, Wales beyond the Severn shore,
And all the fertile land within that bound,
To Owen Glendower; and, dear coz, to you
The remnant northward, lying off from Trent.
And our indentures tripartite are drawn,
Which being sealèd interchangeably—
A business that this night may execute—
Tomorrow, cousin Percy, you and I   80
And my good lord of Worcester will set forth
To meet your father and the Scottish power,

67 here is] Q1; heere's F1

64 **Bootless** without success. (But Hotspur quibbles on the sense 'barefoot.')
weather-beaten (a) buffeted by wind and rain (b) defeated by the weather. On Holinshed's ascription to Glendower of magic ability to raise foul weather and thus hinder his enemy, see Appendix, 1.3.83 and 3.1.61.
65 **without boots** An echo of earlier discussions about muddy roads; see 2.1.81–2 and notes.
67 **our right** the territory that is rightfully ours
68 **order ta'en** arrangements made (*OED*, *order, sb.* 14)
69 **Archdeacon** i.e. the Archdeacon of Bangor, in whose house, according to Holinshed, the deputies of the rebel leaders divided up the realm among them; see Appendix, 3.1.0.1–2.
70–6 **three limits . . . Trent** See Appendix for

Holinshed. The *Severn* flows southwards from Shrewsbury into the Bristol Channel; the *Trent* flows south and east and then northerly from Stoke-on-Trent (not far from Shrewsbury) into the Humber estuary.
70 **limits** territories, regions defined by boundaries (*OED*, *sb.* 3)
71 **from . . . hitherto** up to this boundary-line defined by the Rivers Trent and Severn. (The actor gestures.)
74 **all . . . bound** i.e. presumably the lowlands between the Severn and the Welsh hills
77 **indentures tripartite** an agreement *drawn* (drawn up) in triplicate, each copy sealed *interchangeably* (l. 78)—i.e. with the seals of all three signatories, one copy to be kept by each. See Appendix for Holinshed.
79 **this night may execute** can be carried out tonight

As is appointed us, at Shrewsbury.
My father Glendower is not ready yet,
Nor shall we need his help these fourteen days.
Within that space you may have drawn together
Your tenants, friends, and neighbouring gentlemen.

GLENDOWER

A shorter time shall send me to you, lords;
And in my conduct shall your ladies come,
From whom you now must steal and take no leave,   90
For there will be a world of water shed
Upon the parting of your wives and you.

HOTSPUR

Methinks my moiety, north from Burton here,
In quantity equals not one of yours.
See how this river comes me cranking in,
And cuts me from the best of all my land
A huge half-moon, a monstrous cantle out.
I'll have the current in this place dammed up,
And here the smug and silver Trent shall run
In a new channel, fair and evenly.   100
It shall not wind with such a deep indent
To rob me of so rich a bottom here.

GLENDOWER

Not wind? It shall, it must; you see it doth.

---

97 cantle] F1; scantle Q1   103 wind?] Q2; ~ ∧ Q1

---

84 **father** father-in-law, as at l. 142.
86 **may have drawn** will be able to draw
87 **tenants** those whose landholdings entailed feudal obligations
89 **conduct** safe conduct, escort, as at l. 192
93 **moiety** share
   Burton Burton-on-Trent
95 **comes me cranking in** comes twisting in on my portion. Hotspur's objection may be that the Trent turns northwards after leaving Burton; if it were to continue eastwards into the Wash instead of joining the Humber, he would possess Lincolnshire and part of Nottinghamshire now lost to him. On *me*, see note at 2.4.100.

97 **cantle** Qq's *scantle* is possible in *OED*'s sense of 'a small piece or portion, a scantling', but the only other citation given is later (Robert Vilvain, *Theoremata Theologica*, 1654, 194), and in the present instance the initial *s* could well be a contamination from *monstrous*, the previous word. The F1 reading, *cantle*, better fits the sense; it means 'a projecting corner or angle of land, a portion sheared off'. Compare *Antony* 3.10.6: 'The greater cantle of the world is lost.'
99 **smug** smooth
102 **bottom** river valley (but actually a lowland plain)

MORTIMER

Yea, but mark how he bears his course, and runs me up
With like advantage on the other side,
Gelding the opposèd continent as much
As on the other side it takes from you.

WORCESTER

Yea, but a little charge will trench him here
And on this north side win this cape of land;
And then he runs straight and even.   110

HOTSPUR

I'll have it so. A little charge will do it.

GLENDOWER

I'll not have it altered.

HOTSPUR   Will not you?

GLENDOWER No, nor you shall not.

HOTSPUR Who shall say me nay?

GLENDOWER Why, that will I.

HOTSPUR

Let me not understand you, then; speak it in Welsh.

GLENDOWER

I can speak English, lord, as well as you;
For I was trained up in the English court,
Where, being but young, I framèd to the harp

104–7 Yea . . . you] POPE (*omitting* Yea *and* how); *as verse*, F1, *ending* course, | side, | much, | you; *as prose*, Q1

104–7 **Yea . . . you** See collation. On F1's unconvincing lineation, see Introduction, p. 105. Metrical irregularity is marked as in other parts of the scene: l. 104 is hypermetric in the arrangement of lines adopted here, l. 110 is short, and at ll. 113–15 the middle short line, 'Who shall say me nay?', could be paired with either the preceding or following short lines to produce a satisfactory pentameter. All these irregularities seem rhetorically effective.

104 **me** See note at 2.4.100.

106 **Gelding . . . continent** cutting off something vital from the opposite bank. The *continent* is that which should contain the river, as in *Dream* 2.1.92, where flooding streams 'have overborne their continents'. Mortimer's point is that the Trent's original southerly course, from Stoke-on-Trent to Burton-upon-Trent, deprives Mortimer of as large a potential

share as the Trent's subsequently northerly course deprives Hotspur. Mortimer diplomatically urges the advantage of compromise, whereas Glendower (whose share is not even threatened by this dispute) is characteristically outraged by any proposal to tamper with nature.

108 **charge** expenditure
trench divert by means of a trench (*OED*, v. 4a)

117 **lord** 'Glendower is losing patience with Hotspur and becomes formal. He no longer calls Hotspur "cousin Percy"' (Wright).

118 **trained . . . court** See Appendix for historical background.

119 **framèd to the harp** set to harp accompaniment. Glendower may have composed the *ditties*, or poems, as well, for the ability to write songs and sonnets was the proper accomplishment of a courtier.

Many an English ditty lovely well,   120
And gave the tongue a helpful ornament—
A virtue that was never seen in you.
HOTSPUR
Marry, and I am glad of it with all my heart!
I had rather be a kitten and cry mew
Than one of these same metre ballad-mongers.
I had rather hear a brazen can'stick turned,
Or a dry wheel grate on the axle-tree,
And that would set my teeth nothing on edge,
Nothing so much as mincing poetry.
'Tis like the forced gait of a shuffling nag.   130
GLENDOWER Come, you shall have Trent turned.
HOTSPUR
I do not care. I'll give thrice so much land
To any well-deserving friend;
But in the way of bargain, mark ye me,
I'll cavil on the ninth part of a hair.
Are the indentures drawn? Shall we be gone?
GLENDOWER
The moon shines fair; you may away by night.

---

126 can'stick] Q1 (cansticke); Candlestick F1   128 on] Q1 (an)

120 **ditty** Often used to signify the words of a
song, as distinct from the music, as in *As
You Like It* 5.3.32–3: 'Though there was
no great matter in the ditty, yet the note
was very untuneable.'
121 **gave . . . ornament** gave to the words
the assisting ornament of musical expression; also, gave to the English language a capacity for expressive elegance
and the graceful addition of a Welsh accent
122 **A virtue** an accomplishment
125 **metre ballad-mongers** On derogatory
attitudes towards metrical ballads, see
2.2.42 and note. Hotspur, never the
courtier, derides courtly 'making' of
poetry as though it were indistinguish-
able from street ballad-mongering. (First
recorded use of *ballad-monger* in *OED*.)
126 **brazen can'stick turned** bronze candlestick turned on a lathe. Humphreys and
Wilson (*NCS*) cite Stow, *Survey of London*
(ed. C. L. Kingsford (Oxford, 1908), i.
277) on the Lothbury founders, who 'cast

candlesticks . . . and do afterward turn
them . . . to make them smooth and bright
with turning and scrating (as some do
term it) making a loathsome noise to the
by-passers'.
127 **dry wheel** Compare the proverb 'A dry
cart-wheel cries the loudest' (Dent
C109.1).
    axle-tree axle
128 **set . . . edge** A familiar expression (Dent
T431).
    nothing not at all
129 **mincing** tripping in an affectedly dainty
manner, as in *Merchant* 3.4.67–8: 'and
turn two mincing steps | Into a manly
stride'.
130 **forced . . . nag** 'jerky steps of a hobbled
horse' (Wilson, *NCS*). The metre demonstrates the irregularity.
135 **cavil . . . hair** To split hair, or regard
hair as valueless, is a commonplace idea
(Dent H19 and H32). It recurs at 3.3.57–8.
136 **drawn** drawn up

I'll haste the writer, and withal
Break with your wives of your departure hence.
I am afraid my daughter will run mad,   140
So much she doteth on her Mortimer.   *Exit*

MORTIMER

Fie, cousin Percy, how you cross my father!

HOTSPUR

I cannot choose. Sometime he angers me
With telling me of the mouldwarp and the ant,
Of the dreamer Merlin and his prophecies,
And of a dragon and a finless fish,
A clip-winged griffin and a moulten raven,
A couching lion and a ramping cat,
And such a deal of skimble-skamble stuff
As puts me from my faith. I tell you what: 150
He held me last night at least nine hours
In reckoning up the several devils' names
That were his lackeys. I cried 'Hum', and 'Well, go to',
But marked him not a word. O he is as tedious
As a tirèd horse, a railing wife,
Worse than a smoky house. I had rather live
With cheese and garlic in a windmill, far,

138 **writer** scrivener drawing up the indentures
    withal at the same time
139 **Break with** inform, disclose knowledge to
142 **cross** vex by contradiction. Compare *come 'cross* at l. 167.
144–8 **the mouldwarp . . . cat** See Appendix for Shakespeare's borrowing from Holinshed in a different context. A *mouldwarp* is a mole, literally an earth-thrower, or one that *warps* (throws) up the *mould* (soil). G. R. French, *Shakespeareana Genealogica* (1869), 64, confirms that the dragon, lion, and white wolf (compare wild boar) were the crests respectively of Glendower, Hotspur, and Edmund Mortimer. A *griffin* is a fabulous beast, usually with the head and wings of an eagle and the body and hindquarters of a lion, common in heraldry. *Couching* and *ramping* are Hotspur's sardonic way of expressing the heraldic terms *couchant*, lying down with head erect, and *rampant*, rearing on the hind legs with the forelegs pawing the air and the head in profile. Ordinary *cats* (l. 148)

are not common in heraldry. Equally idiosyncratic are the beasts deprived of locomotion: the *finless fish*, *clip-winged griffin* suggestive of a domestic fowl, and *moulten raven*. *Merlin* is the wizard of Arthurian legend.
147 **moulten** having moulted (only recorded use in *OED*)
149 **skimble-skamble** nonsensical (a word coined by Shakespeare)
150 **puts me from my faith** 'makes me so incredulous that I can no longer believe even my creed as a Christian' (Kittredge)
152 **several** various
153 **go to** Used to express incredulity, like 'Don't tell me', 'You don't say', etc. Hotspur has employed such expressions to pretend polite astonishment, while scarcely listening.
155–6 **railing . . . house** Compare the proverb 'A smoking house and a chiding wife make a man run out of doors' (Dent H781) and Proverbs 10: 26, 19: 13, and 27: 15.
157 **cheese . . . windmill** Traditionally poor fare and noisy accommodations. The

Than feed on cates and have him talk to me
In any summer-house in Christendom.
MORTIMER

In faith, he is a worthy gentleman,   160
Exceedingly well read, and profited
In strange concealments, valiant as a lion
And wondrous affable, and as bountiful
As mines of India. Shall I tell you, cousin?
He holds your temper in a high respect
And curbs himself even of his natural scope
When you come 'cross his humour. Faith, he does.
I warrant you that man is not alive
Might so have tempted him as you have done
Without the taste of danger and reproof.   170
But do not use it oft, let me entreat you.
WORCESTER

In faith, my lord, you are too wilful-blame,
And since your coming hither have done enough
To put him quite besides his patience.
You must needs learn, lord, to amend this fault.

167 come] Q1; doe F1

cheese and garlic are contrasted with *cates*, or delicacies, in l. 158, and the windmill with Glendower's still more voluble and incessant noise. Perhaps, too, Hotspur suggests that the garlic smell would be exacerbated by having the fumes constantly blown in one's face, as when a foul-breathed person talks uninterruptedly. Shakespeare frequently associates garlic with beggarly fare and foul breath, as in *Measure* 3.2.170 and *Coriolanus* 4.6.98. In *2 Henry VI* (4.7.11), similarly, it is reported of Jack Cade that 'his breath stinks with eating toasted cheese'. Nym complains of being fed on bread and cheese in Falstaff's service in *Merry Wives* 2.1.122, and in the same play there are repeated jests about the Welsh partiality for cheese (2.2.268 and 5.5.80 and 134). The familiar phrase 'to live in a windmill' is aimed more at the noisiness; see Dent W452 and citations.
159 **summer-house** a place for recreation, affordable only by the very rich; see citations in Humphreys.
161 **profited** proficient
162 **strange concealments** occult practices, secret art

valiant as a lion A familiar comparison (Dent L308).
163 **wondrous** On adjectives as adverbs, see note at 2.4.355.
164 **India** perhaps America; both the East and West Indies are cited in Shakespeare as sources of wealth (*Merry Wives* 1.3.67, *Errors* 3.2.131, etc.)
165 **temper** temperament
166 **scope** freedom of speech
167 **come 'cross** contradict; see *cross* at l. 142.
169 **Might** who could
tempted provoked
170 **Without . . . reproof** without experiencing a reproof with dangerous consequences
171 **use** practise
172 **too wilful-blame** blameworthy for too much self-will. Compare the phrase with infinitive in *Romeo* 3.5.169: 'You are to blame', printed thus in Q2 but as 'too blame' in F1 (also in F1 text of *Henry VIII* 4.2.101), and evidently interpreted as 'too blameworthy'. Humphreys and Wilson (*NCS*) cite other instances.
174 **besides** out of
patience (trisyllabic)

Though sometimes it show greatness, courage, blood—
And that's the dearest grace it renders you—
Yet oftentimes it doth present harsh rage,
Defect of manners, want of government,
Pride, haughtiness, opinion, and disdain,   180
The least of which haunting a nobleman
Loseth men's hearts and leaves behind a stain
Upon the beauty of all parts besides,
Beguiling them of commendation.

HOTSPUR

Well, I am schooled. Good manners be your speed!
Here come our wives, and let us take our leave.

    Enter Glendower with Lady Percy and Lady Mortimer

MORTIMER

This is the deadly spite that angers me:
My wife can speak no English, I no Welsh.

GLENDOWER

My daughter weeps. She'll not part with you;
She'll be a soldier too, she'll to the wars.   190

MORTIMER

Good father, tell her that she and my Aunt Percy
Shall follow in your conduct speedily.

    Glendower speaks to her in Welsh, and she answers
    him in the same

186.1 *Lady Percy and Lady Mortimer*] DYCE; *the Ladies.* Q1

176 **blood** high spirit. Choleric men were regarded as temperamentally inclined not only to bold, warlike valour, but to rash quarrelsomeness, arrogance, jealousy of rivals, suspiciousness, discontent, etc. Compare Coriolanus, Mercutio, Cassius, and others (Bamborough, 93–4).

177 **dearest** (a) noblest and best (b) costliest. Compare 3.2.123.
    grace credit

178 **present** represent, show

179 **want of government** lack of self-control

180 **opinion** self-conceit, arrogance, as in *LLL* 5.1.2–4: 'Your reasons . . . have been . . . learned without opinion', and *Troilus* 1.3.349

182 **Loseth** causes the loss of

183 **parts besides** other good qualities

184 **Beguiling** fraudulently depriving

185 **be your speed** give you good fortune. A familiar tag (Dent Appendix B, SS17, and *PLED* M623.11). Hotspur answers by wryly hoping that Worcester's emphasis on mannerly restraint may prove valuable when it comes time for battle (Wilson, *NCS*).

186 **and** Humphreys and others cite examples of *and* used to connect an affirmation and a command, as for example at 5.4.33.

187 **spite** vexation, as in Jonson, *Every Man In His Humour*, 1.3.30 (1616 text): 'I ha' no boots, that's the spite on't.'

191 **Aunt Percy** Edmund de Mortimer, the fifth Earl of March and heir presumptive to the throne, was indeed nephew to Hotspur's wife, but the Sir Edmund de Mortimer with whom Shakespeare conflates him was Lady Percy's younger brother; see 2.3.78 where Lady Percy refers to him as 'my brother Mortimer'.

GLENDOWER

   She is desperate here; a peevish self-willed harlotry,
   One that no persuasion can do good upon.
          The Lady speaks to Mortimer in Welsh

MORTIMER

   I understand thy looks. That pretty Welsh
   Which thou pourest down from these swelling heavens
   I am too perfect in; and, but for shame,
   In such a parley should I answer thee.
          The Lady speaks again in Welsh
   I understand thy kisses and thou mine,
   And that's a feeling disputation.   200
   But I will never be a truant, love,
   Till I have learned thy language; for thy tongue
   Makes Welsh as sweet as ditties highly penned,
   Sung by a fair queen in a summer's bow'r,
   With ravishing division, to her lute.

GLENDOWER

   Nay, if you melt, then will she run mad.
          The Lady speaks again in Welsh

MORTIMER

   O, I am ignorance itself in this!

193–4 She … upon] POPE (*eliding* She's, desp'rate, *and* One); *as verse*, F1, *ending* heere:, Harlotry, | vpon; Q1 *prints* She is desperate here *as verse, the remainder as prose*   194.1 *to Mortimer*] CAPELL (*subs.*); *not in* Q1   198.1 *speaks*] MALONE (*subs.*); *not in* Q1

193–4 **She … upon** These two somewhat irregular lines are printed in Q1 (see collation) as an uncertain mixture of verse and prose, and in F1 as three imperfect lines of verse. See Introduction, p. 105.
193 **desperate here** adamant and unpersuadable on this point, i.e. on her determination to accompany Lord Mortimer (which she has just reiterated)
   harlotry See 2.4.382 and note, and *Romeo* 4.2.14: 'A peevish self-willed harlotry it is.' Here the term is used to suggest 'womanish stubbornness'.
194 **persuasion** reasoning
195 **That pretty Welsh** i.e. your eloquent tears
196 **swelling heavens** eyes brimming with tears
197 **perfect** proficient
198 **In such a parley** in a similar discourse of

tears. *Parley* suggests both a conference about terms with an adversary and a public debate, anticipating *disputation* in l. 200.
200 **feeling disputation** discourse conducted through touch and mute interchange of feelings; one that is heartfelt, as contrasted with a formal *disputation*, or debate, in Latin using rhetorical and artificial terms
201 **truant** inattentive or absent pupil (continuing the figure of scholarly disputation)
203 **highly penned** eloquently composed, in high style
205 **division** ornamentation or variation, usually a rapid melodic passage. See *Romeo* 3.5.29: 'Some say the lark makes sweet division.'
206 **melt** (in tears)

GLENDOWER

She bids you on the wanton rushes lay you down
And rest your gentle head upon her lap,
And she will sing the song that pleaseth you,   210
And on your eyelids crown the god of sleep,
Charming your blood with pleasing heaviness,
Making such difference 'twixt wake and sleep
As is the difference betwixt day and night
The hour before the heavenly-harnessed team
Begins his golden progress in the east.

MORTIMER

With all my heart I'll sit and hear her sing.
By that time will our book, I think, be drawn.

GLENDOWER

Do so; and those musicians that shall play to you
Hang in the air a thousand leagues from hence,   220
And straight they shall be here. Sit and attend.

Hotspur and Mortimer sit

HOTSPUR

Come, Kate, thou art perfect in lying down;
Come, quick, quick, that I may lay my head in thy lap.

LADY PERCY (*sitting*) Go, ye giddy goose.

The music plays

221.1 *Hotspur and Mortimer sit*] This edition; *not in* Q1   224 *sitting*] This edition; *not in* Q1

208 **wanton** luxurious, soft (as in *2 Henry IV* 1.1.148), or fresh, green, and luxuriant (as in *Dream* 2.1.99)
  rushes (used as floor-covering in homes and on the theatre stage)
211 **crown the god of sleep** make sleep supreme ruler
212 **Charming** subduing as with a spell
  heaviness drowsiness
215 **heavenly-harnessed team** horse-drawn chariot of the sun
216 **progress** state journey, emphasizing the sun's royalty
218 **book** written document, deed, the *indentures tripartite* of l. 77
  drawn 'finished in a fair copy and ready to be sealed' (Kittredge)
222–45 **Come . . . day** A passage of uncertain mixture of verse and prose; see collation. Q1 gives 242–4 as prose, though the remainder of this speech is in verse. The F1 lineation may have no authority, for much of F1's rendering of Q's prose into

verse is manifestly defective, and designed to use up space, but in this passage it seems plausible.
222 **perfect in** expert at, as at l. 197.
222–3 **lying down . . . lap** The bawdy quibbles on *lying*, *head* and *lap* are also used by Hamlet, when he offers to lie in Ophelia's lap, meaning his head upon her lap, and hints jestingly at 'country matters' (*Hamlet* 3.2.108–16).
224 **giddy goose** A familiar comparison (Dent G347.1).
224.1 **music plays** An instrumental piece, not as accompaniment for the lady's song, and presumably played off-stage (in the tiring-house behind the stage), since the musicians are said by Glendower to 'Hang in the air' (l.220). Whether Glendower is to be perceived as a powerful magician in thus summoning music is a complex question. In general his claims to magical powers are undercut by Hotspur's sardonic witticisms; the eccentric

HOTSPUR

Now I perceive the devil understands Welsh;

And 'tis no marvel he is so humorous.

By'r lady, he is a good musician.

LADY PERCY

Then should you be nothing but musical,

For you are altogether governed by humours.

Lie still, ye thief, and hear the lady sing in Welsh.   230

HOTSPUR I had rather hear Lady, my brach, howl in Irish.

LADY PERCY Wouldst thou have thy head broken?

HOTSPUR No.

LADY PERCY Then be still.

HOTSPUR Neither, 'tis a woman's fault.

LADY PERCY Now God help thee!

HOTSPUR To the Welsh lady's bed.

LADY PERCY What's that?

HOTSPUR Peace, she sings.

Here the Lady sings a Welsh song

Come, Kate, I'll have your song too.   240

LADY PERCY Not mine, in good sooth.

HOTSPUR Not yours, in good sooth!

---

227 he is] Q1 ; hee's F1   242–5 Not … day] *as verse*, F1, *omitting* Heart; *as prose*, Q1

Welsh paterfamilias and windbag is demystified by the hot-tempered rationalist and sceptic. Later, Glendower's superstitious belief in prophecies prevents him from becoming an effective military force at Shrewsbury. See S. Zitner, 'Staging the Occult', in *Mirror up to Shakespeare*, ed. J. C. Gray (Toronto, 1984), 138–48.

225 **the devil understands Welsh** i.e. he has responded to Glendower's command in Welsh—a language only the devil can understand

226 **humorous** capricious, whimsical

230 **thief** A term of reproach used affectionately, like *scoundrel*.

231 **brach** bitch hound
   howl in Irish Compare *As You Like It* 5.2.102–3: 'Pray you, no more of this; 'tis like the howling of Irish wolves against the moon.'

232 **head broken** a cracking or rupturing of the skin, not a skull fracture, as in 2.1.28 (see note)

234 **still** silent; but Hotspur may play on the

sense of 'quiescent'.

235 **Neither** i.e. I won't do that either. Hotspur is perhaps being ironic in averring that silence is a woman's weakness (compare the common saying 'a woman's fault', Dent W671.1, and 1.3.235–7, in which Hotspur's own volubility is compared to a 'woman's mood'), or he may be saying that it would be unmanly for him to be still and submit to the singing. In either case, his bawdy quibble on *still* in the sense of 'sexually passive' asserts a masculine aggressiveness that is apparent in his next line about the Welsh lady's bed.

236 **God help thee** i.e. you're incorrigible; only God could help you now. (But Hotspur plays upon *help* in another sense, that of assisting with an amour.)

239.1 **the Lady sings a Welsh song** Presumably she is accompanied by the off-stage consort that performed at l. 224.1 (Long, 77).

Heart, you swear like a comfit-maker's wife.
'Not you, in good sooth', and 'As true as I live',
And 'As God shall mend me', and 'As sure as day',
And givest such sarsenet surety for thy oaths
As if thou never walk'st further than Finsbury.
Swear me, Kate, like a lady as thou art,
A good mouth-filling oath, and leave 'In sooth',
And such protest of pepper-gingerbread,   250
To velvet-guards and Sunday citizens.
Come, sing.

LADY PERCY I will not sing.

HOTSPUR 'Tis the next way to turn tailor, or be redbreast-
teacher. An the indentures be drawn, I'll away within
these two hours; and so, come in when ye will.   *Exit*

GLENDOWER
Come, come, Lord Mortimer, you are as slow
As hot Lord Percy is on fire to go.

---

258 hot] F1 (Hot, Q4; *Hot*ₐ Q5); Hot. Q1 (*perhaps taking* 'Hot.' *as an abbreviation for* 'Hotspur')

---

243 **Heart** i.e. by Christ's heart
   comfit-maker's confectioner's. London
   citizens and their wives were laughed at
   for their Puritan mannerisms of speech,
   like Margery Eyre in *Shoemakers' Holiday*
   or the Grocer's wife in *The Knight of the
   Burning Pestle*, whose oaths are no stron-
   ger than 'by my troth', 'faith', and 'I warrant' (Dekker, ed. Bowers, 2.3.111–42,
   etc.). Cowl and Morgan and others cite
   Falstaff in *2 Henry IV* 1.2.33 on the rascally 'yea-forsooth knave' of a citizen who
   refuses to lend him money, and Lyly,
   Pap with a Hatchet (ed. Bond, iii. 403):
   'Martin will not swear, but with indeed,
   in sooth, and in truth he'll cog the die of
   deceit.' Familiar forms are to be found in
   Dent L374, G173.1, and D57.1.
245 **mend** amend
246 **sarsenet** i.e. resembling sarsenet cloth
   in silken fine-spun softness and insub-
   stantiality. Compare Jonson, *Alchemist*,
   2.2.89–90: 'taffata-sarsnet, soft, and
   light | As cobwebs'.
247 **Finsbury** a field north of London and
   Moorfields (compare *Moorditch*, 1.2.74,
   and note), used by the London citizenry
   for archery and recreation. For references
   in Jonson, see F. C. Chalfant, *Ben Jonson's
   London* (1978), 78–9.

248 **me** The ethical dative, as at 2.4.100
   (see note).
250 **protest of pepper-gingerbread** a pro-
   testation or affirmation made as of hot-
   spiced gingerbread, such perhaps as one
   might obtain at the *comfit-maker's*
   (l. 243); citizens' fare, mildly spicy but
   crumbling in the mouth
251 **velvet-guards** Generally synonymous
   with *Sunday citizens*, those who trim, or
   'guard', their best clothes in velvet but
   cannot afford all-velvet garments. Compare *Merchant* 2.2.141–2: 'Give him a
   livery | More guarded than his fellows.'
   Humphreys cites Dekker, *Seven Deadly
   Sins* (ed. Grosart, ii. 24): 'O velvet-
   guarded thieves! O yea-and-by-nay
   cheaters! O civil, O grave and right
   worshipful cozeners!'
254–5 'Tis . . . **teacher** i.e. don't sing, then,
   if you've no mind to; singing will only
   turn one quickly into a tailor or one who
   instructs caged birds to sing before they
   are sold. 'Hotspur's contempt for music is
   equalled only by his contempt for the
   bourgeoisie' (Hemingway). Tailors sang
   at their work, like the *weavers* at 2.4.127,
   and were considered effeminate (see note
   at 2.4.239). *Next* means 'nearest', as at
   2.1.9.

By this our book is drawn; we'll but seal,
And then to horse immediately.   260
MORTIMER With all my heart.   *Exeunt*

3.2   *Enter the King, the Prince of Wales, and Lords in*
         attendance

KING HENRY

Lords, give us leave. The Prince of Wales and I
Must have some private conference; but be near at
         hand,
For we shall presently have need of you.   *Exeunt Lords*
I know not whether God will have it so
For some displeasing service I have done,
That in his secret doom out of my blood
He'll breed revengement and a scourge for me;
But thou dost in thy passages of life
Make me believe that thou art only marked
For the hot vengeance and the rod of heaven   10
To punish my mistreadings. Tell me else
Could such inordinate and low desires,

3.2.0.1 *the Prince*] Q1 (*Prince*)   0.1–2 *Lords in attendance*] ROWE (*subs.*); *others.* Q1

---

259 **By this** by this time. The action anticipated at l. 218 is now complete.
    book agreement
    but just
3.2 Location: See Appendix for Holinshed's description of a similar meeting at the royal court in Westminster. Shakespeare nowhere mentions Westminster in the play, but invites us to imagine this scene at the court; Prince Hal has been repeatedly reminded that he is to go 'to the court in the morning' (2.4.277–8, 323–4, 524).
1–2 **give us leave . . . conference** See Appendix for a different report in Holinshed. *Give us leave* is a conventional formula of request for privacy (Dent L167.1).
5 **displeasing service** This hint of guilt and fearfulness of divine vengeance is touched on elsewhere in the Henriad, as when in *Richard II* Henry IV speaks of his 'unthrifty' son as a 'plague' hanging over the Lancastrian house (5.3.1–3), or in *2 Henry IV* reflects upon the 'by-paths and indirect crook'd ways' he used to gain the 'troublesome' crown on his head

(4.5.184–7). Henry V, too, before the Battle of Agincourt, prays to God 'Not today' to 'think upon the fault | My father made in compassing the crown' (*Henry V*, 4.1.280–2). The motif of guilt for Richard's death, though muted in *1 Henry IV*, is suggested here and at l. 43 (see note); see also the possible hint of guilt in King Henry IV's longing to conduct a crusade (Appendix, 1.1.19–22, and Introduction, pp. 36–7).
6 **doom** judgement
  blood offspring, family
8 **passages** courses, proceedings
9–11 **that thou . . . mistreadings** The flexible syntax allows two meanings: (a) you are unavoidably designated as the *scourge* (l. 7) of heaven to punish my missteps or misdeeds (b) you yourself are marked for heaven's *vengeance* because of my sins. In either case, 'Heaven is punishing me through you' (Humphreys).
11 **else** if that is not the case
12 **inordinate** (a) immoderate (b) 'unworthy of your rank' (Humphreys)

Such poor, such bare, such lewd, such mean attempts,
Such barren pleasures, rude society
As thou art matched withal and grafted to,
Accompany the greatness of thy blood
And hold their level with thy princely heart?

PRINCE HENRY ⌈*kneeling*⌉

So please your majesty, I would I could
Quit all offences with as clear excuse
As well as I am doubtless I can purge   20
Myself of many I am charged withal.
Yet such extenuation let me beg
As, in reproof of many tales devised,
Which oft the ear of greatness needs must hear
By smiling pickthanks and base newsmongers,
I may, for some things true, wherein my youth
Hath faulty wandered and irregular,
Find pardon on my true submission.

KING HENRY

God pardon thee! Yet let me wonder, Harry,
At thy affections, which do hold a wing   30
Quite from the flight of all thy ancestors.
Thy place in Council thou hast rudely lost,
Which by thy younger brother is supplied,
And art almost an alien to the hearts

---

18 *kneeling*] This edition; *not in* Q1

13 **bare** paltry, wretched, undisguised, as at
1.3.108
  lewd low, base
  attempts undertakings
14 **rude society** unrefined companionship
15 **withal** with (also at l. 21)
17 **hold their level** claim equality
18–28 **So . . . submission** Holinshed describes
  the Prince as 'kneeling down before his
  father' (194), and such a gesture seems
  called for in this scene, although its
  timing cannot be accurately determined.
19 **Quit** acquit myself of
20 **doubtless** sure
22–8 **Yet . . . submission** 'Let me beg so
  much extenuation that upon confutation
  of many false charges I may be pardoned
  some that are true' (Dr Johnson).
23 **in reproof** upon disproof
24 **greatness** the great
25 **pickthanks** those who 'pick a thank', or

curry favour, especially by informing
against others. See Appendix for Holinshed.
  newsmongers talebearers
30 **affections** inclinations
30–1 **hold . . . from** fly a course quite contrary to. (A figure from falconry.)
32 **rudely** violently. Perhaps a muted
  reference to the story, probably apo-
  cryphal, of Hal's having been jailed for
  boxing the ears of the Lord Chief Justice,
  alluded to in *2 Henry IV* 1.2.182–6 and
  5.2.70–83. The story can be found in Sir
  Thomas Elyot's *The Governor*, 1531, Book
  II, chap. vi, and in Hall, Holinshed, Stow's
  Chronicles, and *Famous Victories*. Or the
  reference here may simply be to Hal's
  escapades with Falstaff; see Introduction,
  p. 20.
34 **art** thou art

Of all the court and princes of my blood.
The hope and expectation of thy time
Is ruined, and the soul of every man
Prophetically do forethink thy fall.
Had I so lavish of my presence been,
So common-hackneyed in the eyes of men,   40
So stale and cheap to vulgar company,
Opinion, that did help me to the crown,
Had still kept loyal to possession
And left me in reputeless banishment,
A fellow of no mark nor likelihood.
By being seldom seen, I could not stir
But like a comet I was wondered at,
That men would tell their children, 'This is he!'
Others would say, 'Where, which is Bolingbroke?'
And then I stole all courtesy from heaven,   50
And dressed myself in such humility
That I did pluck allegiance from men's hearts,
Loud shouts and salutations from their mouths,
Even in the presence of the crownèd King.
Thus did I keep my person fresh and new,
My presence, like a robe pontifical,

36 **The hope . . . time** the hopes men had for
you, for your life
38 **do** The plural follows the collective subject 'soul of every man'.
39–88 **Had I . . . sight** Humphreys (200–1)
cites earlier instances of a traditional
warning against royal over-familiarity in
Hoccleve, *Regement of Princes* (EETS extra
ser. 72 (1897), ll. 2423 ff.), and *Three
Prose Versions of the Secreta Secretorum*
(EETS extra ser. 74 (1898), 12–13).
39 **lavish** unrestrained, with suggestion of
wild, licentious
40 **common-hackneyed** The original sense
of *hackney* as an ordinary riding horse
kept for hire, a hack, is as yet unhack-
neyed in Shakespeare's use of the term.
42 **Opinion** public opinion
43 **loyal** Mahood (35) notes here a betrayal
of guilt; the *loyal* response of true Englishmen would have been to honour
possession, i.e. Richard's possession of the
crown, and Richard himself. The ambivalent guilt continues in *mark*, l. 45, a
word used in l. 9 above of those who are

'marked | For the hot vengeance and the
rod of heaven'.
44 **reputeless** inglorious (only recorded use
in *OED*)
45 **likelihood** prospect of success
47 **comet** Like the 'meteors of a troubled
heaven' in 1.1.10, comets often portend
disorder.
50 **I stole . . . heaven** I assumed a bearing
of heavenly graciousness, or Christ-like
meekness. Henry's assumption of *humility* (l. 51) to win popular favour, here and
in 4.3.81–4, is reminiscent of Absalom's
rebellion against King David in 2 Samuel
15: 5–6, of Henry's own courting of the
common people and his entry into London in *Richard II* (1.4.31–6, 5.2.18–20),
and of Richard of Gloucester's false humility in *Richard III* (2.1.72, 3.7.95, etc.).
56–7 **My presence . . . wondered at** A
familiar idea, as in Dent M20 (Appendix
C): 'A maid oft seen, a gown oft worn, are
disesteemed and held in scorn.'
56 **pontifical** suited to the dignity of a bishop
or prelate

Ne'er seen but wondered at; and so my state,
Seldom, but sumptuous, showed like a feast
And won by rareness such solemnity.
The skipping King, he ambled up and down   60
With shallow jesters and rash bavin wits,
Soon kindled and soon burnt; carded his state,
Mingled his royalty with cap'ring fools,
Had his great name profanèd with their scorns,
And gave his countenance, against his name,
To laugh at gibing boys and stand the push
Of every beardless vain comparative;
Grew a companion to the common streets,
Enfeoffed himself to popularity,
That, being daily swallowed by men's eyes,   70
They surfeited with honey and began
To loathe the taste of sweetness, whereof a little
More than a little is by much too much.
So when he had occasion to be seen
He was but as the cuckoo is in June,

59 won] QI (wan)   72 To loathe] T. JOHNSON (1710); *as part of l.* 71, QI

57 **state** magnificence, solemn pomp
58 **Seldom** Adjectival, as in *Sonnets* 52.4: 'For blunting the fine point of seldom pleasure'.
59 **such solemnity** i.e. the formal impressiveness appropriate to a *feast* (l. 58) or festival
61 **rash** Synonymous with 'Soon kindled and soon burnt' in the next line. Compare *2 Henry IV* 4.4.48: 'rash gunpowder'.
   bavin brushwood used as kindling, as in the proverb 'The bavin burns bright but it is but a blaze' (Dent B107).
62 **carded his state** debased his royal dignity by mingling it with *cap'ring fools* (l. 63). To *card* is to stir, or mix, together, and hence to adulterate. *OED*, v.¹ 2, cites Greene, *Quip for an Upstart Courtier* (1592, ed. Grosart, xi. 275): 'You Tom Tapster . . . that card your beer . . . half small and half strong.' *Carding* is also the process of combing out wool to remove impurities, an action that could suggest here the racking, or extortion, of Richard's kingdom (Davison).
64 **with their scorns** by the reputation of his favourites for scornful manners
65 **gave . . . name** lent his authority and his demeanour, to the detriment of his royal

dignity and contrary to his kingly title
66–7 **To laugh . . . comparative** to find amusement in young blades who jeer and scoff, and submit himself to the impudence of every frivolous youngster who practises his wit in making insulting comparisons. King Henry describes Richard as one who joins on equal terms the game of trading clever insults with his inferiors, like Prince Hal, of whom Falstaff says in 1.2.75–7: 'Thou . . . art indeed the most comparative, rascalliest, sweet young prince.'
69 **Enfeoffed himself** gave himself up entirely, as one might surrender a *fief*, or landed estate, to absolute possession (fee simple)
71 **surfeited with honey** A familiar expression, as in *Romeo* 2.6.11–12: 'The sweetest honey | Is loathsome in his own deliciousness', Proverbs 25: 15 and 26, and Dent H560, with other references. The image of satiation returns in l. 84: 'glutted, gorged, and full'.
75 **cuckoo** See note at 2.4.342 and the saying 'No one regards the June cuckoo's song' (Dent C894.1). Henry describes Richard as offensive to sight (*aspect*, l. 82), to hearing (the cuckoo), and to taste (too much honey).

Heard, not regarded—seen, but with such eyes
As, sick and blunted with community,   .
Afford no extraordinary gaze,
Such as is bent on sun-like majesty
When it shines seldom in admiring eyes;   80
But rather drowsed and hung their eyelids down,
Slept in his face and rendered such aspect
As cloudy men use to their adversaries,
Being with his presence glutted, gorged, and full.
And in that very line, Harry, standest thou;
For thou hast lost thy princely privilege
With vile participation. Not an eye
But is aweary of thy common sight
Save mine, which hath desired to see thee more—
Which now doth that I would not have it do,   90
Make blind itself with foolish tenderness.   *He weeps*

PRINCE HENRY

I shall hereafter, my thrice gracious lord,
Be more myself.

KING HENRY   For all the world
As thou art to this hour was Richard then
When I from France set foot at Ravenspurgh,
And even as I was then is Percy now.
Now, by my sceptre, and my soul to boot,
He hath more worthy interest to the state

91 *He weeps*] JOHNSON; *not in* Q1

77 **community** commonness, ordinary occurrence (*OED*, 5)
79 **sun-like** On the commonplace association of sun and royalty, see 1.2.185 and
2.4.393–4 and *Sonnets* 7.1–4, etc.
82 **in his face** right before his eyes, not con-
cealing the lack of respect
   aspect (stress on second syllable) look,
regard
83 **cloudy** sullen, frowning, darkened by
misfortune (extending the image of the
sun begun at l. 79).
85 **line** degree, category. Compare note at
1.3.168.
87 **vile participation** base fellowship
90 **that** that which
91 **tenderness** i.e. tears. As Wilson (*NCS*)
notes, the King weeps in Holinshed (194)

and in *Famous Victories* (ll. 546–52), although these interviews occur under circumstances closer to those of *2 Henry IV*
4.5.
93 **Be more myself** A familiar theme (Dent
O 64.1) sounded by Henry IV in 1.3.5.
   For all the world in every respect
95 **Ravenspurgh** Bolingbroke's return from
exile and his landing at this Yorkshire
seaport are told in *Richard II* (2.2.51,
2.3.31–5) and referred to elsewhere in
1 Henry IV at 1.3.246 and 4.3.77.
97 **to boot** as well
98–9 **He hath . . . succession** Hotspur has a
better claim to the kingdom through
merit than your merely hereditary claim
of succession unbolstered by the substance of worthy deeds

Than thou the shadow of succession.
For of no right, nor colour like to right,　　　　　100
He doth fill fields with harness in the realm,
Turns head against the lion's armèd jaws,
And, being no more in debt to years than thou,
Leads ancient lords and reverend bishops on
To bloody battles and to bruising arms.
What never-dying honour hath he got
Against renownèd Douglas!—Whose high deeds,
Whose hot incursions and great name in arms
Holds from all soldiers chief majority
And military title capital　　　　　　110
Through all the kingdoms that acknowledge Christ.
Thrice hath this Hotspur, Mars in swaddling clothes,
This infant warrior, in his enterprises
Discomfited great Douglas, ta'en him once,
Enlargèd him and made a friend of him,
To fill the mouth of deep defiance up
And shake the peace and safety of our throne.
And what say you to this? Percy, Northumberland,
The Archbishop's grace of York, Douglas, Mortimer,
Capitulate against us and are up.　　　　　120

107 renownèd] Q1 (renowmed)　　110 capital$_\Lambda$] Q2; ~ . Q1

100 **of . . . to right** possessing no rightful claim, not even the semblance of such a claim
101 **harness** armour; hence (transferred sense, plural) men in armour
102 **Turns head** directs a resistance or insurrection (*OED*, *head*, 29, 30)
lion's Henry echoes Falstaff's commonplace association of the lion with royalty at 2.4.262. It recurs at 3.3.144.
103 **being . . . thou** On Shakespeare's alteration of Hotspur's age to make him equal with Hal, see Appendix and Introduction, p. 14. Compare the common expression 'to be in debt to years' (Dent D167.1).
104 **bishops** The military role of bishops under feudalism is evident in the warlike involvement of the Archbishop of York (1.3.264–7, 4.4.1–41), the Archbishop of Canterbury in *Henry V* (1.1–2), etc.
105 **bruising** crushing
107 **Whose** (referring to Hotspur, not Douglas)
108 **hot** zealous, violent

109 **Holds** The singular verb with plural subject is common.
majority pre-eminence (playing, too, on the paradox that the young Hotspur holds chief *majority*, being of full age, among men older than he)
110 **capital** chief, principal
112 **Thrice** See Appendix for historical background.
114 **ta'en him once** See Appendix for Shakespeare's inconsistency regarding the capture of Douglas.
115 **Enlargèd** freed
116 **To fill . . . up** to swell the roar of deep defiance, or to fill defiance's appetite to the full
119 **The . . . York** his grace the Archbishop of York. See 1.3.266 and note.
120 **Capitulate** draw up articles of agreement; literally, draw up in chapters, or under heads or articles, as in *Coriolanus* 5.3.82
up up in arms

But wherefore do I tell these news to thee?
Why, Harry, do I tell thee of my foes,
Which art my nearest and dearest enemy?
Thou that art like enough, through vassal fear,
Base inclination, and the start of spleen,
To fight against me under Percy's pay,
To dog his heels and curtsy at his frowns,
To show how much thou art degenerate.

PRINCE HENRY

Do not think so. You shall not find it so.
And God forgive them that so much have swayed   130
Your majesty's good thoughts away from me!
I will redeem all this on Percy's head,
And in the closing of some glorious day
Be bold to tell you that I am your son,
When I will wear a garment all of blood
And stain my favours in a bloody mask,
Which, washed away, shall scour my shame with it.
And that shall be the day, whene'er it lights,
That this same child of honour and renown,
This gallant Hotspur, this all-praisèd knight,   140
And your unthought-of Harry chance to meet.
For every honour sitting on his helm,
Would they were multitudes, and on my head
My shames redoubled! For the time will come
That I shall make this northern youth exchange
His glorious deeds for my indignities.
Percy is but my factor, good my lord,

123 **dearest** (a) best-beloved, precious (b) direst, bitterest, as in *Hamlet* 1.2.182: 'my dearest foe'. Compare 3.1.177.
124 **like** likely
vassal servile
125 **Base inclination** inclination for baseness
start of spleen sudden burst of capricious ill humour. See 2.3.75 and note, also 5.2.19.
130–1 **them . . . from me** A reference to the *pickthanks* and *base newsmongers* in l. 25 (see note).
135 **all of blood** The image suggests also the redness of the sun (associated with royalty) sinking in the west 'in the closing of some glorious day' (l. 133), thereby

reinforcing a pun on *sun* and *son* at l. 134.
136 **favours** features, but suggesting also tokens, or insignia, serving as chivalric decoration as at 5.4.71 and 95 (Humphreys)
138 **lights** dawns
141 **unthought-of** disregarded, lightly valued; the opposite of *all-praisèd* in l. 140. Compare *unminded* at 4.3.58.
142 **honour** chivalric ornament, 'favour'; see l. 136 above, and 5.4.71.
146 **indignities** unworthy qualities, shameful conduct; synonymous with 'my shame' at l. 137 and 'My shames' at l. 144
147 **factor** agent

To engross up glorious deeds on my behalf;
And I will call him to so strict account
That he shall render every glory up,   150
Yea, even the slightest worship of his time,
Or I will tear the reckoning from his heart.
This in the name of God I promise here,
The which if he be pleased I shall perform,
I do beseech your majesty may salve
The long-grown wounds of my intemperature.
If not, the end of life cancels all bonds,
And I will die a hundred thousand deaths
Ere break the smallest parcel of this vow.

KING HENRY

A hundred thousand rebels die in this.   160
Thou shalt have charge and sovereign trust herein.
        Enter Blunt
How now, good Blunt? Thy looks are full of speed.

BLUNT

So hath the business that I come to speak of.
Lord Mortimer of Scotland hath sent word

---

154 he ... perform] Q1; I performe, and doe suruiue F1   156 intemperature] F1; intemperance Q1   157 bonds] Q1 (bands)   161.1 *Enter Blunt*] F1; *after l.* 162, Q1

148 **engross up** amass, buy up wholesale, with a quibble on *deeds*: (a) brave acts (b) written legal instruments of purchase (Wilson, *NCS*)
150 **he ... up** Hal's premise is that 'one who subdues a champion succeeds to all the honours that the champion has won'—a premise to which Hotspur also subscribes at the moment of his death in 5.4.77–9 (Kittredge).
151 **worship of his time** honour of his lifetime
152 **the reckoning** i.e. the factor's account (Wilson, *NCS*)
155 **salve** heal
156 **intemperature** This F1 reading (see collation) is attractive for its quibble on 'abnormal or distempered condition of the body' (*OED*), including as it does the medieval connotation of *salve* and *wounds* as well as the moral sense of 'intemperateness of action or passion' found also in Qq's *intemperance* (Wilson, *NCS*). The F1 correction of the Qq reading is unlikely to be compositorial, despite Humphreys's

observation that compositor A had previously set *distemperature* at 3.1.32 (since the work from cast-off copy on e5ᵛ would have been done some time prior to f1, coming at the end rather than the beginning of the setting of f1–3ᵛ), and as an editorial improvement it is too felicitous to seem random.
157 **bonds** QqF1 *bands* was originally a phonetic variant of *bonds*, though now largely differentiated in use. A proverbial idea; see Dent D148: 'Death pays all debts.'
159 **parcel** constituent part. The phrase 'part and parcel' emphasizes this idea of an essential portion (*OED, part, sb.* 1c, 18).
161 **charge** command (of troops)
    sovereign (a) supreme (b) granted by royal authority
164 **Lord Mortimer of Scotland** See Appendix for Shakespeare's wrong assumption that the Scottish earls of March were Mortimers, owing to a misreading of Holinshed.

That Douglas and the English rebels met
The eleventh of this month at Shrewsbury.
A mighty and a fearful head they are,
If promises be kept on every hand,
As ever offered foul play in a state.

KING HENRY

  The Earl of Westmorland set forth today,   170
With him my son, Lord John of Lancaster;
For this advertisement is five days old.
On Wednesday next, Harry, you shall set forward;
On Thursday we ourselves will march. Our meeting
Is Bridgnorth. And, Harry, you shall march
Through Gloucestershire; by which account,
Our business valuèd, some twelve days hence
Our general forces at Bridgnorth shall meet.
Our hands are full of business. Let's away!
Advantage feeds him fat while men delay.   *Exeunt*   180

3.3   *Enter Falstaff and Bardolph*

FALSTAFF Bardolph, am I not fallen away vilely since this
last action? Do I not bate? Do I not dwindle? Why, my
skin hangs about me like an old lady's loose gown; I am

3.3.0 *Bardolph*] DERING MS (*Bardolff*), F1 (*Bardolph*); *Bardol* Q1   1 Bardolph] DERING MS (Bardolffe), F1 (*Bardolph*); Bardoll Q1

---

167 A The *As* in l. 169 seems to require an
    anticipatory sense of *As* here: 'As mighty
    and as fearful an army they are . . . as ever
    offered foul play.'
172 **this advertisement** these tidings
174 **meeting** place of rendezvous
175 **Bridgnorth** a town in Shropshire, on the
    Severn, about twenty miles south-east
    of Shrewsbury on the Coventry–Bir-
    mingham–Bawborth–Shrewsbury road.
    Humphreys, citing J. Crofts in *TLS*, 8 Jan.
    1931, notes that the King, in sending
    Prince Hal through Gloucestershire,
    chooses for him a rather longer route,
    requiring the Prince to start a day sooner
    than his father; but Shakespeare then
    seems to forget this arrangement, for in
    4.2 the Prince encounters Falstaff near
    Coventry, on the other route. Presumably
    the Prince is to gather forces as he mar-
    ches through northern Gloucestershire.

176–7 **by which . . . valuèd** according to
    which computation of time, the business
    we have in hand being carefully estimated
180 **Advantage feeds him fat** opportunity
    (for rebellion) flourishes. *Him* means
    'himself'. Compare the proverb 'Delay
    breeds danger' (Dent D195). Holinshed
    stresses the King's need for haste; see
    Appendix l. 164.
3.3 Location: The tavern in Eastcheap, as in
    2.4.
1 **fallen away** shrunk
2 **action** engagement. Falstaff speaks comic-
    ally of the Gad's Hill robbery (or of his
    near-capture by the sheriff) as though it
    were a fight with the enemy. Prince Hal
    speaks similarly at 2.4.20 (see note).
    bate abate, lose weight
3 **loose gown** a shapeless attire decorously
    suited to matronliness. (Humphreys gives
    a citation.)

withered like an old apple-john. Well, I'll repent, and that
suddenly, while I am in some liking. I shall be out of heart
shortly, and then I shall have no strength to repent. An I
have not forgotten what the inside of a church is made of,
I am a peppercorn, a brewer's horse. The inside of a
church! Company, villainous company, hath been the
spoil of me.   10

BARDOLPH Sir John, you are so fretful you cannot live long.

FALSTAFF Why, there is it. Come sing me a bawdy song;
make me merry. I was as virtuously given as a gentleman
need to be, virtuous enough: swore little, diced not above
seven times—a week, went to a bawdy-house not above
once in a quarter—of an hour, paid money that I
borrowed—three or four times, lived well and in good
compass; and now I live out of all order, out of all
compass.

BARDOLPH Why, you are so fat, Sir John, that you must   20
needs be out of all compass, out of all reasonable compass,
Sir John.

FALSTAFF Do thou amend thy face, and I'll amend my life.

15–17 times—... quarter—... borrowed—] HANMER; times ... quarter ... borrowed Q1

4 **apple-john** an apple that keeps a long
time, and is edible when its skin is
shrivelled. So called because it is supposed
to ripen about St John the Baptist's day,
24 June, and to be eaten two years later.
In *2 Henry IV* 2.4.4–8 the Prince jokes
that Falstaff and apple-johns are alike in
being 'dry, round, old, withered knights'.

5 **suddenly** right away
liking (a) inclination (b) fleshly condition; at ease and pleasure. See also next
note.
out of heart (a) disinclined, disheartened
(b) out of condition (*OED*, *heart*, *sb.* 21).
Mahood (47) suggests the further meaning 'out of the Prince's heart', following
upon the common meaning of *in some
liking*, namely 'held in some affection'.

6 **strength** (a) strength of purpose (b)
strength of body (Humphreys)

8 **peppercorn** unground dried pepper
berry, small and dry like the *shotten herring* (2.4.124), *poulter's hare* (2.4.421),
apple-john (3.3.4), and other objects to
which Falstaff is comically compared; see
note at 2.4.124.

brewer's horse a horse that is old, withered, and decrepit. Cowl and Morgan cite
Dekker, *If this be not a Good Play, the Devil
is in It* (1611): 'as noble-men use their
great horses, when they are past service:
sell 'em to brewers and make 'em dray-
horses' (3.1.10–11). Kittredge also cites
The Trial of Chivalry (*c.* 1601), sig. D4: 'I
have been stumbling up and down all this
night like a brewer's horse that has ne'er
a good eye in his head' (3.1.2–4).

11 **fretful** Compare the pun in 2.2.2, where
Falstaff 'frets like a gummed velvet'. Bardolph responds to Falstaff's succession of
word-plays in ll. 4–6 by suggesting that
Falstaff is (a) spiritually vexed (b) physically frayed.

12 **there is it** there it is

13 **given** inclined, as at 2.4.411

17–18 **good compass** reasonable limits.
Living within and out of compass are both
proverbial ideas (Dent C577 and C577.1).
Bardolph responds at l. 21 with the
unavoidable pun on *compass*, meaning
'circumference', 'girth', but is repaid with
a jest at his expense.

Thou art our admiral, thou bearest the lantern in the
poop, but 'tis in the nose of thee. Thou art the Knight of
the Burning Lamp.

BARDOLPH Why, Sir John, my face does you no harm.

FALSTAFF No, I'll be sworn, I make as good use of it as many
a man doth of a death's-head or a *memento mori*. I never
see thy face but I think upon hell-fire and Dives that lived   30
in purple; for there he is in his robes, burning, burning.
If thou wert any way given to virtue, I would swear by thy
face; my oath should be, 'By this fire, that's God's angel'.
But thou art altogether given over, and wert indeed, but
for the light in thy face, the son of utter darkness. When
thou rann'st up Gad's Hill in the night to catch my horse,

33 that's] Q3 that Q1

24 **admiral** flagship, as in *Antony* 3.10.2:
'Th' Antoniad, the Egyptian admiral'.
lantern Bardolph's red nose, inflamed by
drink, is likened to a flagship lantern used
to guide the fleet. Steevens (1793) cites
Dekker, *The Wonderful Year*, 1603 (ed.
Grosart, i. 138–9) who may be borrowing from Shakespeare: 'The Hamburgers
offered I know not how many dollars, for
his company in an East-Indian voyage, to
have stood o' nights in the poop of their
Admiral, only to save the charges of
candles.'

25–6 **Knight of the Burning Lamp** The
mock-chivalric name parodies the titles
given to heroes of medieval romance,
such as the 'Knight of the Green Sword',
one of the titles of the hero of *Amadis of
Gaul* (translated from the French by
Anthony Munday, *c.*1590). Beaumont
and Fletcher's *The Knight of the Burning
Pestle* (*c.*1607) burlesques the same
fashion. Compare also the Knight of the
Sun alluded to at 1.2.14 (see note).

29 **death's-head . . . *mori*** Skulls engraved on
rings served as reminders of death, and
actual skulls might be kept on desks etc.,
as in *St. Jerome in His Study*, painted by
Jan Massys in 1535. Compare *2 Henry IV*
2.4.224–5: 'Do not speak like a death's
head; do not bid me remember mine end.'
Cowl and Morgan cite Fletcher, *The
Chances* (1613–25): 'they keep death's
heads in rings, | To cry *Memento*'
(1.5.39–40), and Marston, *The Dutch
Courtesan* (1603–4): 'As for their death,

how can it be bad, since their wickedness
is always before their eyes and a death's
head most commonly on their middle finger' (1.2.49–52).

30–1 **Dives . . . purple** *Dives*, the Latin used
in the Vulgate translation of the Bible for
'rich man', was commonly taken for the
proper name of the rich man in Christ's
parable who was 'clothed in purple'
during his sumptuous life but went to hell
(Luke 16: 19–31). Falstaff remembers
the story of Dives and Lazarus again at
4.2.24–5. The association with Dives
recurs in *2 Henry IV* 1.2.32, and of Bardolph's face with hell-fire in *Henry V*
2.3.36–7.

33 **By . . . angel** An oath that appears also in
Misogonus (*c.*1570), 3.1.239: 'By this fire
that burns that's God's angel, I swear a
great oath' (Dent G264.1). It is derived
indirectly from Exodus 3: 2: 'And the
angel of the Lord appeared unto him in a
flame of fire', or Psalm 104: 4: 'He
maketh his angels spirits, and his minis-
ters a flaming fire', or from a similar text
in Hebrews 1: 7.

35 **son of utter darkness** Compare 'sons of
darkness' at 2.4.165 (see note). The *outer
darkness* of the King James version, rendered *utter darkness* in Tyndale's 1526
translation, the Bishops' Bible, Geneva
Bible, and others of the period, and meaning 'further out, indefinitely remote' (see
OED, outer, a. 1 and *utter a.* 1), occurs in
Matthew 8: 12, 22: 13, and 25: 30
(Humphreys).

if I did not think thou hadst been an *ignis fatuus* or a ball
of wildfire, there's no purchase in money. O, thou art a
perpetual triumph, an everlasting bonfire-light! Thou
hast saved me a thousand marks in links and torches,   40
walking with thee in the night betwixt tavern and tavern;
but the sack that thou hast drunk me would have bought
me lights as good cheap at the dearest chandler's in
Europe. I have maintained that salamander of yours with
fire any time this two-and-thirty years, God reward me for
it!

BARDOLPH 'Sblood, I would my face were in your belly!

FALSTAFF God-a-mercy! So should I be sure to be heart-
burned.

Enter the Hostess

How now, Dame Partlet the hen? Have you inquired yet   50
who picked my pocket?

HOSTESS Why, Sir John, what do you think, Sir John? Do
you think I keep thieves in my house? I have searched, I
have inquired, so has my husband, man by man, boy by

49.1 *Enter the Hostess] after l.* 50, Q1 (*Enter host.*)

37 **ignis fatuus** will-o'-the-wisp (Latin for
'foolish fire'), a phosphorescent light
hovering over marshy ground

37–8 **ball of wildfire** will-o'-the-wisp or
similar phosphorescent phenomenon.
OED's earliest citation from 1663 seems
to have overlooked the present example in
which Falstaff links *wildfire* with *ignis
fatuus*. It can also mean a discharge of
highly flammable substance used in warfare and in display as a kind of fireworks;
with a suggestion, too, of erysipelas and
other inflammatory reddening diseases of
the skin (see Wilson, *NCS*). Falstaff's
image of wildfire racing up a hill suggests
the common phrase 'like wildfire'; see
Lucrece 1523.

39 **triumph** illuminated victorious procession or public celebration, or the
illumination itself
   everlasting bonfire-light With possible
suggestion of the *hell-fire* to which Falstaff
repeatedly consigns Bardolph's red face,
in ll. 28–35 above and *2 Henry IV*
2.4.320–2. Compare the Porter's 'everlasting bonfire' in *Macbeth* 2.3.19.

40 **marks** worth two-thirds of a pound; see
note at 2.1.53.

links torches, flares

42 **me** at my expense

43 **good cheap** cheaply (compare French
faire bon marché)
   dearest most expensive

44 **salamander** a kind of lizard supposed to
be able to thrive in fire. Cowl and Morgan
cite Greene, *2 Tritameron of Love* (ed.
Grosart, iii. 142): 'Pliny in his *Natural
Histories* saith, the salamander delighteth
in the fire.'

47 **I . . . belly** 'I wish it were in your belly (for
me)' (Dent B299) is a colloquial way of
retorting to some irritating insult or circumstance. Compare the modern phrases
'to eat one's words' or 'stow it!'. At
ll. 48–9 Falstaff jestingly considers the
literal consequence: heartburn, or in-
digestion.

50 **Dame Partlet** Traditional name for a hen,
as in Chaucer's Nun's Priest's Tale, and
hence for a woman who scolds and fusses.
In *Winter's Tale*, Leontes accuses Anti-
gonus of allowing himself to be 'woman-
tired, unroosted | By thy dame Partlet
here' (2.3.74–5). Chaucer's Pertilote is
also Chaunticleer's favourite 'paramour'.

boy, servant by servant. The tithe of a hair was never lost in my house before.

FALSTAFF Ye lie, hostess. Bardolph was shaved and lost many a hair; and I'll be sworn my pocket was picked. Go to, you are a woman, go.

HOSTESS Who, I? No, I defy thee! God's light, I was never   60
called so in mine own house before.

FALSTAFF Go to. I know you well enough.

HOSTESS No, Sir John, you do not know me, Sir John. I know you, Sir John. You owe me money, Sir John, and now you pick a quarrel to beguile me of it. I bought you a dozen of shirts to your back.

FALSTAFF Dowlas, filthy dowlas. I have given them away to bakers' wives; they have made bolters of them.

HOSTESS Now, as I am a true woman, holland of eight shillings an ell. You owe money here besides, Sir John, for   70

55 tithe] THEOBALD; tight QI   57 Bardolph] DERING MS (Bardolffe), FI (*Bardolph*); Bardoll QI   68 they] QI; and they FI   69–70 eight shillings] QI (viii s.)

55 **tithe** tenth part. The QqFI reading, *tight*, might seem at first to be one of Mistress Quickly's malapropisms, as Hemingway suggests; but in performance the point would be obscured by similarity of pronunciation, and this similarity of sound may also have produced an error in the printed text.

hair a valueless item, as in 3.1.135 (see note)

57–8 **shaved . . . hair** After quibbling on the literal meaning of *hair* at l. 55 by observing that Bardolph's beard has been *shaved* in the tavern and thereby *lost* to him, Falstaff plays on *shaved* in the sense of 'cheated and robbed of his money' and on *lost many a hair* in the sense of 'made bald by syphilis' (compare *Dream* 1.2.86–7). *Shave* often implies causing discomfiture (*OED, v.* 3b). The suggestion of the tavern as a bawdy-house, where customers might suffer this customary double consequence of lechery, is echoed repeatedly in the double entendres of this scene.

59 **you are a woman** Alluding to the common defamatory expression 'to be a woman' (Dent W637.1 and W707.1). As a woman, Falstaff suggests, the Hostess is capable of infinite deception. When the Hostess responds to Falstaff's allegation by protesting her innocence, as though it were a serious misdemeanour to be a woman at all, however, she unwittingly and characteristically offers herself as a further target for Falstaff's wit.

62 **I know you well enough** A common tag (Dent K171.1), but in this context the idea of *knowing* a woman takes on comically carnal implications that the Hostess does not comprehend. Falstaff returns to this risible bantering about the Hostess's femininity at ll. 108–25 below.

66 **to your back** A phrase denoting possession. *OED, to,* 17b gives a later attribution, N. O. Boileau's *Lutria*, ii. 126 (1682): 'This paltry Jack | Had scarce a shoe to's foot, a rag to's back.'

67 **Dowlas** a coarse linen named after Doulas in Brittany. Place-names are common in the naming of cloth in this play, as with Kendal green (2.4.215), sarsenet (i.e. Saracen cloth, 3.1.246), and holland (l. 69 below).

68 **bolters** fabric used to sift meal. To *bolt* is to sift.

69 **holland** fine linen, originally from the Netherlands; see l. 67 above and note, and *2 Henry IV* 2.2.20, where Poins is said to wear a holland shirt.

70 **ell** a measure of 45 inches formerly used in England. Mistress Quickly exaggerates the cost of her linen, just as Falstaff disparages it; according to Linthicum, 98, even fine linen could be had for 4*s.* per yard (Wilson, *NCS*).

your diet and by-drinkings, and money lent you, four-
and-twenty pound.

FALSTAFF He had his part of it. Let him pay.

HOSTESS He? Alas, he is poor, he hath nothing.

FALSTAFF How, poor? Look upon his face. What call you
rich? Let them coin his nose, let them coin his cheeks. I'll
not pay a denier. What, will you make a younker of me?
Shall I not take mine ease in mine inn but I shall have my
pocket picked? I have lost a seal-ring of my grandfather's
worth forty mark.   80

HOSTESS O Jesu, I have heard the Prince tell him, I know not
how oft, that that ring was copper!

FALSTAFF How? The Prince is a jack, a sneak-up. 'Sblood,
an he were here, I would cudgel him like a dog, if he
would say so.

> *Enter the Prince, with Peto, marching, and Falstaff*
> *meets them playing upon his truncheon like a fife*

71–2 four-and-twenty] F1; xxiiii. Q1   72 pound] Q1; pounds F1   83–4 'Sblood, an he] Q1
(Zbloud and hee); and if hee F1   85.1 *with Peto*] THEOBALD: *not in* Q1   85.2 *them* THEOBALD;
him Q1

71 **diet and by-drinkings** board and drinks
between meals
76 **rich** (a) the opposite of *poor* (b) highly
inflamed in the nose and face (although
OED, 6c, cites nothing before 1610—
John Boys, *Works* (1629 ed.), 528:
'having left nothing rich excepting a rich
nose')
 coin Falstaff facetiously suggests that
money could be made out of the valuable
'metal' (see 2.4.338 and note) in Bardolph's rubicund face, or that his likeness
could be stamped on coins in the manner
of kings and emperors.
77 **denier** 'a small copper coin valued at the
tenth part of an English penny' (Cot-
grave), and hence, especially in negative
expressions, the type of a very small coin
 younker fashionable young man (compare German *junker*), prodigal, green-
horn, like the handsomely trimmed
'younker' in the prime of youth in *3
Henry VI* 2.1.23–4, 'prancing to his
love', or the gaily festooned vessel in
Merchant 2.6.14–19 that sets forth 'like a
younger [i.e. a young man, a young mas-
ter] or a prodigal', only to return at length
in tattered beggary. Such a prodigal son
might well have his pockets picked in a

tavern. The prodigal re-emerges at
4.2.33 (see note).
78 **take . . . inn** A familiar expression (Dent
E42).
79 **seal-ring of my grandfather**'s finger-ring
bearing a seal or signet, often valued, as
here, as an heirloom. Compare the 'agate
ring' at 2.4.67 (see note). Cowl and Morgan cite Charles Cotton, *The Scoffer Scoffed*
(1675), 20: 'A man would think that he
had lost | The half of his estate almost, | At
least his grandfather's seal-ring, | Or some
most dear-beloved thing.'
80 **forty mark** £26. 13s. 4d. See 2.1.53 and
note.
83 **jack** knave, rascal
 sneak-up servile or cringing fellow, a
sneak (first recorded use in *OED*)
84 **like a dog** A common comparison (Dent
D506.1).
85.1 *with Peto* Peto is not named here in
QqF1 (see collation), and does not speak
in the scene, but is addressed at l. 189. See
2.4.486.1 and Introduction, pp. 102–3,
on the question of whether Peto or Poins
accompanies the Prince here.
85.2 *truncheon* officer's staff; the *cudgel*
(l. 84) that Falstaff had threatened in
Hal's absence to use on him, now

How now, lad, is the wind in that door, i'faith? Must we
all march?

BARDOLPH Yea, two and two, Newgate fashion.

HOSTESS My lord, I pray you hear me.

PRINCE HENRY What sayst thou, Mistress Quickly? How   90
doth thy husband? I love him well; he is an honest man.

HOSTESS Good my lord, hear me.

FALSTAFF Prithee let her alone, and list to me.

PRINCE HENRY What sayst thou, Jack?

FALSTAFF The other night I fell asleep here behind the arras
and had my pocket picked. This house is turned bawdy-
house; they pick pockets.

PRINCE HENRY What didst thou lose, Jack?

FALSTAFF Wilt thou believe me, Hal? Three or four bonds of
forty pound apiece, and a seal-ring of my grandfather's.   100

PRINCE HENRY A trifle, some eightpenny matter.

HOSTESS So I told him, my lord, and I said I heard your grace
say so; and, my lord, he speaks most vilely of you, like a
foul-mouthed man as he is, and said he would cudgel you.

PRINCE HENRY What, he did not!

HOSTESS There's neither faith, truth, nor womanhood in me
else.

FALSTAFF There's no more faith in thee than in a stewed
prune, nor no more truth in thee than in a drawn fox;

---

91 doth] Q1; does F1

transformed into an instrument to accompany marching

86 **is the wind in that door** is that the way the wind blows? A familiar phrase; Dent W419 and *Much Ado* 2.3.91: 'Sits the wind in that corner?' *Door* means quarter here.

88 **Newgate fashion** two by two, like prisoners being conveyed to the city prison (called Newgate after one of London's seven main gates), or from the prison to their trial. The earliest citation in *OED*. Kittredge quotes Dekker, *Satiromastix* (3.1.235–6): 'Why, then, come, we'll walk arm in arm, as though we were leading one another to Newgate.'

99 **bonds** deeds obligating the signatory to pay a certain sum to the holder of the bond

108–9 **stewed prune** Associated with bawdy-houses and whores, as in *Measure* 2.1.86–103, *2 Henry IV* 2.4.135, and *Merry Wives* 1.1.258; also suggesting the wrinkles of dryness and age.

109 **drawn fox** a hunted fox, driven from cover and relying solely on his cunning; or possibly a fox eviscerated and dragged to lay a false trail. The appropriateness to Mistress Quickly is again physically unflattering.

and for womanhood, Maid Marian may be the deputy's   110
wife of the ward to thee. Go, you thing, go.

HOSTESS Say, what thing, what thing?

FALSTAFF What thing? Why, a thing to thank God on.

HOSTESS I am no thing to thank God on, I would thou
shouldst know it! I am an honest man's wife, and, setting
thy knighthood aside, thou art a knave to call me so.

FALSTAFF Setting thy womanhood aside, thou art a beast to
say otherwise.

HOSTESS Say, what beast, thou knave thou?

FALSTAFF What beast? Why, an otter.   120

PRINCE HENRY An otter, Sir John? Why an otter?

FALSTAFF Why? She's neither fish nor flesh; a man knows
not where to have her.

HOSTESS Thou art an unjust man in saying so. Thou or any
man knows where to have me, thou knave, thou!

111 thing] Q1; nothing F1   114 no thing] Q5; nothing Q1   124 an] Q1; *not in* F1

110 **Maid Marian** a disreputable character from morris dances and May games, usually played by a man, sometimes paired with Robin Hood, though not in the earliest tradition. She had become a byword for slatternly behaviour among Puritan-leaning audiences. Kittredge and Humphreys cite *Misogonus* 2.4.75–6: 'This a smirking wench indeed, this a fair Maid Marion, she is none of these coy dames.'

110–11 **may be the deputy's wife of the ward** i.e. may serve as a model of respectability indeed, like the wife of a dignified local official empowered to act as magistrate in the absence of an alderman and thought of as likely to be a Puritan

111 **to thee** compared to you

113 **a thing to thank God on** 'i.e., she is as God made her' (Wilson, *NCS*). Having called the Hostess 'you thing', and thereby aroused her suspicion of being called something like 'you cunt' (see Partridge, *sb. thing*) or 'you whore', Falstaff turns aside the insult with an equivocation that allows the term to be interpreted in other ways, but does not deny the sexual meaning.

114 **I am . . . on** In her eagerness to deny Falstaff's insinuation of wantonness, the Hostess unwittingly characterizes herself as beyond redemption.

115–6 **setting . . . aside** The Hostess uses this phrase in the conventional polite sense (*OED, set, v.* 139d): except for your

knighthood, without wishing to speak against the rank of knighthood. Falstaff replies (ll. 117–8) in a different sense (*OED*, 139e): overruling your womanhood as of no value or pertinence. Being no woman, the Hostess is a beast.

117 **a beast** Falstaff's formulation could easily be interpreted in the figurative sense of 'unreasonable, unmannerly' (*OED*, 15), but the Hostess, never content to let well enough alone and ever a literalist, gives Falstaff the irresistible opportunity to come up with another extempore comparison.

120 **otter** As an aquatic mammal with fin-like legs and webbed feet, the otter seems not only poised between species, but anatomically androgynous.

122 **neither fish nor flesh** A common saying, 'neither fish nor flesh (nor good red herring)' (Dent F319).

123 **where to have her** A familiar expression (Dent K186) meaning 'how to take her', 'how to understand her', but with the suggestion here of sexual taking, or carnal knowledge, to which Mistress Quickly adds unintended comic emphasis.

125 **where to have me** She means, 'how to understand and take advantage of me', and seemingly remains unaware of the sexual implications. The Prince, unable to resist the fun, purports to come to her aid (ll. 126–7), but hints that she is to be commended for her sexual availability.

PRINCE HENRY Thou sayst true, hostess, and he slanders
thee most grossly.

HOSTESS So he doth you, my lord, and said this other day
you owed him a thousand pound.

PRINCE HENRY Sirrah, do I owe you a thousand pound?   130

FALSTAFF A thousand pound, Hal? A million. Thy love is
worth a million; thou owest me thy love.

HOSTESS Nay, my lord, he called you Jack, and said he
would cudgel you.

FALSTAFF Did I, Bardolph?

BARDOLPH Indeed, Sir John, you said so.

FALSTAFF Yea, if he said my ring was copper.

PRINCE HENRY I say 'tis copper. Darest thou be as good as
thy word now?

FALSTAFF Why, Hal, thou knowest, as thou art but man, I   140
dare; but as thou art prince, I fear thee as I fear the
roaring of the lion's whelp.

PRINCE HENRY And why not as the lion?

FALSTAFF The King himself is to be feared as the lion. Dost
thou think I'll fear thee as I fear thy father? Nay, an I do,
I pray God my girdle break.

PRINCE HENRY O, if it should, how would thy guts fall about
thy knees! But, sirrah, there's no room for faith, truth,
nor honesty in this bosom of thine; it is all filled up with
guts and midriff. Charge an honest woman with picking   150

---

129 owed] Q1 (ought)   135 Bardolph] DERING MS (Bardolffe), F1 (*Bardolph*); Bardol Q1
141 art] Q1 ; art a F1   145 an] Q1 (and); if F1

---

128 **this other** the other
129 **owed** Q1's 'ought' is a variant inflec-
tional form; see *OED*, *owe*, *v.* A. 4, and
ought, v.
131–2 **Thy love is worth a million** Proverbial after Shakespeare (Dent L553).
Falstaff exonerates himself from the accusation by means of a syllogism: (a) you
owe me your love (b) your love is worth a
million (c) therefore you owe me a
million.
133 **Jack** knave, as at 5.4.136
138–9 **as good as thy word** A familiar expression (Dent W773.1).
144 **The King . . . lion** On the association of
the lion with kingship, see 2.4.262 and
note. The *roaring* (l. 142) of the lion is

associated with fear-inducing royal
displeasure in Proverbs 19 : 12 and 20 : 2
(Wilson, *NCS*; Noble, 173).
146 **I pray . . . break** Falstaff uses a common
form of asseveration—see Dent G116.1
and citations—but invites comic interpretation because of his huge girth. See
also the saying 'ungirt, unblessed' (Tilley
U10), suggesting a moral dimension to
Falstaff's failure to gird his loins.
148–9 **there's . . . honesty** An echo of
Mistress Quickly's 'There's neither faith,
truth, nor womanhood' at l. 106. A
familiar tag; see Dent T567 and F34.
149 **bosom** cavity, belly (*OED*, *sb.* 4), not
breast
150 **midriff** diaphragm

thy pocket! Why, thou whoreson, impudent, embossed
rascal, if there were anything in thy pocket but tavern
reckonings, memorandums of bawdy-houses, and one
poor pennyworth of sugar-candy to make thee long-
winded, if thy pocket were enriched with any other injuries but these, I am a villain. And yet you will stand to
it; you will not pocket up wrong. Art thou not ashamed?

FALSTAFF Dost thou hear, Hal? Thou knowest in the state of
innocency Adam fell; and what should poor Jack Falstaff
do in the days of villainy? Thou seest I have more flesh   160
than another man, and therefore more frailty. You confess then you picked my pocket?

PRINCE HENRY It appears so by the story.

FALSTAFF Hostess, I forgive thee. Go make ready breakfast.
Love thy husband, look to thy servants, cherish thy
guests. Thou shalt find me tractable to any honest reason;
thou seest I am pacified still. Nay, prithee, be gone.

Exit Hostess

164–71 Hostess ... again] Q1; *as verse*, F1, *ending* thee: | Husband, | Guests: | reason: | still. |
gone. | Lad? | answered? | Beefe: | thee. | againe.   165 cherish] Q1; and cherish F1
166 guests] Q1 (ghesse)

151 **embossed** (a) swollen, bulging (b)
driven to exhaustion and foaming at the
mouth; said of a hunted animal

152 **rascal** (a) scoundrel (b) immature and
inferior deer. Hal gives an ironic twist to
Falstaff's image of the royal lion's *whelp*
(l. 142) by suggesting that the lion is now
cornering a prey that is paradoxically
lean and inferior, yet also swollen and
embossed.

153 **memorandums** mementoes

154–5 **long-winded** According to Wright,
sugar was given to fighting cocks to
prolong their breath. Its more common
use was to sweeten wine, as at 2.4.21 (see
note).

155–6 **injuries** grounds for complaint, or
affronts to your dignity

156–7 **stand to it** fight stoutly, persevere in
your insistence (*OED*, *stand*, v. 76c)

157 **pocket up** A common expression (Dent
I70), meaning 'to submit to', 'swallow',
with a play on the *pocket* of a garment at
ll. 151–6.

158–9 **state of innocency** The Prayer Book
service for matrimony describes matrimony as 'an honourable estate, instituted

of God in Paradise, in the time of man's
innocency' (Milward, 111).

160–1 **more flesh . . . frailty** Falstaff plays
the sophist with the biblical proverb 'The
flesh is weak' (Matthew 26 : 41 and Mark
14 : 38, Psalm 39 : 4; see Dent F363), by
confounding the literal meaning of *flesh*
with its tropological meaning of
'depraved human nature'. In Greene's
Friar Bacon and Friar Bungay (xiii. 96),
Margaret announces her decision to
marry with 'The flesh is frail' (l. 2079).
See also *Merry Wives* 3.5.45–6. A pre-
fatory instruction for Confirmation in the
Anglican liturgy warns children to be
wary of 'the frailty of their own flesh' that
will prompt them 'to fall into sundry kinds
of sin' (Milward, 109; Noble, 173).

166 **guests** The spelling used in F1, 'Guests',
appears to be F1's modernization of the
word that variously appears as 'ghesse'
(Q1), 'ghests' (Q2), and 'Ghestes' (Q5).
OED gives 'gess', 'gesse', 'guess', and
'guesse' as sixteenth- and seventeenth-
century plural forms of *guest*.

167 **pacified still** always easily pacified,
ready to make it up

Now, Hal, to the news at court: for the robbery, lad, how
is that answered?

PRINCE HENRY O, my sweet beef, I must still be good angel   170
to thee. The money is paid back again.

FALSTAFF O, I do not like that paying back. 'Tis a double
labour.

PRINCE HENRY I am good friends with my father and may do
anything.

FALSTAFF Rob me the Exchequer the first thing thou dost,
and do it with unwashed hands too.

BARDOLPH Do, my lord.

PRINCE HENRY I have procured thee, Jack, a charge of foot.

FALSTAFF I would it had been of horse. Where shall I find   180
one that can steal well? O for a fine thief, of the age of
two-and-twenty or thereabouts! I am heinously unprovided. Well, God be thanked for these rebels, they
offend none but the virtuous. I laud them, I praise them.

PRINCE HENRY Bardolph!

BARDOLPH My lord?

PRINCE HENRY (*giving letters*)

Go bear this letter to Lord John of Lancaster,
To my brother John; this to my Lord of Westmorland.

                                     ⌈*Exit Bardolph*⌉

Go, Peto, to horse, to horse, for thou and I
Have thirty miles to ride yet ere dinner-time. ⌈*Exit Peto*⌉   190

168 court: for] THEOBALD; court for QI   170 beef] QI (beoffe)   181 the age of] QI; *not in*
FI   182 two-and-twenty] FI; xxii. QI   185 Bardolph] DERING MS (Bardolffe), FI (*Bardolph*);
Bardoll QI   187 *giving letters*] This edition; *not in* QI   188 *Exit Bardolph*] DYCE; *not in*
QI   190 *Exit Peto*] CAMBRIDGE; *not in* QI

169 **answered** accounted for
170 **sweet beef** unsalted beef, ox, recalling
     'ribs' and 'tallow' at 2.4.108, 'roasted
     Manningtree ox' at 2.4.436, and
     anticipating 'martlemas' in *2 Henry IV*
     2.2.97.
177 **with unwashed hands** A familiar ex-
     pression (Dent H125) meaning 'at once,
     without waiting to observe the proprieties
     and without scruple'.
179 **charge of foot** (as promised at 2.4.526)
180–4 **I would . . . virtuous** The recurring
     jest about Falstaff uncomfortably on foot
     rather than on horseback here seems to
     remind Falstaff of the Gad's Hill robbery,
     when the Prince acted the part of 'a fine
     thief, of the age of two-and-twenty or

thereabouts' (ll. 181–2), and helped to
deprive Falstaff of his horse. Falstaff would
like another such companion to help him
turn the wars to his own advantage; war
is a God-sent opportunity for all but *the
virtuous* (l. 184).
182–3 **unprovided** ill-equipped
188–190 *Exit Bardolph, Exit Peto* These
exits might possibly be delayed until the
Prince leaves at l. 196. See collation.
189 **Peto** On the conjectural substitution
here of Poins by some editors, see
Introduction, pp. 102–3.
190 **thirty . . . dinner-time** 'This fixes the
time of the scene as early morning' (Wilson, NCS).

Jack, meet me tomorrow in the Temple Hall
At two o'clock in the afternoon.
There shalt thou know thy charge, and there receive
Money and order for their furniture.
The land is burning. Percy stands on high,
And either we or they must lower lie.   *Exit*

FALSTAFF

Rare words, brave world! Hostess, my breakfast, come!
O, I could wish this tavern were my drum!   *Exit*

4.1   *Enter Hotspur, Worcester, and Douglas*

HOTSPUR

Well said, my noble Scot. If speaking truth
In this fine age were not thought flattery,
Such attribution should the Douglas have
As not a soldier of this season's stamp
Should go so general current through the world.
By God, I cannot flatter; I do defy
The tongues of soothers! But a braver place
In my heart's love hath no man than yourself.
Nay, task me to my word; approve me, lord.

DOUGLAS Thou art the king of honour.   10

No man so potent breathes upon the ground
But I will beard him.

     Enter a Messenger with letters

---

192 o'] Q2 (a); of Q1   196 *Exit*] DYCE; *not in* Q1   198 *Exit*] *not in* Q1; *Exeunt.* Q2; *Exeunt omnes.* F1
   4.1.0 *Enter ... Douglas*] Q2; *not in* Q1   1–90 HOTSPUR] Q2; *Per.* Q1   12–13 But ... you] CAPELL; *printed on three lines,* Q1, *ending* him. | there? | you.   12 *a Messenger*] F1; *one* Q1   *with letters*] Q1; *not in* F1

191 **Temple Hall** i.e. Inner Temple Hall of the Inns of Court, as in *1 Henry VI* 2.4.3, a popular meeting-place.
194 **furniture** equipment
197 **brave** splendid
198 **I could . . . drum** I wish I could always rally at this tavern, respond to its call as to a martial instrument in time of war; or possibly Falstaff would like to make the tavern reverberate with the excitement of his setting forth.
4.1 Location: The rebel camp near Shrewsbury.
2 **fine** refined (Hotspur suggests 'subtle')
3 **attribution** praise, tribute

4–5 **As . . . world** that no one else minted in this present age with the stamp of soldier on him should be so widely accepted and acclaimed, like current coin
6–7 **defy . . . soothers** denounce and distrust the language of flatterers. Hotspur uses *defy* in a similar sense at 1.3.227.
7 **braver** better and more distinguished, as befits a brave man
9 **task . . . approve me** challenge me to make good my word, test me
11 **ground** earth
12 **But I will beard him** but that I will defy him in open combat

HOTSPUR   Do so, and 'tis well.—

What letters hast thou there?— I can but thank you.

MESSENGER These letters come from your father.

HOTSPUR

Letters from him? Why comes he not himself?

MESSENGER

He cannot come, my lord. He is grievous sick.

HOTSPUR

Zounds, how has he the leisure to be sick

In such a jostling time? Who leads his power?

Under whose government come they along?

MESSENGER

His letters bears his mind, not I, my lord.   20

WORCESTER

I prithee tell me, doth he keep his bed?

MESSENGER

He did, my lord, four days ere I set forth,

And at the time of my departure thence

He was much feared by his physicians.

WORCESTER

I would the state of time had first been whole

Ere he by sickness had been visited.

His health was never better worth than now.

HOTSPUR

Sick now? Droop now? This sickness doth infect

The very life-blood of our enterprise;

'Tis catching hither, even to our camp.   30

He writes me here that inward sickness—

---

13 thou] QI ; *not in* FI   17 Zounds, how] QI ; How FI   sick] QI ; sicke now FI   20 bears] QI ;
bear Q7   lord] CAPELL; mind QI   31 sickness—] ROWE; sickness, QI ; sickness holds him
CAPELL; sickness stays him (OXFORD)

13 **I can but thank you** Hotspur finishes his
compliment to Douglas after a characteristic self-interruption; see note at
2.3.86, and Hal's parody of this trait in
2.4.102–5 (Kittredge, Wilson, *NCS*).
16 **sick** See Appendix for Shakespeare's rearrangement of the chronology.
18 **jostling** clashing, contending. QqFI's
justling is a variant spelling.
19 **government** command
20 **letters bears** *Letters* (compare Latin *lit-*

terae, an epistle) is not uncommonly singular in sense in Shakespeare.
24 **feared** feared for
25 **time** the times
31 **sickness** Probably the QqFI text is defective (see collation), though the short line
may suggest Hotspur's characteristically
impatient self-interruption as he peruses
the contents of the letter. OXFORD completes the line thus: 'sickness stays him'.

And that his friends by deputation
Could not so soon be drawn, nor did he think it meet
To lay so dangerous and dear a trust
On any soul removed but on his own.
Yet doth he give us bold advertisement
That with our small conjunction we should on,
To see how fortune is disposed to us;
For, as he writes, there is no quailing now,
Because the King is certainly possessed   40
Of all our purposes. What say you to it?

WORCESTER

Your father's sickness is a maim to us.

HOTSPUR

A perilous gash, a very limb lopped off.
And yet, in faith, it is not. His present want
Seems more than we shall find it. Were it good
To set the exact wealth of all our states
All at one cast? To set so rich a main
On the nice hazard of one doubtful hour?
It were not good, for therein should we read
The very bottom and the soul of hope,   50
The very list, the very utmost bound
Of all our fortunes.

32–3 And . . . meet] Q1 ; *relineation with* Could not *as part of l.* 32, CAPELL

---

32 **by deputation** through those acting as Northumberland's deputies, as at 4.3.87.
33 **drawn** drawn together, mustered
   meet appropriate
35 **On . . . own** on anyone other than himself
36 **bold advertisement** admonition to be bold, or confident advice
37 **conjunction** combined force
   on go on
40–1 **the King . . . purposes** See Appendix for Holinshed.
44–5 **His . . . more** his absence seems at present more serious
46 **To . . . states** to stake the total of the resources of each of us. *Exact* is stressed on the first syllable.
47 **cast** cast of the dice
   main (a) stake in gambling (b) army
48 **nice** sensitive, precarious

hazard (a) game at dice (b) venture (*OED*, 1 and 2; Wilson, *NCS*)
49–52 **therein . . . fortunes** by hazarding all, we should survey or discover the very foundation and essence of our hopes, the very limits and furthest extremities of our fortunes. *Soul* (essential nature) suggests also 'sole', and *list* in the sense of 'boundary, limit' (*OED*, *sb.*[1] 8) is applied particularly to the edge, or selvage, of cloth (Humphreys; Wilson, *NCS*). Mahood (23) argues a nautical strain of imagery as well, with *cast* (l. 47) suggesting the cast of a net, *main* a naval expedition (as in 'Spanish main'), *hazard* a trading venture, *bottom* a ship or sea-bed, *list* the heeling of a ship to one side, and *bound* the sense of destination.

DOUGLAS

   Faith, and so we should. Where now remains
   A sweet reversion, we may boldly spend
   Upon the hope of what is to come in.
   A comfort of retirement lives in this.

HOTSPUR

   A rendezvous, a home to fly unto,
   If that the devil and mischance look big
   Upon the maidenhead of our affairs.

WORCESTER

   But yet I would your father had been here.   60
   The quality and hair of our attempt
   Brooks no division. It will be thought
   By some that know not why he is away
   That wisdom, loyalty, and mere dislike
   Of our proceedings kept the Earl from hence.
   And think how such an apprehension
   May turn the tide of fearful faction
   And breed a kind of question in our cause.
   For well you know we of the off'ring side
   Must keep aloof from strict arbitrament,   70
   And stop all sight-holes, every loop from whence
   The eye of reason may pry in upon us.

53–5 Faith … in] COLLIER 1877–8, conj. Walker; *printed on three lines,* Q1, *ending* should, | reuersion, | in; *on four lines,* F1, *ending* should, | reuersion, | hope | in; CAMBRIDGE *conjectures a line missing after* reuersion; STEEVENS 1773 *prints in four lines, ending* should, | reversion, | what | in   55 is] F1; tis Q1

53–5 **Faith . . . in** See collation for various proposals as to lineation. The phrase 'Where . . . reversion' is variously interpreted as beginning a new sentence, as here, or as continuing directly from *we should* in l. 53. The F1 emendation of *tis* to *is* in l. 55 is generally accepted.

54 **reversion** inheritance one expects to obtain at a future time

56 **comfort of retirement** comforting support and refuge to fall back on (first recorded use in *OED* of *retirement,* as at 5.4.5)

58 **look big** look threatening. A popular expression, as in *Shrew* 3.2.230: 'Nay, look not big, nor stamp, nor stare', *Winter's Tale* 4.3.101, and *Henry VIII* 1.1.119. Cowl and Morgan cite T. Heywood, *Wise-Woman of Hogsdon* (c.1604), 4.1 (Pearson reprint, v. 337): 'I'll go, although the devil and mischance look big', suggesting proverbial use.

59 **maidenhead** i.e. beginning, untried state

61 **hair** kind, nature; synonymous with *quality.* From the expression 'of one hair', of one colour and external quality (*OED,* 6). Kittredge cites *Sir Thomas More,* 3.2.91 (ed. Brooke, 399): 'A fellow of your hair'.

62 **Brooks** tolerates

64 **loyalty** i.e. to the Crown
   mere out and out, downright

66 **apprehension** (a) idea that is grasped (b) apprehensiveness

67 **fearful** timorous

69 **off'ring side** insurgent party, taking the offensive against established authority

70 **strict arbitrament** rigorously impartial inquiry

71 **loop** loophole

This absence of your father's draws a curtain
That shows the ignorant a kind of fear
Before not dreamt of.

HOTSPUR   You strain too far.
I rather of his absence make this use:
It lends a lustre and more great opinion,
A larger dare to our great enterprise,
Than if the Earl were here; for men must think,
If we without his help can make a head   80
To push against a kingdom, with his help
We shall o'erturn it topsy-turvy down.
Yet all goes well, yet all our joints are whole.

DOUGLAS
As heart can think. There is not such a word
Spoke of in Scotland as this term of fear.
            Enter Sir Richard Vernon

HOTSPUR
My cousin Vernon, welcome, by my soul.

VERNON
Pray God my news be worth a welcome, lord.
The Earl of Westmorland, seven thousand strong,
Is marching hitherwards; with him Prince John.

HOTSPUR
No harm. What more?

VERNON   And further I have learned   90
The King himself in person is set forth,
Or hitherwards intended speedily
With strong and mighty preparation.

HOTSPUR
He shall be welcome too. Where is his son,

85.1 *Richard*] Q1 (*Ri*:)

73 **draws** draws open or aside
74 **a kind of fear** a fearfulness on our part, or
   a reason to mistrust and fear for the
   soundness of our cause
75 **strain too far** exaggerate
77 **opinion** renown, estimation
78 **dare** daring
80 **make a head** raise an armed force, as at
   3.1.61.
82 **o'erturn . . . down** A popular tag (Dent
   T165).

83 **Yet** still
   joints limbs
84 **As heart can think** A familiar expression
   (Dent H300.1).
86 **My cousin Vernon** See Appendix for historical information.
87–93 **Pray . . . preparation** See Appendix
   for Holinshed and Daniel.
90 **No harm** A familiar tag (Dent *PLED*,
   H169.11).
92 **intended** on the verge of departure

The nimble-footed madcap Prince of Wales,
And his comrades, that doffed the world aside
And bid it pass?
VERNON   All furnished, all in arms;
All plumed like estridges that with the wind
⌐   ⌐
Bating like eagles having lately bathed,   100
Glittering in golden coats like images,
As full of spirit as the month of May
And gorgeous as the sun at midsummer;
Wanton as youthful goats, wild as young bulls.
I saw young Harry with his beaver on,
His cuisses on his thighs, gallantly armed,

---

98 with] Q1; wing ROWE; vie COWL AND MORGAN   98–100 wind | . . . | Bating] OXFORD; wind
| Baited Q1

95 **nimble-footed** Hotspur's sarcastic remark
suggests cowardice or idle capering, but
see Appendix for admiring reports of
Prince Henry's swiftness in the
chronicles.

96 **comrades** (accent on second syllable)
doffed has put, or tossed, aside, carelessly
disregarded; a coalesced form of 'do off'.
QqF1 'daft' (compare *Othello* 4.2.176:
'Every day thou doff'st [Q1; "dafts" in
F1] me with some device') is a variant
form. It is sometimes emended to present
tense (e.g. Hanmer; Wilson, *NCS*) or read
as ambiguously present and past tense,
like *bid* in the next line (Humphreys).

97 **bid it pass** 'Let the world pass' was a
familiar saying, and a drinking-song
refrain appropriate to revellers. Compare
Shrew, Induction 1.5; 'Let the world
slide', and 2.140: 'Let the world slip';
other citations in Kittredge and in Dent
W879: 'Let the world wag.'

97–100 **All furnished . . . bathed** In their
armour, with their headpieces and
horses' trappings decked out with
feathers, the Prince of Wales and his comrades reminded Vernon of ostriches under
spread wings and also freshly-bathed
eagles *bating*, or beating, their wings *with
the wind*, i.e. in the wind. A difficult
passage, in which a line may have been
lost after *wind*, possibly as the result of
damage to the beginning and end of a
manuscript leaf that also produced a
lacuna at l.31 above. Critics have
proposed that *estridges* means 'goshawks'

(e.g. Francis Douce, *Illustrations of Shakespeare and of Ancient Manners*, 1807, i.
435), though a passage from Nashe's
Unfortunate Traveller (ed. McKerrow, ii.
272; cited by G. R. Coffman, *MLN*, 42
(1927), 317–9, and Humphreys, 201–2)
provides a suggestive source for the metaphor of spread ostrich wings resembling
the wings of Pegasus (l. 110 below) and of
eagles pursuing their prey. Compare, too,
Spenser's *Faerie Queene*, I. xi. 34, for the
metaphor of an eagle 'fresh out of the
ocean wave' assaying his 'newly-budded
pinions'. *With* in l. 98 is sometimes
emended to 'wing' (Rowe), and *Baited*, l.
100 (the QqF1 reading), is sometimes
interpreted to mean 'refreshed' or
'renewed' (Wilson, *NCS*). To *bate* in falconry is 'to beat the wings impatiently
and flutter away from the fist or perch'
(*OED*, *v.*¹ 2). The QqF1 *Baited*, indeterminately past tense or past participle, may
have resulted from contamination with
bathd on the same line.

101 **coats** (a) coats of mail (b) heraldic coats
of arms
images gilded effigies, of saints or (more
probably) of warriors

104 **Wanton** sportive, frisky. Compare the
expression 'as wanton as a whelp' (Dent
W38.1).

105 **beaver** face-guard (from Old French
bave, 'saliva'), hence, helmet; or perhaps
his beaver is *up*, as in *Hamlet* 1.2.229.

106 **cuisses** thigh-armour. QqF1 *cushes* is a
phonetic variant.

Rise from the ground like feathered Mercury,
And vaulted with such ease into his seat
As if an angel dropped down from the clouds
To turn and wind a fiery Pegasus 110
And witch the world with noble horsemanship.

HOTSPUR

No more, no more! Worse than the sun in March
This praise doth nourish agues. Let them come.
They come like sacrifices in their trim,
And to the fire-eyed maid of smoky war
All hot and bleeding will we offer them.
The mailèd Mars shall on his altars sit
Up to the ears in blood. I am on fire
To hear this rich reprisal is so nigh
And yet not ours. Come, let me taste my horse, 120
Who is to bear me like a thunderbolt
Against the bosom of the Prince of Wales.
Harry to Harry shall, hot horse to horse,
Meet and ne'er part till one drop down a corse.
O that Glendower were come!

VERNON   There is more news:
I learned in Worcester as I rode along
He cannot draw his power this fourteen days.

109 dropped] Q2 (dropt); drop Q1   117 altars] Q1; altar Q4–5, F1   120 taste] Q1; take Q3–5,
F1   124 ne'er] Q2 (ne're); neare Q1   127 cannot] Q5 *corr.*; can Q1

107 **feathered Mercury** The swift messenger
of the gods had 'wingèd heels' (*Henry V*, 2
Prol. 7), and winged cap.
108 **vaulted** he vaulted. Prince Hal's *noble
horsemanship* (l. 111) symbolizes a new-
found discipline able to control the *wanton*
and *wild* (l. 104) energy of his youth so
exuberantly set forth in the natural
images of this speech. Vaulting like this
(as in *Henry V* 5.2.136–7) is a remarkable
feat in full armour.
110 **wind** wheel about (a term in horsemanship)
  Pegasus winged horse of Greek mythology
111 **witch** bewitch
112–13 **Worse . . . agues** The spring sun
was thought to nourish chills and fevers,
such as those of malaria, by drawing up
vapours from marshland, as in *Lear*
2.4.165: 'You fen-sucked fogs, drawn by

the powerful sun.' Cowl and Morgan cite
Thomas Overbury, *Characters* (1615), *A
Canting Rogue*: 'The March sun breeds
agues.'
113 **nourish agues** i.e. give one the shudders
114 **sacrifices in their trim** sacrificial animals
in their ceremonial finery
115 **maid** Bellona, Roman goddess of war.
Compare *Macbeth* 1.2.55: 'Bellona's bridegroom'. Bellona is paired with *Mars*, the
god of war, at l. 117.
117 **mailèd** clad in mail, armour
118 **Up to the ears** A familiar expression (Dent
H268).
119 **reprisal** prize
120 **taste** try (from French *taster*, *tâter*, to
'feel', 'touch', 'try', 'taste')
125–7 **Glendower . . . days** See Appendix for
Holinshed and Daniel.
127 **draw** draw together, assemble (*OED*, 29)

DOUGLAS

That's the worst tidings that I hear of yet.

WORCESTER

Ay, by my faith, that bears a frosty sound.

HOTSPUR

What may the King's whole battle reach unto?   130

VERNON

To thirty thousand.

HOTSPUR   Forty let it be!

My father and Glendower being both away,

The powers of us may serve so great a day.

Come, let us take a muster speedily.

Doomsday is near; die all, die merrily.

DOUGLAS

Talk not of dying. I am out of fear

Of death or death's hand for this one half-year.   *Exeunt*

4.2   *Enter Falstaff and Bardolph*

FALSTAFF Bardolph, get thee before to Coventry; fill me a
bottle of sack. Our soldiers shall march through. We'll to
Sutton Co'fil' tonight.

BARDOLPH Will you give me money, captain?

FALSTAFF Lay out, lay out.

---

128 yet] Q5; it Q1   135 merrily] Q1 (merely)   137 *Exeunt* Q1; *Exeunt Omnes* F1
   4.2.0 *and*] *not in* Q1   *Bardolph*] DERING MS (Bardolffe), F1 (*Bardolph*); *Bardoll* Q1   1 Bar-
dolph] DERING MS (Bardolfe), F1 (*Bardolph*); Bardol Q1   3 Co'fil'] Q1 (cop- | hill)

130 **battle** army
131 **thirty . . . Forty** Perhaps Shakespeare's
   own figures, to emphasize the unequal
   odds; see Appendix for chronicle accounts.
133 **powers of us** forces we have
   serve suffice for
135 **die all, die merrily** May be proverbial;
   compare 'Death's day is doomsday' (Dent
   (?) D161).
137 **for this one half-year** i.e. (with ironic
   understatement) for a little while longer,
   at any rate. Douglas suggests that Hotspur's defeatist talk of dying is bad for
   morale.
4.2 Location: A public road south-east of
   Coventry.
3 **Sutton Co'fil'** Sutton Coldfield, in War-

wickshire, lies about twenty miles beyond
Coventry to the north-west, a long day's
march and rather off the highway from
Coventry through Birmingham to Bridgnorth and Shrewsbury. See note at
3.2.175. The QqF1 reading, 'cop-hill',
probably reflects Shakespeare's spelling of
'Cophil', pronounced 'Cofil' (Wilson,
NCS).
5 **Lay out** pay for it yourself, I've given
you enough already. Compare *Tempest*
2.2.30: 'they will lay out ten [doits] to
see a dead Indian.' As in 2 *Henry IV* 3.2,
where Bardolph is again Falstaff's quarter-
master, the receiving and disbursing of
funds is highly irregular, and always to
Falstaff's personal advantage.

BARDOLPH This bottle makes an angel.

FALSTAFF An if it do, take it for thy labour; an if it make
twenty, take them all; I'll answer the coinage. Bid my
lieutenant Peto meet me at town's end.

BARDOLPH I will, captain. Farewell.   *Exit*   10

FALSTAFF If I be not ashamed of my soldiers, I am a soused
gurnet. I have misused the King's press damnably. I have
got, in exchange of a hundred and fifty soldiers, three
hundred and odd pounds. I press me none but good
householders, yeomen's sons, inquire me out contracted
bachelors, such as had been asked twice on the banns
—such a commodity of warm slaves as had as lief hear
the devil as a drum, such as fear the report of a caliver
worse than a struck fowl or a hurt wild duck. I pressed me
none but such toasts-and-butter, with hearts in their   20

---

7 An ... an] Q1 (And ... and)   9 at] Q1; a Q5; at the F1   11 soused] Q1 (souct)   13 a
hundred and fifty] Q1 (150.)   13–14 three hundred] Q1 (300.)   15 yeomen's] Q2 (Yeo-
mens); Yeomans Q1   19 fowl] ROWE (1714); foule Q1

---

6 **makes an angel** will bring the total expenditure up to the value of an angel (a
coin showing the angel Michael piercing a
dragon, valued in 1465 at 6s. 8d., but
later (1553) at 10s.)

7–8 **An if... coinage** Falstaff adroitly parries
Bardolph's request for more funds by
taking his word *makes* to mean 'brings in,
coins', facetiously suggesting that Bardolph can profit by each such transaction.

8 **I'll answer the coinage** I'll be answerable
for any coinage the bottle 'makes', I'll
take responsibility for any illegal profits
you make. Private coinage, like Falstaff's
irregular handling of finances, was
illegal.

9 **Peto** On Peto's role as lieutenant, see
Introduction, p. 103.

11–12 **soused gurnet** a pickled small fish
with a disproportionately large spiny
head. A slender delicacy from the food
shops once again, like 'rabbit-suckers'
and 'shotten herring' (see 2.4.124 and
note), and comically inappropriate by
comparison with Falstaff. A familiar term
of opprobrium, after Shakespeare at least;
OED, 1b, cites *Wily Beguiled* (c.1602),
Prol. l. 24: 'Out, you soused gurnet.'

12 **King's press** royal commission to 'im-

press', compel military service. For a contemporary example of abuse, see ll. 21–2
below and note.

14 **good** substantial, wealthy

15 **yeomen's sons** As holders of small landed
estates, yeomen were generally prosperous enough to be able to buy out their
sons' military service.
    contracted engaged to be married

16 **twice on the banns** Announcements of
intent to marry were (and still are)
declared in church, ordinarily on three
successive Sundays, to enable anyone
knowing an impediment to the marriage
to speak out. QqF1 *banes* is a variant form.

17 **commodity of warm slaves** parcel of
cowards, comfortably off and tied to their
creature comforts. Cowl and Morgan cite
Bailey: '*Warm*, well-lined, or flush in the
pocket'.

18 **caliver** light musket (the same word as
calibre)

19 **struck** wounded

20 **toasts-and-butter** milksops. Malone and
Kittredge cite Fynes Moryson, *Itinerary*,
1617, Pt III, Bk I, chap. iii, p. 53: 'Lon-
doners, and all within the sound of Bow-
Bell, are in reproach called Cockneys, and
eaters of buttered toasts.'

bellies no bigger than pins' heads, and they have bought
out their services; and now my whole charge consists of
ancients, corporals, lieutenants, gentlemen of companies
—slaves as ragged as Lazarus in the painted cloth, where
the glutton's dogs licked his sores; and such as indeed
were never soldiers, but discarded unjust servingmen,
younger sons to younger brothers, revolted tapsters, and
ostlers trade-fallen, the cankers of a calm world and a
long peace, ten times more dishonourable-ragged than

21 **pins' heads** Proverbially small (Dent
P336.1).
21–2 **bought out their services** paid a bribe
(to Falstaff) to be released from military
duty. Steevens (1803) quotes *The Voyage
unto Cadiz*, 1596 (Hakluyt, 1599, i. 607):
'A certain lieutenant . . . was by sound of
drum publicly in all the streets disgraced,
or rather after a sort disgraded, and
cashiered for bearing any farther office at
that time, for the taking of money, by the
way of corruption, of certain pressed
soldiers in the country, and for placing of
others in their rooms, more unfit for service, and of less sufficiency and ability'
(1904 ed., iv. 237).
22 **charge** company
23 **ancients** ensigns, standard-bearers. Falstaff's company has a disproportionate
number of junior and non-commissioned
officers, which makes money for Falstaff;
he has promoted the *warm slaves* he first
recruited (l. 17), thereby gaining more as
they sold out, and now pockets the difference between their pay and the
privates' stipends he gives the new
recruits (Wilson, *NCS*). The QqF1 form,
ancients, is a corruption of *ensigns* resulting from a confounding of *ensyne, enseyne*
with *ancien, ancyen* (*OED*). *Ensign* (compare Latin *insignia*) was used at least
occasionally in Shakespeare's time to signify the standard-bearer as well as the
standard; *OED* cites examples from 1579.
Nevertheless, Shakespeare's original texts
invariably use *ancient* or *aunchient* for the
standard-bearer, and *ensign* (except at
ll. 29–30 below) for the standard, suggesting that he observed a distinction.
Albany's reference in *Lear* to veteran officers as 'th' ancient of war' may explain
why officers could be thought 'ancient'
(5.1.32).
gentlemen of companies 'A Gentleman of
the company is he who is something more

than an ordinary soldier, hath a little
more pay, and doth not stand sentinel'
(Sir James Turner, *Pallas Armata*, 1670–1
(1683), 218). *OED, gentleman*, 16 cites
William Blandy, *The Castle, or Picture of
Policy* (1581), 18b: 'Captain, lieutenant,
ancient, sergeant of a company, corporal,
gentlemen in a company or of the round,
lance passado. These are special; the
other that remain, private or common
soldiers.'
24–5 **Lazarus . . . sores** Regarding the parable of Lazarus the poor man and Dives
the rich man in Luke 16: 19–31, see note
at 3.3.30–1. On painted cloth, compare
2 Henry IV 2.1.138–41, where Falstaff
urges Mistress Quickly to replace her
tapestry with less expensive painted cloth
as wall-hangings, and *As You Like It*
3.2.258.
26 **discarded** discharged
   unjust dishonest
27 **younger sons to younger brothers** Since
only the eldest son stood to inherit title
and property under English law, younger
brothers often went into the military or
other careers; their younger sons were
twice removed from inheritance.
   revolted runaway
28 **trade-fallen** whose business has fallen
away (first recorded use in *OED*)
   cankers canker-worms, which destroy
leaves and buds; also, spreading sores, or
cancers, devouring the social organism.
The notion of *long peace* (l. 29) as a breeder
of enervating corruption is common, as in
Hamlet 4.4.27–8 and Nashe, *Pierce Penniless* (1592), i. 213: 'The cankerworms
that breed on the rust of peace' (cited by
Wilson, *NCS*).
29–30 **more . . . ancient** more dishonour-
able in their raggedness, and more ragged
too, than an old tattered flag—the frayed
condition of which is, after all, a sign of
honour in a flag. Qq1–4 'fazd', 'fazde'

an old feazed ancient. And such have I, to fill up the   30
rooms of them as have bought out their services, that you
would think that I had a hundred and fifty tattered
prodigals lately come from swine-keeping, from eating
draff and husks. A mad fellow met me on the way and told
me I had unloaded all the gibbets and pressed the dead
bodies. No eye hath seen such scarecrows. I'll not march
through Coventry with them, that's flat. Nay, and the
villains march wide betwixt the legs as if they had gyves
on, for indeed I had the most of them out of prison.
There's not a shirt and a half in all my company, and the   40
half-shirt is two napkins tacked together and thrown over
the shoulders like a herald's coat without sleeves; and the
shirt, to say the truth, stolen from my host at Saint
Albans, or the red-nose innkeeper of Daventry. But that's
all one, they'll find linen enough on every hedge.
        Enter Prince Henry and the Earl of Westmorland

---

30 old feazed] Q1 (olde fazd); old faczde Q5; old-fac'd F1   31 as] Q1; that F1   32 tattered Q1
(tottered)   45.1 *Prince ... Westmorland*] ROWE (subs.); *the Prince, Lord of Westmerland* Q1

appear to be variants of the past participle
of *feaze*, 'unravel', 'wear rough at the
end.' *Ancient* as a noun in Shakespeare's
original texts invariably means officer or
standard-bearer (see note at l. 23 above)
except in this instance, as distinguished
from 'ensign', or banner; F1's 'old-fac'd
Ancient' (Q5: 'faczde') suggests that the
F1 editor or compositor regarded the
phrase here as referring to a worthy old
officer.

32 **tattered** QqF1 *tottered* is here a variant
form.

33 **prodigals** The story of the prodigal son,
from Luke 15: 11–32, is elsewhere
associated with Falstaff in *Merry Wives*
4.5.6, where his chamber is 'painted
about with the story of the Prodigal', and
in *2 Henry IV* 2.1.139, where Falstaff
again knows the story through a painted
cloth. See also *younker*, 3.3.77 and note.

34 **draff** hogwash, swill
    husks Noble, 277, notes that *husks* is
used in the Geneva and Rheims Bibles at
Luke 15: 16, instead of *cods* as in the
Bishops' Bible. Presumably Shakespeare
knew the story in the Geneva version.

37 **that's flat** that's for certain, as at 1.3.218
(see note)

38 **gyves** fetters

39 **out of prison** Convicts were not uncommonly released on condition that they
enlist; Wilson, *NCS*, notes that 'The Privy
Council emptied the London prisons in
1596 to furnish recruits for the Cadiz
expedition', citing E. P. Cheyney, *A History of England, 1588–1603* (1914), ii.
49–50.

40 **not** Sometimes emended to *but*, following
Rowe, but see 5.3.36 and 2.4.125 for
other examples of this Falstaffian idiom.

42 **without sleeves** The tabard, or herald's
official dress emblazoned with the
sovereign's arms, was sleeveless.

43 **my host** Usual way of referring to an innkeeper.

43–4 **Saint Albans . . . Daventry** towns
north-west of London, on the road to
Coventry

44–45 **that's all one** no matter

45 **hedge** Wet washing, spread to dry on
hedges, was easily stolen, as in *Winter's
Tale* 4.3.5; see J. Dover Wilson, *Life in
Shakespeare's England* (1920), 241–2.

45.1 **Prince Henry** Hal was sent by his
father through Gloucestershire (see note
at 3.2.175), yet here appears to be on the
more northerly route through Coventry.

PRINCE HENRY　How now, blown Jack? How now, quilt?

FALSTAFF　What, Hal, how now, mad wag? What a devil dost thou in Warwickshire? My good lord of Westmorland, I cry you mercy. I thought your honour had already been at Shrewsbury.　　50

WESTMORLAND　Faith, Sir John, 'tis more than time that I were there, and you too; but my powers are there already. The King, I can tell you, looks for us all. We must away at night.

FALSTAFF　Tut, never fear me. I am as vigilant as a cat to steal cream.

PRINCE HENRY　I think to steal cream indeed, for thy theft hath already made thee butter. But tell me, Jack, whose fellows are these that come after?

FALSTAFF　Mine, Hal, mine.　　60

PRINCE HENRY　I did never see such pitiful rascals.

FALSTAFF　Tut, tut, good enough to toss; food for powder, food for powder. They'll fill a pit as well as better. Tush, man, mortal men, mortal men.

WESTMORLAND　Ay, but, Sir John, methinks they are exceeding poor and bare, too beggarly.

---

54 at] This edition; all Q1; all to F1

---

46 **blown** (a) swollen (b) short of wind. At 2.4.322, Falstaff asserts that grief 'blows a man up like a bladder'.
　quilt i.e. thickly padded; with a play on *Jack*, *OED, sb.*² 1b, a quilted soldier's tunic (Joseph Hunter, *New Illustrations of the Life, Studies, and Writings of Shakespeare*, 1845, ii. 52).

49 **cry you mercy** beg your pardon (for not having greeted you more promptly); as at 1.3.212

53–4 **must away** must march

54 **at night** The Q1 reading, *all night*, seems implausible and could easily be a compositorial error for *at night*, especially if spelt *al* (compare 5.4.55 and elsewhere) in the printer's copy. F1 seems to have perceived the need for emendation.

55 **fear** doubt, worry about
　vigilant wakeful, ready to travel all night

57–8 **I think . . . butter** i.e. the proverb

about the cat stealing cream (Dent C167) applies to you in a fleshly sense, since you have grown fat from all your thefts. Cream would be churned into butter in just such a 'tun', or large barrel (2.4.432), as Falstaff carries around with him.

62 **toss** toss on a pike
　food for powder cannon-fodder, fit only to be shot at or to die in battle (*OED, food, sb.* 1d)

63 **pit** mass grave

66–8 **bare . . . bareness** Westmorland means 'threadbare', but Falstaff quibblingly uses *bareness* to mean 'leanness' (*OED*, 2b). He also puns in *poor*, answering Westmorland's meaning 'of inferior quality', with a comic allusion to his recruits' lack of financial means as runaway tapsters or younger sons of younger brothers (ll. 26–7). Falstaff knows well enough where their poverty comes from.

FALSTAFF Faith, for their poverty I know not where they
    had that, and for their bareness, I am sure they never
    learned that of me.

PRINCE HENRY No, I'll be sworn, unless you call three fingers   70
    in the ribs bare. But sirrah, make haste. Percy is already
    in the field.   *Exit*

FALSTAFF What, is the King encamped?

WESTMORLAND He is, Sir John. I fear we shall stay too long.
                                             ⌈*Exit*⌉

FALSTAFF
    Well, to the latter end of a fray and the beginning of
        a feast
    Fits a dull fighter and a keen guest.   *Exit*

4.3   *Enter Hotspur, Worcester, Douglas, and Vernon*

HOTSPUR
    We'll fight with him tonight.

WORCESTER   It may not be.

DOUGLAS
    You give him then advantage.

VERNON   Not a whit.

HOTSPUR
    Why say you so? Looks he not for supply?

VERNON
    So do we.

HOTSPUR   His is certain, ours is doubtful.

WORCESTER
    Good cousin, be advised, stir not tonight.

VERNON
    Do not, my lord.

---

72 *Exit*] Q1; *not in* F1   74.1 *Exit*] CAPELL; *not in* Q1   75–6 Well … guest] *as verse*, POPE (*with*
Well on a separate line); *as prose*, Q1   76 *Exit*] CAPELL; *Exeunt*. Q1
    4.3.0 *Douglas, and Vernon*] Q1 (*Doug: Vernon*)

67, 68 **for** as for
70 **three fingers** three finger-breadths (of
    fat). The Prince underscores Falstaff's jest
    that obesity is hardly 'bareness'.
75–6 **to … guest** Falstaff uses the proverb 'It
    is better coming to the beginning of a feast
    than the end of a fray' (Dent C547) to
    contrast his own appetite for food with

Westmorland's appetite for war.
76 **keen** with keen appetite
4.3 Location: The rebel camp near Shrews-
    bury.
2 **then** i.e. if you wait (addressed to Wor-
    cester, not Hotspur)
3 **supply** reinforcements

DOUGLAS   You do not counsel well.
You speak it out of fear and cold heart.
VERNON
Do me no slander, Douglas. By my life,
And I dare well maintain it with my life,
If well-respected honour bid me on,   10
I hold as little counsel with weak fear
As you, my lord, or any Scot that this day lives.
Let it be seen tomorrow in the battle
Which of us fears.
DOUGLAS
Yea, or tonight.
VERNON   Content.
HOTSPUR   Tonight, say I.
VERNON
Come, come, it may not be. I wonder much,
Being men of such great leading as you are,
That you foresee not what impediments
Drag back our expedition. Certain horse
Of my cousin Vernon's are not yet come up.   20
Your uncle Worcester's horse came but today,
And now their pride and mettle is asleep,
Their courage with hard labour tame and dull,
That not a horse is half the half of himself.
HOTSPUR
So are the horses of the enemy
In general journey-bated and brought low.
The better part of ours are full of rest.
WORCESTER
The number of the King exceedeth our.

---

14 Which ... fears] F1; *as part of l.* 13, Q1   16 I wonder much] T. JOHNSON; *as part of l.* 17,
Q1   21 horse] Q5; horses Q1   28 our] Q1; ours Q6, F1

---

10 **well-respected** well-weighed, carefully
considered (as opposed to fanatical)
17 **leading** experience in military leadership
19 **expedition** rapid progress
horse cavalry. On *horse* as plural form,
see note at 2.1.3.
22 **pride and mettle** natural vigour, or spirit
(the two words are synonymous)

26 **journey-bated** worn out and dejected,
'abated', by their journey
28 **our** See collation for F1's emendation of
Q1 *our* to *ours*, but the use of *our* is sub-
stantiated and recurs at 5.4.154. *OED,
our,* 2 cites Daniel, *Civil Wars* (1601), vi.
61: 'We rule who live; the dead are none
of our.'

For God's sake, cousin, stay till all come in.
> *The trumpet sounds a parley.*
> *Enter Sir Walter Blunt*

BLUNT

I come with gracious offers from the King,   30
If you vouchsafe me hearing and respect.

HOTSPUR

Welcome, Sir Walter Blunt; and would to God
You were of our determination!
Some of us love you well; and even those some
Envy your great deservings and good name
Because you are not of our quality,
But stand against us like an enemy.

BLUNT

And God defend but still I should stand so,
So long as out of limit and true rule
You stand against anointed majesty.   40
But to my charge. The King hath sent to know
The nature of your griefs, and whereupon
You conjure from the breast of civil peace
Such bold hostility, teaching his duteous land
Audacious cruelty. If that the King
Have any way your good deserts forgot,
Which he confesseth to be manifold,
He bids you name your griefs, and with all speed
You shall have your desires with interest
And pardon absolute for yourself and these   50
Herein misled by your suggestion.

HOTSPUR

The King is kind; and well we know the King
Knows at what time to promise, when to pay.

29.1 *parley* trumpet-call announcing an
 embassy from one side to the other (sounded off-stage)
29.2 *Blunt* On Shakespeare's enhancement
 of Blunt's role, see Appendix.
31 **respect** attention
33 **determination** persuasion, affiliation
34 **those some** those same persons among us
 (who love you)
35 **Envy** begrudge
36 **quality** party, fellowship (*OED*, 5; compare the actors' *quality* or profession)
38 **defend** forbid
 still always
39 **limit** prescribed bounds of allegiance
 true rule good order and obedience
42 **griefs** grievances
 whereupon upon what ground
45 **If that** if
51 **suggestion** instigation, evil suggestion, as
 in 2 *Henry IV* 4.4.45, *Macbeth* 1.3.134,
 Othello 2.3.340–1.

My father and my uncle and myself
Did give him that same royalty he wears,
And when he was not six-and-twenty strong,
Sick in the world's regard, wretched and low,
A poor unminded outlaw sneaking home,
My father gave him welcome to the shore;
And when he heard him swear and vow to God   60
He came but to be Duke of Lancaster,
To sue his livery and beg his peace
With tears of innocency and terms of zeal,
My father, in kind heart and pity moved,
Swore him assistance, and performed it too.
Now when the lords and barons of the realm
Perceived Northumberland did lean to him,
The more and less came in with cap and knee,
Met him in boroughs, cities, villages,
Attended him on bridges, stood in lanes,   70
Laid gifts before him, proffered him their oaths,
Gave him their heirs as pages, followed him
Even at the heels in golden multitudes.
He presently, as greatness knows itself,

72 heirs as pages,] F4 (Heires, as Pages,), SINGER (*following* Malone *conj.*, *1780*); heires, as Pages
Q1 pages, followed] Q1 *corr.* (Pages followed) (*Huntington Library Bunbury–Devonshire copy*);
Pagesfollowed Q1 *uncorr.* (*British Library and Trinity College Cambridge copies*)

54–73 **My father . . . multitudes** Compare this account with *Richard II* 2.1.224–300, 2.3.1–151 (esp. 148–51), and 3.3.101–20, and Holinshed ii. 853.

56 **six-and-twenty** See Appendix for Holinshed.

58 **unminded** disregarded

62 **sue his livery** make suit (in the Court of Wards, through his attorneys) to take possession of his inheritance. The dukedom, held by John of Gaunt as tenant of the Crown, legally reverted to the Crown at Gaunt's death, but York and Bolingbroke justly complain in *Richard II* (2.1.201–5, 2.3.129–30) that Richard has denied Bolingbroke's right given him by letters patent 'to sue | His livery'.
beg his peace seek reconciliation with the King. In *Richard II* Richard chooses to 'deny his [Bolingbroke's] offered homage' (2.1.204).

63 **terms of zeal** loyal protestations

68 **The more . . . knee** high and low offered

their allegiance through the conventional gesture of bending the knee with cap in hand. (Humphreys gives contemporary citations.)

70 **Attended** waited for
lanes rows along both sides of the high road

72 **Gave . . . pages** See collation. The comma after 'heires' in QqF1 requires emendation, since the fathers would scarcely have served as pages, and since pages normally precede, rather than follow, the person they serve (Humphreys). The pages are to serve 'as hostages for their fathers' loyalty' (Wilson, *NCS*).

73 **golden** (a) auspicious, celebrating, as in *As You Like It* 1.1.5 and *2 Henry IV* 5.3.95, 99 (b) richly attired

74 **as greatness knows itself** as his authority comes to perceive its own might; or, since authority sooner or later must recognize its own might

256

Steps me a little higher than his vow
Made to my father while his blood was poor
Upon the naked shore at Ravenspurgh,
And now, forsooth, takes on him to reform
Some certain edicts and some strait decrees
That lie too heavy on the commonwealth,   80
Cries out upon abuses, seems to weep
Over his country's wrongs; and by this face,
This seeming brow of justice, did he win
The hearts of all that he did angle for;
Proceeded further— cut me off the heads
Of all the favourites that the absent King
In deputation left behind him here,
When he was personal in the Irish war.

BLUNT

Tut, I came not to hear this.

HOTSPUR   Then to the point.

In short time after he deposed the King,   90
Soon after that deprived him of his life,
And in the neck of that tasked the whole state;
To make that worse, suffered his kinsman March –
Who is, if every owner were well placed,
Indeed his king – to be engaged in Wales,
There without ransom to lie forfeited;
Disgraced me in my happy victories,

---

79 strait] Q1 (streight)   82 country's] Q5 *corr.* (Countries); Countrey Q1

75 **me** The ethical dative, as in 2.4.100 (see
   note) and also at l. 85.
76 **while his blood was poor** while his spirit,
   or temper, was still humbled; but with a
   sardonic suggestion also of lineage that is
   subject to challenge
78–80 **to reform . . . commonwealth** See
   Appendix for Holinshed.
79 **strait** overly strict
81 **Cries out upon** denounces. The description here of Henry's hypocritical wooing
   of the common people is reminiscent of
   Henry's own confession at 3.2.50 ff. and
   of Absalom's rebellion against King David
   in 2 Samuel 15. Compare also *Richard II*
   1.4.23–36.
82 **face** pretence; synonymous with *seeming
   brow of justice* in l. 83
85 **cut me off** cut off; see note at l. 75 above.
87 **In deputation** as deputies, as in 4.1.32

(see note)
88 **personal** personally engaged
92 **in the neck of that** immediately after that,
   as in *Sonnets* 131.11; see *OED*, *neck*, 4. 'A
   race-course expression' (Wilson, *NCS*).
   tasked imposed taxes upon. See Appendix for Holinshed.
94 **if . . . placed** if everyone were given his
   rightful due
95 **engaged** held as hostage, pledged as a
   guarantee, as at 5.2.43; similar to *impawned* at l. 108. A pun on the meaning
   'betrothed' is probably not intended, even
   though (as Eric Rasmussen pointed out to
   me) Shakespeare seems to pre-date the
   earliest *OED* citation of that meaning in
   All's Well 5.3.96 and *Dream* 1.1.138.
96 **lie forfeited** remain prisoner, unreclaimed
97 **Disgraced . . . victories** made my very
   victories on his behalf the occasion

Sought to entrap me by intelligence;
Rated mine uncle from the Council-board;
In rage dismissed my father from the court;   100
Broke oath on oath, committed wrong on wrong,
And in conclusion drove us to seek out
This head of safety, and withal to pry
Into his title, the which we find
Too indirect for long continuance.

BLUNT

Shall I return this answer to the King?

HOTSPUR

Not so, Sir Walter. We'll withdraw awhile.
Go to the King, and let there be impawned
Some surety for a safe return again,
And in the morning early shall mine uncle   110
Bring him our purposes. And so farewell.

BLUNT

I would you would accept of grace and love.

HOTSPUR

And maybe so we shall.

BLUNT   Pray God you do.   *Exeunt*

4.4   *Enter the Archbishop of York and Sir Michael*

ARCHBISHOP

Hie, good Sir Michael, bear this sealèd brief

113 And] Q1 ; And't F1   *Exeunt*] F1 ; *not in* Q1
    4.4.0 *the*] F1 ; *not in* Q1   *and*] Q2 ; *not in* Q1   *Michael*] Q1 (*Mighell*) (*and elsewhere in this scene*)

of my disgrace (e.g. by demanding
the prisoners, 1.3.23ff.)
98 **intelligence** secret information obtained
from spies. See Appendix for Holinshed.
99 **Rated** 'drove away by chiding or scolding' (Onions). The incident here recalled
is at 1.3.14–21.
100 **dismissed   my   father** (recalling
    1.3.122–3)
103 **head of safety** armed force for our self-
defence, as at 1.3.282, perhaps with play
on *head* meaning 'source' (Cowl and Morgan)
    withal in addition
105 **indirect** devious, irregular, both in the
line of succession and in a moral sense
108 **impawned** pledged as security. Westmorland (5.2.28 and 43) of the King's
army is to be left at the rebel camp as a

guarantee for the 'safe return' of 'mine
uncle' Worcester (ll. 109–10) and his
delegation.
111 **Bring him our purposes** convey to him
(the King) our proposals and terms
113 **maybe so we shall** See Appendix for
Holinshed.
4.4 Location: Presumably at the Archbishop of York's palace, though in the
theatre we know only that the Archbishop is conferring with a subordinate.
0.1 *Archbishop of York* See Appendix for
historical information.
    Sir Michael an unhistorical person serv-
ing in the Archbishop of York's household,
either as a priest, for whom the title of 'Sir'
would be appropriate, or as a knight
1 **brief** letter, or dispatch. See Appendix for
Holinshed.

With wingèd haste to the Lord Marshal;
This to my cousin Scrope, and all the rest
To whom they are directed. If you knew
How much they do import, you would make haste.
SIR MICHAEL My good lord, I guess their tenor.
ARCHBISHOP Like enough you do.
Tomorrow, good Sir Michael, is a day
Wherein the fortune of ten thousand men
Must bide the touch; for, sir, at Shrewsbury,   10
As I am truly given to understand,
The King with mighty and quick-raisèd power
Meets with Lord Harry. And I fear, Sir Michael,
What with the sickness of Northumberland,
Whose power was in the first proportion,
And what with Owen Glendower's absence thence,
Who with them was a rated sinew too
And comes not in, o'erruled by prophecies,
I fear the power of Percy is too weak
To wage an instant trial with the King.   20
SIR MICHAEL
Why, my good lord, you need not fear;
There is Douglas and Lord Mortimer.
ARCHBISHOP No, Mortimer is not there.
SIR MICHAEL
But there is Mordake, Vernon, Lord Harry Percy,
And there is my lord of Worcester, and a head
Of gallant warriors, noble gentlemen.
ARCHBISHOP
And so there is. But yet the King hath drawn
The special head of all the land together:
The Prince of Wales, Lord John of Lancaster,
The noble Westmorland, and warlike Blunt,   30

2 **Lord Marshal** See Appendix for historical
information. *Marshal* is trisyllabic; compare French *maréchal*.
3 **my cousin Scrope** See Appendix for historical information.
4 **To whom** to those to whom
10 **bide the touch** stand the test, as gold is
'tried' by the touchstone
14 **the sickness of Northumberland** See Appendix for Holinshed.
15 **in . . . proportion** of greater magnitude

than any other
16 **Owen Glendower's absence** See Appendix for Holinshed and Daniel.
17 **rated sinew** main strength or support on
which to reckon
21–3 **Why . . . there** Lineation follows Q1,
but the metrical irregularity is close to
prose.
23 **Mortimer is not there** See Appendix for
historical information.
28 **special head** noble leadership

259

And many more corrivals and dear men
Of estimation and command in arms.
SIR MICHAEL

Doubt not, my lord, they shall be well opposed.
ARCHBISHOP

I hope no less, yet needful 'tis to fear;
And, to prevent the worst, Sir Michael, speed.
For if Lord Percy thrive not, ere the King
Dismiss his power he means to visit us,
For he hath heard of our confederacy,
And 'tis but wisdom to make strong against him.
Therefore make haste. I must go write again   40
To other friends, and so farewell, Sir Michael.   *Exeunt*

5.1   *Enter the King, the Prince of Wales, Lord John of*
        Lancaster, Sir Walter Blunt, and Falstaff
KING HENRY

How bloodily the sun begins to peer
Above yon bosky hill! The day looks pale
At his distemp'rature.
PRINCE HENRY   The southern wind
Doth play the trumpet to his purposes,

31 more] Q1 (mo)   36 not,] Q2; ∼ʌ Q1
5.1.0.1 the Prince] Q1 (*Prince*)   0.2 Lancaster, Sir] HANMER; *Lancaster, Earle of Westmerland*
sir Q1   *and*] Q2; *not in* Q1   2 bosky] Q2 (busky); bulky Q1

31 **more** QqF1 'mo' or 'moe' occurs only this
   once in *1 Henry IV*, 'more' some sixty-one
   times, and there seems no basis for the
   distinction, though the two words are historically distinct.
   corrivals partners
   dear estimable, noble
32 **estimation** esteem, value
34 **needful 'tis to fear** Compare the proverb
   'It is good to fear the worst' (Dent W912).
35 **prevent** forestall
37 **he means to visit us** An anticipation of
   5.5.34–8 and *2 Henry IV* 1.1.132–5. See
   Introduction p. 15.
5.1 Location: The King's camp near
   Shrewsbury. Throughout Act 5, the sense
   of space in the theatre is fluid; we are
   somewhere on the battlefield. As ll. 12–13
   make clear, the actors are costumed in
   armour.
1 **bloodily** Compare the proverb 'A red

morning foretells a stormy day' (Dent
M1175).
2 **bosky** bushy, covered with thickets. The
   Q2–5F reading 'busky' is a spelling
   variant. The apparent, though faint, reading of Q1, 'bulky', has been defended by
   Shaaber (*MLN*, 54 (1939), 276–8) and
   Humphreys in the sense of 'looming', 'im-
   posing', but 'bulky' would be an easy error
   for the Q1 compositor to make if his Q0
   copy read 'buʃky'. The kerning hazard
   might have damaged the Q0 impression or
   it may be that the faintness of Q1 is the
   result of kerning. F1 avoids kerning with
   'busky'.
3 **his distemp'rature** its (the sun's) un-
   healthy appearance. Compare 3.1.32 and
   see note.
4 **Doth . . . purposes** acts like a trumpeter
   signalling what the sun portends

And by his hollow whistling in the leaves
Foretells a tempest and a blust'ring day.
KING HENRY
　Then with the losers let it sympathize,
　For nothing can seem foul to those that win.
　　　　The trumpet sounds.
　　　　Enter Worcester ⌈and Vernon⌉
　How now, my lord of Worcester? 'Tis not well
　That you and I should meet upon such terms　　　　10
　As now we meet. You have deceived our trust,
　And made us doff our easy robes of peace
　To crush our old limbs in ungentle steel.
　This is not well, my lord, this is not well.
　What say you to it? Will you again unknit
　This churlish knot of all-abhorrèd war,
　And move in that obedient orb again
　Where you did give a fair and natural light,
　And be no more an exhaled meteor,
　A prodigy of fear, and a portent　　　　20
　Of broachèd mischief to the unborn times?
WORCESTER　Hear me, my liege:
　For mine own part, I could be well content
　To entertain the lag end of my life
　With quiet hours, for I protest
　I have not sought the day of this dislike.

8.2 *and Vernon*] THEOBALD; *not in* Q1　25 I] Q1; I ᴕᴐ F1

7　**sympathize** accord, have an affinity
8　**nothing . . . win** Compare the proverb 'He
　　laughs that wins' (Dent L93).
8.1　***trumpet sounds*** another parley, as at
　　4.3.29.1.
8.2　***Vernon*** This character is not mentioned
　　in this scene, in dialogue or stage direc-
　　tions, and says nothing; previously, Hot-
　　spur mentions only 'mine uncle' as emis-
　　sary to King Henry (4.3.110), despite
　　Vernon's presence when Hotspur makes
　　his announcement. Nonetheless, Ver-
　　non's presence in 5.1 as part of a delega-
　　tion seems clearly necessary in order to
　　explain his debate with Worcester in 5.2
　　over the 'liberal and kind offer of the King'
　　(l. 2). Perhaps Shakespeare had not
　　thought ahead when he wrote this scene,
　　and did not revise later.

12　**easy** comfortable, loose-fitting
17　**obedient orb** concentric sphere in which
　　all subjects, like the planets and the stars,
　　should revolve obediently about their
　　kingly centre (comparable to the earth) in
　　fixed courses. The Ptolemaic earth-
　　centred universe was a familiar model for
　　political and social hierarchy, as in *Troilus*
　　1.3.84ff.
19　**exhaled meteor** See note at 1.1.10 on
　　shooting stars as prophetic of disorder.
20　**prodigy of fear** fearful omen of evil,
　　synonymous with *portent*
21　**broachèd . . . times** calamity set flowing
　　(as one might 'broach', or tap, a cask) so
　　as to threaten future generations
24　**entertain** occupy, fill up, as in *Lucrece*
　　1361
26　**the day of this dislike** this time of discord

KING HENRY

You have not sought it? How comes it, then?

FALSTAFF Rebellion lay in his way, and he found it.

PRINCE HENRY Peace, chewet, peace!

WORCESTER

It pleased your majesty to turn your looks   30
Of favour from myself and all our house;
And yet I must remember you, my lord,
We were the first and dearest of your friends.
For you my staff of office did I break
In Richard's time, and posted day and night
To meet you on the way, and kiss your hand,
When yet you were in place and in account
Nothing so strong and fortunate as I.
It was myself, my brother, and his son
That brought you home, and boldly did outdare   40
The dangers of the time. You swore to us,
And you did swear that oath at Doncaster,
That you did nothing purpose 'gainst the state,
Nor claim no further than your new-fall'n right,
The seat of Gaunt, dukedom of Lancaster.
To this we swore our aid. But in short space
It rained down fortune show'ring on your head,
And such a flood of greatness fell on you—
What with our help, what with the absent King,
What with the injuries of a wanton time,   50
The seeming sufferances that you had borne,
And the contrarious winds that held the King
So long in his unlucky Irish wars
That all in England did repute him dead—
And from this swarm of fair advantages

---

28 **lay . . . found it** 'The thief's excuse when discovered in possession of stolen goods' (Wilson, *NCS*)

29 **chewet** chough, jackdaw, i.e. chatterbox; also, a pie of minced meat or fish

30–71 **It pleased . . . enterprise** See Appendix for Holinshed.

32 **remember** remind

34–5 **For . . . time** For this episode, see *Richard II* 2.2.58–9 and 2.3.26–7, and Holinshed in Appendix.

35 **posted** rode post-haste

38 **Nothing** not at all

41–5 **You swore . . . Lancaster** Compare 4.3.60–5 and Holinshed in Appendix.

44 **new-fall'n** recently fallen to your lot (by the death of John of Gaunt)

45 **Gaunt** On the name, see note at 2.2.63.

50 **injuries** abuses
   wanton ungoverned, ill-managed, arbitrary, extravagant

51 **sufferances** sufferings, wrongs

You took occasion to be quickly wooed
To grip the general sway into your hand;
Forgot your oath to us at Doncaster;
And, being fed by us, you used us so
As that ungentle gull, the cuckoo's bird, 60
Useth the sparrow; did oppress our nest,
Grew by our feeding to so great a bulk
That even our love durst not come near your sight
For fear of swallowing; but with nimble wing
We were enforced, for safety's sake, to fly
Out of your sight and raise this present head,
Whereby we stand opposèd by such means
As you yourself have forged against yourself
By unkind usage, dangerous countenance,
And violation of all faith and troth 70
Sworn to us in your younger enterprise.

KING HENRY
These things indeed you have articulate,
Proclaimed at market crosses, read in churches,
To face the garment of rebellion

---

65 safety's] QI (safety)   71 your] QI; *not in* FI   72 articulate] QI; articulated FI

---

56 **occasion** the opportunity
60 **ungentle . . . bird** rude nestling, the cuckoo's unfledged chick. The original meaning of *bird* is 'nestling'. Because cuckoos lay their eggs in other birds' nests, they are often the model of parasitical overwhelming of those who have provided support, as in *Lear* 1.4.214 and *Antony* 2.6.28.
63 **our love** we who loved you
64 **swallowing** being swallowed
65 **safety's** QqF1 'safety'; on the uninflected noun used instead of a possessive, see note at 1.2.146.
67 **opposèd by such means** goaded into opposition by such factors
69 **unkind** unnatural and ungrateful
    dangerous countenance menacing demeanour and conduct
70 **troth** plighted word
71 **younger** at its outset
72–82 **These . . . confusion** Henry's characterization of rebellion reflects the warnings of the homily 'Against Disobedience and Rebellion', required to be read in

church four times a year after the Northern Rising of 1569: 'The most rash and hare-brained men, the most greatest unthrifts, that have most lewdly wasted their own goods and lands, those that are over the ears in debt, and such as for thefts, robberies, and murders dare not in any well-governed commonwealth where good laws are in force, show their faces . . . . They would pretend sundry causes, as the redress of the commonwealth . . . or reformation of religion . . . they have made a great show of holy meaning by beginning their rebellions with a counterfeit service of God . . . they display and bear about ensigns and banners, which are acceptable unto the rude ignorant common people' (Milward, 120–1).
72 **articulate** articulated, set forth in articles. The *-ate* form of the participle is common, as in 'create' and 'consecrate' in *Dream* 5.1.394 and 404.
74 **face** trim, adorn, cover (deceptively) with another 'facing' of material

263

With some fine colour that may please the eye
Of fickle changelings and poor discontents,
Which gape and rub the elbow at the news
Of hurly-burly innovation.
And never yet did insurrection want
Such water-colours to impaint his cause,   80
Nor moody beggars, starving for a time
Of pell-mell havoc and confusion.

PRINCE HENRY

In both your armies there is many a soul
Shall pay full dearly for this encounter,
If once they join in trial. Tell your nephew,
The Prince of Wales doth join with all the world
In praise of Henry Percy. By my hopes—
This present enterprise set off his head—
I do not think a braver gentleman,
More active-valiant or more valiant-young,   90
More daring or more bold, is now alive
To grace this latter age with noble deeds.
For my part, I may speak it to my shame,
I have a truant been to chivalry;
And so I hear he doth account me too.
Yet this before my father's majesty:
I am content that he shall take the odds
Of his great name and estimation,

---

83 your] Q1; our F1   88 off] F1; of Q1   90 active-valiant] THEOBALD; actiue, valiant
Q1   valiant-young] THEOBALD; valiant yong Q1

---

75 **colour** (a) hue (b) outward semblance
76 **changelings** renegadoes, turncoats
77 **rub the elbow** To cross one's arms and
    rub the elbows was to express delight (see
    Dent E100), like rubbing one's hands
    today. Compare *LLL* 5.2.109, where a
    love-struck wooer is described as having
    'rubbed his elbow thus' in pleasure at a
    witty observation on love.
78 **hurly-burly innovation** tumultuous in-
    surrection
79 **want** lack
80 **water-colours** i.e. thin excuses (compare
    colour in l. 75, and see note), transparent
    and flimsy
    impaint depict (*OED* records only one
    other, later usage)

his its
81 **moody** sullen, discontented
    beggars i.e. the *poor discontents* of l. 76,
    starving ('eager') for insurrection as a
    means of livelihood. *Beggars* is a direct
    object of *want* in l. 79.
82 **pell-mell havoc** disordered plundering
83 **both your** i.e. both the King's and the
    rebels'. The emendation to *both our* in F1
    is followed by some modern editors.
87 **hopes** i.e. hopes of salvation
88 **This . . . head** setting aside this present
    enterprise of rebellion, not reckoning it to
    his account
89 **braver** finer
92 **latter** modern
98 **estimation** reputation

And will, to save the blood on either side,
Try fortune with him in a single fight.   100
KING HENRY
And, Prince of Wales, so dare we venture thee,
Albeit considerations infinite
Do make against it. No, good Worcester, no,
We love our people well; even those we love
That are misled upon your cousin's part.
And, will they take the offer of our grace,
Both he and they and you, yea, every man
Shall be my friend again, and I'll be his.
So tell your cousin, and bring me word
What he will do. But if he will not yield,   110
Rebuke and dread correction wait on us,
And they shall do their office. So, be gone.
We will not now be troubled with reply.
We offer fair; take it advisedly.
                    Exeunt Worcester ⌈and Vernon⌉

PRINCE HENRY
It will not be accepted, on my life.
The Douglas and the Hotspur both together
Are confident against the world in arms.
KING HENRY
Hence, therefore, every leader to his charge,
For on their answer will we set on them,
And God befriend us as our cause is just!   120
                    Exeunt. The Prince and Falstaff remain

114.1 *Exeunt Worcester and Vernon*] THEOBALD (*Exit Worcester, with Vernon*); *Exit Worcester*
QI   120.1 *The Prince and Falstaff remain*] QI (*manent Prince, Falst.*)

102 **Albeit** (literally) although it be that, although on the other hand. The subjunc-
tive has the force of 'were it not that'. The
King does not accept the Prince's offer; in
view of the King's military superiority and
Hotspur's reputation as a fighter, the risk
is too great. This non-historical challenge, not found in Holinshed, portrays
Hal's spirit, and anticipates his single
combat with Hotspur during the battle.
105 **cousin's** kinsman's, here nephew's
106 **grace** pardon

111 **wait on us** are in attendance, awaiting
my royal command
112 **office** duty, function
114 **take it advisedly** best consideration will
urge you to accept
116 **the Hotspur** Douglas is usually called
'the Douglas,' but on the unusualness of
prefixing *the* to an untitled name like
'Hotspur', see note at 1.3.259.
119 **on their answer** i.e. when they refuse,
as we expect they will

FALSTAFF Hal, if thou see me down in the battle and bestride
me, so; 'tis a point of friendship.

PRINCE HENRY Nothing but a colossus can do thee that
friendship. Say thy prayers, and farewell.

FALSTAFF I would 'twere bedtime, Hal, and all well.

PRINCE HENRY Why, thou owest God a death.   ⌈*Exit*⌉

FALSTAFF 'Tis not due yet; I would be loath to pay him
before his day. What need I be so forward with him that
calls not on me? Well, 'tis no matter; honour pricks me
on. Yea, but how if honour prick me off when I come on?   130
How then? Can honour set to a leg? No. Or an arm? No.
Or take away the grief of a wound? No. Honour hath no
skill in surgery, then? No. What is honour? A word.
What is in that word honour? What is that honour? Air.
A trim reckoning. Who hath it? He that died o' Wednesday. Doth he feel it? No. Doth he hear it? No. 'Tis insensible, then? Yea, to the dead. But will it not live with the

---

121–4 Hal . . . farewell] *as prose*, POPE; *as verse*, Q1, *ending at* battel | friendship. | friendship, |
farewell.   126 *Exit*] HANMER; *not in* Q1   130 Yea] Q1; *not in* F1   131 then? Can] Q2; then
can Q1   136 'Tis] Q1; Is it F1   137 will it] Q2; wil Q1

---

121 **bestride** stand over (a fallen man) in
order to defend him, as in *Errors* 5.1.192,
Macbeth 4.3.4, *2 Henry IV* 1.1.207

122 so well and good

123 **colossus** See *Caesar* 1.2.136, where
Shakespeare reflects the common belief
that the huge statue of Helios, one of the
seven wonders of the ancient world, stood
astride the entrance to the harbour of
Rhodes.

125 **bedtime** Suggested by 'Say thy prayers'
(Elton).

126 **thou owest God a death** Proverbial
(Dent G237). The thought and the prob-
able pun on *debt* are seemingly
anticipated in 1.3.186 (see note), and
recur in *2 Henry IV* 3.2.227: 'We owe
God a death.' Kittredge cites the *Sermons*
of Henry Smith (d. 1591; 1609 ed., 598),
as evidence of the proverb's meaning: 'I
owe God a death, as his Son died for me.'
Exit Prince Henry leaves at, or near, this
point, but could do so at l. 127, 128, or
129 if Falstaff addresses the first sentence
or two of his speech to the departing
Prince.

127–8 **'Tis . . . day** Dent p. 21, n. 9, cites an

anonymous poem attributed by Bond to
Lyly (iii. 451): 'Who youngest dies he
doth [but] pay | a debt he owes before the
day.' See also Dent T290.

128–9 **forward . . . me** alacritous in responding to the creditor who does not yet
demand payment of me

129 **pricks** spurs (with pun in next line). A
familiar   expression   (Dent   *PLED*
H572.11).

130 **prick me off** mark me off the list (of the
living). To *prick* is to make a hole, or mark,
by pricking, dotting, as in *Caesar* 4.1.1:
'These many, then, shall die. Their names
are pricked.' The image may also suggest
Death's dart.

131 **set to a leg** rejoin a severed leg or set a
broken one

132 **grief** pain, as at 1.3.51.

133 **A word** Compare the formula 'X is but a
word' applied to faith, virtue, friendship,
honour, etc. (Dent *PLED* W781.11).

135 **A trim reckoning** 'A pretty balance
sheet!' (Wilson, *NCS*)

136–7 **insensible** not perceptible to the
senses

living? No. Why? Detraction will not suffer it. Therefore
I'll none of it. Honour is a mere scutcheon. And so ends
my catechism.   *Exit*   140

5.2   *Enter Worcester and Sir Richard Vernon*
WORCESTER

O no, my nephew must not know, Sir Richard,
The liberal and kind offer of the King.
VERNON

'Twere best he did.
WORCESTER   Then are we all undone.

It is not possible, it cannot be,
The King should keep his word in loving us;
He will suspect us still, and find a time
To punish this offence in other faults.
Suspicion all our lives shall be stuck full of eyes;

5.2.0 *and*] F1 ; *not in* Q1   3 are we] Q1 ; we are F1   undone] Q5 ; vnder one Q1   8 Suspicion]
ROWE (1714); Supposition Q1

138 **Detraction** slander
     suffer allow
139 **scutcheon** the lowest form of heraldic
device, a funereal tablet featuring a coat
of arms and mourning emblems to be
displayed in funeral processions, on
tombs in churches, over gates, etc. To Falstaff, honour is 'nothing but a cheap piece
of heraldry to grace funerals' (Wilson,
NCS).
140 **catechism** religious instruction and
statement of faith in the form of question
and answer. Falstaff's sardonic catechism
may owe something to the more
lugubrious soliloquy of Basilisco in
*Soliman and Perseda, c.*1590, in which the
speaker asks, Where is Hercules, where
is Priam, where is Achilles, etc., and
answers his own question with the refrain
'Dead' (Kyd, *Works*, ed. Boas,
5.3.63–76). See Introduction, p. 27.
5.2 Location: The rebel camp. The fluid
sense of space is evident as Worcester and
Vernon return to camp and are met by
Hotspur and Douglas.
1–25 **O no . . . King** See Appendix for
Holinshed.
   3 **undone** ruined. Qq1–4 read 'vnder one';
Wilson (*NCS*) suggests that Shakespeare
wrote 'und one' and the Q printer 'corrected' it.
7 **in** in punishing

8 **Suspicion** QqF1's reading, 'supposition'
can be defended in the sense of 'a notion
held without certainty or assurance';
such a meaning is perhaps consonant
with Virgil's Fama, a monster with as
many eyes, ears, and mouths as there are
feathers on her body (*Aeneid* iv. 181–8).
Yet Virgil and his later imitators such as
Chaucer, *House of Fame*, and Spenser,
Faerie Queene, I. iv. 31, in which Envy is
'ypainted full of eyes', are closer in their
imagery to Suspicion than to mere Supposition. Shakespeare's Rumour 'painted
full of tongues' in the Induction to *2 Henry
IV* is more malicious than Shakespeare's
other uses of 'supposition' would suggest;
to him the term generally means only
'something assumed to be true', even in a
positive sense, as in *Errors* 3.2.50 and
Much Ado 4.1.238. Daniel's *Philotas*
(1604) speaks of 'Suspicion full of eyes
and full of ears' (3.3 Chorus, l. 1150), and
Dekker's *Welsh Ambassador* (*c.*1623?) of
'Suspicion sealing up her hundred eyes'
(4.3.54), specifically equating Virgil's
Fama with Suspicion in the spirit of the
proverb 'Suspicion has double eyes' (Dent
S1017). Shakespeare's line is hypermetrical, and may be defective in some other
way, but 'Suspicion' offers an improvement.

For treason is but trusted like the fox,
Who, never so tame, so cherished, and locked up,   10
Will have a wild trick of his ancestors.
Look how we can, or sad or merrily,
Interpretation will misquote our looks,
And we shall feed like oxen at a stall,
The better cherished still the nearer death.
My nephew's trespass may be well forgot;
It hath the excuse of youth and heat of blood,
And an adopted name of privilege,
A hare-brained Hotspur governed by a spleen.
All his offences live upon my head   20
And on his father's. We did train him on,
And, his corruption being ta'en from us,
We as the spring of all shall pay for all.
Therefore, good cousin, let not Harry know
In any case the offer of the King.
        Enter Hotspur and Douglas, ⌈with Soldiers⌉

VERNON

Deliver what you will; I'll say 'tis so.

Here comes your cousin.

HOTSPUR   My uncle is returned.

Deliver up my lord of Westmorland.

Uncle, what news?

WORCESTER

The King will bid you battle presently.   30

DOUGLAS

Defy him by the lord of Westmorland.

10 never] Q1; ne're F1   12 merrily] Q1 (merely)   25.1 *Enter ... Soldiers*] CAPELL (*subs.*);
Enter Percy. Q1; *Enter Hotspurre* F1 (*placed after* 'cousin' *in l.* 27)   27 Here ... cousin] F1; *as
part of l.*26, Q1   29 news?] Q1; newe-? F1

10 **never so** be he never so
11 **trick** trait, as at 2.4.390
12 **or sad or merrily** either serious or cheer-
    ful
13 **misquote** (first recorded use in *OED*)
18 **an adopted name of privilege** a nickname
    ('hotspur') that licenses rashness
19 **spleen** intemperate impulse. See note at
    2.3.75 and also 3.2.125.
20 **live** See note at 1.2.177.
21 **train** entice, draw
22 **his . . . us** since (it is alleged) his guilt

originated in us, as from a poisoned spring
25.1 *with Soldiers* No soldiers are men-
    tioned in QqF1, but Hotspur's address at
    l. 75 to 'fellows, soldiers, friends' seems to
    require more of an audience than Worces-
    ter, Vernon, and Douglas.
26 **Deliver** report
28 **Deliver up** release as hostage or 'surety';
    see note at 4.3.108.
31 **Defy . . . Westmorland** Westmorland,
    now returning to the King's camp, can
    convey the rebels' message of defiance.

268

HOTSPUR

Lord Douglas, go you and tell him so.

DOUGLAS

Marry, and shall, and very willingly.   *Exit Douglas*

WORCESTER

There is no seeming mercy in the King.

HOTSPUR

Did you beg any? God forbid!

WORCESTER

I told him gently of our grievances,
Of his oath-breaking, which he mended thus,
By now forswearing that he is forsworn.
He calls us rebels, traitors, and will scourge
With haughty arms this hateful name in us.   40
      Enter Douglas

DOUGLAS

Arm, gentlemen, to arms! For I have thrown
A brave defiance in King Henry's teeth,
And Westmorland that was engaged did bear it,
Which cannot choose but bring him quickly on.

WORCESTER

The Prince of Wales stepped forth before the King,
And, nephew, challenged you to single fight.

HOTSPUR

O, would the quarrel lay upon our heads,
And that no man might draw short breath today
But I and Harry Monmouth! Tell me, tell me,
How showed his tasking? Seemed it in contempt?   50

VERNON

No, by my soul. I never in my life
Did hear a challenge urged more modestly,
Unless a brother should a brother dare

---

33 **Marry, and shall** indeed I will. A familiar
    tag (Dent M699.1).
34 **seeming** semblance of
38 **forswearing** swearing falsely, perjuring
    himself
42 **brave** proud, haughty
43 **engaged** held as hostage; compare *im-
    pawned* at 4.3.108 (see note).

44 **cannot choose but** cannot do otherwise
    than
49 **Monmouth** a name for Harry from the
    Welsh town in which he was born
50 **showed his tasking** appeared his giving of
    the challenge. Compare *task* in 4.1.9.
52 **urged** proposed, put forward

To gentle exercise and proof of arms.
He gave you all the duties of a man,
Trimmed up your praises with a princely tongue,
Spoke your deservings like a chronicle,
Making you ever better than his praise
By still dispraising praise valued with you;
And, which became him like a prince indeed,   60
He made a blushing cital of himself,
And chid his truant youth with such a grace
As if he mastered there a double spirit
Of teaching and of learning instantly.
There did he pause. But let me tell the world,
If he outlive the envy of this day,
England did never owe so sweet a hope,
So much misconstrued in his wantonness.

HOTSPUR

Cousin, I think thou art enamourèd
On his follies. Never did I hear   70
Of any prince so wild a liberty.
But be he as he will, yet once ere night
I will embrace him with a soldier's arm,
That he shall shrink under my courtesy.
Arm, arm, with speed! And, fellows, soldiers, friends,

71 liberty] Q1 (libertie); libertine CAPELL

54 **gentle** befitting noble birth
   proof of arms test of martial skill
55 **duties** due respect, the praise that manliness deserves
56 **Trimmed . . . praises** adorned his praise of you
59 **still . . . you** constantly disparaging praise itself as not sufficient to measure your true worth. Words cannot do justice to Hotspur's merit. A hyperbole that goes beyond the Prince's actual speech in 5.1.83ff., but captures the generosity of the tribute.
61 **blushing cital of himself** modest account of his merits and truancy; a citation or summons of himself, a calling of himself to account and as witness to Hotspur's chivalry (first recorded use in *OED* of *cital*)
64 **instantly** simultaneously
66 **envy** ill-will, malignity

67 **owe** own
68 **misconstrued** (accent on second syllable)
   wantonness sportiveness of youth. See *wanton* at 4.1.104.
71 **liberty** licence, reckless lack of restraint. Hotspur has never heard such overstepping of bounds reported of any prince. *Libertine*, proposed by Capell and adopted by many editors, is possible, since, as Humphreys notes, Shakespeare could have written *libertie*, but unnecessary.
73–4 **I will . . . courtesy** Hotspur puns sardonically: (a) I will embrace this flattering prince and outdo the courtesy he has purported to show me (b) I will engage him in a duel of arms and force him to retire and suffer defeat, daunted by my nobler spirit. *Shrink* can also mean 'shiver', as in *As You Like It* 2.1.9.

Better consider what you have to do
Than I, that have not well the gift of tongue,
Can lift your blood up with persuasion.
    Enter a Messenger
MESSENGER My lord, here are letters for you.
HOTSPUR I cannot read them now.   80
  O gentlemen, the time of life is short!
To spend that shortness basely were too long
If life did ride upon a dial's point,
Still ending at the arrival of an hour.
An if we live, we live to tread on kings;
If die, brave death, when princes die with us!
Now for our consciences, the arms are fair
When the intent of bearing them is just.
    Enter another Messenger
SECOND MESSENGER
  My lord, prepare. The King comes on apace.
HOTSPUR
  I thank him that he cuts me from my tale,   90
For I profess not talking. Only this:
Let each man do his best.   *He draws his sword*
              And here draw I
A sword, whose temper I intend to stain
With the best blood that I can meet withal
In the adventure of this perilous day.
Now, Esperance! Percy! And set on.
Sound all the lofty instruments of war,
And by that music let us all embrace;

---

85 An] Q1 (And)   88.1 *another Messenger*] F1 ; *another* Q1   89 SECOND MESSENGER] CAPELL;
Mes. Q1   91 talking.] Q2 (talking,), F1 (talking:); talking$_\wedge$ Q1   92 *He draws his sword*] This
edition; *not in* Q1   draw I] Q1 ; I draw F1   93 A sword] POPE; *as part of l.* 92, Q1   whose] Q1 ;
Whose worthy F1   94 withal] CAPELL; withall. Q1 ; withall, Q2   95 day.] Q2; day, Q1

76–8 **Better . . . persuasion** be better moved
    by consideration of what you have to do
    than I, a weak orator, could move you
    thereto by persuasive rhetoric
81–4 **the time . . . hour** See Appendix for
    chronicles. 'The time of life is short' may
    be proverbial (Dent T332.1).
82–4 **To spend . . . hour** a life basely spent
    would be too long even if human life las-
    ted only the single hourly movement of
    the hand of the dial (or sundial), always

    ending at the termination of that one
    hour
86 **brave** glorious
87 **for** as for
    fair just
90 **cuts me from my tale** stops me talking
91 **I profess not talking** talking is not my
    profession
95 **adventure** chances
96 **Esperance! Percy!** See 2.3.68 and note,
    and Appendix for Holinshed.

For, heaven to earth, some of us never shall
A second time do such a courtesy.   100
        Here they embrace. The trumpets sound. Exeunt

5.3   *The King enters with his power. Alarum to the battle.*
        Then enter Douglas, and Sir Walter Blunt dressed as
        the King

BLUNT

What is thy name, that in the battle thus
Thou crossest me? What honour dost thou seek
Upon my head?

DOUGLAS   Know then my name is Douglas,
And I do haunt thee in the battle thus
Because some tell me that thou art a king.

BLUNT They tell thee true.

DOUGLAS

The Lord of Stafford dear today hath bought
Thy likeness, for instead of thee, King Harry,
This sword hath ended him. So shall it thee
Unless thou yield thee as my prisoner.   10

BLUNT

I was not born a yielder, thou proud Scot,

100.1 Here] Q1; *not in* F1   Exeunt] ROWE (*subs.*); *not in* Q1

5.3.0.1 enters] Q1; *entreth* F1   to] Q1; *vnto* F1   0.2–3 *dressed as the King*] WILSON, NCS
(*subs.*); *not in* Q1   1–3 What ... head?] HANMER; *printed in two lines*, Q1, *ending* me, |
head?   1 the] T. JOHNSON (1710); *not in* Q1   11 a ... Scot] Q1; to yeeld, thou proud Sot Q5;
to yeeld, thou haughty Scot F1

99 **heaven to earth** i.e. I'll wager heaven
versus earth, infinity to something finite
5.3 Location: Shrewsbury battlefield. The
stage directions in QqF1 do not indicate
an exeunt at the end of the previous
scene, and run together in one paragraph
the embracing of the rebels, the sounding
of the trumpets, and the King's entry,
thereby suggesting the fluidity of scene
'change', especially in a battle sequence.
F1 does not mark a new scene here.
Capell's notation of a scene change is
technically correct if, as seems likely, the
rebels leave before (or while) the King
comes on stage. The *trumpets sound*
(5.2.100.1) presumably in response to
Hotspur's command 'Sound all the lofty
instruments of war' (5.2.97), but they
may also seem to greet the entry of the
King (see Long, 79). Space is fluid in the

theatre; we move indeterminately from
the rebels' camp in 5.2 to the field of
battle. Battle action is segmented iconi-
cally into a series of conflicts between two
adversaries, interspersed with *alarums* or
calls to battle by drums or trumpets (Nay-
lor, 160). *Alarums* are often associated (as
perhaps here and at l. 29.2, certainly at
5.4.0.1) with *excursions*, or issuing forth
on stage of groups of soldiers. During the
alarum at 5.3.0.1 the King and his *power*
(his forces) leave.

1–3 **What ... head** Mislined in QqF1 as two
lines of verse, seemingly to save space; see
collation and Introduction, p. 105.
7 **Stafford** See Appendix for Holinshed and
Daniel.
   dear dearly, at high price
7–8 **bought | Thy likeness** paid for his
resemblance to you

And thou shalt find a king that will revenge
Lord Stafford's death.
>   *They fight. Douglas kills Blunt.*
>   *Then enter Hotspur*

HOTSPUR

O Douglas, hadst thou fought at Holmedon thus,
I never had triumphed upon a Scot.

DOUGLAS

All's done, all's won; here breathless lies the King.

HOTSPUR Where?

DOUGLAS Here.

HOTSPUR

This, Douglas? No, I know this face full well.
A gallant knight he was; his name was Blunt,   20
Semblably furnished like the King himself.

DOUGLAS (*to the body*)

A fool go with thy soul whither it goes!
A borrowed title hast thou bought too dear.
Why didst thou tell me that thou wert a king?

HOTSPUR

The King hath many marching in his coats.

DOUGLAS

Now, by my sword, I will kill all his coats!
I'll murder all his wardrobe, piece by piece,
Until I meet the King.

HOTSPUR   Up and away!
Our soldiers stand full fairly for the day.
>   *Exeunt, leaving Blunt's body*
>   *Alarum. Enter Falstaff, solus*

13.1 *They* Q1; *not in* F1   *Douglas kills Blunt*] Q1; *Blunt is slaine* F1   13.2 *enter* Q1; *enters*
F1   16 won; here] Q2 (won: here) won here Q1   22 *to the body*] This edition; *not in* Q1   A
fool] CAPELL: Ah foole, Q1   29.1 *Exeunt*] F1; *not in* Q1   *leaving Blunt's body*] This edition; *not
in* Q1   29.2 Alarum] Q1 (*Alarme*); *Alarum, and* F1

15 **triumphed** (accent on second syllable)
16 **breathless** i.e. dead
21 **Semblably furnished** similarly dressed
    and armed, dressed to resemble the King
22 **A fool . . . goes** i.e. may the stigma 'A fool'
    accompany your soul whithersoever it
    goes (for having dressed in King Henry's
    garb). Capell's emendation of QqF1's 'Ah
    foole' has been accepted because of
    many analogues in colloquial speech;
    e.g. Whetstone, *1 Promos and Cassandra*

(1578), 2:4.15: 'Go, and a knave [go]
with thee.' Dent G150.1 cites others.
25 **coats** richly embroidered vests worn over
    armour and featuring coats of arms. See
    note at 4.2.42 on the tabard, or herald's
    coat. Douglas responds using the word
    coats in its literal sense of *wardrobe* (l. 27).
29 **stand . . . day** enjoy a position that bids
    fair to win the day
29.1 *Exeunt* Modern editors do not indicate
    a scene change here, because Blunt's

FALSTAFF Though I could scape shot-free at London, I fear   30
the shot here; here's no scoring but upon the pate. Soft,
who are you? Sir Walter Blunt. There's honour for you.
Here's no vanity! I am as hot as molten lead, and as
heavy too. God keep lead out of me! I need no more
weight than mine own bowels. I have led my ragamuffins
where they are peppered. There's not three of my hun-
dred-and-fifty left alive, and they are for the town's end,
to beg during life. But who comes here?
        Enter the Prince

PRINCE HENRY
What, stands thou idle here? Lend me thy sword.
Many a nobleman lies stark and stiff   40
Under the hoofs of vaunting enemies,
Whose deaths are yet unrevenged. I prithee lend me thy
sword.

35 ragamuffins] QI (rag of Muffins)   36–7 hundred-and-fifty] DERING MS, ROWE; 150 QI
37 are] QI; *not in* FI   42 yet] QI; *not in* FI   I prithee] QI; Prethy FI

body is still on-stage, but this may still be
the case at what is conventionally marked
as the beginning of 5.4. FI does not mark
a new scene at either point. On the
alarum, see head-note to this scene.

30 **shot-free** without paying the *shot*, or
reckoning, due in a tavern. Compare
1.3.214–5 (see note) and 5.4.113 about
'scot and lot'. Falstaff plays also on the
notion of escaping the *shot* (l. 31) of
battle.

31 **scoring** continues the pun: (a) notching
or slashing with battle weapons (b) scoring a tavern reckoning by notches on a
tally stick or chalk marks on the tavern
door, as at 2.4.25

33 **Here's no vanity** (ironically), if this
doesn't illustrate my catechism about the
emptiness of honour, then nothing does.
Perhaps, too, Falstaff sardonically suggests that Sir Walter is troubled no more
with the *vanity* of worldliness from which
Falstaff, in his mock piety, begged to be
excused in 1.2.77: 'I prithee trouble me
no more with vanity.'

33–4 **hot … heavy** A familiar coupling; see
Dent H356.1 'Too heavy and too hot',
and Dent L134, 'as heavy as lead'.

35–6 **I have … peppered** Falstaff has exposed his troops to heavy fire in order to
collect the pay of the slain. Humphreys
(153) and Wilson (*Fortunes*, 85) cite contemporary instances of this not uncom-

mon abuse. Anticipated in 4.2.62–4.

36 **not** See note at 4.2.40 and also 2.4.125
for this Falstaffian idiom.

37 **town's end** at the outskirts of a town,
especially at the gates of a walled town,
where beggars congregated to take advantage of traffic on the main road. Mentioned also in 4.2.9.

39 **What** Shakespeare often means 'Why' in
such a question, and the comma may be
in error.

   stands A possible form of the second person singular, in place of *stand'st*, for verbs
ending in dentals (Abbott, 340). Compare
gets, l. 49 below. Humphreys cites *Hamlet*: 'thou . . . Revisits thus' (FI text,
1.4.52–3) and others. *Stand'st* is more
common, however, and J. Dover Wilson
(*The Manuscript of Shakespeare's 'Hamlet'*,
Cambridge, 1934, p. 291) regards the Q
text as based on an incorrect reading of
Shakespeare's manuscript.

42–3 **Whose . . . sword** Printed as a single
line of prose in QI and abbreviated to an
imperfect verse line in FI. The Prince
speaks verse in this scene, but breaks the
pentameter cadence with the refrain-like
'lend me thy sword' heard first at l. 39
and again at l. 48. The tension between
verse and prose nicely catches the dis-
tancing of Hal from Falstaff, whose idiom
remains prose.

FALSTAFF O Hal, I prithee give me leave to breathe a while.
Turk Gregory never did such deeds in arms as I have done
this day. I have paid Percy, I have made him sure.

PRINCE HENRY

He is, indeed, and living to kill thee.

I prithee lend me thy sword.

FALSTAFF Nay, before God, Hal, if Percy be alive, thou gets
not my sword, but take my pistol if thou wilt.   50

PRINCE HENRY

Give it me. What, is it in the case?

FALSTAFF Ay, Hal, 'tis hot, 'tis hot. There's that will sack a
city.

   The Prince draws it out, and finds it to be a bottle of sack

PRINCE HENRY

What, is it a time to jest and dally now?

       He throws the bottle at him   *Exit*

FALSTAFF Well, if Percy be alive, I'll pierce him. If he do
come in my way, so; if he do not, if I come in his willingly,
let him make a carbonado of me. I like not such grinning
honour as Sir Walter hath. Give me life, which if I can
save, so; if not, honour comes unlooked for, and there's
an end.   *Exit*   60

53.1 *to be*] Q1; *not in* Q5   *it out, and finds it to be*] Q1; *out* F1   54.1 *He . . . Exit*] Q1; *Exit. Throwes it at him* F1   60 *Exit*] F1; *not in* Q1

45 **Turk Gregory** *Turk* is a synonym for any
ferocious and bloodthirsty tyrant. *Gregory*
may suggest either Hildebrand, Pope
Gregory VII (1073–85), whom Foxe and
other Protestant polemicists denounced
as an inordinately violent man (Humphreys, Hemingway), or Pope Gregory
XIII (1572–85), who, as Wilson (*NCS*)
observes, 'blessed if he did not instigate
the Massacre of St Bartholomew, and
promised plenary indulgence to anyone
who would murder Elizabeth'. In 1579,
Wilson shows, Gregory XIII figured 'with
Nero and the Grand Turk as one of "The
Three Tyrants of the World" in coloured
prints sold on the streets of London'
(citing J. E. Neale, *Queen Elizabeth* (1934),
225, 248).

46 **paid Percy** settled his account, killed
Percy. Compare 2.4.210–11: 'seven of
the eleven I paid', and 5.4.42 and 113.
made him sure made sure of him. But the

Prince, in the next line, plays on *sure* in
the sense of 'safe and sound'.

49 **gets** See note at l. 39.

52 **'tis hot** Falstaff's excuse for having his
pistol in its *case* (l. 51), or holster, instead
of at the ready, according to Wilson
(*NCS*), is that the pistol is red-hot from
repeated firing, and must be put aside to
cool.
sack despoil (with obvious pun)

55 **pierce** A short vowel—'perse'—allows a
quibble on 'Percy'. Compare *LLL* 4.2.79:
'Master Person, quasi pers-one . . .
pierced.'

56 **so** well and good, as at 5.1.122

57 **carbonado** rasher of meat, scored across
and grilled. Compare 'ribs' and 'tallow' in
2.4.108.

59–60 **there's an end** (a) that concludes the
whole subject treated in my catechism (b)
thus life ends. A common tag (Dent
E113.1).

275

2/2⁸

5.4   *Alarum. Excursions. Enter the King, Prince Henry,*
           Lord John of Lancaster, and the Earl of Westmorland

KING HENRY

   I prithee, Harry, withdraw thyself; thou bleedest too
       much.

   Lord John of Lancaster, go you with him.

LANCASTER

   Not I, my lord, unless I did bleed too.

PRINCE HENRY

   I beseech your majesty make up,

   Lest your retirement do amaze your friends.

KING HENRY   I will do so.

   My lord of Westmorland, lead him to his tent.

WESTMORLAND

   Come, my lord, I'll lead you to your tent.

PRINCE HENRY

   Lead me, my lord? I do not need your help.

   And God forbid a shallow scratch should drive   10

   The Prince of Wales from such a field as this,

   Where stained nobility lies trodden on,

   And rebels' arms triumph in massacres!

LANCASTER

   We breathe too long. Come, cousin Westmorland,

   Our duty this way lies. For God's sake, come.

                   ⌈*Exeunt Lancaster and Westmorland*⌉

5.4.0.1 *Prince Henry*] MALONE; *the Prince* Q1   0.2 *and the*] *not in* Q1   6–7 I will ... tent] F1;
as a single line, Q1   15.1 *Exeunt ... Westmorland*] CAPELL; *not in* Q1

5.4 Location: The scene continues at
   Shrewsbury field. Whether Blunt's body
   is removed at some point or remains on-
   stage during Hotspur's death cannot be
   determined. If it remains, then the scene
   break here is no more complete than at
   5.3.29.1.

0.1 *Excursions* parties of soldiers issuing
   forth, as perhaps also is intended at
   5.3.0.1 and 5.3.29.1.

1 **I prithee ... much** Lineation follows Q1.
   The extra-metrical character contributes
   to a sense of haste and abruptness.
   thou bleedest too much See Appendix for
   Holinshed.

4 **make up** advance, bring up your forces,
   as at l. 57

5 **retirement** falling back (first recorded use
   in *OED*; see 4.1.56)

     amaze alarm, fill with consternation

6–7 **I will ... tent** Printed as one line in Qq;
   see collation. The F1 lineation is followed
   here. Capell's lineation, breaking the line
   after 'Westmorland', is a possible conjecture, but must be regarded as uncertain in
   a passage with such fluid boundaries between prose and verse.

12 **stained** i.e. (a) with blood and dirt (b)
   with dishonour

14 **breathe** pause for breath, as at l. 46, and
   at 2.4.241

15.1 ⌈*Exeunt . . . Westmorland*⌉ This
   exeunt, not marked in QqF1, could possibly be delayed until l. 23, when Prince
   Henry also leaves. Prince Henry either
   apostrophizes his departing brother or
   speaks this praise within his hearing.

PRINCE HENRY

By God, thou hast deceived me, Lancaster!
I did not think thee lord of such a spirit.
Before I loved thee as a brother, John,
But now I do respect thee as my soul.

KING HENRY

I saw him hold Lord Percy at the point   20
With lustier maintenance than I did look for
Of such an ungrown warrior.

PRINCE HENRY

O, this boy lends mettle to us all!   *Exit*
          Enter Douglas

DOUGLAS

Another king? They grow like Hydra's heads.
I am the Douglas, fatal to all those
That wear those colours on them. What art thou
That counterfeit'st the person of a king?

KING HENRY

The King himself, who, Douglas, grieves at heart
So many of his shadows thou hast met
And not the very King. I have two boys   30
Seek Percy and thyself about the field;
But, seeing thou fall'st on me so luckily,
I will assay thee, and defend thyself.

DOUGLAS

I fear thou art another counterfeit;
And yet, in faith, thou bearest thee like a king.
But mine I am sure thou art, whoe'er thou be,

23.1 *Enter Douglas*] F1 ; *not in* Q1   33 and] Q1 ; *so* F1

---

20 **at the point** at swords' points
21 **lustier maintenance** more vigorous bearing and action
24 **Another king** See Appendix for Holinshed.
   Hydra's heads As fast as one of its numerous heads was cut off, the Lernian Hydra grew others in its place, until it was vanquished by Heracles in one of his seven labours. The comparison was commonplace (Dent H278).

26 **colours** colours in the King's coat of arms
29 **his shadows** i.e. those disguised as the King, having form without substance
31 **Seek** who seek
32 **luckily** occurring by chance and producing happy results
33 **assay thee** put you to the test
   and On the connecting of an affirmation and a command with *and*, see note at 3.1.186.
36 **mine** i.e. my victim

And thus I win thee.
> *They fight; the King being in danger, enter the Prince*
> *of Wales*

PRINCE HENRY

Hold up thy head, vile Scot, or thou art like
Never to hold it up again! The spirits
Of valiant Shirley, Stafford, Blunt are in my arms.   40
It is the Prince of Wales that threatens thee,
Who never promiseth but he means to pay.
> *They fight. Douglas flieth*

Cheerly, my lord. How fares your grace?
Sir Nicholas Gawsey hath for succour sent,
And so hath Clifton. I'll to Clifton straight.

KING HENRY   Stay and breathe awhile.

Thou hast redeemed thy lost opinion,
And showed thou mak'st some tender of my life
In this fair rescue thou hast brought to me.

PRINCE HENRY

O God, they did me too much injury   50
That ever said I hearkened for your death.
If it were so, I might have let alone
The insulting hand of Douglas over you,
Which would have been as speedy in your end
As all the poisonous potions in the world,
And saved the treacherous labour of your son.

37.1 *the Prince*] Q1 (*Prince*)   37.2 *of Wales*] Q1; *not in* F1   57 Sir] Q1 (S.)

37.1 **the King being in danger** See Appendix
  for Holinshed and Daniel.
38 **like** likely
40–5 **Shirley, Stafford, Blunt . . . Gawsey . . .**
  Clifton See Appendix for Holinshed and
  Daniel.
42 **pay** i.e. (a) settle a debt (b) kill, as at l. 113
  below and 5.3.46 (see note). On promis-
  ing and paying, compare 4.3.53.
43 **Cheerly** A cry of encouragement.
47 **opinion** reputation, as at 4.1.77
48 **thou mak'st some tender of** you have
  some regard for; with the suggestion also

of a monetary metaphor in *tender*, an offer
of money in discharge of a debt (*OED*,
tender, sb. 2)
51 **hearkened for** sought eagerly to hear of,
  lay in wait for. In *Famous Victories*
  (ll. 93–4, 455–7) and the chronicles, suspicions of the Prince's impatience for his
  father's life are much more explicit. See
  Introduction, p. 21.
53 **insulting** scornfully triumphing, as in
  1 Henry VI 1.2.138–9: 'that proud in-
  sulting ship | Which Caesar and his
  fortune bare'.

278

KING HENRY

Make up to Clifton; I'll to Sir Nicholas Gawsey.

Exit King

Enter Hotspur

HOTSPUR

If I mistake not, thou art Harry Monmouth.

PRINCE HENRY

Thou speak'st as if I would deny my name.

HOTSPUR

My name is Harry Percy.

PRINCE HENRY   Why then I see   60

A very valiant rebel of the name.

I am the Prince of Wales; and think not, Percy,

To share with me in glory any more.

Two stars keep not their motion in one sphere,

Nor can one England brook a double reign

Of Harry Percy and the Prince of Wales.

HOTSPUR

Nor shall it, Harry, for the hour is come

To end the one of us; and would to God

Thy name in arms were now as great as mine!

PRINCE HENRY

I'll make it greater ere I part from thee,   70

And all the budding honours on thy crest

I'll crop to make a garland for my head.

HOTSPUR

I can no longer brook thy vanities.

They fight.

Enter Falstaff

60 Why then I see] ROWE (1714); *as part of l.* 61, Q1   67 Nor] F1; Now Q1   73.1 *They*] Q1; *not in* F1

57 **Make up** advance, as at l. 4
64 **Two . . . sphere** For an earlier instance of this astronomical metaphor, see note at 5.1.17. Each moving heavenly body was assigned its own sphere in Ptolemaic astronomy. Compare the proverb 'Two suns cannot shine in one sphere' (Dent S992).

65 **brook** endure
67 **Nor** The F1 reading. Q1's *now* is an easy mistake for the printer to have made.
71 **honours** chivalric ornaments, or 'favours', as at 3.2.142
73 **vanities** empty boasts

FALSTAFF Well said, Hal! To it, Hal! Nay, you shall find no
    boy's play here, I can tell you.

> *Enter Douglas. He fighteth with Falstaff, who falls*
> *down as if he were dead. ⌈Exit Douglas.⌉ The Prince*
> *killeth Percy*

HOTSPUR

O Harry, thou hast robbed me of my youth!
I better brook the loss of brittle life
Than those proud titles thou hast won of me;
They wound my thoughts worse than thy sword my
    flesh.
But thoughts, the slaves of life, and life, time's fool,   80
And time, that takes survey of all the world,
Must have a stop. O, I could prophesy,
But that the earthy and cold hand of death
Lies on my tongue. No, Percy, thou art dust,
And food for—   *He dies*

PRINCE HENRY

For worms, brave Percy. Fare thee well, great heart!

75.1 who] F1 ; *he* Q1   75.2 Exit Douglas] CAPELL; *not in* Q1   80 thoughts, the slaves] Q1
(thoughts the slaues); thought's the slaue Q2–5, F1   83 earthy and] Q1 ; earth and Q2 ; Earth,
and the F1   85 He dies] ROWE; *not in* Q1   86 thee] Q1 ; *not in* F1

74 **Well said** Well done
75 **boy's play** '(It is) no child's (boy's) play' is
    a familiar expression (Dent C324).
75.2 **Exit Douglas** The timing of Douglas's
    exit, not marked in QqF1, is uncertain.
    Conceivably he remains on stage a few
    moments longer, for at 5.5.19 we learn
    that he saw 'The noble Percy slain'—a
    phrase that could refer to the actual kill-
    ing. Why does he not come to the aid of
    Hotspur? Earlier, at l. 42.1, Douglas fled
    before Prince Henry. If, as Seymour
    Connor (*UTSE*, 27 (1948), 215–21)
    speculates, Douglas forbears to enter the
    fray, and thereupon flees a second time
    before Hal, the Prince would be in a
    position to act magnanimously toward
    the 'noble Scot' (5.5.17) whom Hal
    addressed earlier as 'vile Scot' (5.4.38).
75.2–3 *The Prince killeth Percy* See Appen-
    dix for the chronicles.
    killeth i.e. mortally wounds
77 **brittle life** A commonplace idea (Dent
    L251.1).
78 **those . . . me** For the idea that the cham-
    pion in such a contest wins all the honours
    of his vanquished rival, see ll. 71–2 above

and note at 3.2.150.
80–2 **But . . . stop** but thoughts (which are
    dependent on our physical existence), and
    life (which is the plaything of time, subject
    to its merest whim), and even time itself
    (which exercises control over all earthly
    existence), must come to an end. Compare
    Revelation 10:6: 'there should be no lon-
    ger time' (Kittredge). The Q1 reading is
    preferable to that of Qq2–5 and F1 (see
    collation) because it preserves the plural
    thoughts of l. 80, and because it effectively
    sees *thoughts, life,* and *time* as all coming to
    a stop, whereas the non-authoritative
    emendation of Q2 reduces the idea to a
    series of sententious moralisms: 'thought
    is the slave of life', etc.
81 **survey** (accent on second syllable)
82 **prophesy** Compare Dent M514: 'Dying
    men speak true.' Gaunt in *Richard II*
    2.1.5–8 and 31ff. says: 'Methinks I am a
    prophet new inspired, | And thus expiring
    do foretell of him', etc. See also *Hamlet*
    5.2.347.
84–6 **dust . . . worms** Compare Dent E30:
    'Earth must go to earth (Dust to dust)',
    from Ecclesiastes 3: 20, and M253: 'A

Ill-weaved ambition, how much art thou shrunk!
When that this body did contain a spirit,
A kingdom for it was too small a bound;
But now two paces of the vilest earth   90
Is room enough. This earth that bears thee dead
Bears not alive so stout a gentleman.
If thou wert sensible of courtesy
I should not make so dear a show of zeal.
But let my favours hide thy mangled face;
    He covers Hotspur's face
And, even in thy behalf, I'll thank myself
For doing these fair rites of tenderness.
Adieu, and take thy praise with thee to heaven!
Thy ignominy sleep with thee in the grave,
But not remembered in thy epitaph!   100
    He spieth Falstaff on the ground
What, old acquaintance, could not all this flesh
Keep in a little life? Poor Jack, farewell!
I could have better spared a better man.
O, I should have a heavy miss of thee
If I were much in love with vanity.
Death hath not struck so fat a deer today,
Though many dearer, in this bloody fray.
Embowelled will I see thee by and by.

91 thee] Q7; the Q1   95.1 *He ... face*] This edition; *not in* Q1   97 rites] Q1 (rights)   100.1 *He ... ground*] Q1; *not in* F1   108 Embowelled] Q1 (Inboweld)

man is nothing but worms' meat.' For a stage interpretation, see Introduction, p. 79.

87 **Ill-weaved . . . shrunk** Compare Dent C432: 'Like northern [i.e. poorly woven] cloth, shrunk in the wetting'.

88–91 **When that . . . enough** Compare Dent F582: 'Six feet of earth make all men equal', and *Richard II* 3.3.153–4.

92 **stout** valiant

93 **sensible of courtesy** able to hear my praise

94 **dear** heartfelt
   zeal warm admiration

95 **favours** something given as a mark of favour or ceremonial decoration and worn conspicuously as a badge; sometimes a knot of ribbon, glove, or scarf worn as a love-token, but more probably here the twisted silken band in the Prince's

colours joining his crest to his helmet (C. W. Scott-Giles, *Sh's Heraldry* (1950), 91) or the plumes of his helmet described in 4.1.98 (H. Hartman, *PMLA*, 46 (1931), 720). In a magnanimous gesture, Hal bestows on the dead Hotspur the honour Hal has won.

104 **heavy** (a) sorrowful, momentous (b) weighty

105 **vanity** frivolity, as at 1.2.77

107 **dearer** playing upon *deer*, l. 106, with the double sense of (a) dearer to the heart, as at l. 94 (b) nobler, as in 1.1.62 and 4.4.31

108 **Embowelled** disembowelled for embalming and burial. Humphreys notes an allusion to the 'assay', or ceremony of embowelling the deer and awarding the paunch to the hounds, as described in Madden, 65.

Till then, in blood by noble Percy lie.   *Exit*
     Falstaff riseth up

FALSTAFF Embowelled! If thou embowel me today, I'll give   110
  you leave to powder me and eat me too tomorrow.
  'Sblood, 'twas time to counterfeit, or that hot termagant
  Scot had paid me, scot and lot too. Counterfeit? I lie, I am
  no counterfeit. To die is to be a counterfeit, for he is but
  the counterfeit of a man who hath not the life of a man;
  but to counterfeit dying, when a man thereby liveth, is to
  be no counterfeit, but the true and perfect image of life
  indeed. The better part of valour is discretion, in the
  which better part I have saved my life. Zounds, I am afraid
  of this gunpowder Percy, though he be dead. How if he   120
  should counterfeit too and rise? By my faith, I am afraid
  he would prove the better counterfeit. Therefore I'll make
  him sure; yea, and I'll swear I killed him. Why may not
  he rise as well as I? Nothing confutes me but eyes, and
  nobody sees me. Therefore, sirrah (*stabbing him*), with a
  new wound in your thigh, come you along with me.
     He takes up Hotspur on his back.
     Enter Prince Henry and Prince John of Lancaster

110 Embowelled . . . embowel] Q1 (Inbowled . . . inbowel)   125 (*stabbing him*)] CAPELL (*subs.*);
not in Q1   126.1 *He takes up*] Q1 ; *Takes* F1   126.2 *Prince Henry and Prince John*] Q2 (*Prince and
Iohn*); *Prince Iohn* Q1

109 **in blood** Humphreys (160) notes a
  double meaning, since, in the continuing
  metaphor of hunting the deer, *in blood*
  means in full vigour, full of life. The ironic
  application to the shamming Falstaff cannot be evident to Hal, who, like the
  audience, believes that Falstaff is dead. In
  the next moment, however, Falstaff
  shows the metaphor to be literally true, by
  appearing to rise from the dead.
111 **powder** (a) sprinkle fresh meat with salt
  or powdered spice, and pickle in the 'pow-
  dering tub' for preserving, as one would
  do to a slain deer (b) embalm in brine, as
  one would do to a slain warrior
112 **termagant** savage and blustering, like
  the supposed Mohammedan god of
  medieval and Renaissance lore; see Spenser, *Faerie Queene*, VI. vii. 47: 'And oftentimes by Turmagant and Mahound
  swore'. Hamlet would have players
  whipped 'for o'er-doing Termagant. It
  out-Herods Herod' (*Hamlet* 3.2.13).
113 **paid** killed, as in 5.3.46 (see note), and
  5.4.42

scot and lot making final payment. The
  play on words in *scot* recalls 1.3.214–15
  (see note). The expression became commonplace (Dent S159).
118 **The better . . . discretion** This ancient
  idea is found, for example, in Vincentio
  Saviolo's observation *Of Honour* that
  'without them [i.e. wisdom and discretion]
  a man is not to be accounted valiant, but
  rather furious' (*Saviolo His Practice*, 1595,
  sig. Bb, quoted in Cowl and Morgan). Falstaff's influential formulation of the
  proverb (Dent D354) is his own, and
  characteristically gives undue prominence to *discretion*.
   part Several possible meanings: (a) constituent part (b) quality (c) theatrical role
  (choosing between the parts of Valour
  and Discretion) (d) sexual member (Jorgensen, *ShakS*, 9 (1976), 141–58).
126.1 **He takes . . . back** In Ulpian Fulwell's
  Like Will to Like (1562–8), the devil carries off Nichol Newfangle the Vice to hell
  on his back. The familiarity of the stage
  image from this and other morality plays

PRINCE HENRY

Come, brother John; full bravely hast thou fleshed
Thy maiden sword.

LANCASTER   But soft, whom have we here?
Did you not tell me this fat man was dead?

PRINCE HENRY I did; I saw him dead,   130
Breathless and bleeding on the ground.—Art thou alive?
Or is it fantasy that plays upon our eyesight?
I prithee, speak. We will not trust our eyes
Without our ears. Thou art not what thou seem'st.

FALSTAFF No, that's certain, I am not a double man; but if
I be not Jack Falstaff, then am I a jack. There is Percy.
        He throws down Hotspur's body
If your father will do me any honour, so; if not, let him kill
the next Percy himself. I look to be either earl or duke, I
can assure you.

PRINCE HENRY

Why, Percy I killed myself, and saw thee dead.   140

FALSTAFF Didst thou? Lord, Lord, how this world is given to
lying! I grant you I was down and out of breath, and so
was he; but we rose both at an instant, and fought a long
hour by Shrewsbury clock. If I may be believed, so; if not,
let them that should reward valour bear the sin upon their
own heads. I'll take it upon my death, I gave him this
wound in the thigh. If the man were alive and would deny
it, zounds, I would make him eat a piece of my sword.

136.1 *He throws ... body*] CAPELL (*subs.*); *not in* Q1   146 take it upon] Q1; take't on F1

(see Introduction, p. 26) links Falstaff in
this significant action with inventive cunning and spiritual reprobation.

127 **fleshed** initiated in bloodshed, given a
first taste (as with a hawk or hound, to in-
flame its appetite for killing)

135 **double man** (a) apparition, counterpart
of a living man (b) two men, Falstaff with
Hotspur on his back

136 **jack** knave

142 **lying** (a) telling lies (b) lying still

143 **at an instant** simultaneously

144 **Shrewsbury clock** (presumably in the
church tower)

146 **take it upon my death** swear as at the

moment of death, with my eternal soul at
risk. The oath appears to be even more
solemn than in Kittredge's paraphrase:
'Swear with death as the penalty for perjury.'

148 **eat . . . sword** 'To eat one's sword' is a
familiar phrase (Dent *PLED* S1053.11). It
is often paired with the metaphor of 'eating words', as here, where Falstaff would
make Hotspur swallow his words of denial
or 'eat' (be stabbed by) Falstaff's sword.
Compare Marston's *Histriomastix* (*c*.1599),
Act 5 (ed. Wood, iii. 287): 'Swallow those
words, or thou shalt eat my sword.'

LANCASTER

This is the strangest tale that ever I heard.

PRINCE HENRY

This is the strangest fellow, brother John.   150

Come, bring your luggage nobly on your back.

For my part, if a lie may do thee grace,

I'll gild it with the happiest terms I have.

　　　A retreat is sounded

The trumpet sounds retreat; the day is our.

Come, brother, let us to the highest of the field,

To see what friends are living, who are dead.

　　　　　　　　　　　　　Exeunt Prince Henry and Lancaster

FALSTAFF I'll follow, as they say, for reward. He that
rewards me, God reward him. If I do grow great, I'll grow
less; for I'll purge and leave sack, and live cleanly as a
nobleman should do.　　　　　　　*Exit, with Hotspur's body*   160

2/28

5.5　　*The trumpets sound. Enter the King, the Prince of Wales,
Lord John of Lancaster, the Earl of Westmorland, with
Worcester and Vernon prisoners*

KING HENRY

Thus ever did rebellion find rebuke.

149 ever] Q1; e're F1　　154 our] Q1; ours Q2　　156.1 *Exeunt ... Lancaster*] CAPELL (*subs.*);
Exeunt. Q1　　158 great] Q1; great again F1　　160 *Exit ... body*] CAPELL (*subs.*); *Exit.*
Q1　　5.5.0.1 *the Prince*] Q1 (*Prince*)　　0.2 *the Earl*] Q1 (*Earle*)

152 **a lie** i.e. this lie of yours. Wilson (*NCS*)
and Humphreys regard ll. 152–3 as
offered in an aside to Falstaff, since
disclosure to Prince John would vitiate the
promise. Yet for Prince Hal to conspire in
such secrecy would imply an intimacy
with Falstaff that no longer exists. The
Prince offhandedly and recklessly invites
Falstaff to exploit a reputation for valour
at Hal's expense and without fear of Hal's
open contradiction, but Hal certainly is
not about to deny to John his statement
that 'Percy I killed myself' (l. 140).
　grace credit, favour (with an ironic suggestion of a spiritual grace that is surely
not forthcoming)

153 **happiest** most felicitous and favourable

153.1 *retreat* a trumpet-call either from the
rebel side signalling defeat or from the
loyalist side signalling withdrawal from
successfully completed combat, as in
1 Henry VI 2.2.3

154 **our** ours, as at 4.3.28 (see note)

155 **highest** highest vantage-point

157 **I'll . . . reward** Wilson (*NCS*) and
Humphreys, citing Turbervile's *Book of
Hunting* (1576), 135 and 244–5, note
that Falstaff follows like a hunting-hound
that has brought down the quarry and
hopes to be rewarded with a portion at the
ceremonial of assay and breaking up.
Compare note at l. 108 and Madden, 65.

159 **purge** (a) lose weight by means of pur-
gative drugs (b) repent, void sin

5.5 Location continues to be Shrewsbury
field. In terms of Shakespeare's theatre, it
is overly specific to indicate another part
of the field where the King presumably
has his command post.

0.1 *trumpets sound* a signal for a royal
entrance, perhaps one of special solemnity to mark the victory (Long, 80). The
retreat (5.4.153.1) has already been
sounded.

0.3 *Worcester and Vernon prisoners* See
Appendix for Holinshed.

1 **rebuke** (a) check, repulse (b) reproof

Ill-spirited Worcester, did not we send grace,
Pardon, and terms of love to all of you?
And wouldst thou turn our offers contrary?
Misuse the tenor of thy kinsman's trust?
Three knights upon our party slain today,
A noble earl, and many a creature else
Had been alive this hour,
If like a Christian thou hadst truly borne
Betwixt our armies true intelligence.   10

WORCESTER
What I have done my safety urged me to;
And I embrace this fortune patiently,
Since not to be avoided it falls on me.

KING HENRY
Bear Worcester to the death, and Vernon too.
Other offenders we will pause upon.

> *Exeunt Worcester and Vernon, guarded*

How goes the field?

PRINCE HENRY
The noble Scot, Lord Douglas, when he saw
The fortune of the day quite turned from him,
The noble Percy slain, and all his men
Upon the foot of fear, fled with the rest;   20
And, falling from a hill, he was so bruised
That the pursuers took him. At my tent
The Douglas is; and I beseech your grace
I may dispose of him.

KING HENRY   With all my heart.

PRINCE HENRY
Then, brother John of Lancaster,
To you this honourable bounty shall belong.
Go to the Douglas and deliver him
Up to his pleasure, ransomless and free.

---

2 not we] Q1; we not F1   14 the] Q1; *not in* F1   15.1 *Exeunt ... guarded*] THEOBALD: *Exit Worcester and Vernon* F1; *not in* Q1

2 **spirited** (pronounced in two syllables)
5 **Misuse . . . trust** misrepresent the *true intelligence* (l. 10) entrusted to you for Hotspur, and thereby abuse Hotspur's trust
tenor purport. Alternatively, the word might be read as *tenure* (an acceptable

modernization), authority, control.
20 **Upon the foot of fear** in panic
21–2 **falling . . . took him** See Appendix for Holinshed.
26 **this honourable bounty** the honour of this bounteous act

His valours shown upon our crests today
Have taught us how to cherish such high deeds   30
Even in the bosom of our adversaries.

LANCASTER

I thank your grace for this high courtesy,
Which I shall give away immediately.

KING HENRY

Then this remains, that we divide our power.
You, son John, and my cousin Westmorland
Towards York shall bend you with your dearest speed,
To meet Northumberland and the prelate Scrope,
Who, as we hear, are busily in arms.
Myself and you, son Harry, will towards Wales,
To fight with Glendower and the Earl of March.   40
Rebellion in this land shall lose his sway,
Meeting the check of such another day;
And since this business so fair is done,
Let us not leave till all our own be won.   *Exeunt*

36 bend you] Q4; bend, you Q1   41 lose] Q1 (loofe)

29 **valours** (The plural use for an abstract
   quality is not uncommon.)
   crests i.e. helmets
33 **give away** i.e. pass along, confer on
   Douglas

36 **bend you** direct your course
   dearest most urgent
39 **towards Wales** See Appendix for Holinshed's different account.
41 **his** its
44 **leave** leave off

SHAKESPEARE'S CHRONICLE SOURCES

THE Introduction includes a discussion of Shakespeare's use of his chronicle sources. Since the most important of those sources are readily available in Bullough's *Narrative and Dramatic Sources*, volume 4, they are not reprinted at length here. What follows instead is a point-by-point comparison of Shakespeare's text with pertinent excerpts from Holinshed, Daniel, Stow, and others, arranged scene by scene and line by line. Page numbers in parentheses, e.g. Holinshed (181) or Stow's *Chronicles* (219), are to Bullough's edition, volume 4. References to Daniel's *Civil Wars* are by book and verse, e.g. iii. 97, and may be found in Bullough or any edition of the poem. On the few occasions when the material in Holinshed being referred to is not in Bullough's selections, reference is to the original 1587 edition by volume and page, e.g. iii. 520. This Appendix also includes historical information from the *Dictionary of National Biography* *(DNB)* and other standard sources.

1.1.0.1 *Lord John of Lancaster*] This third son (1389–1435) of Henry IV became Duke of Bedford in 1411. He appears in *Henry V* and in *1 Henry VI* as Regent of France after Henry V's death.
   1 shaken … wan] Holinshed alludes to the 'unquiet reign' of Henry IV, and reports how, after a failed attempt on his life in 1401, Henry lacked the confidence to 'compose or settle himself to sleep for fear of strangling'. Such was the 'suspected state' of a king 'holding his regiment with the hatred of his people, the heart grudgings of his courtiers, and the peremptory practices of both together' (181).
19–22 As far … levy] According to Holinshed, King Henry was asked in 1400 by the Emperor of Constantinople for aid against the Turks, but did not himself propose a crusade until the end of his reign (iii. 519). Shakespeare brings the event forward in time, thereby permitting his audience to wonder whether Henry's unspoken motives for this crusade may not have included expiation for the death of Richard II. On Henry's covert sense of guilt, see note at 3.2.5. Yet Henry may well have had political reasons also. In *2 Henry IV* the dying King Henry intimates to his son that his motive was to head off political rebellion by busying his restive peers with a holy cause abroad, and he advises his son to act accordingly (4.4.209–16).
   31 gentle cousin] Ralph Neville, first Earl of Westmorland (1364–1425), sided with Henry IV against Richard II in 1399, and remained a loyal follower of the Lancastrians at Shrewsbury and afterwards. His wife was Henry IV's half-sister.
   38 Mortimer] Sir Edmund de Mortimer (1376–1409), son of the third Earl of March, married Glendower's daughter after his capture at Brynglas (the Battle of Nesbit, June 1402), and was brother-in-law to

Hotspur, since 'Kate', really 'Elizabeth', was Edmund's elder sister. This Sir Edmund, however, was never Earl of March or heir to the throne. Shakespeare, following Daniel's *Civil Wars*, conflates Sir Edmund with his nephew Edmund, the fifth Earl of March, who was recognized by Richard II as heir presumptive to the Crown in 1398 after the death of Edmund's father, Roger, the fourth Earl of March, whom Richard had originally proclaimed his heir in 1385. (The Earl of Worcester refers to the 1398 proclamation at 1.3.145–6.) Holinshed, too, confuses the two Mortimers, for he reports that when the forces of Herefordshire were led against Glendower 'under the conduct of Edmund Mortimer Earl of March', this earl was 'taken prisoner', and goes on to explain that King Henry 'was not hasty to purchase the deliverance of the Earl March' by ransoming him from Glendower 'because his title to the crown was well enough known'. King Henry accordingly 'suffered him to remain in miserable prison, wishing both the said earl and all other of his lineage out of this life with God and his saints in heaven, so they had been out of the way, for then all had been well enough as he thought' (182). In Holinshed, again, it is the Earl of March who marries Glendower's daughter (184). Holinshed appears not to realize that the Earl of March fought victoriously against the Scots in September 1402, whereas Edmund Mortimer was captured some three months earlier.

40 the irregular and wild Glendower] Owen Glendower (1359?–1416?) headed a Welsh rebellion against Henry IV on Henry's succession, and captured Sir Edmund de Mortimer in June 1402, releasing him after the marriage of Edmund to Glendower's daughter. Holinshed describes Glendower as 'robbing and spoiling within the English borders' (182)—that is, engaged in the 'irregular' and 'wild' tactics of guerrilla warfare—and reports that King Henry, troubled by Glendower 'and his unruly complices, determined to chastise them, as disturbers of his peace' (180).

43–6 Upon . . . spoken of] Holinshed reports that 'The shameful villainy used by the Welshwomen towards the dead carcasses was such as honest ears would be ashamed to hear and continent tongues to speak thereof' (182). The Battle of Nesbit took place on 22 June 1402.

52 Holy Rood Day] Holinshed reports the Battle of Holmedon as taking place 'on the Rood day in harvest' (183). Shakespeare has made virtually contemporaneous two battles, that on 14 September in which the Scottish forces were defeated by Hotspur and his allies (including the fifth Earl of March), and that in which Edmund Mortimer was captured, on 22 June, nearly three months earlier.

52–3 Hotspur . . . Percy] Sir Henry Percy (1364–1403), eldest son of the first Earl of Northumberland. He assisted Henry IV to the throne, but broke with him and proclaimed a rebellion in June 1403. According to history, he was killed by Henry IV at the Battle of Shrewsbury on 16 June.

53 Archibald] Archibald, fourth Earl of Douglas, first Duke of Touraine

(1369?–1424), defeated and captured by the fifth Earl of March and Hotspur in Northumberland in September 1402. Holinshed's account, because of a missing comma, obscures the fact of Douglas's capture, and it is not mentioned in this first scene of Shakespeare's play (see information given at ll. 71–2 below), although King Henry appears later to know that Douglas was once captured by Hotspur (3.2.114). At the Battle of Shrewsbury, where he was an ally of Hotspur, Douglas was again captured (as Shakespeare describes in Act 5).

57 by discharge of their artillery] Holinshed refers to the 'violence of the English shot' (183) as decisive, meaning the English archers by whom the battle was won, but Shakespeare had guns in mind; compare 'vile guns' in 1.3.63.

68 two-and-twenty] Holinshed reports 'three-and-twenty knights' slain (183).

71–2 Mordake . . . Douglas] Holinshed reports that among the prisoners taken at Holmedon 'were these, Mordacke Earl of Fife, son to the governour Archembald Earl Douglas, which in the fight lost one of his eyes' (183). The lack of a comma after *governour* led Shakespeare to characterize Mordake as Douglas's son. In fact the captured man was Murdac, or Murdoch, Stewart, known as the Earl of Fife until the death of his father in 1420, when he became the second Duke of Albany. He was kept prisoner in England from 1402 until 1415, when he was exchanged for Sir Henry Percy, second Earl of Northumberland and son of Hotspur (*DNB*). Contrast 3.2.114, where Shakespeare appears to know that Douglas was once captured by Hotspur.

72–3 Atholl . . . Menteith] Shakespeare follows Holinshed in this list of those captured (183), and also in assuming that Menteith is a separate person, when historically the name was one of the titles of 'Mordake', Earl of Fife.

78 my lord Northumberland] Henry Percy, first Earl of Northumberland (1342–1408), the Northumberland of *Richard II* who was alienated from King Richard and joined Henry of Lancaster.

94 I shall . . . Fife] Holinshed: 'and especially they were grieved because the King demanded of the Earl and his son such Scottish prisoners as were taken at Holmedon and Nesbit; for of all the captives which were taken in the conflicts foughten in those two places, there were delivered to the King's possession only Mordake Earl of Fife, the Duke of Albany's son, though the King did divers and sundry times require deliverance of the residue, and that with great threatenings' (184).

95 Worcester] Thomas Percy, Earl of Worcester (1344?–1403), younger brother of the first Earl of Northumberland, deserted Richard II for Henry IV in 1399, but joined the Percy rebellion against Henry in 1403. He was captured and beheaded at the Battle of Shrewsbury.

96 Malevolent . . . aspects] According to Holinshed, Worcester's 'study was ever (as some write) to procure malice, and set things in a broil' (184).

99 I have sent] In Holinshed it is the Percys who take the initiative for a confrontation. See next note.

103 Windsor] According to Holinshed, the Percys, at Worcester's instigation, 'came to the King unto Windsor upon a purpose to prove him' (184).

1.2.0 *Enter ... Falstaff*] According to Holinshed, Prince Henry's conduct was under some suspicion in 1411 because of the 'great resort of people' that 'came to his house' and the 'companions agreeable to his age' with whom 'he spent the time in such recreations, exercises, and delights as he fancied' (193, 195). Shakespeare portrays this merry companionship as occurring much earlier in the reign.

121 vizards] Stow, in his *Chronicles*, reports of Prince Hal that 'being accompanied with some of his young lords and gentlemen, he would wait in disguised array for his own receivers, and distress them of their money' (219).

123 Eastcheap] Stow, in his *Chronicles*, reports an affray in 1410 between the men of 'the King's son being in Eastcheap at supper, after midnight' and men of the court, in which 'the Mayor and Sheriffs' had to intervene. The son in question may or may not have been Prince Henry (216).

1.3.83 great magician] Here, as in 3.1, Shakespeare takes a hint from Holinshed, who reports of Glendower that '(as was thought) through art magic, he caused such foul weather of winds, tempest, rain, snow and hail to be raised, for the annoyance of the King's army, that the like had not been heard of; in such sort, that the King was constrained to return home' (182–3).

148–50 And then . . . expedition] Holinshed: 'which Edmund at King Richard's going into Ireland was proclaimed heir apparent to the crown and realm' (184).

243 madcap Duke] Impulsiveness and idiosyncrasy are not especially evident in Shakespeare's portrait of the Duke of York in *Richard II* or in *Woodstock*; but Humphreys cites Holinshed's description of 'a man rather coveting to live in pleasure than to deal with much business' (iii. 485), and a similar description in Hardyng's *Chronicle* tells of one who went hunting and hawking while the other peers were gathered in council and parliament (340). York did retire from the court after Henry IV's coronation in 1399, and lived thus until his death in 1402 (*DNB*).

269 the Lord Scrope] Holinshed describes the Archbishop of York as 'brother to the lord Scroope, whom King Henry had caused to be beheaded at Bristol' (186). See 4.4. This 'brother'—actually a distant cousin—was William Scroop, or Scrope, Earl of Wiltshire (1351?–99), loyal to Richard, arrested by Henry IV in 1399 and executed; his death is cited in *Richard II* 3.2.142.

2.3.1–13 But . . . opposition] This letter by an unnamed respondent gives particular form to Holinshed's observation that 'when the matter came to trial, the most part of the confederates abandoned them [i.e. Hotspur and his allies in arms], and at the day of the conflict left them alone' (186).

19–20 my lord . . . action] According to Holinshed, 'certain articles' introduced to win support among the nobility for the Percys' cause were devised 'by the advice of Richard Scroope, Archbishop of York' (186).

2.4.527–8 The money . . . advantage] Stow, in his *Chronicles*, reports that when the receivers, who had been robbed by Hal himself among others, had complained as to 'how they were robbed in their coming unto him, he would give them discharge of so much money as they had lost, and besides that they should not depart from him without great rewards for their trouble and vexation, especially they should be rewarded that best had resisted him and his company, and of whom he had received the greatest and most strokes' (219).

3.1.0.1–2 *Enter . . . Glendower*] Holinshed writes of the three-way negotiations among Hotspur, Glendower, and 'Edmund Earl of March' as follows: 'they by their deputies, in the house of the Archdeacon of Bangor [in northwest Wales], divided the realm amongst them' (185). The leaders did not meet personally, as in Shakespeare.

12–16 At my nativity . . . coward] Holinshed reports that 'strange wonders happened (as men reported) at the nativity of this man, for the same night he was born, all his father's horses in the stable were found to stand in blood up to the bellies' (184). Holinshed appears to be speaking in fact of Edmund Mortimer's birth, but the imprecise reference ('the nativity of this man') and the mention of Owen Glendower in the previous sentence easily allow for misinterpretation. Elsewhere, Holinshed mentions a 'blazing star' in 1402 that foretold Glendower's defeat of Lord Grey (iii. 519).

61 Three times] Of the three campaigns mentioned in Holinshed, in 1400, 1402, and 1405 (iii. 519–20, 530), the last came after Shrewsbury; but perhaps, as Humphreys suggests, Shakespeare consulted Hardyng's *Chronicle* in which 'the King Henry thrice to Wales went', only to be afflicted by 'mists and tempests' so foul 'that he had never power | Glendower to annoy' (p. 359).

70–6 three limits . . . Trent] Shakespeare takes these divisions from Holinshed, who reports that, by the tripartite covenant, 'all England from Severn and Trent, south and eastward, was assigned to the Earl of March; all Wales, and the lands beyond Severn westward, were appointed to Owen Glendower; and all the remnant from Trent northward, to the lord Percy' (185).

77 indentures tripartite] Holinshed reports that the deputies of the rebel lords caused 'a tripartite indenture to be made and sealed with their seals' (185).

118 trained . . . court] Glendower studied law at Westminster, and, as squire to the Earl of Arundel, served Henry of Lancaster (*DNB*).

Holinshed reports that Glendower became an 'utter barrister, or an apprentice of the law', and adds that others 'have written that he served this King Henry the Fourth, before he came to attain the crown, in room of an esquire' (180).

144–8 the mouldwarp . . . cat] Hotspur's ridiculing of Glendower's favourite heraldic emblems may borrow some language from Holinshed in a different context. Holinshed reports that the three-way dividing of England's map 'was done (as some have said) through a foolish credit given to a vain prophecy, as though King Henry was the mouldwarp, cursed of God's own mouth, and they three were the dragon, the lion, and the wolf, which should divide this realm between them. Such is the deviation (saith Hall) and not divination of those blind and fantastical dreams of the Welsh prophesiers' (185). Hall's earlier account attributes this prophecy to 'the deviation and not divination of that mawmet Merlin' (the third year of King Henry the IV, fol. xx).

3.2.0 *Enter . . . attendance*] According to Holinshed, 'The court was then at Westminster' when Prince Henry 'got knowledge' that 'certain of his father's servants were busy to give information against him, whereby discord might arise betwixt him and his father; for they put into the King's head not only what evil rule (according to the course of youth) the Prince kept to the offence of many, but also what great resort of people came to his house, so that the court was nothing furnished with such a train as daily followed the Prince. These tales brought no small suspicion into the King's head, lest his son would presume to usurp the crown, he being yet alive' (193). The Prince knelt down before his ailing father, professed his loyalty in the presence of certain lords of the court, and was embraced with tears and reconciliation. Historically, the event took place in 1411 or 1412, well after the Battle of Shrewsbury, at a time when the King was 'grievously diseased' and 'caused himself in his chair to be borne into his privy chamber' (194)—circumstances closer to the father-son interview of *2 Henry IV* than to that of *1 Henry IV*. Stow, *Chronicles*, gives a similar report (217).

1–2 give us leave . . . conference] In Holinshed, the King interviews his son 'in the presence of three or four persons, in whom he had confidence' (194).

25 pickthanks] According to Holinshed, 'Thus were the father and the son reconciled, betwixt whom the said pickthanks had sown division' (195, first appearing in 1587 edition).

103 being . . . thou] Hotspur, born in 1364, was historically twenty-three years Prince Hal's senior. Shakespeare equalizes the ages to stress their rivalry, as in Daniel's *Civil Wars*; Daniel speaks of Hotspur's 'young undanger'd hand' (iii. 109).

112 Thrice] Holinshed records three major engagements in 1388 and 1402 (iii. 465 and 520). At the first, the then Douglas was slain, but Hotspur was captured (Humphreys).

114 ta'en him once] In 1.1.70–2, Shakespeare appears to have assumed from Holinshed's ambiguously pointed English chronicle that Hotspur captured Mordake, 'son to beaten Douglas', rather than Douglas himself. The correct information here in 3.2 could have been learned from Holinshed's *Histories of Scotland* (ii. 254), where the capture of Douglas is clearly reported (Humphreys).

164 Lord Mortimer of Scotland] Holinshed reports that one of King Henry's northern allies, 'the Scot, the Earl of March', earnestly called upon Henry at the time of Shrewsbury 'to make haste and give battle to his enemies, before their power by delaying of time should still too much increase'. This same lord, historically George Dunbar, Earl of the 'March', or borderland, of Scotland, is referred to earlier by Holinshed as 'George Earl of March', an ally of Hotspur against Douglas at Holmedon (188, 183). The confusing similarity to the title of the English Earl of March evidently led Shakespeare to assume that the Scottish earls of March were also Mortimers.

4.1.16 sick] By timing this illness to coincide with the Battle of Shrewsbury—in Holinshed it comes earlier, at a less critical juncture (186)—Shakespeare adds to the rebels' difficulty and to Hotspur's impetuous valour as contrasted with the evasions of his father (Humphreys).

40–1 the King . . . purposes] Holinshed describes the King as 'understanding their cloaked drift' (187).

86 My cousin Vernon] Holinshed reports merely that Sir Richard Vernon was one of the chieftains of the Percys' army at Shrewsbury (189). Shakespeare has substantially augmented his role.

87–93 Pray . . . preparation] Holinshed, who does not mention a separate force marching under Westmorland and Prince John of Lancaster, credits King Henry himself with such speed 'that he was in sight of his enemies, lying in camp near to Shrewsbury, before they were in doubt of any such thing' (188). Holinshed gives a larger military role to the King than does Shakespeare. Daniel, *Civil Wars*, stresses the 'swift approach and unexpected speed' of the King upon the rebels, bringing dismay into their souls (iii. 99).

95 nimble-footed] 'He was passing swift in running, in so much that he with two other of his lords by force of running, without any manner of hounds or greyhounds, or without bow or other engine, would take a wild buck or doe at large in a park' (*The First English Life of King Henry the Fifth, c.*1513, ed. C. L. Kingsford (Oxford, 1911), 17). This account is repeated almost verbatim by Stow, *Annals of England*, 547, and substantially by William Harrison, *Description of England* (in Holinshed, i. 226). Holinshed summarizes the view of most chroniclers (iii. 583): 'In strength and nimbleness of body from his youth few to him comparable' (quoted by Humphreys, 124).

125–7 Glendower . . . days] Although Glendower himself was historically absent from the battle (*DNB*), Holinshed reports that 'The Welshmen also, which before had lain lurking in the woods, mountains, and marshes, hearing of this battle toward, came to the aid of the Percys, and refreshed the wearied people with new succours' (190). Shakespeare intensifies the odds against Hotspur by following Daniel, *Civil Wars*, who stipulates that 'The joining with the Welsh they had decreed | Was hereby stopped', i.e. prevented by King Henry's 'swift approach and unexpected speed' (iii. 99).

131 thirty ... Forty] Holinshed puts the Percys' force at 14,000 (189), but neither he nor Daniel estimates the size of the King's army. As Wright and Humphreys observe, Wyntown's *Cronykil of Scotland* (Book IX, chap. 24, l. 2485) estimates 30,000, and the ballad of 'The Battle of Otterburn' relates that, when 'the Percy and the Douglas met', the former was faced by 'forty thousand ... and four' (stanza 35), but we cannot be sure Shakespeare consulted these sources. Hall says that 'on both parts were above forty thousand men assembled' (cited by Hemingway).

4.3.29.2 *Blunt*] Shakespeare has enhanced Blunt's role by giving him a mission assigned in Holinshed (189) to Thomas Presbury, Abbot of Shrewsbury, and a clerk of the Privy Seal.

56 six-and-twenty] When Bolingbroke landed at Ravenspurgh, according to Holinshed (iii. 498), there were 'with him not past threescore persons'.

78–80 to reform ... commonwealth] Holinshed reports: 'Moreover, he undertook to cause the payment of taxes and tallages to be laid down and to bring the King to good government' (iii. 498).

92 tasked] In Holinshed the rebels complain that 'whereas taxes and tallages were daily levied, under pretence to be employed in defence of the realm, the same were vainly wasted, and unprofitably consumed' (186–7).

98 intelligence] In Holinshed the rebels complain that 'through the slanderous reports of their enemies, the King had taken a grievous displeasure with them' (187).

113 maybe so we shall] Holinshed reports that by the persuasions of the King's ambassadors, with their offer of pardon, 'the lord Henry Percy began to give ear unto the King's offers, and so sent with them his uncle the Earl of Worcester, to declare unto the King the causes of those troubles' (189).

4.4.0 *Archbishop of York*] According to Holinshed, this prelate was 'Richard Scroope, Archbishop of York, brother to the lord Scroope, whom King Henry had caused to be beheaded at Bristol' (186), but see 1.3.269 above. This Scrope supported Henry IV against Richard II in 1399, but, like the Percys, grew disaffected. Eventually he joined the rebellion portrayed in *2 Henry IV* 4.1–2, and was induced by treachery to surrender to Westmorland. He was executed at York in 1405.

1 brief] According to Holinshed, Scrope advised the Percys in the devising of 'certain articles' that were shown to 'divers noblemen,

and other states of the realm', moving them 'to favour their purpose' (186).

2 Lord Marshal] i.e. Thomas Mowbray, third Earl of Nottingham (1388–1305), son of Thomas Mowbray, first Duke of Norfolk, who was banished in *Richard II* 1.3, with forfeiture of his estates. The son, resentful of exclusion from his father's honours, eventually joined the rebellion of 1405 portrayed in *2 Henry IV* 4.1–2, where he was induced by treachery to surrender and was executed without trial.

3 my cousin Scrope] Possibly Sir Stephen Scrope of *Richard II* 3.2.91–218, or his son Henry, third Baron Scrope of Masham (1376?–1415), who, as Shakespeare shows in *Henry V* 2.2, was executed for his complicity in a plot to dethrone Henry V. Several Scropes were opposed to Henry IV and his son (see 1.3.269 above); perhaps Shakespeare uses this family name here without further precision.

14 the sickness of Northumberland] Holinshed reports that 'The Earl of Northumberland himself was not with them, but being sick, had promised upon his amendment to repair unto them (as some write) with all convenient speed' (186).

16 Owen Glendower's absence] Holinshed reports that the Percys marched toward Shrewsbury in 1403 'upon hope to be aided (as men thought) by Owen Glendower, and his Welshmen' (187), and were assisted by Welsh troops (though Glendower is not specifically mentioned, and in fact he was not present) during the battle itself (190). Daniel, *Civil Wars* (iii. 99), is closer to Shakespeare in denying a Welsh presence; Shakespeare adds the touch about prophecies (l. 18) as consistent with Glendower's character. Compare 4.1.125–7 above.

23 Mortimer is not there] In fact, the fifth Earl of March never took part in the Percys' rebellion; he was honourably treated, but strictly guarded, by Henry IV on the occasion of the Lancastrian revolution, and was eventually restored to his estates. Glendower's son-in-law, Sir Edmund de Mortimer, was, like Glendower, absent from Shrewsbury.

5.1.30–71 It pleased ... enterprise] According to Holinshed, 'when the two armies were encamped, the one against the other, the Earl of Worcester and the lord Percy with their complices sent the articles (whereof I spake before) ... to King Henry ... which articles in effect charged him with manifest perjury, in that (contrary to his oath received upon the Evangelists at Doncaster, when he first entered the realm after his exile) he had taken upon him the crown and royal dignity, imprisoned King Richard, caused him to resign his title, and finally to be murdered. Divers other matters they laid to his charge, as levying of taxes and tallages, contrary to his promise, infringing of laws and customs of the realm, and suffering the Earl of March to remain in prison, without travailing to have him delivered.' The King countered with an offer of pardon, to which Hotspur favourably responded by sending his uncle Worcester to declare once more 'unto the King the causes of those troubles' and to negotiate further (189).

34–5 For . . . time] According to Holinshed, 'Sir Thomas Percy, Earl of Worcester, lord steward of the King's house . . . brake his white staff' (iii. 499–500).

41–5 You swore . . . Lancaster] According to Holinshed, 'At his coming unto Doncaster, the Earl of Northumberland and his son Sir Henry Percy . . . with the Earl of Westmorland came unto him, where he sware unto those lords that he would demand no more but the lands that were to him descended by inheritance from his father and in right of his wife' (iii. 498). Shakespeare does not mention Doncaster in *Richard II*.

5.2.1–25 O no . . . King] According to Holinshed, after King Henry had 'condescended unto all that was reasonable at his hands to be required . . . the Earl of Worcester (upon his return to his nephew) made relation clean contrary to that the King had said, in such sort that he set his nephew's heart more in displeasure towards the King than ever it was before, driving him by that means to fight whether he would or not' (190). Shakespeare provides Worcester with an interlocutor and a plausible motive.

81–4 the time . . . hour] Holinshed reports that in his battle oration Hotspur urged his men to consider that 'better it is to die in battle for the commonwealth's cause, than through cowardlike fear to prolong life, which after shall be taken from us, by sentence of the enemy' (188). Stow and Daniel have similar speeches.

96 Esperance! Percy!] Holinshed reports as follows: 'then suddenly blew the trumpets, the King's part crying "S. George! Upon them!"'; the adversaries cried "*Esperance! Percy!*", and so the two armies furiously joined' (190).

5.3.7 Stafford] Holinshed reports that the rebels pressed forward so strongly at the King's position and with such vehemence that they slew the King's standard-bearer, Sir Walter Blunt, and slew among others 'the Earl of Stafford, that day made by the King constable of the realm' (190–1). This association of Blunt and Stafford, together with Holinshed's observation in the next paragraph that Douglas 'slew Sir Walter Blunt, and three other' (191), may have suggested to Shakespeare that Stafford was one of those dressed in the King's clothing. Holinshed does not make it clear that there were two Blunts; but Shakespeare may have learned this fact from Daniel (*Civil Wars*, iii. 112), for in *2 Henry IV* 1.1.16–17 Lord Bardolph reports 'both the Blunts | Killed by the hand of Douglas'.

5.4.1 thou bleedest too much] Although, according to Holinshed, the Prince 'was hurt in the face with an arrow, so that divers noblemen that were about him would have conveyed him forth of the field, yet he would not suffer them so to do, lest his departure from amongst his men might haply have stricken some fear into their hearts' (191).

24 Another king] Of the encounter of the King and Douglas, Holinshed writes: 'the King crying "Saint George, victory!" brake the array of his enemies, and adventured so far that (as some write) the Earl Douglas strake him down' (191). Though the King was subsequently 'raised', Holinshed does not report who rescued him on this occasion.

37.1 *the King being in danger*] Holinshed reports simply that 'The Prince that day holp his father like a lusty young gentleman' (191). Shakespeare seems more directly indebted to Daniel, *Civil Wars*, who apostrophizes Hal thus: 'Hadst thou not there lent present speedy aid | To thy endangered father nearly tired, | Whom fierce encount'ring Douglas overlaid, | That day had there his troublous life expired' (iii. 111).

40–5 Shirley, Stafford, Blunt ... Gawsey ... Clifton] Among the English slain, according to Holinshed, were 'the Earl of Stafford ... Sir Hugh Shorlie, Sir John Clifton, Sir John Cokaine, Sir Nicholas Gausell, Sir Walter Blunt', and others (191). Daniel, *Civil Wars*, lists as casualties 'Heroical courageous Blunt', 'Magnanimous Stafford', and 'valiant Shorly' (iii. 111–13).

75.2–3 *The Prince killeth Percy*] Holinshed reports of King Henry that 'The other on his part,' that is, others among his army, 'encouraged by his doings, fought valiantly, and slew the lord Percy called Sir Henry Hotspur' (191), and Stow, too, reports merely that 'Hen. Percy, whilst he went before his men in the battle, pressing upon his enemies, was suddenly slain, which being known the King's enemies fled' (191, n. 6). Shakespeare has greatly augmented Prince Hal's role, partly following Daniel, *Civil Wars*, who prophesies in advance of the battle that 'There shall young Hotspur with a fury led | Meet with thy forward son as fierce as he' (iii. 97).

5.5.0.3 *Worcester and Vernon prisoners*] Holinshed reports that among the captives were 'the Earl of Worcester, the procurer and setter forth of all this mischief', and 'Sir Richard Vernon', both of whom were 'condemned and beheaded' (191–2; see l. 14).

21–2 falling ... took him] According to Holinshed, the Earl of Douglas, put to flight with others of the rebels, 'for haste, falling from the crag of an high mountain, brake one of his cullions [i.e. testicles], and was taken, and for his valiantness, of the King frankly and freely delivered' (191). Shakespeare adds Prince Hal's role in making the magnanimous gesture of release 'ransomless and free' (l. 28).

39 towards Wales] By contrast, Holinshed reports that 'the King, having set a stay in things about Shrewsbury, went straight to York'. Only after the York expedition did Henry determine 'to go into North Wales, to chastise the presumptuous doings of the unruly Welshmen' (192).

INDEX

An asterisk indicates that the note supplements information given in *OED*.

JANE AUSTEN	Catharine and Other Writings
	Emma
	Mansfield Park
	Northanger Abbey, Lady Susan, The Watsons, and Sanditon
	Persuasion
	Pride and Prejudice
	Sense and Sensibility
ANNE BRONTË	Agnes Grey
	The Tenant of Wildfell Hall
CHARLOTTE BRONTË	Jane Eyre
	The Professor
	Shirley
	Villette
EMILY BRONTË	Wuthering Heights
WILKIE COLLINS	The Moonstone
	No Name
	The Woman in White
CHARLES DARWIN	The Origin of Species
CHARLES DICKENS	The Adventures of Oliver Twist
	Bleak House
	David Copperfield
	Great Expectations
	Hard Times
	Little Dorrit
	Martin Chuzzlewit
	Nicholas Nickleby
	The Old Curiosity Shop
	Our Mutual Friend
	The Pickwick Papers
	A Tale of Two Cities

American Literature

British and Irish Literature

Children's Literature

Classics and Ancient Literature

Colonial Literature

Eastern Literature

European Literature

History

Medieval Literature

Oxford English Drama

Poetry

Philosophy

Politics

Religion

The Oxford Shakespeare